"The failure of the current prohibitionist cannabis policy has led to an international debate in search of other regulatory models for cannabis. A first departure from the prohibitionist model in many countries has been the decriminalization of the consumption and possession of cannabis for personal use, which de facto allowed the emergence of Cannabis Social Clubs as a risk reduction initiative within that prohibitionist framework. This model of self-organization of consumption has been reproduced informally in many countries and has become an alternative system of production and legal supply.

This book analyses the international repercussions of the Cannabis Social Club model and highlights the advantages and limitations of this route of access to cannabis. It is a must read for those looking for new alternative regulatory models for cannabis."

Juan Muñoz Sánchez, *Professor of Criminal Law, University of Málaga, Spain*

"The emergence of the Cannabis Social Club model in legal, quasi-legal and wholly illegal incarnations in different countries around the world poses both a threat and an opportunity to existing drug policy regimes. This timely and important collection collated by Mafalda Pardal provides interdisciplinary and international insights into this novel model of drug supply and will be of interest to those working in fields as diverse as drug policy, social movements, criminology and cultural studies. An excellent contribution to the literature."

Gary Potter, *Reader in Criminology & Research Director, Lancaster University, UK*

"Cannabis policy is changing throughout the Western world. While full legalization in North America captures the headlines, more relevant for European debate are the Cannabis Social Clubs that have emerged in the last 20 years. This collection of essays on how the clubs have grown and interacted throughout the world, from Uruguay and New Zealand to Spain and Belgium, provides many insights into an important innovation in drug policy."

Peter Reuter, *Distinguished University Professor, School of Public Policy and Department of Criminology, University of Maryland, USA*

"Current prohibitionist drug policies have shown to be ineffective to reduce harms related to drug consumption and trafficking. Although many national governments are not ready to change the paradigm regarding drug policies, Cannabis Social Clubs emerge to be an alternative to implement harm reduction policies in prohibitionist contexts. The experiences of these Clubs in Europe, New Zealand and Uruguay give us hope to think about a regulatory drug policy based on human rights and individual liberties for cannabis consumption. This book gives us evidence on how the Cannabis Social Clubs worked in different contexts, what the barriers for their implementation are and how they have provided a setting to create transnational collaborative spaces towards a drug policy reform. Combining this evidence with the effects of emerging cannabis regulatory frameworks implemented in Canada and at the state level in the United States gives us a complete scenario on how we can move away from prohibition and start thinking on international and comprehensive policy reforms."

Laura Atuesta, *Full Professor – Researcher, Center for Research and Teaching in Economics (CIDE), Mexico*

The Cannabis Social Club

As cannabis legalization reforms are underway, there is some concern that non-profit, 'middle ground' options may remain under-researched and thus less visible. This book offers an in-depth account of one of the possible 'middle ground' models for the supply of cannabis: the Cannabis Social Club.

Cannabis Social Clubs (CSCs) are typically formal, non-profit associations of adult cannabis users who produce and distribute that substance close to or at cost price among themselves. They constitute an user-driven model for the supply of cannabis. In most jurisdictions, CSCs remain a grassroots, unregulated initiative of groups of users, but the model has been legalized in Uruguay and Malta, and it has featured recent debates and legislative proposals in other countries. This book brings together contributions from internationally respected scholars, drawing on case studies, empirical findings and policy reflections, from a range of countries (such as Belgium, Canada, New Zealand, Spain, Uruguay, USA), and a consideration of the CSC model from different disciplinary backgrounds. Part I provides detailed analysis of where and how CSCs have been operating, and a critical analysis of their key features and relationship with institutional actors. Part II discusses several policy outcomes and proposes a design of a regulatory market, as well as considering whether the CSC model might be suited for adaptation to the supply of other substances.

The Cannabis Social Club is important reading for academics in the fields of drug policy analysis, criminology, economics, policy studies and anthropology. It will also be of interest to policy makers, journalists and law-enforcement personnel.

Mafalda Pardal (PhD) is Senior Analyst at RAND Europe, and serves as European Lead at the RAND Drug Policy Research Center. During the time this book was prepared Dr Pardal was Research Fellow and Assistant Professor in Criminology at Ghent University. Her research interests include the study of illicit markets and drug policy.

Drugs, Crime and Society
Series Editors: Jack Spicer and Mark Monaghan

This new series will be a natural home for research on the topic of drugs and crime, bringing together original, innovative and topical books that, broadly conceived, address the role and impact of drugs and drugs policy on crime, criminality the criminal justice system and its agents. Aiming to showcase cutting edge theory and research in the area, it will serve as a focal point around which the field can continue to develop and flourish. Welcoming both research monographs and edited volumes, the series will serve as an outlet for exceptional early career researchers, established scholars and productive collaborations between those working in the field, across the globe

The Cannabis Social Club
Mafalda Pardal

The Cannabis Social Club

Edited by
Mafalda Pardal

Routledge
Taylor & Francis Group
LONDON AND NEW YORK

First published 2023
by Routledge
4 Park Square, Milton Park, Abingdon, Oxon OX14 4RN

and by Routledge
605 Third Avenue, New York, NY 10158

Routledge is an imprint of the Taylor & Francis Group, an informa business

British Library Cataloguing-in-Publication Data
A catalogue record for this book is available from the British Library

Library of Congress Cataloging-in-Publication Data
A catalog record has been requested for this book

ISBN: 978-0-367-51906-3 (hbk)
ISBN: 978-0-367-51908-7 (pbk)
ISBN: 978-1-003-05567-9 (ebk)

DOI: 10.4324/9781003055679

Typeset in Times New Roman
by Taylor & Francis Books

For Lola.

Contents

List of illustrations xi
List of contributors xiii
Series Editors' Foreword xviii
Acknowledgements xx
List of abbreviations xxii

1 Introduction: 30 years of Cannabis Social Clubs: looking back and looking ahead 1
MAFALDA PARDAL

PART I 18

2 Cannabis Social Clubs in Europe: a transnational social movement network in the making? 18
MELISSA BONE, MAFALDA PARDAL, ÒSCAR PARÉS AND TOM DECORTE

3 A friendly match? The relationship between Cannabis Social Clubs and regulators in Uruguay 39
CLARA MUSTO

4 What are the barriers and prospects for establishing Cannabis Social Clubs in New Zealand? 57
MARTA RYCHERT AND CHRIS WILKINS

5 The Spanish Social Club: what's in a name? 73
ISIDRO MARÍN-GUTIÉRREZ AND MÓNICA HINOJOSA-BECERRA

6 Legal or not: a comparative analysis of Belgian and Uruguayan Cannabis Social Club members' profile and policy preferences 93
ELIANA ÁLVAREZ, ROSARIO QUEIROLO, LORENA REPETTO AND MAFALDA PARDAL

PART II 114

7 Bringing Foucault to Cannabis Social Clubs (through the notion of counter-conduct) 114
PIETER RONDELEZ AND MAFALDA PARDAL

8 CSC + 2: can the Cannabis Social Club model be a buffer against market distortions? 133
DAVIDE FORTIN

9 Cannabis legalization in Washington: policy evolution and emerging evidence from the first nine years 155
JULIA DILLEY, CAISLIN FIRTH AND BEAU KILMER

10 From compassion to commercial: what got left behind in the transition to legal cannabis in Canada 187
RIELLE CAPLER AND DANIEL BEAR

11 Drug Social Clubs – the next social club generation? 209
VENDULA BELACKOVA, MARTA RYCHERT, CHRIS WILKINS AND TOM DECORTE

Index 237

Illustrations

Figures

3.1 Evolution of the number of total cannabis users registered with the IRCCA, 2014–2021 46
5.1 A party organized by AECA in Huelva (1999) 74
5.2 Meeting prior to the creation of the FAC at the AMEC headquarters in Madrid (2002) 74
5.3 A party of the ARSECSE association in Seville (2002) 77
5.4 Celebration of Saint Canuto in Vigo (2008) 78
5.5 A 'Cannabis Cup' of the Bellaflor in Málaga (2002) 80
5.6 Cannabis varieties presented to the ARSECSE Cup in Seville (2003) 80
5.7 CannabisSur Conference in Málaga (2001) 81
5.8 Expocannabis in the city of Córdoba (1999) 82
5.9 Expocannabis in Barcelona (2004) 83
5.10 Demonstration in Madrid in favor of the legalization of cannabis (2002) 84
5.11 Demonstration in favor of cannabis in Madrid (2001) 84
5.12 Meeting of the FAC-Sur in Lucena, Córdoba (October 19, 2011) 86
6.1 CSC members' self-reported cannabis use evolution by country 101
6.2 Organization of activities by CSCs by country 103
6.3 CSC members' participation in activities by country 103
6.4 Agreement with regulations by country 105
6.5 CSC members' agreement with Uruguayan rules for CSCs by country 106
8.1 Pricing across supply channels 142
9.1 Active cannabis licenses in Washington in fiscal year 2020 163
9.2 Monthly number of cannabis retailer making sales* in Washington 164
9.3 Percentage of WA residents in communities with different levels of cannabis retailer density (access density, quartiles), 2014–2016 165

9.4 Monthly cannabis retail sales in Washington, July 2014–July 2020 165
9.5 Monthly sales of cannabis by product type in Washington, July 2014–October 2017 166
9.6 Regression-based estimates for price per 10 mg THC by product/subtype over time in Washington 167
9.7 Adult cannabis current use and frequent-use prevalence, by quarter, Behavioral Risk Factor Surveillance System, Washington, QI 2009–2016 170
9.8 Annual number of cannabis-related exposures reported to Poison Centers, Washington State, 2009–2019 172
9.9 Cannabis originating from Washington that was seized in other states 176

Tables

2.1 Contacts with other CSCs (in the same country and in other countries) 24
2.2 Reported conflicts between CSCs 25
2.3 Reported incidents between CSCs and police and judiciary 27
2.4 Collaboration with professionals and professional services 28
3.1 Number of registers by province circa 2020 48
6.1 Key features of the online surveys for Belgian and Uruguayan CSC members 97
6.2 CSCs members' sociodemographic characteristics by country 98
6.3 Cannabis use and self-reported knowledge about cannabis content by country 99
8.1 Supply and demand assumed relationship 140
9.1 Cannabis collective gardens and cooperatives in Washington 159
9.2 Self-reported youth cannabis use prevalence and accessibility, 2010–2018 168
11.1 Possible functions and activities of drug social clubs per type of psychoactive substance use 224

Contributors

Eliana Álvarez is a research assistant at the Department of Social Sciences at the Universidad Católica del Uruguay (UCU). She has a master's degree in Public Policies. Her work focuses on the implementation of the cannabis policy in Uruguay. Since 2016, she has participated in different research projects, including the Latin American Marijuana Research Initiative (LAMRI). Her masters' dissertation, 'Impact Evaluation of the Cannabis Sales at Pharmacies on Use and Risk Perception', received a grant from the Uruguayan National Agency for Research and Innovation. She has published articles in *Addiction* and the *International Journal of Drug Policy.*

Daniel Bear is a Professor in the Faculty of Social and Community Services at Humber College in Toronto, Canada. He has a PhD and MSc in Social Policy from the London School of Economics and Political Science, and a BA in Sociology (Honours) from the University of California at Santa Cruz. Dr Bear's research focuses on the intersection of the criminal justice system, drugs, and social justice.

Vendula Belackova is an Adjunct Senior Lecturer at the Social Policy Research Centre, Faculty of Arts and Social Sciences, University of New South Wales, Australia. In her previous role as a Senior Project Officer at the Uniting Medically Supervised Injecting Centre in Sydney and lecturer at Charles University in Prague, she has conducted interdisciplinary research into drug policy in Europe, Australia, and the United States. Vendula completed a Fulbright postgraduate fellowship at the College of Social Sciences at the Florida State University and Endeavour Visiting Research fellowship at the National Drug and Alcohol Research Centre in Sydney.

Melissa Bone, PhD, is an Associate Professor at the University of Leicester, UK. Melissa researches drug policy from a human rights perspective and she has recently published a monograph with Routledge entitled *Human Rights And Drug Control: A New Perspective.* Melissa also examines how to engage people who use drugs in drug policy debates and reform discussions through the 'Drug Policy Voices' ESRC-funded research project. Additionally, Melissa researches the legal landscape of cannabis social clubs throughout Europe, cannabis activism and medical cannabis laws in the UK.

Rielle Capler, MHA, PhD. Dr Capler has engaged in research, advocacy, knowledge translation, service provision, organizational development, community organizing, consulting and advising on policy nationally and internationally in relation to cannabis for over 20 years. Rielle received the Governor General of Canada's Queen Elizabeth II Diamond Jubilee Medal for her contribution to society through her work with medical cannabis, including foundational work with the first compassion club in Canada. Rielle's research focus is on harm reduction, access and equity related to cannabis and other plant medicines. Rielle is a Postdoctoral Research Fellow at the British Columbia Center on Substance Use.

Tom Decorte is Professor of Criminology and director of the Institute for Social Drug research (ISD) at Ghent University (Belgium). He co-founded the Global Cannabis Cultivation Research Consortium (GCCRC) and is trustee of the Board of the European Society for Social Drug research (ESSD) and of the International Society for the Study of Drug Policy (ISSDP). His research interests include patterns of substance use, the supply side of cannabis markets, and the implementation of local drug monitoring systems. He has been adviser to a range of organizations on policies to improve public health relating to the use of drugs around the world.

Julia Dilley is a Senior Research Scientist and Epidemiologist with Multnomah County Health Department and State of Oregon Public Health Division (USA). For more than 20 years Julia has supported public health in Washington, Oregon, Alaska and New Mexico by studying effects of cannabis, alcohol, tobacco and drug policies, and improving public health data quality for surveillance and evaluation. Julia leads a research study of cannabis legalization impacts in Washington and Oregon, examining local policies and cannabis market variation. She also co-chairs a national subcommittee of the Council of State and Territorial Epidemiologists that is developing cannabis surveillance best practices.

Caislin Firth, PhD, MPH, is a social epidemiologist interested in unpacking how public policies shape social and built environments and their influence on health inequities. With a background working in local government in the Pacific Northwest (USA), Caislin's research goes beyond answering the question 'Do population health interventions (e.g. cannabis legalization) improve health?' by also considering what works, for whom and in which contexts. In practice, Caislin has studied the underlying causes of inequities in substance use, criminal justice, mobility and transportation outcomes and the relationship between neighbourhood environments and health.

Davide Fortin, PhD is an economist at Panthéon-Sorbonne University where his interest lies at the intersection of the fields of health economics and industrial organization. His research explores the economics of cannabis regulation, focusing on the interrelation across cannabis markets (industrial, light, medical and recreational) as well as the integration of cannabis into the European health system. Davide has developed a methodology for drug market sizing for UNODC and is adjunct lecturer at University of Padua. He collaborates with MPG consulting to advise government agencies in designing cannabis markets.

Mónica Hinojosa-Becerra is Professor at the Universidad Nacional de Loja (Ecuador), where she coordinated the Social Communication Career (2015), and has been the Dean of the Faculty of Education, Art and Communication (2016). She has a PhD in Audiovisual Communication from the University of Málaga (Spain). She has been a Professor at the Universities of Málaga (Spain), Cordoba (Spain), Universidad de las Américas (Ecuador) and Universidad Espíritu Santo (Ecuador). She is the Director of Tvmedia2 Producciones.

Beau Kilmer is the McCauley Chair in Drug Policy Innovation and director of the Drug Policy Research Center at RAND. His research lies at the intersection of public health and public safety, with special emphasis on drug policy and crime. Kilmer's publications have appeared in leading journals such as *New England Journal of Medicine* and *PNAS*, and his commentaries have been published by *Los Angeles Times, New York Times, Wall Street Journal* and other outlets. He co-authored a book on cannabis legalization and the future of fentanyl.

Isidro Marín-Gutiérrez, PhD in Social Anthropology and Degree in Political Science and Sociology from the University of Granada. He is currently Assistant Professor at the University of Seville (Spain) and has been a Professor-Researcher at the Universidad Técnica Particular de Loja (UTPL) (2013–2021) (Ecuador), as well as Associate Professor at the University of Huelva (2004–2013) (Spain). He is a member of the Technical Council of the scientific journal of communication and education Comunicar, and of the E6 Research Group and COIDESO. He is the Director of the research group DocumentaUTPL.

Clara Musto, PhD in Cultural and Global Criminology (University of Kent and University of Utrecht), currently works at the Criminology research group of the School of Social Science of Universidad de la República, Uruguay (NACVI). Her interests include violence and urban development, drug policy, organized crime, and crimes of the powerful. She was a researcher of Monitor Cannabis Uruguay, a team specialized in the monitoring and evaluation of cannabis regulation in the country.

Òscar Parés has an undergraduate degree in philosophy and anthropology and a master's degree in drug addiction from the Universidad de Barcelona. He worked for the Government of Catalonia's Program on Substance

Abuse, coordinating nightlife risk-reduction programmes and the regulation of Cannabis Social Clubs. Òscar is a founding member of the Drug Policy Unit of the Universitat Autònoma de Bellaterra (UAB). Currently, in his role as Deputy Director of the ICEERS Foundation, Òscar promotes educational, drug reform and research projects on Cannabis Social Clubs and is the lead organizer of the World Ayahuasca Conference.

Rosario Queirolo is Associate Professor at the Department of Social Sciences, Universidad Católica del Uruguay. She has a PhD in Political Science from the University of Pittsburgh. Her two main research areas are comparative politics and drugs policies. She studies electoral behaviour and public opinion in Latin America. Her book *The Success of the Left in Latin America* was published by University of Notre Dame Press. Queirolo is also studying the impact of cannabis legalization(s), and of Cannabis Social Clubs as an alternative. She has published articles in *Addiction, International Journal of Drug Policy, Drug and Alcohol Review*, among others.

Lorena Repetto is Assistant Professor at the Political Science Department (Universidad de la República, Uruguay). She is a PhD student in political science at Universidad de la República. She has a specialization in Methods and a Master in Public Policy. Lorena does research in political science, particularly in public policy, security policies and cannabis regulation. She has published on these topics in *Addiction, International Journal of Drug Policy* and other journals.

Pieter Rondelez is a PhD researcher at Ghent University, Faculty of Political and Social Sciences. His research is focused on the study of radical change by social movements and the role of social scientists in this process. Furthermore, he is currently developing methods in order to study social change by using Foucault's governmentality approach.

Marta Rychert is a Senior Research Officer at the Shore & Whāriki Research Centre, College of Health, Massey University, New Zealand. Her work lies at the intersection of health, policy and law, with particular focus on drug policy change, cannabis law reform and regulation of other psychoactive products including new psychoactive substances (NPS) and new drug delivery systems (e.g. vaping). Her research projects have been funded by the NZ Health Research Council and Marsden Royal Society of New Zealand. Prior to her academic appointments, she worked in the European Union Drugs Agency (EMCDDA) in Portugal.

Chris Wilkins, Associate Professor, is the leader of the drug research team at the Shore & Whāriki Research Centre, College of Health, Massey University, New Zealand. Dr Wilkins has research expertise in drug trends, drug markets, and drug policy. In 2020, he co-edited *Legalizing Cannabis: Experiences, Lessons and Scenarios* with Professor Tom Decorte and

Professor Simon Lenton. Chris Wilkins has been an invited speaker by the European Monitoring Centre for Drugs and Drug Addiction (EMCDDA), and at the United States National Institute for Drug Abuse Community Epidemiology Working Group (CEWG).

Series Editors' Foreword

The idea for this book series emerged in 2019. From conversations at different conferences and with a growing awareness of a proliferation of modules and programmes across a range of different universities, it became apparent that there was no natural home for drugs-related research of monograph length. We were approached by Routledge to see if we might want to intervene, to develop a series where the latest research in the field of drugs and crime and the role and understanding of drugs in society and the responses to them could be published. Our aim, in creating this series, is to bring together original, innovative and topical books from scholars of all career stages. The series plans to be methodologically diverse, theoretically sophisticated and international in its outlook. With drug policy reform gathering traction, yet many drug harms intensifying, now more than ever such learning is required.

Of course 2019 was a different time. Since then, the Covid-19 pandemic has altered the way we live and also the way we understand the world. But in the field of drugs policy there is often as much continuity as change. In terms of continuity, the early signs from the pandemic are that despite the various unprecedented restrictions placed on daily life in the form of national lockdowns, the demand for substances for the purposes of intoxication has remained stable, and the suppliers have proved to be remarkably innovative and adaptable. Even where change is identified, continuity often follows. High-profile evolutions in UK heroin and crack cocaine markets referred to as 'County Lines' over recent years, for example, have primarily led to familiar responses by boosting police powers to respond to the issue and the political scapegoating of various groups held to be responsible.

Yet, anyone exposed to the drugs field at the moment is likely to have the distinct feeling that change is afoot. In fact, change may not be the right term. Drug policy development, innovation, or remembering the past may be better. There is increasing recognition by various actors that the drug problem cannot be solved through enforcement alone. In various parts of England and Wales, alternative approaches are being developed, often at the behest of Police and Crime Commissioners of different political persuasions. Diversion schemes are one such example, but we are also seeing senior police figures recommending a suite of different measures to tackle the record levels of drug-related harm and death that is currently being experienced across the UK. Such policies include the (re)introduction of heroin-assisted treatment programmes in the North East of England, Glasgow and the West Midlands. There are also continuing calls for the development of safe-injection facilities, although to date these have not materialized.

Elsewhere, most visibly in North America, the legalisation of cannabis for recreational as well as medicinal use has gathered apace. Cannabis has been legalized for recreational use in 18 States as well as at the Federal level in Canada. Although lagging behind, in October 2021 Luxembourg became the first country in Europe to permit adults to grow up to four plants of cannabis at home, making it the first country on the continent to legalize the production and consumption of the drug, recognizing that prohibition had failed in its primary aim to deter people from using drugs. No longer are the decriminalization policy of Portugal or the coffee shops of Amsterdam the automatic reference points for people citing how drugs are dealt with differently elsewhere.

The politics of drug policy is such that now more than ever a home for the copious amount of drug research taking place is needed, if only to start the painstaking process of debunking myths and learning from what is happening elsewhere. It is our vision that this series can contribute to this undertaking and can be at the forefront of understanding this rapidly changing area of policy and practice. Mafalda Pardal's edited collection on Cannabis Social Clubs is an excellent example of scholarship in this area and represents a superb addition to the series. Boasting contributions across a range of international contexts, it provides insights of how these models operate in Europe, South America and North America. Various theoretical perspectives are drawn on throughout, from Foucault to legal studies, providing sophisticated analysis. In addition to providing valuable historical context, the book also charts the position of Cannabis Social Clubs in relation to contemporary trends and considers what may lie ahead in the future. Being essential reading for anyone interested in this area, while making a valuable contribution to the drugs field more generally, we welcome this timely text to 'Drugs, Crime and Society'.

Jack Spicer – *University of the West of England, UK*
Mark Monaghan – *University of Birmingham, UK*

Acknowledgements

The idea for this book project probably came up around 2015 with the start of my PhD research project on the topic of Cannabis Social Clubs (CSCs). I have had great mentors along the way, who have enriched my own understanding of drug policy and (drug) research, and it has been a privilege to continue to work alongside them to this day. A special acknowledgement to those who have been the closest to this intellectual journey: Tom Decorte (Ghent University, Belgium) and Letizia Paoli (Katholieke Universiteit Leuven, Belgium). I owe a great debt of gratitude to many other colleagues, in particular to Julie Tieberghien, Frédérique Bawin, Marthe Ongenaert, and the team at the Institute for Social Drug Research at Ghent University, and to the colleagues at RAND Europe and the RAND Drug Policy Research Center.

In the course of my research on CSCs I have held fellowships from the Research Foundation Flanders (FWO) and from the Research Council of Ghent University, which have allowed me to spend time in Belgium and abroad studying this phenomenon. Special thanks to Rosario Queirolo and her team (Universidad Católica del Uruguay, Uruguay), who have hosted me during my research stay in 2018 and have become dear *compañeras de viaje* since then.

While the first step for this book was a solo one, soon enough that PhD project became a gateway to multiple (and much welcomed) research collaborations and exchanges. This book is a reflection of that.

I am also very grateful to the many scholars who have contributed their time and expertise to review the chapters included in this book:

Xabier Arana (University of Basque Country, Spain)
Rebecca Askew (Manchester Metropolitan University, UK)
Liz Barrett (UNSW Sydney, Australia)
Marcos Baudean (ORT University Uruguay, Uruguay)
Frédérique Bawin (Ghent University, Belgium)
Anne Line Bretteville-Jensen (Norwegian Institute of Public Health, Norway)
Jonathan Caulkins (Carnegie Mellon University, USA)
Steven Debbaut (Ghent University, Belgium)
Edmond Fehoko (Auckland University of Technology, New Zealand)
Rebecca Jesseman (Canadian Centre on Substance Use and Addiction, Canada)

Dirk Korf (Amsterdam University, The Netherlands)
Simon Lenton (Curtin University, Australia)
Amber Marks (Queen Mary University of London, UK)
Alice Mattoni (University of Bologna, Italy)
Rosalie Pacula (University of Southern California, USA)
Bryce Pardo (RAND Corporation, USA)
Rosario Queirolo (Catholic University of Uruguay, Uruguay)
Toby Seddon (University of Manchester, UK)
Alex Stevens (University of Kent, UK)
Todd Subritzky (La Trobe University, Australia)

To all the CSC representatives, cannabis growers, cannabis users, and all others who have contributed to the development of this work: thank you!

Finally, the deepest *obrigada* to my family for their never-failing enthusiasm and support.

List of abbreviations

ACAC	Asociación Coruñesa de Amigos do Cánabo
ADEUC	Asociación de Estudios y Usos del Cannabis de Córdoba
AECA	Asociación de Estudios de Cannabis de Asturias
AECA	Asociación de Estudios sobre el Cannabis Al-Andalus
AMA	Asociación Manchega Antiprohibicionista
AMEC	Asociación Madrileña de Estudios sobre el Cannabis
AMIC	Asociación Mallorquina para la Información del Cannabis
ARSEC	Asociación Ramón Santos de Estudios Sobre el Cannabis
ARSECSE	Asociación Ramón Santos de Estudios del Cannabis de Sevilla
BC	British Columbia
CAMCD	Canadian Association of Medical Cannabis Dispensaries
CatFAC	Federació d'Associacions de Cànnabis de Catalunya
CBD	Cannabidiol
CCCB	Barcelona Cannabis Tasters Club
CDSA	Federal Controlled Drugs and Substances Act
CLCB	Cannabis Legalisation and Control Bill
ConFAC	Confederación de Federaciones de Asociaciones Cannábicas
CSC	Cannabis Social Club
DOH	Department of Health
DSC	Drug Social Clubs
DUI	Driving under the influence
EMCDDA	European Monitoring Centre for Drugs and Drug Addiction
ENCOD	European Coalition for Just and Effective Drug policies
FAC	Federación de Asociaciones Cannábicas
FBI	Federal Bureau of Investigation
FEDCAC	Federació d'Associacions Cannàbiques Autoregulades de Catalunya
ICEERS	The International Center for Ethnobotanical Education, Research and Services
IRCCA	Institute for the Regulation and Control of Cannabis
LCB	Liquor Control Board
MODA	Misuse of Drugs Act
MP	Member of Parliament

NGO	Non-Governmental Organization
NORML	National Organization for the Reform of Marijuana Laws
NPS	New psychoactive substances
NSDUH	National Survey on Drug Use and Health
NWHIDTA	Northwest High Intensity Drug Trafficking Areas
NZ-NORML	New Zealand – National Organization for the Reform of Marijuana Laws
NZ-RSA	Royal New Zealand Returned and Services' Association
OPS	Overdose Prevention Sites
PWUD	People who use drugs
SMO	Social Movement Organization
SUD	Substance use disorder
THC	Tetrahydrocannabinol
UKCSC	United Kingdom Cannabis Social Club
UNDRIP	United Nations Declaration on the Rights of Indigenous Peoples
WAMM	Wo/Men's Alliance for Medical Marijuana
WOLA	Washington Office on Latin America

1 Introduction

30 years of Cannabis Social Clubs: looking back and looking ahead

Mafalda Pardal

Cannabis Social Clubs: an introduction

The typical definition of a Cannabis Social Club (CSC) is likely to include all or a combination of the following elements: 1) the CSC as a non-profit association; 2) the CSC as a group created by and for adult cannabis users; 3) the CSC as a collective and closed system for the supply of cannabis. This is also the case in the various characterizations of CSCs included in this volume. As such, a CSC seems to involve some degree of formalization (as registered associations), which helps distinguish this type of cannabis supply from other more informal social supply arrangements. The CSCs have also by and large adhered to a non-profit ethos. This has placed CSCs on the non-commercial and 'middle ground' spectrum of cannabis supply models (Caulkins & Kilmer, 2016; Caulkins et al., 2015). The involvement of users in the establishment and management of these associations has also been central to their functioning: these are indeed described as associations of cannabis users, characterized as being a "remarkable demonstration of consumer agency in cannabis production and distribution" (Belackova & Wilkins, 2018, p. 27). The cannabis produced by the CSCs is only made available to members, creating a closed system of supply. Activism or advocacy are also underlying drivers and part of the working of (some of) these associations as well (Bone et al., this volume; Marín, 2008; Queirolo et al., 2016). Most CSCs are in fact functioning in contexts where the supply of cannabis or CSCs are not regulated and might constitute a breach of the applicable laws.

The documented CSC practices to date confirm the presence of CSCs with the core features listed above. However, there are different understandings of what a CSC entails and how it should function (Bone et al., this volume; Pardal et al., 2020), and several authors have discussed the appearance and coexistence of "multiple versions of the model" (Decorte et al., 2017, p. 47; Jansseune et al., 2019; Martínez, 2015; Montañés, 2017; Pardal, 2018a; Sánchez & Collins, 2018). Some groups, (self-)defined as CSCs, have diverted from those core characteristics, and in doing so have altered the shape of the model.

DOI: 10.4324/9781003055679-1

This chapter serves as an introduction to the core topic of this book, providing an overview of how the CSC model has evolved through time and across different settings.[1]

CSC prototype(s)

Before the first actual CSC was created, and within the broader drug user movement, there are other examples of user associations formed with the purposes of providing a space for the collective or social use of a substance, facilitating its production, providing peer support and harm reduction services, and/or engaging in activism or lobbying (Belackova et al., this volume; Hunt et al., 2010; Montañés & Oomen, 2009; Pardal, 2016). An early documented instance is that of the so-called Club des Hashischins (Club of the Hashish-Eaters). This Club was active in Paris (1844–1849) and held monthly meetings where its (elite) members explored 'altered states of consciousness', primarily by using hashish. More recent examples include the case of the Junkie Unions, created in the late 1970s/early 1980s in the Netherlands. These were groups primarily formed by heroin users, which run unofficial needle exchange initiatives, shared information about methadone prescription programmes, and were involved in a range of other protest and awareness-raising events (Bennett et al., 2011; Efthimiou-Mordaunt, 2015; Friedman et al., 1987; Friedman et al., 2007). Cannabis buyers' clubs and compassion clubs in North America have also provided cannabis (particularly for medical purposes) and spaces for socialization among their circle of members since the 1990s (Capler & Bear, this volume; Feldman & Mandel, 1998; Grinspoon, 2003; Reiman, 2008).

The 'Spanish model'

There is consensus in the literature as to Spain being the birthplace of the CSC model (Arana & Montañés, 2011; Barriuso, 2012; Belackova & Wilkins, 2018; Belackova et al., 2016; Blickman, 2014; Calafat et al., 2000; Coombes, 2014; Ghehiouèche & Zemouli, 2016; Hunt et al., 2010; Kilmer et al., 2013; Marín & Hinojosa, 2017; Obradors-Pineda et al., 2021; Parés & Bouso, 2015). While cannabis activism and different activist groups were already active in the country (Marín, 2009; Montañés, 2017), the first cannabis associations that seem to have been on the basis of the later appearance of CSCs were established in the 1990s. In particular, the creation (in 1991) of the Asociación Ramón Santos de Estudios sobre el Cannabis (ARSEC) played a pioneering role in that process (Calafat et al., 2000; Casals & Marks, 2015; Gamella & Rodrigo, 2004; Madera, 2017). ARSEC is an association based in Barcelona, formally constituted (i.e. complying with the general procedures and registration as an association with the Registro de Asociaciones de la Generalitat de Cataluña) (Muñoz, 2015), whose stated goals included the study of cannabis-related issues, as well as the sharing of that information among the members (Arana & Montañés, 2011; Montañés, 2017; Parés & Bouso, 2015). Following an enquiry sent to the public prosecutor concerning the legality of a collective crop for members of the association, and making this initiative public (including to the media) (Barriuso, 2011, 2012; Martínez, 2015; Montañés, 2017; Muñoz, 2015), in 1993 ARSEC planted about 200 plants for the 100–150 members of the association at the time (Barriuso, 2012; Marks, 2019; Parés & Bouso, 2015). The police intervened and confiscated the plants, but while the case was still being considered in court several other associations were created with a similar form and purpose (Arana & Montañés, 2011; Barriuso, 2011, 2012; Madera, 2017; Marín, 2009; Montañés, 2017) in what has been termed the 'Catalan breach' (Martínez, 2015; Parés & Bouso, 2015). This first wave of 'associations for the study of cannabis' (Decorte et al., 2017) led by ARSEC and the associations that have followed its footsteps share a number of core features.

These were very public initiatives: the associations were registered in a public registry, contacted and informed the media about their activities, consulted public actors. As such, they had a rather public or overt profile. In addition, the supply of cannabis, on the basis of a collective cultivation and closed distribution to members, was already a characteristic of these first associations. At the same time, the associations were also engaged in the broader activist movement (Barriuso, 2011; Madera, 2017; Martínez, 2015; Montañés, 2017). With regards to the size of these associations (and thus of the closed circuit of supply established for members), the available accounts point to some variability. Taking the case of ARSEC, the reports around the start of the first experiment with collective cultivation indicate a membership base of around 100–150 users (Montañés, 2017; Parés & Bouso, 2015), while later reports (circa 1999), mention that the association had more than 3000 members (Calafat et al., 2000; Gamella & Rodrigo, 2004).

The start of the following decade marks another milestone for the development of CSCs in Spain. It is in 2001 that the first association adopting the denomination of 'Cannabis Social Club' appears: the Club de Catadores de Cannabis de Barcelona (CCCB) (Arana & Parés, 2020; Barriuso, 2005; Muñoz, 2015). Differently than the previous 'associations for the study of cannabis', the CCCB of Barcelona and the subsequent emerging associations across the country explicitly indicated they would engage in collective cultivation of cannabis and provide their members a (private) space for the consumption of that substance (Jansseune et al., 2019; Marín, 2009; Martínez, 2015; Muñoz, 2015). As Barriuso (2011) (who himself had an active role within the CSC movement) explains:

> little by little, the associations began to formalize their set-up: from being registered as 'cannabis research' associations they went on to become 'cannabis users' associations and included the creation of private spaces for consumption and social cultivation in their statutes.
>
> (p. 3)

While the earlier associations also engaged in the cultivation of cannabis to supply their members, this was not included in the bylaws of the associations – which referred only to 'study' or 'research' related to cannabis. To that effect, several authors have emphasized the impact of a legal analysis conducted by Muñoz & Soto, 2001, which was highly influential in how CSCs organized their activities (Arana & Montañés, 2011; Barriuso, 2005, 2011; Jansseune et al., 2019; Montañés, 2017; Muñoz, 2015). From that analysis, four aspects emerged as essential to guarantee (in theory)[2] CSCs' adherence to the Spanish legal framework and have been integrated into CSCs' functioning: 1) having a commitment to harm reduction, for instance by reducing the risk of substance adulteration; 2) establishing a closed supply system (i.e. access to the CSCs and the cannabis they produce is restricted to members and membership is only possible for regular/previous cannabis users) and mainly for "immediate consumption" at the premises of the association (to avoid diversion to non-members); 3) limiting the amounts supplied to members to meet their personal use needs only (the underlying rationale also being a reduction of potential diversion to non-members); 4) applying a low price (or providing the substance free of cost), and without the intent of generating profit (Muñoz & Soto, 2001).

Some characteristics associated with the first wave of the 'associations for the study of cannabis' became more consistently part of the CSCs' way of functioning. For example: being non-profits, and ensuring that the (limited) revenues generated with the supply of cannabis to members were reinvested in the social and other activities of the Clubs (Barriuso, 2011). The new emphasis on providing a private space for the consumption of cannabis became also enshrined into CSCs' way of working (Barriuso, 2011, 2012; Belackova et al., 2016), and it is connected to both the idea of restricting access and limiting diversion, as well as to the broader social agenda of these associations (which also organized other events for members). The arrangements around collective cultivation were also further developed, with CSCs typically relying on in-house cultivation (by volunteer or paid members of the clubs) (Barriuso, 2011), as a guarantee of quality of the product being supplied and of the closed system of production and distribution.

Expansion of the model, replicas and new variants

As other CSCs were created across Spain and in the absence of a clear legal framework for their operation, these associations felt the need to form a coalition, a supra-organization that could represent and guide them, and so the first CSC Federation (called Federación de Asociaciones Cannábicas, FAC) was established in 2003 (Alvarez et al., 2016; Arana & Montañés, 2011; Arana & Parés, 2020; Barriuso, 2011, 2012; Belackova et al., 2016; Belackova & Wilkins, 2018; Jansseune et al., 2019; Madera, 2017; Marín, 2009; Montañés, 2017; Val, 2017).[3] Initially, the FAC gathered around 20 CSCs (Arana & Montañés, 2011; Arana & Parés, 2020; Barriuso, 2011, 2012; Jansseune et al., 2019), and subsequently regional branches of that Federation were created (e.g. CATFAC in Catalonia, EUSFAC in the Basque Country) (Belackova & Wilkins, 2018). In the years that followed, several other CSC Federations were formed in Spain (e.g. FEDCAC in Catalonia) (Belackova et al., 2016; Belackova & Wilkins, 2018; Jansseune et al., 2019; Montañés, 2017; Pardal et al., 2020). The key contribution of CSC Federations, as described by Belackova & Wilkins (2018) has been to provide "frameworks for self-regulation of CSCs" and to represent "their members in seeking legal recognition from authorities" (p. 27) (see also: Alvarez et al., 2016; Arana & Parés, 2020). For instance, these Federations have published guidelines on how their affiliated CSCs should operate (Alvarez et al., 2016; Arana & Parés, 2020; Arnoso & Elgorriaga, 2016; Barriuso, 2012; Jansseune et al., 2019; Kilmer et al., 2013; Montañés, 2017), covering instructions about the administration of the clubs, the requirements for membership, collective cannabis cultivation, the distribution of the cannabis among members and the venue of the clubs (Belackova & Wilkins, 2018; Decorte et al., 2017). In practice, as different CSC Federations typically put forward their own framework of self-regulation, multiple interpretations of the model can be found – which to some extent reflect the divergent views of the groups involved, their preferred strategies and underlying ideologies (Bone et al., this volume; Jansseune et al., 2019). CSC Federations are not unique to Spain: similar umbrella CSC associations have been formed, for instance, in France (Decorte, 2015), in the UK (Bone & de Hoedt, 2018; Decorte, 2015), among other European countries (Bone et al., this volume), or in Uruguay (Musto, this volume). Also pan-European initiatives, such as the case of the European Coalition for Just and Effective Drug Policies (ENCOD), have engaged with the development of the CSC model and represented CSCs in the public debate (Blickman, 2014; Calafat et al., 2000; Pardal et al., 2020). For instance, ENCOD has issued a Code of Conduct for European CSCs (first published in 2011, with an updated version released in 2020).[4] Despite these efforts to consolidate and harmonize the practices of CSCs, the available reports suggest that CSC Federations have only represented a relatively small number of the active CSCs (Arana & Parés, 2020; Belackova et al., 2016; Belackova & Wilkins, 2018; Blickman, 2014; Jansseune et al., 2019; Parés-Franquero et al., 2019). And even the Clubs affiliated with a particular CSC Federation may, in practice, not always adhere to its respective code of conduct or guidelines (Jansseune et al., 2019).

In addition to the creation of CSC Federations, the presence of CSCs in Spain continued to grow in the years after the creation of the first CSC in Barcelona (Decorte et al., 2017; Madera, 2017; Marín & Hinojosa, 2017; Martínez, 2015; Montañés, 2017; Muñoz, 2015; Parés & Bouso, 2015). Most sources documenting CSCs in that country agree that around 2011 (and especially in the period between 2011 and 2014),[5] a substantive increase in the number of active CSCs took place, against a backdrop of economic crisis in the country (Arana & Parés, 2020; Blickman, 2014; Jansseune et al., 2019; Martínez, 2015; Parés & Bouso, 2015). Martínez (2015) describes this development as "a cannabis boom, understood as a massive and almost indiscriminate opening of clubs" (p. 100, own translation). While estimating the total number of CSCs remains challenging, the more recent accounts available (drawing on informal sources, interviews, registers from public authorities, etc.) point to about 700–800 to around 1000 CSCs operating in the whole country (c.2016–2017) (Decorte et al., 2017; Montañés, 2017; Sánchez & Collins, 2018; Val, 2017).[6]

Beyond the Spanish borders, CSCs appeared in other countries too – although the amount of evidence on the presence and *modus operandi* of CSCs varies across countries. For instance, the entrance and development of the CSC model in Belgium is well documented (Decorte, 2014, 2015; Pardal, 2018a, 2018b), and some recent research into the situation of CSCs in the UK has also been conducted (Bone & de Hoedt, 2018). Other settings have received less research attention so far (Blickman, 2014). In any case, in addition to Spain, CSCs have been reportedly active in the following countries: Austria, Belgium, Czech Republic, France, Germany, Hungary, Ireland, Italy, the Netherlands, Poland, Romania, Slovenia, Switzerland, UK (Arana & Montañés, 2011; Belackova et al., 2016; Belackova & Wilkins, 2018; Blickman, 2014; Bone & de Hoedt, 2018; Coombes, 2014; Decorte, 2014, 2015; Decorte et al., 2017; Ghehiouèche et al. 2016; Goumaz et al., 2014; Lakhdar, 2018; Montañés, 2017; Pardal et al., 2020; Pardal, 2018b; Zobel et al., 2014). We could find indications of CSCs present in European countries since the late 1990s (e.g. in the Czech Republic and Poland) (Pardal et al., 2020), and for instance in Belgium from 2006 onwards (Decorte, 2014, 2015; Pardal, 2018b) but the appearance of CSCs across Europe seems to have mainly occurred in more recent years, in particular from around 2010 onwards (Blickman, 2014; Bone & de Hoedt, 2018; Pardal et al., 2020).

CSCs are not exclusively an European phenomenon though. There have been a few attempts to establish CSCs in New Zealand, for instance (Belackova et al., 2016; Belackova & Wilkins, 2018; Decorte, 2014, 2015; Rychert & Wilkins, this volume). Most notably, the CSC model has been one of the supply options legalized and regulated in Uruguay since 2013 (Decorte et al., 2017; Levayer, 2017; Musto, this volume; Pardal et al., 2019; Queirolo, 2020; Queirolo et al., 2016; Zobel, Marthaler, & Broers, 2014).[7] This represents a milestone in the development of the CSC model as it was the first time CSCs were formally regulated at the national level.[8] As of November 2021, according to the national institute overseeing the implementation of the new cannabis law (*Instituto de Regulación y control del cannabis,* IRCCA) there are 213 registered CSCs, serving a total of 6452 club members (IRCCA, 2021). In this country, the general framework for the functioning of (legal) CSCs is defined by law: the clubs can have between 15–45 members, both the CSCs and their members need to register in a national database, the clubs can cultivate up to 99 plants, and may distribute a maximum of 40 grams (or 480 grams per year) (Pardal et al., 2019; Queirolo, 2020). Other mentions of CSCs in South America were found in the literature reviewed as well: for instance, in Argentina, Chile, and Colombia (Belackova et al., 2016; Belackova &

Wilkins, 2018; Decorte, 2014, 2015) – some of these and other 'novel' settings are explored in more detail in this chapter.

'Ceci n'est pas un CSC': different types of CSCs enter the scene

The multiplication of CSCs in Spain as well as the appearance of CSCs in several other countries has implied to some extent a transformation ('shapeshifting' – see Pardal (2018a)) of some features of the model (Arana & Parés, 2020; Belackova & Wilkins, 2018; Blickman, 2014; Decorte, 2019; Decorte et al., 2017; Decorte & Pardal, 2017; Jansseune et al., 2019; Levayer, 2017; Marín, 2009; Martínez, 2015; Montañés, 2017; Pardal et al., 2020; Parés & Bouso, 2015; Sánchez & Collins, 2018). The research in this area has discussed the presence of different "types of clubs" (Blickman, 2014, p. 9), a "proliferation of a variety of CSC models" (Belackova & Wilkins, 2018, p. 31; but also: Montañés, 2017), whose "practices were significantly different" (Arana & Parés, 2020, p. 308). Multiple factors may have contributed to this, including the lack of a (clear) regulatory framework in most jurisdictions where CSCs are active, but also a diversity of views with regards to the self-regulatory practices of CSCs, and the involvement of different actors in the management of these associations (Belackova & Wilkins, 2018; Pardal, 2018a; Parés & Bouso, 2015). This is not to say that the earlier Spanish-inspired CSC model – as described in the previous sections, is extinct. The available evidence suggests that while some of those features have been preserved, some variants of the initial model have appeared alongside (Sánchez & Collins, 2018).

One important deviation to the original ethos of the model has to do with its business model. Since their early start, the CSCs have been established as non-profit associations. However, there have been reported cases of actors using CSCs to set up "profitable businesses" (Alvarez et al., 2016; Blickman, 2014; Caulkins et al., 2015; Decorte, 2014; Decorte et al., 2017; Muñoz, 2015). For instance, in Spain, as more and more CSCs were created from 2011 onwards, other types of associations emerged too (Arana & Parés, 2020; Jansseune et al., 2019; Martínez, 2015; Parés & Bouso, 2015). Arana and Parés (2020) noted that:

> although their statutes were very similar to those of CSCs, their practices were significantly different: they had more members (close to 10.000 in some cases); their operations were less transparent, and their volume of business indicated that they were making considerable profits.
>
> (p. 308)

For instance, some of these 'commercial' clubs sought new members among tourists on the streets and online (Decorte et al., 2017; Martínez, 2015), traded municipal permits, or had front men in the board of directors of the association (i.e. "people who are paid money to assume responsibility for a potential crime in the case of conviction", Arana and Parés (2020, p. 319)). Most of these cases have been reported in a context where the CSC model is not regulated,[9] and there has been critique from within the CSC movement concerning this exploitation of the model by "so-called CSCs" for business purposes which in their view "devalues" it of its core features (Arana & Parés, 2020; Martínez, 2015).

As already hinted in relation to the previous point (but not exclusively a reflection of business model), we find CSCs in many 'sizes'. Some CSCs and Federations have introduced caps to the number of members the associations can accept; in Uruguay this is defined by law (CSCs can have a maximum of 45 members). Even so, one can find CSCs with less than 10 members (Pardal et al., 2020), to CSCs with hundreds (Decorte, 2015; Kilmer et al., 2013; Marín, 2008; Pardal, 2018a; Pardal et al., 2020), and even thousands of members (Arana & Parés, 2020; Blickman, 2014; Calafat et al., 2000; Decorte et al., 2017; Marín, 2008).

Further, in terms of 'who' is accepted as member, there has also been a noteworthy development. Generally, the CSCs have been composed of adult users of cannabis – regardless of the purpose of use. In practice, that has resulted in a mix of (primarily) recreational but also (some) medical usage among CSC membership (Arana & Montañés, 2011; Barriuso, 2005; Decorte, 2015; Decorte et al., 2017; Jansseune et al., 2019; Kilmer et al., 2013; Pardal et al., 2020). Nevertheless, the literature in this area has also documented some cases of 'medical' CSCs, i.e. CSCs that only admit individuals using cannabis for medical purposes. Such CSCs have been established in Belgium, Italy, Switzerland, and in the UK (Decorte, 2015; Goumaz et al., 2014; Pardal, 2018b; Pardal & Bawin, 2018; Pardal et al., 2020). For instance, at this type of CSC in Belgium, candidate members are asked to present a physician prescription or medical record to be able to enroll in the association. These clubs have different arrangements concerning the distribution of cannabis to their members (e.g. type of delivery, frequency of distribution) and the types of products made available (Pardal & Bawin, 2018).

The description of the origins of CSCs in Spain (and in other countries) reflect some degree of pubic engagement. Those leading the initiatives made their intentions known, contacted the public authorities about the start of collective cannabis plantations, and later on started formally registering as associations – which implies submitting bylaws outlining the goals, structure and functioning of the CSCs, and which identifies the association and some of its members (e.g. location of the CSC premises, identification of those with a leadership function within the association). In Uruguay, registration in a national database (the registry data is not publically available though) is required by law (Queirolo, 2020). The CSCs have maintained, in general, a public profile, but there are also indications that some CSCs prefer to remain more underground (e.g. not completing formal registration, not engaging with the media, not participating in public initiatives) (Arana & Parés, 2020; Pardal, 2018a). Furthermore, while CSCs have introduced – even in unregulated contexts – a system of supply of cannabis for members, there are also associations that self-define as CSCs but are not active suppliers (Jansseune et al., 2019; Pardal, 2016, 2018a; Pardal & Decorte, 2018; Pardal et al., 2020). This may be a result of strategic preferences, but also the (direct or indirect) consequence of judicial action. Such CSCs exclusively engage with (other forms of) activism – organizing public demonstrations, participating in other activist forums or organizations, building political alliances, among other activities.[10]

Another core feature of CSCs relates to the collective cultivation of cannabis within the association. The cultivation of cannabis was "a form of resistance, affirmation and protest for legal change" (Alvarez et al., 2016, p. 78). It has also been a way of (self-)guaranteeing access to a product (perceived to be) of higher quality (Barriuso, 2011; Belackova et al., 2016; Decorte, 2015). Arana and Parés (2020) noted that "by growing their own cannabis, club members are able to control its quality" (p. 307). Research in this area has nevertheless noted that some CSCs are also purchasing the cannabis they supply to their members outside of the CSC (i.e. from other illicit market actors) (Barriuso, 2012; Jansseune et al., 2019; Pardal et al., 2020). In practice, such clubs function in a similar way to 'buyers clubs', in the sense that they are not producing cannabis in-house but rather buying it in bulk from external actors. This represents a deviation from the original functioning of the model, which Barriuso (2012) criticized as follows:

> among the false clubs that are appearing in some parts of the Spanish state, the 'back door' is becoming generalized, so that it [cannabis] is systematically bought on the black market and then distributed to the members, without one being able to know how it was cultivated and opening up the door to covert profit-making.
>
> (p. 15, own translation)

Finally, one other characteristic of CSCs concerns their 'social' role (Marín-Gutiérrez & Hinojosa-Becerra, this volume). Also in this regard, there are different degrees of involvement across CSCs. Having an area for social contact among CSC members and allowing the consumption of cannabis in the premises of the CSC has been a typical characteristic of these associations, especially in Spain (Barriuso, 2011, 2012; Jansseune et al., 2019; Marks, 2019; Muñoz, 2015; Pardal et al., 2020; Zobel et al., 2014). This has been seen by CSC members as a safe space where they can socialize without feeling stigmatized for their use of cannabis (Belackova et al., 2016). CSCs' social role has also been linked to harm reduction goals and initiatives. For instance, CSCs have organized workshops and training around risk reduction (for staff and members) and have sought collaboration with drug prevention and other health professionals (Arana & Parés 2020; Arana & Sanchez, 2016; Decorte, 2014, 2015). In their more day-to-day practice, CSCs also act as a point of information and advice about cannabis use for their respective members (Arana & Sanchez, 2016), and host different social activities for them (Jansseune et al., 2019; Pardal et al., 2020).

A note on recent developments

There are other recent cases of grassroots experiments with CSCs or cannabis associations, emerging especially in the last decade. Beyond Europe, such initiatives can be found, for instance, in Central and South America (i.e. Costa Rica, Argentina, Brazil, Chile and Ecuador) and in the African continent (i.e. South Africa). A first common characteristic across these settings is that the initiatives have been taking place within prohibitionist frameworks, often testing perceived legal ambiguities. One of the respondents explained that the associations (in Chile) have chosen "the judicial route as a strategy to achieve a change because the legislative route would be much slower" (KI12). As an example, in Brazil, the instrument of preventive *habeas corpus* has been used (individually and collectively) to secure protection from the risk of imprisonment related to the cultivation of cannabis for medical purposes (Dos Santos et al., 2020; Dos Santos & Rosas, 2021; Lambert & Martins, 2018; Policarpo & Martins, 2019). In practice, this has meant that those – including cannabis associations – with that safe conduct are able to cultivate cannabis, and that the police will not confiscate or detain those involved. Most respondents have nevertheless noted that given the limited room for manoeuvre within these prohibitionist frameworks, the active associations tended to focus exclusively on medical cannabis (e.g. Argentina, Brazil, Chile, Costa Rica). While there might have been some attempts to establish associations for broader (recreational) purposes (e.g. in Costa Rica), these 'medical cannabis associations' have mainly gathered patients and their family. In fact, in Argentina and Brazil, for example, mothers of ill children (suffering from rare diseases) have been central actors in the cannabis movement and within these associations (KI1, KI3, KI4, KI9). In this regard, one respondent noted that this has meant that "there is no stigmatization around the theme or their engagement – they are actors that can sensitize the public opinion" (KI4). At the same time, it was noted that this is "still a conservative activism" (KI1) and that the movement remains small. The South African context offers a different case of cannabis associativism, where the medical aspect is less present and where the self-regulatory codes developed by the associations resemble those of other European CSCs (in terms of the requirements for membership, of how collective cultivation is organized, providing a consumption space for members, and setting limits to quantities distributed, etc.). These 'grow clubs' – with a "focus on craft" (KI10) and set up primarily for recreational use - have emerged in that country since 2018–2019 (KI10, KI12), following a ruling from the country's Constitutional Court which "decriminalized personal cannabis use and possession within a private space" (Steynvaart & Wegerif, 2021). Some elements of continuity and change can thus be found in these more recent developments.

Finally, and just as the curtain was closing on this book, Malta has become the second country worldwide, and the first in Europe, to legalize and regulate the CSC model. The new law establishes an Authority on the Responsible Use of Cannabis (ARUC) and foresees the creation of non-profit associations (registered with the ARUC) that can cultivate cannabis "exclusively for its members in a collective manner to distribute it only to those members" (Bill 241, Article 7A). Accordingly, access to the Maltese CSCs will be restricted to members (who are at least 18 years old) and will be able to enrol a maximum of 500 individuals per club. The CSCs will be allowed to distribute a maximum of 7 grams on a single day or more than 50 grams per month. The law puts forward several other requirements concerning the packaging of cannabis products, reporting to ARUC, prohibition of advertisement, among others. At the time of writing, it is unclear whether the CSC model had a presence in Malta prior to the passing of this new legislation (similarly to what had happened in Uruguay) (Pardal et al., 2019; Pardal et al., 2020), so this is likely to be a novelty in implementation.

Themes and structure of this book

This overview of the key milestones in the development of the CSC model in the past 30 years (if one can agree on when to place the start date) touches upon some of the themes and questions that will be further discussed throughout this book. CSCs are a relatively deep-rooted model in Europe and seem to have expanded to other regions as well. It is a model born within a prohibitionist regime, but that has also been integrated into post-prohibition legal frameworks. These geographical, cultural, and legal backgrounds, as well as the diverse views constructed around the model (not least by the groups of users directly implementing it) have translated into different versions or variants of the CSC model. While some consider this (de-)construction of the model as a threat (and in some cases, as a 'misuse' of the concept), others see it as an opportunity for pushing and re-shaping the boundaries of the model.

Part I of this book brings forward new insights from concrete experiences with the CSC model in different settings. **Bone et al.** draw on survey data to examine the CSC landscape in Europe and whether and how a transnational social movement network of CSCs has been or is being constructed. **Musto** focuses on the Uruguayan case, discussing how the CSC model ended up being integrated in that country's cannabis legal reform, as well as exposing the current experiences of implementation of the model – relying on qualitative data from interviews, observations, and a document analysis. **Rychert & Wilkins** draw also on qualitative data to shed light into the New Zealand context, the attempts to set up CSCs, and the barriers and opportunities for future development of the model in the country. **Marín-Gutiérrez & Hinojosa-Becerra** focus on the original CSC setting: Spain. Including visual materials captured by the authors during a period of 20 years (during which they conducted ethnographic research), this contribution identifies and discusses the different meanings and manifestations of a 'social' CSC. **Álvarez et al.** engage in a comparative analysis of survey data among CSC members in Uruguay and Belgium, unveiling who joins these associations, how (much) they use cannabis and how they obtain it, and what their preferences are in terms of cannabis policies.

In Part II, we find a number of reflections on the place and role of CSCs in broader policy designs and discussions. **Rondelez & Pardal** take on Foucault's notion of counter-conduct and apply it to the context of CSCs, untangling CSCs' relationship with peers and with *prima facie* actors of power. **Fortin** sketches a theoretical model wherein the CSC model is included alongside commercial outlets and medical-only suppliers. **Dilley et al.** pay attention to the implementation of a commercial model for the supply of cannabis in Washington (USA), considering the transition from 'cooperatives' and 'collective gardens'. In turn, **Capler & Bear** look at the Canadian case, focusing on the choices made with the introduction of a legal framework for cannabis supply in the country, and what that has meant for earlier grassroots experiments such as the compassion clubs. Finally, **Belackova et al.** explore the notion of 'drug social clubs', considering the opportunities and barriers for users of other substances to self-organize and supply themselves in a re-interpretation of the CSC model.

Notes

1 This is based on a review of the literature. In a first phase, known sources that addressed the topic of CSCs – including own publications, were collected. Following that, more systematic searches using the term 'Cannabis Social Club' and other combinations of words (e.g. cannabis AND association; cannabis AND collective) were run on Google Scholar. The terms were translated to Dutch, French, Portuguese and Spanish and relevant sources in those languages were also reviewed. Sources that described or included information about the functioning or characteristics of CSCs were considered relevant for the purposes of this analysis. Both scientific research as well as grey literature were reviewed. Additional sources were retrieved through snowballing. A total of 63 sources were collected and reviewed thematically on NVivo. In addition, to better understand more recent developments in non-European countries, targeted searches were carried to identify potential settings with CSC and/or CSC-related activity. Key respondents were invited from the following countries: Argentina, Brazil, Chile, Costa Rica, Ecuador, and South Africa. The European Coalition for Just and Effective Drug Policies (ENCOD) was also consulted. This is not meant as a comprehensive overview, but it is used here to illustrate some of the current developments in this area. A brief interview protocol was used that touched upon the following broad topics: history of CSCs/cannabis associations in the country; legal framework; volume of CSCs/cannabis associations in the country; contacts between domestic associations and other similar associations in Europe/other countries; key characteristics of the CSCs/cannabis associations. In total, 13 key informants were interviewed between July and October of 2021, through online video-conferencing platforms. The interviewees were researchers studying CSCs/cannabis associations or representatives of cannabis associations. The notes taken during the interviews were brought into NVivo for analysis. Legal texts and other policy documents (some of which recommended by the interviewees) concerning the selected countries were also consulted.

2 Most court rulings had been favourable to the CSCs until early 2015, but since then different verdicts have been reached – for more on this please see Arana and Parés (2020).

3 There are reports of previous associations formed by cannabis activist collectives, including the Coordinadora Estatal de Organizaciones para la Normalización del Cannabis (1996–2002), which included cannabis associations from different regions

in Spain and later gave way to the creation of FAC (Arana & Montañés, 2011; Calafat et al., 2000; Hunt et al., 2010; Parés & Bouso, 2015).

4 These European Guidelines for Cannabis Social Clubs are available at: https://encod.org/the-european-guidelines-for-cannabis-social-clubs/ (last accessed 20 November 2021).

5 Casals & Marks (2017) consider that this 'exponential' growth was already beginning in 2007 (p. 482). The judicial decisions on cases involving CSCs in the early 2000s, which tended to held that CSCs' activities were not in violation of the Spanish criminal code (Casals & Marks, 2015; Sánchez & Collins, 2018) – and particularly a positive outcome in a court case involving the CSC Pannagh in 2007 (in which the judge ordered the confiscated cannabis to be returned to the association), may have also contributed to the upsurge of CSCs (Arana & Montañés, 2011; Martínez, 2015; Montañés, 2017; Val, 2017).

6 More specifically, CSCs seem to be present in larger numbers in the regions of Catalonia (Blickman, 2014; Decorte et al., 2017; Jansseune et al., 2019; Martínez, 2015; Parés-Franquero et al., 2019; Parés & Bouso, 2015) and the Basque Country (Blickman, 2014; Decorte et al., 2017; Parés-Franquero et al., 2019).

7 Although the new law (Law 19.172) was approved in 2013, the registry of CSCs was only opened in October of 2014 (Pardal et al., 2019; Queirolo et al., 2016).

8 Nevertheless, there have been some (relatively short-lived) attempts to regulate the model at regional and local level in Spain (Arana & Parés, 2020; Decorte & Pardal, 2020).

9 Nevertheless, in Uruguay – where the CSC model is regulated, there have also been indications of the existence of 'unregistered' clubs (i.e. CSCs that are not fully in adherence with the legal framework) and which may be operating as (for-profit) selling points in a grey market (Pardal et al., 2019; Queirolo, 2020).

10 CSCs producing and distributing cannabis have also included these public activism and lobbying initiatives as part of their repertoire of action (Pardal et al., 2020).

References

Alvarez, A., Gamella, J. F., & Parra, I. (2016). Cannabis cultivation in Spain: a profile of plantations, growers and production systems. *International Journal of Drug Policy*, 37, 70–81.

Arana, X., & Montañés, V. (2011). Cannabis cultivation in Spain – the case of Cannabis Social Clubs. In T. Decorte, G. R. Potter, & M. Bouchard (Eds), *World Wide Weed: global trends in cannabis cultivation and its control* (pp. 163–177). Farnham, UK: Ashgate.

Arana, X., & Parés, Ò. (2020). Cannabis Social Clubs in Spain: recent legal developments. In T. Decorte, S. Lenton, & C. Wilkins (Eds), *Legalizing cannabis: experiences, lessons and scenarios*. London and New York: Routledge.

Arana, X., & Sánchez, V. M. (2011). Cannabis cultivation in Spain – the case of Cannabis Social Clubs. In T. Decorte, G. R. Potter, & M. Bouchard (Eds), *World Wide Weed: global trends in cannabis cultivation and its control* (pp. 163–177). Farnham, UK: Ashgate.

Arnoso, A., & Elgorriaga, E. (2016). *Estudio de las pautas de consumo de cannabis en los Clubes Sociales de Cannabis y Evaluación de su eficacia*. Donostia/San Sebastián: Fundación Renovatio.

Barriuso, M. (2005). Propuesta de modelo legal para el cannabis en el Estado Español. *Eguzkilore*, 19, 151–167.

Barriuso, M. (2011). Cannabis Social Clubs in Spain: a normalizing alternative underway. *Series on Legislative Reform of Drug Policies*, 9, 1–8.

Barriuso, M. (2012). Ni prohibición ni mercantilización: buscando el equilibrio en la regulación legal del cannabis. In *Cannabis: usos, seguridad juridica y politicas* (pp. 167–181). Victoria-Gasteiz, Spain: Ararteko.

Belackova, V., Tomkova, A., & Zabransky, T. (2016). Qualitative research in Spanish cannabis social clubs: 'the moment you enter the door, you are minimising the risks'. *International Journal of Drug Policy*, 34, 49–57.

Belackova, V., & Wilkins, C. (2018). Consumer agency in cannabis supply - Exploring auto-regulatory documents of the cannabis social clubs in Spain. *International Journal of Drug Policy*, 54, 26–34.

Bennett, T., Jacques, S., & Wright, R. (2011). The emergence and evolution of drug user groups in the UK. *Addiction Research & Theory*, 19(6), 556–565.

Blickman, T. (2014). Cannabis policy reform in Europe: bottom up rather than top down. *Series on Legislative Reform of Drug Policies*, 28, 1–24.

Bone, M., & de Hoedt, G. (2018). Being the change: charting Greg de Hoedt's cannabis journey. *Drugs and Alcohol Today*, 18, 126–136.

Calafat, A., Juan, M., Becona, E., Fernandez, C., Gil, E., & Llopis, J. J. (2000). Estrategias y organizacion de la cultura pro-cannabis. *Adicciones*, 12, 231–273.

Casals, O., & Marks, A. (2015). *Proceso de regulación de clubes sociales de cannabis en Cataluña*. Retrieved from: http://observatoriocivil.org/wp-content/uploads/2015/02/OC-2015-3-Informe-170-v3.pdf (last accessed 23 March 2022).

Caulkins, J. P., & Kilmer, B. (2016). Considering marijuana legalization carefully: insights for other jurisdictions from analysis for Vermont. *Addiction*, 111(12), 2082–2089.

Caulkins, J. P., Kilmer, B., Kleiman, M. A. R., MacCoun, R. J., Midgette, G., Oglesby, P., Reuter, P. H.et al. (2015). *Considering marijuana legalization: insights for Vermont and other jurisdictions.* Santa Monica, CA: RAND Corporation.

Coombes, R. (2014). Cannabis regulation: high time for change? *British Medical Journal, Feature.* doi: doi:10.1136/bmj.g3382.

Decorte, T. (2014). De Belgische 'Cannabis Social Clubs': middenweg tussen zwarte markt en commerciele beschikbaarheid? *Panopticon*, 35(6), 520–537.

Decorte, T. (2015). Cannabis social clubs in Belgium: organizational strengths and weaknesses, and threats to the model. *International Journal of Drug Policy*, 26, 122–130.

Decorte, T. (2019). *Cannabis regulation in Europe: country report Belgium.* Amsterdam: Transnational Institute.

Decorte, T., & Pardal, M. (2017). Cannabis Social Clubs in Europe: prospects and limits. In R. Colson, & H. Bergeron (Eds), *European Drug Policies: the ways of reform* (pp. 285–299). New York: Routledge.

Decorte, T., & Pardal, M. (2020). Insights for the design of Cannabis Social Club regulation. In T. Decorte, S. Lenton, & C. Wilkins (Eds), *Legalizing cannabis: experiences, lessons and scenarios* (pp. 409–426). London and New York: Routledge.

Decorte, T., Pardal, M., Queirolo, R., Boidi, M. F., Sanchez, C., & Pares, O. (2017). Regulating Cannabis Social Clubs: a comparative analysis of legal and self-regulatory practices in Spain, Belgium and Uruguay. *International Journal of Drug Policy*, 43, 44–56.

Dos Santos, D. R., Henriques, C. J., Brito, E. H. S. (2020). Maconha medicinal: aspectos jurídicos e sociais. *Revista PIXELS*, III (July–December), 72–88.

Dos Santos, R. F., & Rosas, C. A. Da F. (2021). Geografia e cannabis: disputas territoriais no Brasil. *Revista Campo-Território*, 16(43), 48–72. Retrieved from: https://doi.org/10.14393/RCT164303 (last accessed 23 March 2022).

Dos Santos, R. F., & Rosas, C. A. R. F. (2021). *Quantificação das Associações Canábicas do Paraná*. Conference paper: XXVII Semana de Geografia UEPG – Decolonialidade, Posicionalidade e Ensino Remoto.
Efthimiou-Mordaunt, A. (2015). Junkies in the House of the Lord. *Substance Use & Misuse*, 50(8–9),1159–1164.
Feldman, H. W., & Mandel, J. (1998). Providing medical marijuana: the importance of Cannabis Clubs. *Journal of Psychoactive Drugs*, 30(2), 179–186.
Friedman, S. R., Jarlais, D. C. D., Sotheran, J. L., Garber, J., Cohen, H., & Smith, D. (1987). AIDS and self-organization among intravenous drug users. *International Journal of the Addictions*, 22(3), 201–219.
Friedman, S. R., Jong, W. d., Rossi, D., Touze, G., Rockwell, R., Jarlais, D. C. D., & Elovich, R. (2007). Harm reduction theory: users' culture, micro-social indigenous harm reduction, and the self-organization and outside-organizing of users' groups. *International Journal of Drug Policy*, 18, 107–117.
Gamella, J. F., & Rodrigo, M. L. J. (2004). A brief history of cannabis policies in Spain (1968–2003). *Journal of Drug Issues* (Summer), 623–659.
Ghehiouèche, F., & Zemouli, K. R. (2016). Cannabis Social Club: una política para el siglo XXI. Retrieved from: https://faaat.net/think-tank-en/csc-for-cnd/?lang=es (last accessed 25 March 2022).
Goumaz, C., Cau, J., & Broers, B. (2014). Le 'cannabis medical club', un modèle d'accès au cannabis thérapeutique? *Dépendances, Juillet* 2014(53), 20–23.
Grinspoon, L. (2003). The medical marijuana problem. *Journal of Cognitive Liberties*, 2, 63–81.
Hunt, N., Albert, E., & Montañés, V. (2010). User involvement and user organising in harm reduction. In EMCDDA (Ed.), *Harm reduction: evidence, impacts and challenges* (pp. 333–354). Luxembourg: Publications Office of the European Union.
Jansseune, L., Pardal, M., Decorte, T., & Parés Franquero, Ò. (2019). Revisiting the Birthplace of the Cannabis Social Club Model and the Role Played by Cannabis Social Club Federations. *Journal of Drug Issues*, 49(2), 338–354. doi:10.1177/0022042618815690.
Kilmer, B., Kruithof, K., Pardal, M., Caulkins, J. P., & Rubin, J. (2013). *Multinational overview of cannabis production regimes*. Santa Monica, CA: RAND Corporation.
Lakhdar, C. B. (2018). L'inéluctable légalisation du cannabis en France? *Revue d'économie politique*, 6(128), 1101–1122.
Lambert, L., & Martins, L. (2018). O poder judiciário como balcão de direitos: reflexões sobre as estratégias jurídicas para a garantia do uso medicinal da maconha. *Em Sociedade Revista do Departamento de Ciencias Sociais – PUC Minas*, 1 (1), 190–207.
Levayer, L. (2017). Regulación del mercado de cannabis en Uruguay. Génesis, implementación y retos de futuro. In D. P. Martínez (Ed.), *Las sendas de la regulación del cananbis en España* (pp. 314–329). Barcelona: Edicions Bellaterra.
Madera, H. (2017). Autocultivo y autocultivadores de cannabis. Desarollo del movimiento y peritaciones de consumos y cultivos. In D. P. Martínez (Ed.), *Las sendas de la regulación del cannabis en España* (pp. 177–190). Barcelona: Edicions Bellaterra.
Marín, I. (2008). La cultura 'cannábica' en España (1991–2007). (PhD). Universidad de Granada, Granada.
Marín, I. (2009). *Cannabis: el movimiento cannábico en España*. Madrid: Editorial Popular.

Marín, I., & Hinojosa, M. (2017). Veiticinco años del movimiento cannábico español. In D. P. Martínez (Ed.), *Las sendas de la regulación del cannabis en España* (pp. 123–135). Barcelona: Edicions Bellaterra.

Marks, A. (2019). Treating the 'personal' as private: contextualising the normative framework of Cannabis Clubs in Spain within a 'global model of constitutional rights'. *International & Comparative Law Quarterly*, 68(1). doi:10.2139/ssrn.2989771.

Martínez, D. P. (2015). Clubs sociales de cannabis: normalizacion, neoliberalismo, oportunidades politicas y prohibicionismo [EN translated version: Cannabis Social Clubs: normalisation, neoliberalism, political opportunities and prohibition]. *CLIVATGE*, 3, 92–112.

Montañés, V. (2017). Evolución del activismo cannábico en España. In D. P. Martínez (Ed.), *Las sendas de la reguiación del cannabis en España* (pp. 145–159). Barcelona: Edicions Bellaterra.

Montañés, V., & Oomen, J. (2009). Use of drugs and advocacy: a research into the participation of drug user organisations in the design of drug policies on a local and European level. Retrieved from: https://www.academia.edu/4156962/Hunt_Neil_Eliot_Albert_and_Monta%C3%B1%C3%A9s_Virginia_2010_User_involvement_and_user_organising_in_harm_reduction (last accessed 25 March 2022).

Muñoz, J. (2015). La relevancia penal de los Clubes Sociales de Cannabis. *Revista Electrónica de Ciencia Penal y Criminologia*, 17(22), 1–50.

Muñoz, J., & Soto, S. (2001). El uso terapéutico del cannabis y la creación de establecimientos para su adquisicion y consumo. *Revista de Derecho Penal y Criminología*, 2(7), 49–94.

Obradors-Pineda, A., Bouso, J.-C., Parés-Franquero, Ò., & Romaní, J.-O. (2021). Harm reduction and cannabis social clubs: Exploring their true potential. *International Journal of Drug Policy*, 97, 103358.

Pardal, M. (2016). Cannabis Social Clubs through the lens of the drug user movement. *Tijdschrift over Cultuur & Criminaliteit*, 6(2), 47–58.

Pardal, M. (2018a). An analysis of Belgian Cannabis Social Clubs' supply practices: a shapeshifting model? *International Journal of Drug Policy*, 57, 32–41.

Pardal, M. (2018b). The Belgian Cannabis Social Club landscape. *Drugs & Alcohol Today*, 18(2), 73–79.

Pardal, M., & Bawin, F. (2018). The supply of cannabis for medical use through Cannabis Social Clubs in Belgium. *Contemporary Drug Problems*, 45(2), 127–145.

Pardal, M., & Decorte, T. (2018). Cannabis use and supply patterns among Belgian Cannabis Social Club members. *Journal of Drug Issues*, 48(4), 689–709.

Pardal, M., Decorte, T., Bone, M., Parés, Ò., & Johansson, J. (2020). Mapping Cannabis Social Clubs in Europe. *European Journal of Criminology*, 0(0), 1477370820941392. doi:10.1177/1477370820941392.

Pardal, M., Queirolo, R., Álvarez, E., & Repetto, L. (2019). Uruguayan Cannabis Social Clubs: from activism to dispensaries? *International Journal of Drug Policy*, 73, 49–57.

Parés, Ò., & Bouso, J. C. (2015). Cannabis Social Clubs. In *Innovation born of necessity. pioneering drug policy in Catalonia*. New York: Open Society Foundations.

Parés-Franquero, Ò., Jubert-Cortiella, X., Olivares-Gálvez, S., Díaz-Castellano, A., Jiménez-Garrido, D. F., & Bouso, J. C. (2019). Use and habits of the protagonists of the story: Cannabis Social Clubs in Barcelona. *Journal of Drug Issues*, 49(4), 607–624.

Policarpo, F., & Martins, L. (2019). 'Dignidade', doença' e 'remédio': uma análise da construção médico-jurídica da maconha medicinal. *Revista Antropolítica*, 47, 143–166.

Queirolo, R. (2020). Uruguay: the first country to legalize cannabis. In T. Decorte, S. Lenton & C. Wilkins (Eds), *Legalizing cannabis: experiences, lessons and scenarios* (pp. 116–130). London and New York: Routledge.

Queirolo, R., Boidi, M. F., & Cruz, J. M. (2016). Cannabis clubs in Uruguay: The challenges of regulation. *International Journal of Drug Policy*, 34, 41–48.

Reiman, A. E. (2008). Self-efficacy, social support and service integration at medical cannabis facilities in the San Francisco Bay area of California. *Health and Social Care in the Community*, 16(1), 31–41.

Sánchez, C., & Collins, M. (2018). Better to ask forgiveness than permission: Spain's sub-national approach to drug policy. *Global Drug Policy Observatory, Policy Brief* 12 (June), 1–26.

Steynvaart, M., & Wegerif, M. (2021). High time South Africa finalises legalities around cannabis social clubs. *Daily Maverick South Africa*. Retrieved from: https://www.dailymaverick.co.za/article/2021-06-24-high-time-south-africa-finalises-legalities-around-cannabis-social-clubs/ (last accessed 1 December 2021).

Val, I. (2017). Evolución y actualidad de los clubes sociales de cannabis en Euskadi, una mirada retrospectiva de los últimos veinte años. In D. P. Martínez (Ed.), *Las sendas de la regulación del cannabis en España* (pp. 160–176). Barcelona: Edicions Bellaterra.

Zobel, F., Marthaler, M., & Broers, B. (2014). Le modèle des Cannabis Social Clubs. *Dépendances, Juillet* 2014(53), 15–17.

Part 1

2 Cannabis Social Clubs in Europe

A transnational social movement network in the making?

Melissa Bone, Mafalda Pardal, Òscar Parés and Tom Decorte

Background

Cannabis Social Clubs in Europe and beyond

Cannabis social clubs (CSCs or clubs) are typically defined as non-profit collectives where cannabis is produced and distributed among a closed circuit of adult cannabis consumers. The CSC model could also have considerable policy relevance in terms of facilitating and/or co-creating harm reduction initiatives with other drug policy stakeholders, and the model could provide a social space for additional peer to peer support for both recreational and medicinal cannabis consumers. In a more ideological sense, the CSC model has the potential to challenge the present culture of drug control as well, since in most cases it is a grassroots, bottom-up initiative. According to Bone (2020):

> this rare level of consumer control poses a challenge to traditional regulatory thought, where cannabis is controlled by the government, the free market and/or the medical establishment. Thus, the CSC model is unique since it resists the dominant political powers in drug policy design.
>
> (p. 58)

Originating in Spain, CSCs now operate in jurisdictions across the world, in different socio-political contexts and under different legal frameworks. However, apart from in Uruguay, CSCs remain illegal or have otherwise operated at the margins of domestic drug control legislation, risking law enforcement detection. While the model developed in Spain in the early 1990s (Parés & Bouso, 2015),[1] it was the resultant court cases, the Spanish judiciary, media involvement, academic involvement – see the influential report by Muñoz and Soto (2000) commissioned by the government of Andalusia to explore the legality of cannabis establishments at the time - and of course the clubs themselves that planted the initial seeds for the model's success in terms of its growth both domestically and beyond the Spanish border.

The development of the Spanish CSCs inspired citizens in other countries to test the legal limits of their own domestic drug control legislation. For

DOI: 10.4324/9781003055679-2

example, the Belgian CSCs have been challenging the boundaries of Belgian law (Decorte, 2015), particularly a tolerance policy concerning the individual possession of one plant by one person. Although, in 2017 the College of Public Prosecutors explicitly noted that this policy does not apply to the collective possession of cannabis in the context of associations (Pardal, 2018). Pardal (ibid.) draws on research with Belgian CSCs to highlight that their model was inspired by earlier Spanish CSC experiments, which is evidence of a knowledge transfer between activists across countries in Europe.

Much of the existing research focuses on CSCs in Spain and Belgium (Arana & Parés, 2020; Belackova et al., 2016; Decorte et al., 2017; Jansseune et al., 2019; Marín, 2009; Pardal, 2018; Parés et al., 2019), and an accurate in-depth understanding of the CSC phenomenon in Europe was considered to be missing (EMCDDA, 2016). While there were reports of CSCs existing elsewhere in Europe, there was limited or no information about the phenomenon (Blickman, 2014; Decorte & Pardal, 2017). To fill this knowledge-gap, we created and distributed an online survey in 2018–2019, to provide an international, comparative view of CSCs across Europe. The survey mapped the presence of CSCs across the European Union[2] and examined how CSCs operated in those countries (see Pardal et al., 2020a).

Three in four European clubs in our sample (n=61) allowed cannabis consumption on the CSC premises and the same number were involved in cannabis cultivation and distribution. The European CSCs were also engaged in a diverse repertoire of action (when asked about the types of activities they undertook in the last two years). Almost all the clubs in the sample (n=74; 91%) shared information materials, 79% (n=64) held informative events including debates, lectures, and/or workshops, and two in three CSCs (n=54; 67%) organized entertainment events (e.g. a comedy night, musical activities, art exhibitions or competitions). Significantly, for the purposes of this chapter, more than half of the clubs (n=51; 63%) had spent time lobbying and informing key stakeholders and had either organized or participated in other forms of activism related to cannabis policy reform (e.g. protests, demonstrations, collaborations with other CSCs and activists).

Understanding the transnationalization of activist networks

Earlier research has considered CSCs to be important social movement organizations (SMOs) within the broader cannabis movement, which seeks to overturn the current prohibitionist cannabis regime (Marín, 2008; Marín & Hinojosa, 2017). According to the classic definition put forward by McCarthy and Zald (1977), a SMO is "a complex, or formal, organization which identifies its goals with the preferences of a social movement or a countermovement and attempts to implement those goals" (p. 1218). SMOs are important actors within a social movement: they can mobilize people and financial resources, help develop a movement's sense of identity, and ensure continuity of the claims through time (Della Porta & Diani, 2014; Edwards & McCarthy, 2004; Kriesi, 1996; McCarthy, 1996).

As multiple groups/SMOs tend to be active and operating on the same or similar issues, this may give rise to different inter-organizational relationships, characterized by different levels of cooperation (or competition) among them (Della Porta & Diani, 2014). This may also be the case with CSCs, as several of these associations have appeared within and across countries in Europe and therefore 'occupy' the same space. In an earlier study of the Belgian CSC landscape, Pardal (2018) found that cooperation among CSCs in that country was limited and that the field remained somewhat fragmented – despite CSCs seeking collaboration with other secondary organizations (e.g. lobbying organizations, grow shops, etc.) and with CSCs abroad.

Three key processes tend to characterize the transnationalization of social movements. The first is diffusion, defined by Della Porta and Tarrow (2005), as "the spread of movement ideas, practices, and frames from one country to another" (p. 2). Diffusion may occur when SMOs in one country integrate or adopt practices of SMOs in other countries. Underlying transnational diffusion is the communication of information across actors in different places. This can happen through social bonds and personal networks (relational diffusion), through mass media and other forms of mass communication which do not involve a particular social tie (nonrelational diffusion), or even by means of key individuals or 'brokers', who connect "'otherwise unconnected sites" (Tarrow, 2005, p. 104). As noted above, the Spanish CSC boom contributed to the emergence of CSCs in other European countries, which seemed to have adopted similar forms of collective action (although local specificities remain): including (collective) cannabis cultivation and distribution, the sharing of information, organizing informative/educational and social events, lobbying, and protesting activities. In the case of the appearance of CSCs in Uruguay, the available evidence suggests that both international drug experts and activists acted as 'knowledge brokers' in the process leading up to the design and passage of the new law (which integrated CSCs) in that country (von Hoffmann, 2016).

CSCs' activities have also led to the development of various networks and federations of CSCs, which issue good practice guidelines for their operation both domestically and across Europe (Belackova & Wilkins, 2018; Jansseune et al., 2019). For instance, the European Coalition for Just and Effective Drug Policies (ENCOD)[3] grouped together several European CSCs (creating a directory of 'ENCOD registered European Cannabis Social Clubs'), helped frame the goals associated with CSCs and developed a Europe-wide code of conduct for these associations, among other activities in this area (ENCOD, 2011, 2020). This could be seen as an example of transnational coalition formation that involves CSCs and CSC representation (Tarrow, 2005).

A second process that might be observed is internalization, i.e. when protest events are directed against domestic institutions, but for conflicts or decisions that were taken at an international level. Typically, the process goes as follows: there is external pressure from international institutions regarding a policy, which results in its implementation by domestic governments. In turn, this implementation triggers protests – which target the domestic government implementing it (despite it being part of an international policy agenda). Arguably, this element might be observed in the broader cannabis movement as well, as domestic cannabis policies are to some degree tied to the international cannabis prohibition system (as most countries are signatory parties to the UN Conventions, for instance).[4] As such, contention at the domestic level against current cannabis laws could also be seen as a form of internalization.

The third process or strategy is externalization, in which protests on domestic issues are projected at international institutions or foreign actors (Della Porta & Tarrow, 2005; Tarrow, 2005). For example, when CSC representatives and other activists from different countries (e.g. Belgium, Germany, Spain) have exposed their views in public hearings, conferences, and other events hosted at the European Parliament in Brussels,[5] they have externalized their demands.

Beyond forming these networks and transnational bonds, drug reform strategies could align themselves with the prevailing power vector within the policy community, which, according to MacGregor (2017), is important for interdependencies and relationships of trust to emerge; to advance policy change. Goldsmith (2015) additionally notes that there should be an element of strategic alignment where policy change strategies are tailored to key government priorities. The Uruguayan cannabis activists knew this. By forming a legalizing coalition with state officials, they framed the regulation of cannabis through a responsibility lens and developed the Regulación Responsable platform to convince a skeptical public and communicate the advantages of cannabis reform (Castro, 2014; von Hoffman, 2016). This legal change also came about in a favorable political context where in addition to the important role played by “pro-legalization leaders in strategic political positions”, there were societal concerns with public safety (Queirolo et al., 2019, p. 1313). While the CSC model was not included in a first version of the bill its inclusion was demanded by cannabis activists and young legislators, who were familiar with the developments of CSCs in Spain (Musto, this volume; Pardal et al., 2019).

Our goals

The presence of several groups of activists, with varying ideologies and motivations, engaged in a broader cannabis movement across different settings begs the question of whether and how they are connected. Drawing on novel data from a 2018–2019 survey, this chapter analyses whether CSCs in Europe have built collaborative relationships and whether supra-national organizations have been created to support their efforts (McCammon & Moon, 2015), i.e. whether a transnational social movement network of CSCs has emerged at the European level. Secondly, in our analysis we aim to map out the network of relationships of European CSCs both at the domestic and transnational level.

Methods

The data included in this chapter derives from a 30-item survey (carried out in 2018–2019) which was translated into all the official languages of the EU zone and sent via email and social media to potential participants and gatekeepers. 81 CSCs completed the survey across 13 European countries, most notably Spain, the UK, and Belgium. There was a disparity in how the CSCs defined themselves, compounded by the fact that there is no common agreed upon normative or shared legal definition of what constitutes a CSC (Decorte & Pardal, 2020). As such, we drew on the CSCs' own conceptualization as a sufficient criterion for inclusion in the survey. Basically, if an organization considered itself a CSC, then it was eligible to participate. We employed a mixture of strategies to identify and recruit participants. We conducted exploratory online searches to identify CSCs in Europe, consulted the list of CSCs included on ENCOD's website, attended events and conferences organized by CSCs and other cannabis activists and relied on our own networks of contacts in the field building on our previous research (Bone & de Hoedt, 2018; Decorte et al., 2017; Jansseune et al., 2019; Pardal, 2018, Parés & Bouso, 2015). We created a website and contacted CSCs via email, social media, and/or phone.

The survey included both closed-ended questions analysed with statistical analysis software SPSS 25 and open-ended questions analysed using qualitative analysis software NVivo 12. For the purposes of this chapter, we have also exported all the answers relating to whether there have been knowledge exchanges, collaborations or conflicts between CSCs within and across countries in Europe, and with other key stakeholders, in an excel document and coded the answers thematically. Of a total of 30 questions, 19 questions were closed and collated information on membership numbers, membership criteria, and membership of federations or other international organizations, the operation, and function of each CSC, including the activities and events the club partakes in, staffing costs, the cannabis products available to members, cannabis supply channels, and information relating to cannabis cultivation and the number of growers. Eleven questions were open-ended to collate data on CSC relationships with: other CSC's (both domestically and internationally), the police and the judiciary, the media, professional services, local authorities, and other third parties such as criminal entrepreneurs. For a more comprehensive overview of our approach, please see Pardal et al. (2020a).

Results

The ideology motivations and visions of the European CSCs

When asked if the club is in favor of legal regulation of Cannabis Social Clubs in their own respective country, 78 out of 81 CSCs answered the question, with 74 CSCs indicating actively supporting it. More than half of the clubs indicated they had spent time notifying, lobbying, and informing key stakeholders (n=51; 63%) (Pardal, 2020a). CSC Federations seem to also play a role here, as reported by one of the CSCs:

> A regional federation has been created to serve as an interlocutor with the political powers and the media. In addition, regular meetings are held with different authorities to discuss the different harm reduction and prevention activities carried out by the Association.
>
> (CSC25)

One CSC in the UK has also been contacted by the National Institute for Clinical Excellence (NICE), to help provide national guidance for medical professionals, in response to the UK government's rescheduling of cannabis for medical use in 2018 (see Bone & Potter, 2021 for more detail). A further three CSCs from Spain mentioned the Regulación Responsable platform in relation to policy making as well.

Interestingly, one UK CSC stated that they focus predominately on promoting medical clubs: "We fundraise for new micro medical clubs and help them with admin set up" and another UK CSC expanded on their motivation for helping medical consumers:

> The medical members find the club a safe haven away from isolation at home and a friendly place to come and speak to other patients that use cannabis to help many conditions, this has helped people come out of depressions which always make small symptoms seem bigger. One member who is a liver transplant patient told me this week 'thank you for making me feel normal for the day' after he had his first day at the club. That's why we do what we do. This member has been to prison for growing his own medicine. We have people that work in all kinds of professions and the diversity is incredible to be around at times.
>
> (CSC57)

When asked about the legal regulation of the CSC model, three clubs harnessed human rights discourse when answering, stating that they have formed the clubs "in defense of our rights" (CSC43), to "promote civil disobedience" (CSC71), and that they consider the "final victory" to be "free planting + self-supply" (CSC64), in a similar vein to the ideology espoused by the early Spanish associations in the 1990s. The clubs are aware of other commercial variants of the model (and of the other commercial suppliers) too, but some clubs tried to promote the 'traditional' CSC model to counteract this development:

> We loosely follow the UKCSC framework, we attempt to regulate quality and price in a number of ways. Mostly we educate on how things should be done and try to be in place doing that before big business comes along. We have a commercial club nearby doing their thing too.
>
> (CSC82)

Domestic CSC collaborations

Within our sample, 3 in 4 CSCs (n=61) reported collaborating with other CSCs in their own country. Domestic collaboration was the highest in the UK with 88% of clubs collaborating, 77% in Spain and 62% elsewhere in Europe – see Table 2.1. Most of the CSCs in our sample were members of a CSC Federation or another umbrella organization (n=57, 70%). In some countries, all clubs that participated in our survey claimed to be a member of a CSC Federation (i.e. Austria, Belgium, Ireland, Italy, Romania). There were only 3 EU countries in our sample where there were no reports of CSCs being affiliated with a CSC Federation (i.e. Hungary, Poland, and the Netherlands). In total, 26 CSC Federations or other international organizations were mentioned by our respondents. CSCs which explicitly mentioned federations or other international organizations comprised 72% of the Spanish subsample; 65% of the UK subsample and 71% from other EU countries. The federations or umbrella organizations most frequently mentioned were the European non-profit organization ENCOD (n=14) – an example of a supra-national organization in this area, the UKCSC Federation (n=11),[6] the FAC,[7] and ConFAC[8] in Spain (n=5 respectively) as well as several of its regional branches - including the CatFAC[9] in Catalonia (n=5).

Among the smaller number of CSCs reporting not collaborating with other CSCs in the same country, the reasons put forward to explain this lack of contact related to infighting with other clubs or the non-existence of other CSCs in that country. One CSC further expanded on this stating:

> We had contact with all clubs in Belgium in the past, today still with a few. We are focusing on our own club. Activists tend to start fighting among each other, we had enough of this and focus on doing our own thing.
>
> (CSC70)

Table 2.1 Contacts with other CSCs (in the same country and in other countries)

With CSCs in same country	*N*	*Yes*	*%*	*No*	*%*	*No answer*	*%*
CSCs in Spain	43	33	76.7	9	20.9	1	2.3
CSCs in the UK	17	15	88.2	1	5.9	1	5.9
CSCs elsewhere in Europe	21	13	61.9	5	23.8	3	14.3
Total sample	**81**	**61**	**75.3**	**15**	**18.5**	**5**	**6.2**
With CSCs in other countries	*N*	*Yes*	*%*	*No*	*%*	*No answer*	
CSCs in Spain	**43**	5	11.6	34	79.1	4	9.3
CSCs in the UK	**17**	7	41.2	7	41.2	3	17.6
CSCs elsewhere in Europe	**21**	10	47.6	11	52.4	-	-
Total sample	**81**	**22**	**27.2**	**52**	**64.2**	**7**	**8.6**

At the same time, in two countries where we only recruited one CSC (i.e. in Hungary and Ireland), both CSCs indicated having contacts with other clubs domestically. This suggests that there may be more CSCs active in those countries and which did not participate in the survey. A further 38 CSCs listed individual clubs they collaborated with in their home country. This is evidence of national collaboration between CSCs with one club stating: "We help all the clubs along the coast and have opened up our doors to club admins and managers that want some more advice and help to get to the stage we are at" (CSC57).

In addition, when asked in a previous question about what activities their CSC undertakes to regulate its existence, 24 out of the 78 CSCs who answered this question reported that they were involved in federation-led activities to lobby policy makers and implement domestic and regional legislation such as La Rosa Verda, a regulatory initiative for CSCs in Catalonia. This initiative collected 57,000 citizen signatures to change the law in the Catalonian parliament (Arana & Parés, 2020).

Although 83% of all clubs in our sample answered 'no' when asked separately whether their club had experienced conflicts with other CSCs (Table 2.2), it is interesting to note that only 23 out of the 67 clubs (which indicated not having had conflicts) expanded on their answer. Almost half of those who expanded on their answer (n=11) reported clear conflicts and rivalries. Five of those conflicts related to differing ideologies between CSCs and between members within a club (e.g. those wanting to make a profit and move away from the 'typical' model and those wanting to preserve a non-profit logic): "The main problem was the commercial spirit that some original members wanted to impress upon the society, unlike the rest, so their memberships were rejected, and they founded another club" (CSC17).

Issues related to "competition" (n=1), "envy" (n=1) and "egos" (n=2) between clubs were also mentioned, and one CSC specifically related this to gender:

> We have experienced conflicts, mainly due to a female running the club and male ego's rising. Not wanting to work together in the local area as they have their own agendas.
>
> (CSC50)

Table 2.2 Reported conflicts between CSCs

Incidents with other CSCs	*N*	*Yes*	*%*	*No*	*%*	*No answer*	
CSCs in Spain	**43**	2	4.6	41	95.4	-	-
CSCs in the UK	**17**	4	23.5	11	64.7	2	11.8
CSCs elsewhere in Europe	**21**	5	23.8	15	71.4	1	4.8
Total sample	**81**	**11**	**13.6**	**67**	**82.7**	**3**	**3.7**

Nevertheless, seven clubs reported a good relationship with other CSCs, despite the question on conflicts between clubs being negatively framed (i.e. we did not enquire about the nature of the relationship in general, but specifically asked about problematic contact between CSCs):

> We have a very good relationship with the clubs that are members of the Federation to which we belong.
>
> (CSC8)

The remaining (n=5) responses were neutral with regards to experiencing problems or conflicts with other CSCs:

> No, not really. We never had any practical problems with other clubs. There is a difference in views, visions and approaches with other clubs, but I would not describe that as having problems with them.
>
> (CSC70)

Transnational CSC collaborations

Only one in four CSCs in our sample (n=22; 27%) reported collaborations or contact with CSCs abroad (please see Table 2.1). International collaborations were less common in Spain (n=5; 12%) than in other European countries (n=7; 41% in the UK; n=10; 48% elsewhere in Europe).

One CSC stated that they had made online contact with clubs abroad (CSC20), and another club (CSC63) noted that while they do not collaborate with other clubs, they do collaborate with other cannabis patient organizations in Poland, Croatia, Spain, and the USA. The supranational organization ENCOD was also considered to act as a gatekeeper for one club (CSC66) – as we noted earlier, this was also the umbrella organization most frequently mentioned by the survey respondents. Nevertheless, for one club – which considered itself to be the sole CSC in its respective country, there remains room for improvement in terms of the support provided by the international organizations, and by ENCOD in particular:

> It would be desirable to network real European cooperation and work together on its goals. After all, most of them are in the European Union. Unfortunately, ENCOD does not really help in [anonymized country] either. A legal ring backed by lawyers would certainly speed things up positively.

Additionally, large-scale cannabis fairs and events like Spannabis (Barcelona) were mentioned by one club as facilitating transnational collaborations (CSC75).

The relationship with local authorities, the police, and the judiciary

In general, one in three CSCs (n=28; 35% of our sample) reported having had problems or incidents with police or with the judiciary (see Table 2.3). In Spain, less than half of the CSCs in our sample reported such incidents (n=18; 42% of the subsample). Remarkably, none of the participating clubs from the UK reported problems or incidents with the police or the judiciary. One of these clubs explained this by noting its adherence to guidelines from the UKCSC Federation: "Not to date. We play by the UKCSC guidelines and this keeps us well away from commercial level production that would be targeted" (CSC48).

Elsewhere in Europe about half of the clubs reported incidents with the police (n=10; 48% of the subsample). These clubs were located in Austria, Belgium, Poland, and Slovenia. Some of the reported adverse contact with the criminal justice system included police raids, being prosecuted in court, receiving criminal sentences which involved prison time and/or fines, as one respondent noted: "A lot of problems with police raids, and arrest of our members. Everyone has a court judgment and history in prisons" (CSC81).

In other European countries, such as the Czech Republic, Germany, Hungary, Ireland, Italy, Romania, and the Netherlands, none of the participating CSCs reported such difficulties. Significantly, there is also evidence of clubs working together to protect each other from criminalization and employing the same legal representation, with one CSC stating:

> On one occasion we were given a package of marijuana for the Copa.[10] We had an oral hearing and they filed 25g of weed. It was stated that it was a consignment for self-consumption by members of another association who did not want to fly with cannabis according to lawyers of both associations.
>
> (CSC16)

A number of clubs reported administrative incidents (n=13); referring solely to administrative matters where they had been required to provide documentation to local authorities, process a license with the appropriate local council to legitimize the clubs' activities, or be subject to a one off

Table 2.3 Reported incidents between CSCs and police and judiciary

Incidents with police & judiciary	*N*	*Yes*	*%*	*No*	*%*	*No answer*	*%*
CSCs in Spain	43	18	41.9	25	58.1	-	-
CSCs in the UK	17	-	-	16	94.1	1	5.9
CSCs elsewhere in Europe	21	10	47.6	11	52.4	-	-
Total sample	**81**	**28**	**34.6**	**52**	**64.2**	**1**	**1.2**

"civilian drug investigator check-up" (CSC75), or a visit from a local council inspector. One of the clubs mentions "liaising with the police for large events" (CSC57), and one of the three clubs reporting robberies stated that they had reported theirs to the police (CSC26), demonstrating a level of cooperation with the police and local authorities.

Relationship with professionals and professional services in harm reduction or drug treatment

Two in three CSCs in our sample report collaboration with professionals or professional services in drug prevention, harm reduction or drug treatment (n=57; 70% of the sample) (see Table 2.4). Four in five Spanish CSCs have some collaboration with professionals (n=35; 81% of the subsample). Half of the CSCs we recruited in the UK report some collaboration with professionals (n=9; 53% of the UK subsample). Elsewhere in Europe, 13 clubs report collaboration with professionals or professional services (62% of the subsample). Clubs in Hungary, Slovenia, and the Netherlands report no such collaboration.

Only one CSC reported that professional services have refused to engage in a dialogue and two of the CSCs who answered 'no' did so for ideological reasons, as they did not support prevention strategies. Although noteworthy, this opinion was an anomaly within our sample.

A proportion of CSCs provided workshops and talks at cannabis events for members and other service providers (n=10), as well as giving and receiving training on harm reduction and treatment from the drug organizations they collaborate with (n=16). The Spanish CSCs in particular referred to Energy Control[11] (n=12), ICEERS[12] (n=5) and CSC Federations such as CatFAC (n=1) and FEDCAC[13] (n=1) when discussing training programs, workshops, talks, and the dissemination of relevant information and advice. One CSC also reported testing cannabis products to ensure their safety: "We collaborate with Energy Control. We receive charts and presentations on risk prevention. We also take samples of cannabis for analysis and supervision purposes" (CSC32).

As we discuss elsewhere (Pardal et al., 2020a), the CSCs in our sample undertook a range of activities beyond the cultivation and distribution of cannabis, including sharing information materials and organizing informative

Table 2.4 Collaboration with professionals and professional services

	N	*Yes*	*%*	*No*	*%*	*No answer*	*%*
CSCs in Spain	43	35	81.4	6	13.9	2	4.6
CSCs in the UK	17	9	52.9	7	41.2	1	5.9
CSCs elsewhere in Europe	21	13	61.9	8	38.1	-	-
Total sample	**81**	**57**	**70.4**	**21**	**25.9**	**3**	**3.7**

events, organizing entertainment activities, lobbying, and engaging in protests and demonstrations. With regards to information sharing focusing on harm reduction, 15 CSCs explicitly stated that they disseminated "information" and "advice" to members. Furthermore, 5 CSCs had also undertaken an "expert" role through acting as professional drug treatment services at times:

> We have started speaking to local services to help them understand problematic cannabis use in teens and also for spice [synthetic cannabinoid] users. We have seen first-hand how legal CBD products can be effective at breaking the cycle for spice users and get them into a normal life pattern.
>
> (CSC57)

The CSCs reported collaborating with experts, including doctors (n=10), counsellors (n=4), psychologists (n=6), and a pharmacist (n=1). Clubs have also reported working with community groups and mental health teams and have referred patients to these organizations (n=3), and/or have shared information on a patients' cannabis consumption with their consent (n=3):

> We work with local community groups and project leaders on a variety of projects. We also work with the local carers' networks, outreach teams, and community mental health teams. We share medical information with doctors with the patient's permission about cannabis consumption.
>
> (CSC61)

When asked about collaborations with professional services, the discourse focused on responsible use, as a considerable proportion of CSCs (n=15) highlighted the importance of "risk reduction", "responsible regulation", and "consumer responsibility". Interestingly, one CSC focused on the management of "pleasures" as well as "risks", since the training received from the organization Energy Control emphasized the management of both.

However, there seems to be room for improvement in terms of the relationship established with stakeholders such as professional services. For instance, when asked about the most urgent problems their club was facing,[14] three CSCs referred to the need to improve testing of their supply (CSC32; 48; 63), and one CSC noted that health services lacked the political and institutional will to take patients' needs seriously (CSC69). CSC74 also expanded on the need to develop a stronger, official relationship with service providers given the stigma surrounding cannabis:

> The social and legal stigma makes it very difficult to establish a more solid relationship where research facilities, testing facilities, and information materials would go a long way to adding more credibility to the clubs and inspire people to believe that a positive change is on our doorstep.

The relationship with the media

When asked whether the local, regional or national media had ever reported about their club 77 out of 81 clubs answered the question; 27 CSCs (33%) stated that there had never been any contact with the media. At least two of those reported making a conscious decision not to engage. CSC61 reported that they "have many requests" but refused to engage and CSC58 expanded further, refusing because of their overarching motivation to help patients: "No, we have never tried to gain any attention, our prerogative is to help patients get the access they need". The remaining 50 CSCs (62%) have engaged with the media to varying degrees with one CSC (69) responding: "We try to use the media as much as possible. 20 articles per year".

The clubs engaged with the media at a local, national, and international level. Half of all the CSCs who answered that there had been media involvement, considered it to be at a local and regional level (n=25). These clubs were interviewed on local radio stations, TV programs, and in local newspapers. A proportion of CSCs (n=8) were also involved in national media reporting, focusing on the benefits of the CSC model and how it operates in practice, and a small number of CSCs (n=5) stated that they had engaged with foreign media, including South American, Canadian, German, Italian, French, and other European media organizations.

Out of the 50 CSCs who had engaged with the media, 22 clubs explicitly stated that the reporting had been positive, two clubs answered that there had been a mixture of positive and negative reporting and five clubs answered that the reporting had been negative. Two of the CSCs provide reasons for collaborating with the media, namely: "to normalize the situation of the association' (CSC25) and to 'shake off the stigma suffered by cannabis users" (CSC6). One CSC even harnessed the power of the media to counteract misinformation about the club that was released by the police: "Information given by the police was false, we had to correct and thanks to the media, which publicized our counter information" (CSC41).

Of the five CSCs who stated that there had been negative reporting by the media, two CSCs expanded on their answer, noting that the media "manipulated statements" (CSC64), and "is looking for sensation" (CSC70).

Discussion and conclusions

European CSCs: connected domestically with fewer transnational ties

The results of the survey reveal little evidence of transnational collaborations between CSCs across Europe. Only one in four CSCs reported contacts or collaborations with CSCs from abroad. While there is some evidence of transnational links, including with other stakeholders – i.e., five CSCs stated they had collaborated with foreign media organizations, there remained a general reluctance to initiate transnational collaborations with other European clubs. Indeed, the data suggests a stronger level of domestic connectedness illustrated by the development of CSC Federations, particularly in Spain and the UK, and their contribution to spread practices, ideologies, and legislative initiatives within the CSCs' respective countries. Even so, the results suggest that CSCs across Europe are disconnected overall. Several reasons may help to explain this finding. Perhaps this is because the movement is still in its infancy in some of the countries surveyed; therefore, the focus may still be on building collaborations at the domestic level. Additionally, CSCs could primarily be interested in initiating changes to their own domestic legislation, since European CSCs operate in different socio-legal and political contexts; thus, national collaborations and lobbying efforts are more prominent here. Nonetheless, given the intertwining of international and domestic cannabis policies, protest action organized at the national level by CSCs and other actors could be seen through the prism of internalization, as argued above.

Given the number and history of CSCs in Spain it is also unsurprising that - where we found evidence of collaborative cross-country ties - it is the clubs from other jurisdictions that are most interested to connect and learn from the Spanish CSCs. Thus, there exists a space for international collaborations from other EU CSCs.

It is also worth noting that although the majority of the CSCs surveyed are not currently engaging with CSCs in other European countries, we now find associations self-defining as CSCs in (at least) 13 European countries. This is a striking evolution from the origins of the model in Spain in the 1990s (considering also that no legislation has been passed at the national level legitimizing the functioning of CSCs in Europe). The growth of the model across Europe also indicates that there may have been learning (even if indirectly or without explicit collaborations or brokerage) between groups of cannabis users in different countries, or that the actions of groups of users in one country may have inspired others to follow suit (Pardal, 2018). Furthermore, while we do not explore the internal functioning of the European CSCs in detail here (for more see Pardal et al., 2020a), research in this area has identified both similarities and differences in how CSCs operate – both within and across countries. Again, this could be an indication that there has been some diffusion of practices and learning across countries. At the same time, it also suggests that those setting up CSCs may have cultivated some degree of self-regulatory agency (see also Belackova & Wilkins, 2018): shaping the way CSCs function in line with their ideology and view of the model, to adapt to particular domestic legal contexts, or because of other reasons.

We also found some examples of transnational coalitions or supra-national organizations, which have been formed to support domestic activists in their own national efforts. CSCs noted that these organizations acted as gatekeepers and large cannabis events facilitated networking with other clubs and relevant stakeholders. Several CSCs referred to ENCOD and to the Regulación Responsable platform as well.

While ENCOD can be seen as a more enduring, long-term type of transnational coalition, Regulación Responsable had more of an instrumental purpose, as it was originally focused on the Uruguayan context to promote the legal regulation of cannabis around the time the new Uruguayan cannabis bill was being prepared and discussed (Levayer, 2017). A similar platform was later introduced in Spain though (Montañés, 2017), after Spanish and Uruguayan delegates met at a Spanish cannabis fair and discussed the efficacy of that initiative. While this platform has largely remained inactive since 2018 due to anecdotal reports of infighting between the Spanish CSCs – see Arana and Parés (2020) for more detail on conflicts between the Spanish CSCs – it is interesting to see how clubs in both Spain and Uruguay have influenced each other; since Uruguay also implemented lessons from the Spanish CSCs when reforming their cannabis laws in 2013 – in this case, the transnational links go beyond the European space (Muller & Draper, 2017; Musto, 2018; Pardal et al., 2019).

The broader network of relationships: collaborations and conflicts with other stakeholders

In our analysis we also considered the network of relationships of CSCs with other stakeholders, including with local authorities, the police, and the judiciary, professional services in harm reduction or drug treatment, other relevant professionals, and with the media. It has been suggested that the CSC model could have considerable policy relevance in terms of facilitating and/or co-creating harm reduction initiatives (Belackova et al., 2016; Belackova & Wilkins, 2018). Most of the clubs surveyed reported collaborations with professionals or professional services in drug prevention, harm reduction or drug treatment. However, CSCs noted the need to develop a more professional or official relationship with drug treatment and harm reduction stakeholders.

The survey revealed that the relationship between local authorities, the police, and the judiciary is mixed. While local authorities and the police have collaborated to an extent (e.g. liaising with clubs for large events and predominantly dealing with administrative matters), 28 CSCs in our sample still reported adverse contact with the criminal justice system. These general legal constraints have been also corroborated by other sources, as we noted earlier.

The relationship with the media is largely positive and collaborations have been reported as being useful to normalize the CSC model and shake off the stigma related to cannabis. Building alliances with the media might be important to change public opinion and could help legitimize the model. There is some evidence of a more formalized arrangement with policy-making bodies as well, as the Catalonian CSCs contributed to the La Rosa Verda legal initiative, and a UK CSC noted their contribution to national health guidelines pertaining to medical cannabis.

Overall, there is evidence to suggest that the European CSCs are aligning themselves with powerful stakeholders including the media, professional services, and the police, so that interdependent relationships and trust can build to advance policy change. There is also a clear focus on "responsible use" and "risk reduction" when answering the question on collaborations with professional services. This suggests that some of the European CSCs are aiming to professionalize their movement, in a similar vein to the cannabis activism organizations in Uruguay. This could help CSCs to strategically align their reform strategy with more powerful stakeholders.

The ideologies of the European CSCs

The majority of CSCs undertake lobbying, campaigning, protesting, and other awareness raising activities to promote the legal regulation of CSCs. The lack of legal regulation remained a key theme when asked about the most urgent or important problems facing their club (Pardal et al., 2020a). This could be a point of convergence for CSCs across Europe to develop a more connected transnational network. Although, in trying to achieve the goal of legal regulation, CSCs seem to put forward varying motivations and ideologies.

Some clubs promoted human rights ideology, whereas others focused primarily on health, wellbeing, and offering holistic peer to peer support. Several clubs expressed concern that the cannabis market is being and will continue to be commercialized, though a fraction advocated for commercial clubs or even the continuation of an underground illicit model. While the CSC Federations can go some way towards reducing ideological differences between the clubs, the number of conflicting interests, and ideologies remains high (Jansseune et al., 2019). Arana and Parés (2020) consider that these divergences or conflicts emerge from CSCs' interactions with the cannabis industry and/or the illicit market. For example, Spain is a world leader in the seeds sector, hosting numerous international fairs every year, and it is home to more than 1,000 grow shops (Arana & Parés, 2020; Marín, 2008). Given the origin of the CSC movement emerging through human rights arguments, Spain comprises a useful case study to demonstrate how: "the cannabis law reform agenda is now being driven by an unlikely alliance between commercial business interests and human rights advocates" (Seddon, 2020, p. 14).

Limitations

There are limitations with this online study, particularly since the recruitment approach (i.e. drawing on referral chains and relying on CSC Federations which have their own internal power dynamics) means that the representativeness of the sample cannot be guaranteed. Additionally, the data set is likely to be skewed in favor of CSCs who have a more formalized structure and advocate cannabis reform, since CSC Federations could have a vested interest in promoting clubs who share a similar ideology and working practices. Unregistered, commercially oriented or underground 'shadow clubs' are therefore more likely to be underrepresented, given precisely their hidden nature. In a similar vein, we cannot know for certain how many CSCs are active per country (except for the authors' home countries, to a certain extent, as a stronger knowledge base has been built in Spain, Belgium, and the UK). Indeed, given the difficulties in researching hidden and hard to reach populations and the potential language barriers, it is difficult to conclude how many CSCs received our survey in total. For more detail on the limitations when researching CSCs as a hidden or uninterested population, see Pardal et al., 2020b.

There was also a reluctance to discuss international collaborations with other CSCs and we did not ask detailed or specific questions about activist organizations or federations, as the purpose of the survey was to provide a general overview of the CSC presence across Europe. In addition, while we were able to gather insights into CSCs' collaborative relationships with other CSCs and stakeholders – both domestically and transnationally, our dataset did not allow for a more in-depth consideration of processes of internalization or of externalization. This is because we did not collect data focusing specifically on the nature of protest events (in which CSCs reported being involved), at whom these were directed, or which associations or individuals took part. More in-depth qualitative or ethnographic research would be useful here to build a further rapport and trust between the researchers and the clubs. It could also help to facilitate deeper insights into these processes of transnationalization, and into CSCs' ideologies and motivations – since perspectives surrounding drug policy making can be diverse and often involve questions of values (Askew and Bone, 2019).

Notes

1 In Spain, drug possession and cultivation for personal consumption is not criminalized. Additionally, the practical effect of the 'doctrine of shared consumption' developed by the Spanish Supreme Court allows for drug sharing between individuals in certain circumstances. Though, regarding Cannabis Social Clubs, in 2015, the Spanish Supreme Court clearly stated that "organized, institutionalized and persistent cultivation and distribution of cannabis among an association open to new members is considered drug trafficking" (see EMCDDA, (2019, p. 5); also see Marks (2019) and Arana and Parés (2020) for a thorough overview of the legal developments in Spain).

2 At the time of the survey the UK was still a member of the EU and was included in our study.

3 ENCOD was created in 1993 by several organizations active in the field of drugs, and has become involved in advocating for the CSC model since 2006 (ENCOD, 2018).

4 Nevertheless, particularly in recent years, some jurisdictions have introduced reforms to their domestic cannabis laws (Seddon, 2020).

5 Some examples include: a presentation by Martín Barriuso (representing a Spanish Federation of CSCs) at the European Parliament in December 2010; presentations by Joep Oomen (at the time, coordinator of ENCOD) and Michel Degens (representing a Belgian CSC) at the European Parliament in February 2016; or co-organization by

ENCOD and a MEP of an online conference about recreational cannabis legislation in the EU.

6 United Kingdom Cannabis Social Clubs.

7 Federación de Asociaciones Cannábicas.

8 Confederación de Federaciones de Asociaciones Cannábicas.

9 Federació d'Associacions de Cànnabis de Catalunya.

10 In English: 'cup'. The *Copa* refers to competitions where different CSC representatives bring their best cannabis strains and extractions, there are judges who vote for the winners in each category.

11 Energy Control is a harm reduction project. This Spanish non-profit organization provides information, advice and drug analysis.

12 The International Center for Ethnobotanical Education, Research and Services (ICEERS) is a non-profit organization 'dedicated to transforming society's relationship with psychoactive plants' (ICEERS).

13 Federació d'Associacions Cannàbiques Autoregulades de Catalunya.

14 The most central key issue reported by our survey respondents related to legal concerns and the "lack of regulation" or "legal limbo" in which the CSCs are operating – for a more in-depth discussion of this matter please see Pardal et al. 2020a.

References

Arana, X., & Parés, Ò. (2020). Cannabis social clubs in Spain: Recent legal developments. In Decorte, T., Lenton, S., & Wilkins, C. (Eds.) *Legalizing Cannabis. Experiences, Lessons and Scenarios.* New York: Routledge.

Askew, R. & Bone, M., (2019). Deconstructing prohibitionist ideology: A sociocognitive approach to understand opinions on UK drug policy and the law. *International Journal of Drug Policy*, 74, 33–40. doi:10.1016/j.drugpo.2019.08.001.

Barriuso, M. A. (2011). Cannabis social clubs in Spain: A normalizing alternative underway. Series on Legislative Reform of Drug Policies 9, Transnational Institute 1. Retrieved from: https://www.tni.org/files/download/dlr9.pdf (last accessed 27 March 2022).

Belackova, V., Tomkova, A., & Zabransky, T. (2016). Qualitative research in Spanish Cannabis Social Clubs: 'The moment you enter the door, you are minimizing the risks'. *International Journal of Drug Policy*, 34, 49–57. doi:10.1016/j.drugpo.2016.04.009.

Belackova, V., & Wilkins, C. (2018). Consumer agency in cannabis supply – exploring auto-regulatory documents of the cannabis social clubs in Spain. *International Journal of Drug Policy*, 54, 26–34. doi:10.1016/j.drugpo.2017.12.018.

Blickman, T. (2014). Cannabis policy reform in Europe: Bottom up rather than top down. *Transnational Institute: Series on Legislative Reform of Drug Policies*, 28, 1–16. doi:10.13140/2.1.2977.3603.

Bone, M. (2020). *Human Rights and Drug Control: A New Perspective.* Abingdon: Routledge.

Bone, M., & de Hoedt, G. (2018). Being the change: Charting Greg de Hoedt's cannabis journey. *Drugs and Alcohol Today*, 18, 126–136. doi:10.1108/DAT-01-2018-0001.

Bone, M., & Potter, G. (2021) Medical cannabis in the UK: The (false) dawn of a new era? In Meisel, J., & Corva, D. (Eds.) *The Routledge Handbook of Interdisciplinary Cannabis Research.* New York: Routledge.

Castro, G. (2014). *From Punishment to Markets: Social Movements, the State, and Legal Marijuana in Uruguay.* Presentation at the 5th Uruguayan Congress of Political Science. Asociación Uruguaya de Ciencia Política, 7–10 October 2014.

Decorte, T. (2015). Cannabis Social Clubs in Belgium: Organizational strengths and weaknesses, and threats to the model. *International Journal of Drug Policy*, 26, 122–130. doi:10.1016/j.drugpo.2014.07.016.

Decorte, T., & Pardal, M. (2017). Cannabis Social Clubs in Europe: Prospects and limits. In Colson, R., & Bergeron, H. (Eds.) *European Drug Policies: The Ways of Reform*. New York: Routledge.

Decorte, T., & Pardal, M. (2020). Insights for the design of Cannabis Social Club regulation. Decorte, T., Lenton, S., & Wilkins, C. (Eds.) *Legalizing Cannabis. Experiences, Lessons and Scenarios*. London: Routledge.

Decorte, T., Pardal, M., Queirolo, R., Boidi, M. F., Sánchez, C., & Parés, Ò. (2017). Regulating Cannabis Social Clubs: A comparative analysis of legal and self-regulatory practices in Spain, Belgium and Uruguay. *International Journal of Drug Policy*, 43, 44–56. doi:10.1016/j.drugpo.2016.12.020.

Della Porta, D., & Diani, M. (2014). *Social Movements: An Introduction*. Oxford: Blackwell Publishing.

Della Porta, D., & Tarrow, S. (2005). Transnational processes and social activism: An introduction. In Della Porta, D., & Tarrow, S. (Eds.) *Transnational Protest and Global Activism* (pp. 1–20). Lanham, MD: Rowman & Littlefield Publishers.

Edwards, B., & McCarthy, J. D. (2004). Resources and social movement mobilization. In Snow, D. A., Soule, S. A., & Kriesi, H. (Eds.), *The Blackwell Companion to Social Movements* (pp. 116–152). Malden: Blackwell Publishing.

ENCOD (2011). European Cannabis Social Clubs. Code of conduct. ENCOD. Retrieved from: https://cannabis-social-clubs.eu/en/code-conduct-european-cannabis-social-clubs (last accessed 11 June 2021).

ENCOD (2018). Our mission. ENCOD. Retrieved from: https://encod.org/our-mission/ (last accessed 11 June 2021).

ENCOD (2020). *Guidelines European Cannabis Social Clubs*. ENCOD. Retrieved from: https://encod.org/the-european-guidelines-for-cannabis-social-clubs/ (last accessed 11 June 2021).

EMCDDA(European Monitoring Centre for Drugs and Drug Addiction) (2016). *Models for the Legal Supply of Cannabis: Recent Developments*. Luxembourg: Publications Office of the European Union.

EMCDDA(European Monitoring Centre for Drugs and Drug Addiction) (2019). *Spain County Drug Report 2019*. Madrid: The Spanish National Focal Point. Retrieved from: https://www.emcdda.europa.eu/system/files/publications/11353/spain-cdr-2019.pdf. (last accessed 24 September 2021).

Goldsmith, N. M. (2015). Changing psychedelics policy. In Ellens, J. H., & Roberts, T. B. (Eds.) *The Psychedelic Policy Quagmire*. Santa Barbara, CA: Praeger.

Jansseune, L., Pardal, M., Decorte, T., & Parés, Ò. (2019). Revisiting the birthplace of the Cannabis Social Club model and the role played by Cannabis Social Club Federations. *Journal of Drug Issues*, 49, 338–354. doi:10.1177/0022042618815690.

Kriesi, H. (1996). The organizational structure of new social movements in a political context. In McAdam, D., McCarthy, J., & Zald, M. N. (Eds.) *Comparative Perspective on Social Movements: Political Opportunities, Mobilizing Structures, and Cultural Framing* (pp. 152–184). Cambridge and New York: Cambridge University Press.

Levayer, L. (2017). Regulación del mercado de cannabis en Uruguay. Génesis, implementación y retos de futuro. In Martínez Oró, D. P. (Ed.) *Las sendas de la regulación del cannabis en España* (pp. 314–329). Barcelona: Edicions Bellaterra.

Macgregor, S. (2017). *The Politics of Drugs: Perceptions, Power and Policies.* Basingstoke: Palgrave Macmillan.

Marín, I. (2008). *La cultura cannábica en España (1991–2007)*. Granada: Universidad de Granada.

Marín, I. (2009). *Cannabis: el movimiento cannábico en España.* Madrid: Editorial Popular.

Marín, I., & Hinojosa, M. (2017). Veinticinco años del movimiento cannábico español. In Martínez Oró, D. P. (Ed.) *Las sendas de la regulación del cannabis en España* (pp. 123–135). Barcelona: Edicions Bellaterra.

Marks, A. (2019). Defining personal consumption in drug legislation and Spanish cannabis clubs. *International and Comparative Law Quarterly,* 68(1), 193–223. doi:10.1017/S0020589318000404.

McCammon, J., & Moon, M. (2015). Social movement coalitions. In Della Porta, D., & Diani, M. (Eds.), *The Oxford Handbook of Social Movements.* Oxford: Oxford University Press.

McCarthy, J. D. (1996). Constraints and opportunities in adopting, adapting and inventing. In: McAdam, D., McCarthy, J. D., & Zald, M. N. (Eds.) *Comparative Perspectives on Social Movements* (pp. 141–151). Cambridge: Cambridge University Press.

McCarthy, J. D., & Zald, M. N. (1977). Resource mobilization and social movements: A partial theory. *The American Journal of Sociology,* 82(6), 1212–1241.

Montañés, V. S. (2017). Evolución del activismo cannábico en España. In Martínez Oró, D. P. (Ed.) *Las sendas de la regulación del cannabis en España* (pp. 145–159). Barcelona: Edicions Bellaterra.

Muller, C., & Draper, G. (2017). *Marihuana oficial: crónica de un experimento Uruguayo.* Montevideo: Editorial Sudamericana Uruguaya.

Muñoz, J., & Soto, S. (2000). Uso terapéutico del cannabis y creación de establecimientos para su adquisición y consumo: viabilidad legal. *Boletín Criminológico,* 47, 1–4.

Musto, C. (2018). Regulating cannabis markets: the construction of an innovative drug policy in Uruguay [unpublished doctoral dissertation]. Universiteit Utrecht & University of Kent.

Pardal, M. (2018). The Belgian Cannabis Social Club landscape. *Drugs and Alcohol Today,* 18(2), 80–89. doi:10.1108/DAT-09-2017-0051.

Pardal, M., Bone, M., Decorte, T., Queirolo, R., Parés, Ò., Johansson, J., Álvarez, E., & Repetto, L. (2020b). Hidden and uninterested populations: Methodological insights and unresolved issues from the study of Cannabis Social Clubs. *Methodological Innovations,* 13(3), 1–12. doi:10.1177/2059799120976963.

Pardal, M., Decorte, T., Bone, M., Parés Ò., Johansson, J. (2020a). Mapping Cannabis Social Clubs in Europe. *European Journal of Criminology.* doi:10.1177/1477370820941392.

Pardal, M., Queirolo, R., Álvarez, E., & Repetto, L. (2019). Uruguayan Cannabis Social Clubs: From activism to dispensaries?. *International Journal of Drug Policy,* 73, 49–57. doi:10.1016/j.drugpo.2019.06.022.

Parés, Ò. & Bouso, J. (2015). *Innovation Born of Necessity: Pioneering Drug Policy in Catalonia.* New York: Open Society Foundations.

Parés, Ò., Jubert-Cortiella, X., Olivares-Gálvez, S., Díaz-Castellano, A., Jiménez-Garrido, D. F., & Bouso, J. C. (2019). Use and habits of the protagonists of the story: Cannabis Social Clubs in Barcelona. *Journal of Drug Issues,* 49(4), 607–624. doi:10.1177/0022042619852780.

Queirolo, R., Rossel, C., Álvarez, E., & Repetto, L. (2019). Why Uruguay legalized marijuana? The open window to public insecurity. *Addiction*, 114(7), 1313–1321. doi:10.1111/add.14523.

Seddon, T. (2020). Immoral in principle, unworkable in practice: Cannabis law reform, the Beatles and the Wootton Report. *The British Journal of Criminology*, 60(6), 1567–1584. doi:10.1093/bjc/azaa042.

Tarrow, S. (2005). *The New Transnational Activism*. Cambridge: Cambridge University Press.

von Hoffmann, J. (2016). The international dimension of drug policy reform in Uruguay. *International Journal of Drug Policy*, 34, 27–33. doi:10.1016/j.drugpo.2016.04.015.

3 A friendly match? The relationship between Cannabis Social Clubs and regulators in Uruguay

Clara Musto

Introduction

In 2013, Uruguay broke into the worldwide headlines by becoming the first nation in extensively regulating cannabis. Behind the approval of this law, an odd and at times conflictive combination of national civil society representatives, legislative and executive power entrepreneurs, and transnational networks conflated, to make cannabis regulation happen. This political step was so controversial that the widely known British journal *The Economist* decided to declare Uruguay as "The Country of the Year" for its "path-breaking reform that does not merely improve a single nation but, if emulated, might benefit the world" (Economist, 2013).

Regardless of one's own personal position on the matter, it is unquestionable that this legal change deeply challenged the way in which governments traditionally deal with cannabis. Whereas cannabis prohibition is currently the norm worldwide, the approved Uruguayan law number 19.172 implies a different approach to the use and supply of cannabis. The law defines different types of cannabis use, i.e. recreational, medical, scientific, and industrial, and sets out the related institutional regulatory settings. It outlines three objectives for the new legal framework: to reduce drug-trafficking-related violence; to promote cannabis users' health; and to promote a fair law enforcement policy. In order to achieve these objectives, four policy tools are put forward: (i) problematic drug use education and prevention; (ii) problematic drug users' treatment, rehabilitation, and re-entry; (iii) police action over the illegal cannabis trade; and (iv) a legal cannabis market system.

This new law states that the planting, growing, harvest, and commercialization of cannabis is prohibited unless it is done under certain circumstances. Thus, only Uruguayan residents aged 18 or older can ask to be registered in the Institute for the Regulation and Control of Cannabis (IRCCA) as cannabis users, completing this registration at the post office. The law defines a purchase limit for non-medical cannabis of 40 grams per month to be sold in pharmacies and by CSCs to their members. Registered home growers can cultivate up to six plants and the collective cultivation within CSCs can amount to 99 plants maximum. Three legal and regulated supply models therefore co-exist in Uruguay (albeit users can

DOI: 10.4324/9781003055679-3

only select one supply model at a time): 1) home cultivation; 2) pharmacy sales; 3) CSCs. The law 19.172 and its further regulatory framework also establish a number of conditions for cannabis use. Generally, it is prohibited to smoke in indoor public spaces, to drive under the influence, and to advertise cannabis. In the cases where the established possession limits are surpassed; this is, more than 40 grams per person in the case of buyers and CSC members, or more than 480 grams per year in the case of home growers, it is up to the judge's discretion to establish the existence of a crime, in accordance to the evidence found. Whereas in the retailing system via the adhering pharmacies only a few cannabis strains are available (with a THC content below 10%), no strain restrictions apply to personal cultivation nor to CSCs.

This chapter seeks to improve the understanding of the implementation of the CSC model in Uruguay, focusing particularly on the relationship between CSCs, their representatives and the institutional actors that oversee the implementation of that regulatory framework. In order to do so, the chapter explores different key aspects in the development of the CSC model in the country, namely: 1) how the model was imported in the Uruguayan legal framework; 2) the regulatory framework regarding CSCs; 3) the relationship between CSCs' representatives and public authorities in charge of the implementation of the regulatory framework.

Methods

This chapter focuses on the implementation of the CSC model in Uruguay since the approval of law 19.172, and on the relationship between CSCs and regulators. The analysis draws on multiple sources.

First, I rely on observations obtained from thirteen years following the political process leading up to and following the passage of the new cannabis law (2007–2020). During that period, I attended a number of meetings with political representatives of every political party, including: the Informal Dialogues on cannabis regulation organized by the Uruguayan Drugs Committee, the Transnational Institute and WOLA; meetings of the National Coordinator for Marijuana Regulation conformed by local social organizations; the Responsible Regulation public campaign; meetings of the "advisory group" for cannabis regulation called by the National Drugs Committee, the Frente Amplio[1] programmatic session on the drugs issue, and the cannabis regulation implementation workshops in Denver, Colorado, organized by the Drug Policy Alliance (US), among others.

In addition, I also draw on a number of legal and secondary data. This includes the Cannabis Control and Regulation Law (Law 19.172) passed in December 2013 and the regulatory decree for domestic cultivation, CSCs, and sale at pharmacies (Decree No. 120/014) passed in May 2014. I reviewed the data published at the IRCCA's web page[2] (including the registries for domestic cultivation, CSCs, and sale at pharmacies; and the data on sanctions), and ten reports on the monitoring of the regulated cannabis market (*Informes de monitoreo del Mercado regulado de cannabis*) – which have been published by the IRCCA in May, June, August, September, and November of 2018, January, June, and October of 2019, and in February and May of 2020; which was the last published report.

Third, the analysis builds on qualitative data gathered through interviews. In the first wave, I conducted 38 interviews during the first two years (2014–2016) of the implementation of the law. The interviewees were members of the Uruguayan legislative power, three representing the Partido Nacional, six representing the Frente Amplio, one the Partido Colorado, and one the Partido Independiente (n=11). Four interviews were also conducted with members of the Uruguayan executive: with the General Secretary of the National Drugs Committee; with the first president of the IRCCA; and two with members of the Minister of the Interior. Sixteen interviews were conducted with members of Uruguayan civil society groups both for and against the reform, ranging from cannabis activism to drug treatment institutions. Seven interviews were arranged with Uruguayan professionals specialized in the topic of drugs, including two lawyers, a journalist, a sociologist, a historian, a hemp entrepreneur, and a Uruguayan Pharmacies Union representative.

A second wave of ten interviews and informal talks were conducted in 2020, with cannabis growers and CSC members, the president of the Uruguayan Cannabis Clubs Federation, the former secretary of the IRCCA, the current IRCCA president, and an email exchange with the IRCCA inspectors' team, who declined to be interviewed in depth. Key data was also obtained through extended participant observation at one CSC located in Montevideo that started its activities by the end of 2013.

Results

The import of a model

When the Uruguayan government announced their intention to regulate cannabis at a press conference in June 2012, CSCs and home growing were off the table. What government actors envisioned was a state monopoly for cannabis supply, and the State Cannabis Monopoly for its Commercialization bill was introduced to parliament in August 2012 with that aim. At this memorable press conference, then Minister of Defense Fernández Huidobro argued that "the Uruguayan Ministry of Foreign Affairs will fight internationally for cannabis legalization in the region, because this war [on drugs] was won by the narcos" (Fernández Huidobro; Strategy for Life and Coexistence Press Conference, June 20, 2012).

The push to move forward with cannabis regulation came from a specific group within the Uruguayan government: President José Mujica, Minister of the Interior Eduardo Bonomi, and Minister of Defense, Eleuterio Fernández Huidobro, two of his most trusted collaborators. The three of them not only belong to the same political party within the Frente Amplio coalition, but also share an exceptional and long life experience. Back in the 1960s, Mujica, Bonomi and Fernández Huidobro counted themselves among the co-founders of the National Liberation Movement Tupamaros, a left-wing urban guerrilla group that emerged as a reaction to the rough social and economic situation of the time within a politically convulsed continent.

The Uruguayan government's announcement was sudden and highly controversial, creating a "chaotic moment of punctuation" followed by communicational turmoil (Baumgartner & Jones, 1993; True et al., 2007). According to public polls, more than 60% of Uruguayans disagreed with the government's proposal (Equipos, 2019). The global mass media was eager to delve into the proposal for a first national-level legal cannabis framework, but the absence of specific answers from governmental authorities to questions about the policy tools to be implemented exposed a lack of technical knowledge and expertise in the matter.

In addition to this, the government's announcement was controversial even among the civil society groups that were already advocating for domestic growing and CSCs in parliament, as expressed in the Cannabis Regulation for Its Consumption law presented almost one year before the government´s incursion in the political process. The government repeatedly defended the regulated supply of cannabis appealing to community values such as authority and fairness to counter the disproportionate criminal costs of "the rebellion of illegal drug trafficking" against Latin America (Durán-Martínez, 2015; Garzón-Vergara, 2012; Queirolo et al., 2019; Repeto, 2014).

The governmental emphasis on the violence associated with drug selling contrasted strongly with activism groups that framed cannabis regulation primarily as a solution to a problem of individual autonomy within a 'new rights' agenda, as a matter of liberty and protection of cannabis users. The different emphasis at the deep core policy level – as an authority and fairness moral problem or as a matter of liberty and protection of cannabis users – were associated to different goals of the law, either reducing drug-related violence or improving cannabis users' health and enjoyment of rights; as a harm-reduction tool. These positions were also related to the preferred policy tools to be included in the new legal framework. The main contention at this level was between including a state's monopoly for cannabis production, distribution, and sale – indispensable for the government-, and the inclusion of mechanisms for legal personal cultivation and CSCs, the *sine qua non* condition for the advocacy coalition (Musto, 2018).

Amidst this communicational turmoil, local cannabis activists, and civil society groups warned that: "we do welcome the government's involvement in the discussion, but this should by no means become a regress in the debate […] Personal cultivation and Cannabis Social Clubs are the starting point" (UyPress, 2012).

Both civil society and the sectors of the government that supported cannabis reform knew that if they remained apathetic, cannabis regulation would hardly be achieved. A key informant from the president's party recognized this tension and explained that:

> After the press conference, I talked to [Minister of the Interior] Bonomi and Lucia [Topolansky, senator and spouse of President Mujica] about the personal cultivation issue. I explained to them that strategically we could not afford to be against the social movement and cannabis activism by leaving personal cultivation out, because actually they would be the only ones to support a cannabis legalization proposal.
>
> (Frente Amplio legislator, personal communication, April 2014)

In this scenario, the cannabis growers' networking at the highest political level (Dolowitz & Marsh, 2000; Jones & Newburn, 2006; Stone, 2000) was a necessary condition for the inclusion of CSCs in the new Uruguayan law, and there were many spaces of international knowledge transfer for this experience. For instance, Martín Barriuso, president of the Spanish CSC Pannagh, and former president of a Spanish CSC Federation, visited Uruguay to present the CSC model in different public and private fora during 2011 and 2012. In April 2013, Uruguay's National Drug Board, the University of the Republic, and the civil society organization Proderechos co-sponsored an event on 'Personal cultivation and cannabis clubs' with Martín Barriuso (Spain), Òscar Parés (Spain), and Jorge Hernández (Mexico) as panelists. In parallel, local political entrepreneurs arranged meetings between these actors and Uruguayan civil society groups and government representatives.

Civil society and the section of the government supporting reform needed to find a friendly arrangement in order for cannabis regulation to be approved. Against a backdrop of a majority adverse public opinion, national, and international civil society helped to change the image attached to cannabis reform, to defend the Uruguayan initiative in a rather hostile international conventions arena, and to fill in the gaps of knowledge in order to develop a suitable regulation framework. The contribution of civil society allowed the government's single article bill for a State Cannabis Monopoly for Its Commercialization to be transformed into a comprehensive 44 article law in just a few months, including provisions for both cannabis sale to individuals, personal cultivation, and CSCs.

The regulatory framework

In December 2013, the Cannabis Control and Regulation Law (Law 19.172) was passed after an extremely polarized parliamentary vote. Until the very last moment, when the law was put to the vote, the prospect for cannabis reform was highly uncertain. In a chamber overcrowded with an odd mix of journalists from all around the world, hippies, and people both in dreadlocks and suit and tie, only the Frente Amplio representatives raised their hands to change the country's cannabis policy and legal framework. The law passed with 50 votes in favor and 49 against in the House of Representatives, and 16 votes in favor and 14 against in the Senate.

It then took five months for the Uruguayan government to put in place the first element of the system to legalize cannabis. As throughout the political debate, the recreational use of cannabis was prioritized over medical cannabis, and in May 2014, the government issued the regulatory decree for domestic cultivation, CSCs, and sale at pharmacies (Decree No. 120/014), and set up IRCCA.

The IRCCA is meant to be the key institutional player in the new cannabis regulation model. Its official mission is to: "regulate and control the activities related to the production, commercialization, and use of cannabis for various purposes, as well as promoting and proposing actions aimed at reducing the risks and damages associated with the problematic use of cannabis" (Law 19.172, Article 18). It is a three-part institute composed by a Board, an Executive Director, and an Honorary Advisory Council. The Board is composed of representatives of the National Drug Board, the Ministry of Cattling, Agriculture, and Fisheries; the Ministry of Social Development and the Ministry of Public Health. Board members are appointed based on their "recognized moral and technical reputation" (Article 81) and they have total freedom to choose the frequency of their meetings and all other aspects of their work. The Board is also in charge of appointing the Executive Director and setting his/her salary (all IRCCA's directors have been male thus far) with the government and the funds available in the IRCCA (Article 83).

Lastly, the Honorary Advisory Council is the main consultation group of IRCCA. It is composed of nine members representing the ministries of Education and Culture, Interior, Economy, Industry, Energy, and Mining; the University of the Republic, the Congress of Provincial Governors, the Cannabis Social Clubs, the domestic growers, and the licensees for industrial growing. Regarding CSC representation, the regulatory decree states that the clubs can propose three persons to the Executive Office, which ultimately appoints the members and can directly select a representative if no proposal is submitted (Article 86). As will be shown in the following section, the Honorary Advisory Council is a key institution to guarantee IRCCA's accountability and transparency, but eight years after the law´s approval the Committee has never been convened.

Compared to other experiences of policy development (Barriuso, 2011; Decorte, 2015; Decorte, et al., 2017; Montañés, 2014; Pardo, 2014; Pere, 2015), Uruguay presents an exceptionally strict regulatory framework. During my fieldwork, Uruguayan authorities directly related this output to the particular political process that led to cannabis regulation and the initial rejection of CSCs by the executive power. For instance, one key respondent explained that: "The law defines a rather restrictive framework for cannabis clubs. It was what it could be achieved in that political context; hopefully, we will be able to improve it and make it more flexible in the future" (National Drugs Committee / IRCCA, April 2014).

As introduced in the previous section, the import of CSCs was the result of international cannabis growers' elite networking and activism lobby. The Uruguayan Executive Power originally rejected this type of bottom-up market organization as it would constitute a supply model outside of the State's control. Unlike the executive's insistence on a selling scheme (concretized via the pharmacy sales), domestic cultivation, and CSCs were an essential demand of cannabis activism. Thus, the middle road solution for the government was the inclusion of a tight regulatory framework for CSCs.

Within that framework, and through a rather heavy bureaucratic procedure, which may take up to one year to complete, adult residents can set up CSCs with 15 to 45 members. First, the club must be registered as a non-profit organization at the Ministry of Education and Culture, and the name selected must include the expression "cannabis club". Following that, it must be registered with the IRCCA. In parallel, CSC members must also complete a separate process of individual registration as cannabis users and select a CSC for their cannabis supply. CSCs are restricted to the sole purpose of producing cannabis buds for its members. No external persons are allowed in the club facilities: in order to receive visitors, clubs need to ask for a written permission from IRCCA, justifying the visit. Clubs must have a single location where all the activities are performed: cannabis cultivation, harvesting, processing, storage, and distribution. They must also have a social area – separated from the areas where the growing is performed – for the purpose of the distribution of cannabis among its members, and a bathroom. Cannabis locations must be at 150 meters distance from education, cultural, or sports centers attended by people under 18 years old and drug treatment institutions (IRCCA, 2018).

The law establishes that it is IRCCA's role to define the "minimum conditions of infrastructure, security, and operation that social clubs must meet in order to carry out their activity" (Article 30), and its Board decides on the sanctions for violations. Every authorized club should be visited at least once a year by IRCCA's inspection team of only four inspectors. Possible sanctions – a point I return to later – range from fines to seizure of the product or elements used to commit the infringement, destruction of the product, suspension from the registry, temporary or permanent disqualification, and partial or total (either temporary or permanent) closure of the facilities (Article 95).

Evolution in the implementation of the regulatory framework

After nine months of the law's approval, in August 2014, the cannabis domestic growers' register was the first to be opened. From that point on, Uruguayan residents could ask to be legally allowed to grow up to six plants per household. According to the *Encuesta Nacional en Hogares sobre Consumo de Drogas*, sponsored by the governmental Drugs Observatory conducted in 2014, about 14,000 people declared that they were domestic cannabis growers in Uruguay previous to regulation, predominantly between the ages of 30 and 44, living in Montevideo. This represented 11% of the total population that declared to have consumed cannabis in the past 30 days (OUD, 2014). By July 2017, the approved licenses for domestic cultivation were 6930. One year later, by June 2018, there were 8583 approved licenses.

However, licenses for domestic cultivation need to be renewed every three years, which explain why on August 2018 the registered domestic growers descended to 6735; 1848 people did not renew their licenses. After this, the number of registrants increased from 6912 by January 2019 to 12386 by April 2021 (see Figure 3.1).

In October 2014, the CSC register opened. After a slow start, by July 2016 the registered clubs climbed to 17. By July 2017, there were 63 registered CSCs. The number kept increasing in the following years: by September 2018 there were 107 registered clubs and by April 2021 a total of 171, reaching 5152 members (Figure 3.1). They are located in 12 of the 19 provinces of the country.

More than three years after the law's approval, in May 2017, the registry for cannabis purchasers through pharmacy was the last to be introduced. This was the most dynamic register; only on the first day 539 people registered to legally purchase cannabis. The number exponentially grew through time: by July 2017 there were 6797 registered purchasers, in April 2018 the number climbed up to 23161, and by April 2021 there are 41238 registered pharmacy buyers (Figure 3.1). This evidence seems to show that if people get to choose, they largely prefer to buy cannabis to growing their own or joining a cannabis club. Still, one of the most important limitations of the Uruguayan model is at the retailing level. After eight years of the approval of the law, pharmacies are scarce, concentrated in the territory, and tend to be located in the middle- and upper-class neighborhoods of the capital city of Montevideo. Additionally, supply to pharmacies is limited, according to the last data available between July 2017 and May 2020, 4166 kilograms were sold at pharmacies; 59% in Montevideo and 41% in the rest of the country. As official reports repeatedly

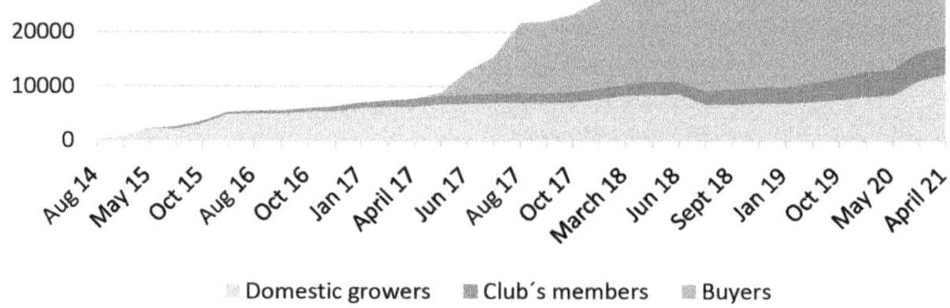

Figure 3.1 Evolution of the number of total cannabis users registered with the IRCCA, 2014–2021

Source: Prepared by the author based on IRCCA´s public registers

highlight, the offer at pharmacies is still limited and does not meet the current demand: "in Montevideo the weekly stock available runs out in two or three days" (IRCCA, 2020, p. 10). By 2021 there are only 16 pharmacies selling cannabis throughout the country, located in 10 of the 19 provinces.

Considering the three ways of access combined, by April 2021 the legal system covered 62667 cannabis users, which amounts to a 26% of the estimated 238000 cannabis users of the country, as reported by the VII *Encuesta Nacional en Población General sobre Consumo de Drogas* of 2018 (IRCCA, 2020). Analysing the geographic distribution of registers, as showed in Table 3.1, there does not seem to be a substitution effect among the different supply channels: in several provinces there are no adhering pharmacies nor CSCs. In three provinces – Artigas, Montevideo, Rocha, and Maldonado – there is roughly the same number of domestic growers as club members, but in most of the provinces CSCs are the minority option.

There are several factors that help interpreting these numbers. From the very beginning of the political process, it was known that registration in a state-controlled database would be the most rejected feature of the law among users (Boidi et al., 2016). This national register aims at restricting the limit of available legal cannabis to up to 40 grams per month per person. It is protected by the Habeas Data law (no. 18337), which establishes a relatively strict judicial procedure for access permissions. The judicial protection of the data prevailed when in March 2021 the new Minister of the Interior – an orthodox war on drugs warrior – publicly demanded that the IRCCA disclosed the addresses of CSCs and home growers to go after possible diversion to the illicit market. Overall, people participating in my research considered the register a violation of personal freedom and privacy, as well as discriminatory – because cannabis is currently the only recreational legal drug for which this type of registration is required, as opposed to alcohol and tobacco.

In addition to the initial rejection of the register; there is a striking lack of public campaigns in Uruguay aiming at endorsing user's registration. As I will analyze in more detail in the next section, the strategy selected by the governmental elite to skew opposition to the law was to confine it into political silence. There are not any messages explaining the benefits of the legal system nor of the advantages of registration.

Still, the domestic cannabis market did changed significantly. Before regulation, most Uruguayan frequent users (68%) reported that they consumed a low-quality type of compressed cannabis smuggled into Uruguay by regional trafficking networks, commonly referred to as '*paraguayo*'. Only 33% of users had access to locally produced cannabis buds in natural state (OUD, 2014). By 2017, this scenario changed dramatically: based on the results of the First National Survey on Cannabis Regulation in Uruguay,[3] an estimate of more than 60% of users were consuming flowers/herbal cannabis, many of them combining multiple legal and illegal ways of accessing the substance. In fact, much of the cannabis is still produced outside the regulated channels. According to the same survey by 2017,

Table 3.1 Number of registers by province circa 2020

Province	*Residents > 18*	*Buyers*	*Pharma-cies*	*Domestic growers*	*CSCs*	*CSCs' members*	*Total registers*	*Registers in 1000 resi-dents > 18*
Maldonado	118301	4474	2	715	26	761	5950	50.3
Flores	18201	464	0	78	0	0	542	29.8
Montevideo	1010307	23077	6	2664	70	2174	27915	27.6
Treinta y Tres	34042	824	0	90	0	0	914	26.8
Lavalleja	43259	832	1	131	0	0	963	22.3
Canelones	375379	5349	0	1401	31	981	7731	20.6
Salto	85042	1378	1	203	4	72	1653	19.4
Rocha	49379	155	0	454	11	343	952	19.3
Paysandú	78589	945	1	329	5	134	1408	17.9
Durazno	39766	579	0	109	1	18	706	17.8
Artigas	4966	689	1	100	2	90	879	17.7
San José	78736	731	1	223	0	0	954	12.1
Colonia	91199	333	0	565	4	128	1026	113
Soriano	58536	463	1	277	0	0	740	12.6
Tacuarembó	62668	283	0	245	0	0	528	8.4
Florida	48395	259	0	154	0	0	413	8.5
Río Negro	3745	96	0	157	1	41	294	7.9
Cerro Largo	58897	160	0	247	1	40	447	7.6
Rivera	71066	119	0	222	2	52	393	5.5
No data	-	28	0	54	0	0	82	-
TOTAL	2408872	41238	14	8.418	158	4834	5449	22.6

Source: Adapted from IRCCA, 2020, p. 7.

45970 people were cannabis growers. This is to say: only 5% of them were officially registered as such with the state.

Systemic pressure

Within this scenario of restrictions in the legal selling, clubs seem to be facing strong incentives to evolve "from activism to dispensaries", as described by Pardal et al. (2019). During interviews, CSCs and growers were very critical about the low engagement of regulators with and understanding of "where the clubs are evolving and why". A member of a CSC and current president of the Uruguayan Cannabis Clubs Federation explains this as follows:

> In December 2019, for example, we [the Clubs representatives] had a meeting with the IRCCA authorities and more than once they highlighted the idea of clubs as "a group of friends who grow cannabis". However, the actual picture is more diverse than that, and actually there are more and more clubs that really don't fit that logic of friends that grow cannabis.
>
> (President of the Uruguayan Cannabis Clubs Federation, interview, May 21, 2020)

In a study conducted in 2015, Queirolo et al. (2016) identified two types of clubs working in Uruguay; an "activist" type and a "group of friends" type (Queirolo, et al., 2016, p. 13). The activist type stemmed from parent organizations linked in some form to previous cannabis-related activism. This type of organization was more frequent among the firsts clubs. The other type of club identified was formed by friends and relatives who gathered in order to have access to good quality cannabis. A new study by Pardal et al. (2019) suggested a shift towards a quasi-dispensary type of CSC, because of the organizational ways that many clubs developed or the paucity of social contact or events among members.

I also found traces of a professionalization shift similar to what Pardal et al. (2019) described. CSCs' members did not want to be identified as activists neither as a "group of friends", but rather as entrepreneurs; "just like when you have any other agricultural enterprise":

> There are Clubs, for example, that after being robbed wanted to report the incident to *Banco de Seguros del Estado* [the state-owned insurance company], just like when you have any other agricultural enterprise, but insurance doesn't apply to cannabis. Why does this happen if it is legal? We pay taxes as everybody else...There isn't a vision of how to develop the regulatory framework, how to update it trying to understand what the clubs' problems really are.
>
> (President of the Uruguayan Cannabis Clubs Federation, interview, May 21, 2020)

My research participants identified some generational gap in this regard, differentiating an "Old Guard" and a "New Guard" of CSCs' representatives. The "Old Guard" developed their growing skills in a context where cannabis was still prohibited. For them, it was essential to differentiate themselves from the commercial interchange of cannabis, emphasizing other social and cultural aspects of the activity, as well as its harm-reduction outputs; assuring quality within a market where pressed/low quality, internationally trafficked cannabis was prominent. For these growers the political establishment was generally regarded as mistrustful:

> Cannabis growers were always far away from the political establishment, from the suit and tie people that speak well and whom many times do not even know what a cannabis plant looks like or how to grow it. There is a natural mistrust in this type of people.
>
> (Journalist, interview, October 17, 2014)

The "New Guard" corresponds to representatives appearing in a context of legal cannabis. For this new generation, the individual users centered logic of the harm-reduction discourse falls short, and does not address their difficulties as producers. They claim for the rights and obligations of legal business. They are interested in developing a virtuous match with regulators and in several instances in my fieldwork, the learning process developed by public agents and inspectors since the approval of the law was highly valued.

Within this general trend, I found three main tensions involved in the current relationship between clubs and IRCCA authorities: regarding the conditions of CSC facilities, production costs, and participation in the decision-making process. From the users' perspective, setting up a club is not an easy task. They first need to overcome the long bureaucratic process required to register as a non-profit organization with the Ministry of Education and Culture, and then apply for IRCCA's authorization (Queirolo, et al., 2016). A first emergent issue is that the IRCCA defines the minimum conditions that club facilities must meet on a case-by-case basis. Among the club members interviewed, the prevalent feeling was that the IRCCA was inconsistent in its requirements across cases, and in certain instances it was almost impossible to meet IRCCA's expectations. In one case, for example, a club presented 53 different possible locations to the IRCCA before they got approval.

The second and possibly the most important tension relates to the 45-member limit of Uruguayan regulatory framework, which was intended to facilitate their control by the state agency. This problem has been discussed in the literature, for example, with reference to large clubs with thousands of members in Spain (Decorte, et al., 2017; Pere, 2015). Cannabis clubs are restricted in terms of membership and production volume, but cannabis production implies economies of scale, where the cost per unit depends on how much is produced. Growers can reduce prices or improve product quality within a certain scale: bigger scales facilitate higher production by spreading production cost over a larger amount of goods.

The limit to membership makes it difficult for clubs to reach financial sustainability without becoming a "rich people's" club. As one grower explains:

> With forty-five people, it just doesn't add up. You would need two or three clubs of forty-five members to share costs, securing the growing sites against robberies. And this, if it's indoors. Outdoors you would need even more clubs working together. How many hours of work it takes depends on how much you have automatized the crop, this is to say, how high your start-up costs are. If the maximum allowed is ninety-nine plants, plus the mother plants that you need to have, it makes 200. It takes like four hours of work to water 200 plants. Add to that all the other work needed for trimming, drying, curing… Add to that the money for the rent, electricity, security… If it is only one club, only rich people can afford it.
>
> (Cannabis grower, interview, November 2014)

The prices of cannabis from clubs are significantly higher than the prices at pharmacies[4] and, as discussed in another chapter of this book (Álvarez et al., this volume), a predominance of "male, aged between 20 and 40 years old, with a university degree, and middle to upper class" among Club´s members is observed (Pardal et al, 2019, p. 52). Most clubs charge a registration fee and then a monthly fee, but many of them have faced important difficulties in achieving economic sustainability while guaranteeing monthly supply. The most important cost that Club´s face relates with safety conditions. Currently, after repeated robberies to outdoor-growing clubs, most clubs located in or close to urban areas grow indoors, which imply much higher functioning costs. The President of the Uruguayan Cannabis Clubs Federation explained:

> There aren't any serious conversations happening about what alternatives we could have to improve security conditions. Now we are putting on the table of negotiations the option of more than one club sharing facilities, which would be very positive to improve our security. Or if at least we would be able to share storage facilities, storing in the same place, and outside of each of the club's headquarters. Only by doing this you can overcome this critical challenge. And for them [the IRCCA] it would be even easier to control and prevent diversions. But what we find among regulators is no willingness to think together about how to develop the club model. What I think is that there is no one inside the government that is thinking about the clubs' potential and has the political will to improve the clubs' situation, to consolidate it. And clubs have a lot of potential. There's a lot of clubs in the IRCCA´s waiting list.
>
> (President of the Uruguayan Cannabis Clubs Federation, interview, May 21, 2020)

During my fieldwork, I had the opportunity of witnessing a police inspection to a club that had been robbed, and to join members when they filed the police report. It was shocking to witness the low priority that the Uruguayan justice system gave to the incident: police officers and prosecutors showed no interest at all in investigating the crime. A few weeks later, the case was dismissed.

The last tension detected in the relationship between regulators and CSC members concerns the establishment of the IRCCA's Honorary Advisory Council and CSCs' participation within that platform. During the political campaign that led to cannabis regulation, the government proposed this body as a way to ensure IRCCA's transparency and accountability. Theoretically, it should be the institutional place where to solve the political tensions related to the implementation, guaranteeing the representation of relevant non-governmental actors as the University of the Republic, a representative of the CSCs, a representative of the domestic growers, and a representative of the industrial licensees at the IRCCA.

From the CSCs' point of view, the possibility of appointing this Council was a strategic step towards further developing the regulatory framework, updating it as required by emergent issues. To this end, the clubs organized themselves in a CSC Federation, which now has 35 members that keep close communication with 35 more clubs. The Federation facilitates knowledge exchange among clubs, not only about the technical aspects of cannabis growing but also about the bureaucratic issues of the regulatory framework. The Cannabis Clubs Federation held a vote to select its representatives at the Council, and in June 2018 informed the IRCCA about the decision:

> Since then, we are still waiting for the IRCCA to convene a meeting. In May 2018, we told the IRCCA that we had our representatives for the National Honorary Council. They told us that we had until June to have the decision certified by a notary public. So we did it. Supposedly, it was going to take 15 more days for the IRCCA to approve it, and 15 more days for the government to approve it. After one month and a half, we went back there asking for their response. They told us that they hadn't had time to process it. We waited for another month, we asked again, and they told us that they were waiting for the industrial licensee to select representatives… But how could it be that for us, hundreds of clubs, the deadline was June 2018 and by the end of the year we were still waiting for the licensees representatives? Then we requested a meeting once again in mid-2019, and the answer was that since national elections were so close, it didn't make any sense to call for a meeting because anyways the IRCCA´s authorities would change… Then we had the national elections, and now nobody is replying at the IRCCA. We have been waiting two years for this meeting: it never happened.
>
> (President of the Uruguayan Cannabis Clubs Federation, interview, May 21, 2020)

In March 2020, a new government took office in Uruguay, formed by a right-wing coalition of parties opposing the Frente Amplio. Similarly to what happened in the 2014 elections, no party or presidential candidate took the initiative to criticize or support the Law. In July 2020 Daniel Radío, from the Partido Independiente, was named head of the National Drugs Committee and therefore president of the IRCCA. During the political process that led to cannabis regulation, Radío was a supporter of the law. Since then, even if the new Minister of the Interior has been endorsing an orthodox war on drugs approach – raising penalties for drug offenses and calling upon the militarization of drug policy – with regards to cannabis the continuity with the previous government's cannabis policy prevailed. As a case in point, when in March 2021 the new Minister of the Interior pressed the IRCCA to have access to the addresses of home growers and CSCs without judicial authorization, Radío defended the Habeas Data procedure and the Minister of the Interior had to finally quit his intention.

Sanctions

While 87 clubs had registered with the IRCCA from 2015 to 2017 (14 registered in 2015, 35 in 2016, and 38 in 2017), sanctions only started to appear in 2017: one club was sanctioned that year, 3 in 2018, and the majority, 22, were sanctioned in 2019. As explained by an interviewee, this lag is due to the long learning curve that clubs experience before they become economically sustainable and are fully operational.

In spite of being home to almost half of the clubs, only six of the sanctioned clubs were located in Montevideo. Canelones, a predominantly rural province bordering Montevideo, is home to 10% of registered clubs but had the same number of sanctions as Montevideo. The province of Maldonado, the country's main tourist destination, hosts 17% of the clubs, five of which received sanctions. The three provinces together concentrate more than 80% of the sanctions. According to my research participants this geographic distribution may be more the reflect of the assiduity of the inspectors' visits than the actual practices of the clubs; as already mentioned, a team of only four inspectors located in Montevideo has the task of controlling CSCs' functioning throughout the country.

In most cases, the sanctions were warnings with requirements of minor changes to club facilities, such as installing a toilet or a CCTV camera. The fines given ranged from 558 USD to 8000 USD. In a few cases, the sanctions included the destruction of surplus production, and in eight cases either the club or the technical manager were disqualified for one to three years.

Conclusions

In this chapter, we saw how the negotiated entry of CSCs into the process of approval of the Cannabis Regulation Law may have further shaped its implementation process. The Uruguayan government, which only envisioned the creation of a state monopoly for the supply of cannabis, originally did not support the CSC model. It were the efforts of cannabis growers' elite networking that contributed to the inclusion of the model in the new framework. Both civil society and the government needed to find a friendly arrangement in order for cannabis reform to be approved. This meant that the initial government's aspiration was transformed into a more comprehensive law in just a few months, including provisions for both cannabis sale to individuals at adhering pharmacies, personal home cultivation, and CSCs.

Yet, this friendly arrangement resulted in a strict regulatory framework for CSCs. In this analysis I identified a number of key tensions that have characterized the development of the model to date and the relationship between clubs and regulators. Specifically, some of the restrictions imposed in relation to the facilities and operations of the clubs, such as the limit of members allowed per CSC and the impossibility of cooperative action between CSCs (e.g. by sharing storage facilities), translated into difficulties for CSCs, which in turn has resulted in a trend from outdoors to indoors cultivation and higher operational costs for clubs. To date, CSCs remain the most expensive way to access cannabis in Uruguay. This analysis also shows – in line with earlier research, that different types of CSCs (an "old" and "new" guard) share this space and may have developed different relationships with regulators. While for the first clubs the emphasis was in the social and cultural aspects of cannabis growing, more recent clubs tend to frame their demand as a matter of rights and obligations of legal business. This new guard is leading the efforts of civil society for developing a virtuous match with regulators.

Overall, an atmosphere of uncertainty has characterized the implementation of the law. This uncertainty is associated with the scarce points of sale (i.e. adhering pharmacies) available, which are highly concentrated in the most advantaged areas of the country. In spite of the large preference of Uruguayan residents for the purchase of cannabis at pharmacies, by 2021 the state system is far from meeting its potential demand. Considering the three ways of access combined, the legal system only reaches 26% of the estimated 238000 last year cannabis users of the country. Within this context, the growing number of CSCs has evolved into a network of federated clubs that advocate for this supply model as a middle option of circular economy, where consumer and producer know each other, developing trust in their exchange.

Another example of this uncertainty relates also to some secrecy around political decisions regarding cannabis – which is another example of the perhaps more distant or unfriendly match between regulators and CSCs. Even though the legal framework foresees a key role of the state and the participation of different interest groups, particularly through IRCCA's Honorary Advisory Council, eight years after the approval of the law these actors have not yet formally met. Nevertheless, the new right-wing Uruguayan government has put forward some reassurance that the option of cannabis regulation taken by the previous government will earn space as a long-term state policy. What this experience may show is how a 'bifurcated' drug policy approach can work in Latin America, with cannabis regulation standing out as a market separation tool while reinforcing an orthodox war on drugs for the rest of the illegal drugs commerce; the shift towards permissiveness in Uruguay poses more of a puzzle than a simple shift.

Notes

1 The Frente Amplio is a left-wing party that won Uruguayan national elections of 2004, 2009, and 2014 with a legislative majority. Throughout this period, thanks to the cooperation between the Frente Amplio and civil society organizations, a wave of social progressive reforms took place. In 2007, Uruguay became the first Latin American country to approve a Consensual Unions law (Law N° 18.246, 27/12/2007) to enhance the legal status of unmarried couples, independently of their sexual orientation. In 2008, the Sexual and Reproductive Health law (Law N° 18.426, 01/12/2008) was passed, aimed at integrating sexual and reproductive teaching in the education system and to legalize abortion. In 2009, the Right to a Gender Identity law (Law N° 18620, 25/10/2009) consecrated the possibility for transgender people to change their ID documents. In the same year, jurisdiction over adoptions was moved to the state (from institutions such as the Church), and unmarried couples were ruled potential adoptive parents. In practice, this implied the possibility for same-sex couples to adopt. In 2013 it was the turn of the Equal Marriage law (Law N° 19.075, 03/05/2013), which not only gave homosexual couples the right of marriage, but also made optional which of the parents' last name is registered first, exposing the previous imposition of the father first as a gender-biased practice (Musto, 2018, p. 63).

2 Please see: http://www.ircca.gub.uy (last accessed June 7, 2021).

3 The First National Survey on Cannabis Regulation in Uruguay was conducted by Monitor Cannabis, the Uruguayan Observatory of Drugs and the INE (National Institute of Statistics) in 2017 based on a representative random sample of the population between 15 and 65 years of age (n=2181).

4 By mid-2021, the price of the 5-gram pack at pharmacies was $U 350, which amounts to less than 2 USD per gram.

References

Barriuso Alonso, M. (2011). Los clubes sociales de cannabis en España. Una alternativa normalizadora en marcha. *Serie reforma legislativa en materia de drogas*, 9, 1–8.

Baumgartner, F., & Jones, B. (1993). *Agendas and Instability in American Politics.* Chicago: University of Chicago Press.

Boidi, F., Queirolo, R., & Cruz, J. (2016). Cannabis consumption patterns among frequent consumers in Uruguay. *International Journal of Drug Policy*, 34, 34–40. doi:10.1016/j.drugpo.2016.05.008.

Decorte, T. (2015). Cannabis Social Clubs? (CSCs) in Belgium: Organizational strengths and weaknesses, and threats to the model. *International Journal of Drug Policy*, 26(1), 122–130. doi:10.1016/j.drugpo.2014.07.016.

Decorte, T., Pardal, M., Queirolo, R., Boidi, M. F., Sánchez Avilés, C., & Parés, O. (2017). Regulating Cannabis Social Clubs: A comparative analysis of legal and self-regulatory practices in Spain, Belgium and Uruguay. *International Journal of Drug Policy*, 43, 44–56. doi:10.1016/j.drugpo.2016.12.020.

Dolowitz, D., & Marsh, D. (2000). Learning from abroad: The role of policy transfer in contemporary policy-making. *Governance: An International Journal of Policy Administration*, 13(1), 5–24. doi:10.1111/0952-1895.00121.

Durán-Martínez, A. (2015). From acquiescence to rebellion? South America and the Global Drug Control Regime. In Idler, A., & Garzón, J. C. (Eds.), *The International Drug Control Regime in the Twenty-first Century.* Boulder, CO: Lynne Rienner.

Economist. (18 December 2013). Earth's got talent. *The Economist*. Retrieved from: https://www.economist.com/leaders/2013/12/18/earths-got-talent (last accessed 24 September 2021).

Equipos. (30 August 2019). *Opinión sobre la ley de regulación de la marihuana. Equipos Mori* Retrieved from: https://equipos.com.uy/opinion-sobre-la-ley-de-regulacion-de-la-marihuana/ (last accessed 24 September 2021).

Garzón-Vergara, J. C. (2012). *The Rebellion of Criminal Networks.* Washington, DC: Woodrow Wilson International Center for Scholars.

IRCCA. (2018). *Resolución 9 – Acta* 166. Montevideo: IRCCA.

IRCCA. (2020). *Mercado Regulado de Cannabis. Informe X.* Montevideo: Presidencia de la República.

Jones, T., & Newburn, T. (2006). *Policy Transfer and Criminal Justice. Exploring US Influence Over British Crime Control Policy.* Maidenhead, UK: Open University Press.

Monitor Cannabis. (2016). *A tres años de su aprobación. Seminario evaluación y monitoreo de la regulación del cannabis.* Montevideo: Monitor Cannabis.

Montañés, V. (2014). *Rompiendo el hielo. La regulación del cannabis en Países Bajos, Colorado y Uruguay.* Donostia/San Sebastián: Fundación Renovatio.

Musto, C. (2018). Cannabis market regulation in Uruguay; the construction of an innovative drug policy [Doctoral dissertation, Utrecht University / Kent University].

NSRC. (2017). *National Survey on Cannabis Regulation.* Montevideo: Instituto Nacional de Estadística.

OUD. (2014). *6ta Encuesta Nacional sobre Consumo de Drogas en Hogares.* Montevideo: Junta Nacional de Drogas.

Pardal, M., Queirolo, R., Álvarez, E., & Repetto, L. (2019). Uruguayan Cannabis Social Clubs: From activism to dispensaries? *International Journal of Drug Policy*, 73, 49–57. doi:10.1016/j.drugpo.2019.06.022.

Pardo, B. (2014). Cannabis policy reforms in the Americas: A comparative analysis of Colorado, Washington, and Uruguay. *International Journal of Drug Policy*, 25, 727–735. doi:10.1016/j.drugpo.2014.05.010.

Pere, D. (2015). Clubes sociales de cannabis: normalización, neoliberalismo,oportunidades políticas y prohibicionismo. *Clivatge*, 3, 92–112.

Queirolo, R., Boidi, M. F., & Cruz, J. M. (2016). Cannabis Clubs in Uruguay: The challenges of regulation. *International Journal of Drug Policy*, 34, 41–48. doi:10.1016/j.drugpo.2016.05.015.

Queirolo, R., Rossel, C., Álvarez, E., & Repetto, L. (2019). Why Uruguay legalized marijuana? The open window of public insecurity. *Addiction*, 114(7), 1313–1321. doi:10.1111/add.14523. Repeto, L. (2014). Regulacion del cannabis: ¿un asunto de seguridad? Entrada y mantenimiento en agenda de un problema de politica publica. *Revista Uruguaya de Ciencia Politica*, 23(1), 6–34.

Stone, D. (2000). Non-governmental policy transfer: The strategies of independent policy institutes. *Governance: An International Journal of Policy and Administration*, 13(1), 45–62. doi:10.1111/0952-1895.00123.

True, J., Jones, B., & Baumgartner, F. (2007). Punctuated-equilibrium theory explaining stability and change in public policymaking. In Sabatier, P. (Ed.), *Theories of the Policy Process.* Boulder, CO: Westview Press.

UyPress. (20 July 2012). Se constituyó la Coordinadora Nacional por la Legalización de la Marihuana uy.press. Retrieved from: https://www.uypress.net/Politica/Se-constituyo-la-Coordinadora-Nacional-por-la-Legalizacion-de-la-Marihuana-uc30735 (last accessed 24 September 2021).

4 What are the barriers and prospects for establishing Cannabis Social Clubs in New Zealand?

Marta Rychert and Chris Wilkins

Introduction

New Zealand has been at the forefront of cannabis law reform debate in recent years. In October 2020, the country held the world's first national referendum involving a detailed legislative bill to legalize recreational cannabis, the Cannabis Legalization and Control Bill (CLCB). Although the referendum failed and cannabis use, possession and supply presently remains prohibited under the Misuse of Drugs Act (MODA), enforcement in relation to cannabis users has relaxed over recent decades (Wilkins & Sweetsur, 2012), with a significant reduction in arrests and the introduction of court diversion and more recently, pre-charge warning schemes. The majority of cannabis users who are prosecuted receive a community sentence or discharge without conviction (MOJ, 2020). In addition, a recent amendment to MODA legislated that personal use and possession of all drugs should not be prosecuted "unless required in the public interest" (s7 (5)); a change that some commentators have described as effectively decriminalizing personal possession of drugs by stealth (Rowe, 2019). In 2018, another amendment to MODA enabled the creation of regulations for a new Medicinal Cannabis Scheme, which became operational in April 2020.

Rates of cannabis use in New Zealand are relatively high by international standards (15% last year prevalence (NZ Health Survey, 2020) and there is a long-standing grassroots cannabis community and tradition of cannabis activism. The New Zealand chapter of National Organization for the Reform of Marijuana Laws (NORML), which originated in North America, dates back to 1979. NZ-NORML has been acting as a hub for cannabis activism over the past 40 years, including by lobbying for the legalization of recreational cannabis and organizing cannabis 'civil disobedience' events (e.g., the annual J-day that features smoking of cannabis in a public space). The Aotearoa Legalise Cannabis Party was established in 1996, and although this political party never won representation in the New Zealand Parliament, two candidates went on to become MPs via the Green Party list. This included New Zealand's first and only MP to identify as a Rastafarian. In 2013, the Whakamana Cannabis Museum opened in Dunedin (a university city in the South Island) and has become another hub for cannabis activism.

DOI: 10.4324/9781003055679-4

Despite the active grassroots cannabis scene, little is known about the adoption and practice of the Cannabis Social Club (CSC) model in New Zealand. There have been a number of high-profile attempts to establish and run CSCs in the past ten years or so, but they ended with closure and arrests. This chapter reviews the recent history of cannabis activism in New Zealand, focusing on recent attempts to establish CSCs. In the second part of the chapter, we consider the opportunities for greater uptake of the CSC model under the Government's proposed Cannabis Legalization and Control Bill (CLCB, the subject of the 2020 cannabis legalization referendum). The CLCB sought to establish a highly regulated largely commercial market for cannabis. The Bill also included unique dedicated provisions for not-for-profit cannabis sales, home-growing, 'social sharing', and micro-cultivator licenses, potentially creating space for legal CSC-like organizations. Although the referendum narrowly failed (with 48.4% voting in support versus 50.7% opposed), the proposed regulatory framework is among the few examples of a detailed regulatory framework for cannabis legalization that accommodates licenses for not-for-profit supply. The CLCB could serve as a template for cannabis law reform in other countries in the future.

Methods

The analysis draws on published records of New Zealand CSCs in traditional and social media, our ongoing research on recreational and medicinal cannabis use in New Zealand, and an in-depth interview with a long-time cannabis campaigner and founder of "the first CSC in New Zealand" (Hopkins, 2011a). The interview was conducted by the first author in August 2020, during a time of intense pre-referendum public debate on the future of cannabis law in New Zealand. We used an unstructured interview guide to (1) examine a pioneering CSC activist's motivations and vision for the CSC model in New Zealand, and (2) explore the harm reduction practices implemented in these pioneering New Zealand CSCs. The interview was used to verify information from published media accounts of CSC activity. We synthesize findings from the interview and review of media sources, and identify barriers that have prevented the CSC model from establishing a more permanent foothold in New Zealand, with focus on cannabis enforcement practice and wider cannabis policing practice. In the second part of the chapter, we analyze CLCB provisions for not-for-profit legal cannabis supply that could serve as a model for other countries in the future.

Cannabis Social Clubs (CSC): definition and the extent of CSC and other social supply in New Zealand

CSCs are not-for-profit voluntary organizations of cannabis users who grow and distribute cannabis for personal use among their members (Barriuso, 2011; Decorte et al., 2017). The model originated in the late 1990s in Spain, where CSCs operate in a legally grey area enabled by the judicial interpretation of drug legislation as permitting possession of cannabis in *private* spaces and the liberal enforcement practice that has supported this view (Barriuso, 2011). In the last two decades, attempts have been made to establish CSCs in a number of other countries, including Belgium and the UK, with varied success. Uruguay is the only country to formally legalize and regulate CSCs via a national law (Queirolo et al., 2016).

The lack of formal legal and regulatory frameworks to support the operation of CSCs (with the notable exception of Uruguay) means the clubs have relied on self-regulation and their existence has often been challenged by the police. A growing body of academic literature has described the diversity across CSCs with respect to club management, membership criteria, and how they grow and distribute cannabis to club members (Pardal, 2018; Pardal et al., 2020). Although there remains some debate around the definition of CSCs, it is generally accepted that transparency, democracy, non-profitability, and commitment to harm-reduction are key elements of the model (Belackova et al., 2016; Decorte et al., 2017; ENCOD, 2011). Under some definitions, registration in a national registry of associations is required (Barriuso, 2011), but this has proved challenging in the context of cannabis prohibition in which many clubs operate today (Pardal et al., 2020).

While little is known about the functioning of formal CSCs in New Zealand, survey data suggests there is significant social supply of cannabis in the country. For example, 65% of those who reported using cannabis in the previous six months in a large online survey purchased cannabis from a "friend, partner or family member" (NZ Drug Trends Survey 2020, unpublished data). In a separate survey question, 21% of cannabis users reported receiving "all" of the cannabis they used in the past six months for "free" (NZ Drug Trends Survey 2020, unpublished data). Yet in a recent survey of medicinal cannabis users in New Zealand (where 95% of respondents accessed cannabis products from sources other than the legal pharmacy option), only 3% accessed cannabis via an "informal club/cooperative" in the past year (compared to 41% who accessed cannabis from a recreational drug dealer), and less than 0.5% identified a club/cooperative as their main source of supply (Rychert, et al., 2020).

Despite the generally low public profile of CSCs in New Zealand, a number of CSCs have opened (and closed) around the country in the past ten years. The next section identifies key characteristics of some high-profile attempts to run CSCs in the country.

The Daktory: the history of the first CSC in New Zealand

On 19 November 2008, a warehouse space in New Lynn, a fringe residential suburb in the city of Auckland, became the site of what was later dubbed "New Zealand's first cannabis club" (Hopkins, 2011a). The 'Daktory' – named after its founder Dakta Green – was open to adults (18 years and older) as a space where they could purchase and consume cannabis (Andrew, 2020). Dakta Green, a long-time cannabis activist (58 years old at the time), described the space as "a nice, secure place where people can get good quality weed at a reasonable price" (Fisher, 2009). The Daktory opened in blatant defiance of the prohibition on use, possession, and sale of cannabis in New Zealand under the Misuse of Drugs Act. Indeed, 'Live like it's legal' was the club's motto.

Daktory club fees and prices

The Daktory charged a membership fee of $20NZD a month (=$14USD or €12EUR) (Fisher, 2009), or a one-off entry fee of $5NZD (=$4USD or €3EUR) (Wikipedia, 2020). The club sold a variety of cannabis strains (sourced from trusted black market suppliers), with prices varying between $10 and $20 per gram (=$7–14USD or €6–12EUR) (NZ Court of Appeal, 2011). At various stages, cannabis was also grown on the premises. Patrons could also bring their own cannabis to consume at the club, and share it with other members on the premises (Hopkins, 2011b).

Consumption venue and club rules

The warehouse occupied by the Daktory featured an open space with couches, music (via a donated stereo sound system), and bongs provided for the smoking of cannabis (Andrew, 2020). Club rules prohibited consumption of alcohol on the premises or entrance under the influence of alcohol. At one point, the club started using a breathalyzer at the door and refused entry to anyone over the legal breath alcohol content driving limit (personal communication with Dakta Green, 14 August 2020). Consumption (or mixing) of cannabis with tobacco was also banned (personal communication with Dakta Green, 14 August 2020).

Membership and club popularity

With "about 30 people" attending the club on the opening day (Andrew, 2020), the Daktory quickly grew in popularity, with information about the CSC spreading via word-of-mouth, NORML networks, online fora, and later mainstream media articles. According to media reports, Auckland's Daktory could attract up to 300–400 members a night (Fisher, 2009). By Christmas 2008 (one month after the club opened), the club had 1,500 members (Fisher, 2009), and in January 2010 an estimated 2,000 members were registered (Edge, 2010). The Daktory did not keep records of registered members due to concerns relating to security and possible prosecution (personal communication with Dakta Green, 14 August 2020). Instead, members were identified by nicknames and membership cards were issued upon payment of the monthly membership fee. Once smartphones became more popular, a photo-verification system was developed, which involved identification of members via a photograph stored on club members' mobile phones (the photograph, taken at club premises, showed a member holding a 'receipt' of membership fee written on a whiteboard) (personal communication with Dakta Green, 14 August 2020).

Initially, Auckland Daktory was open seven days a week but after several months the club temporarily suspended operations for a few weeks to restructure, and then re-opened five days a week (Wednesday–Sunday). This came as a response to the club's growing popularity and the demands of running a club that was "selling pounds of cannabis a week" (personal communication with Dakta Green, 14 August 2020):

> It got overwhelming. By December there would be a hundred or more people queuing at the door. The purpose was never to become the biggest 'tinny house'[1] in the country. The purpose was to make sufficient to pay our way and to pay our [activism] campaign.
>
> (Personal communication with Dakta Green, 14 August 2020)

The hours of operation were also reduced (rather than opening at 4pm, the club started opening at 5pm on week days) to accommodate its neighbors' need to access adjacent carparks during busy traffic hours (personal communication with Dakta Green, 14 August 2020).

Daktory activism

The club operated on a not-for-profit basis with proceeds spent on maintaining the club premises and services (i.e., rent and basic remuneration for members involved in day-to-day operation of the club), and promoting the cause of cannabis law reform (personal communication with Dakta Green, 14 August 2020). This included maintenance of 'Mary Jane the Cannabus', an old Bedford bus owned by NZ-NORML and used for nation-wide pro-legalization campaigning over the years. Between August and November 2010, Dakta Green and other cannabis activists involved in the Daktory drove the Cannabus from the top to the bottom of North Island, stopping in small towns along the way to visit local MPs, promote cannabis law reform and hold 4/20 sessions open to the public (Green, 2010a). Green referred to those pop-up events as "temporary Daktory smoking club[s]" (Green, 2010b). A similar campaign took place between March and May 2008, when Green and other activists drove the 'Cannabus' around the country, visiting 42 towns and cities and organizing public cannabis smoking sessions en route across New Zealand (Karauria, 2008; Wikipedia, 2020).

It was during consultations with local activists around the country that Dakta Green developed the vision of a nationwide network of not-for-profit cannabis clubs (Edge, 2010; Hopkins, 2011b).

> During these talks, overwhelmingly I have found that the not-for-profit model [for legalization] featured in almost every conversation. This is the

> only fair way to move cannabis to the legal market [and] share equitably in the community the benefits of legalization. It is not possible to do that in a for-profit model [that] excludes all those that have suffered financial loss as a consequence of arrests and incarceration that come as a consequence of prohibition.
>
> (Personal communication with Dakta Green, 14 August 2020)

First police raid and conviction

The Auckland Daktory continued to operate for months without complaints from the public or neighbors, and in open defiance of the law, attracting significant media publicity. Then on 9 January 2010 the police executed a search warrant, apparently acting on a call from a journalist who raised questions with the police (Hopkins, 2011b). The police found "246 grams of dried material" alongside a number of cannabis plants (NZ Court of Appeal, 2011). Dakta Green was arrested and faced three cannabis charges ("possessing cannabis for sale", "selling cannabis", and "allowing premises to be used for the consumption of cannabis"). He was initially sentenced to eight months imprisonment, substantially less than the standard starting point of 27 months for this type of offending. The reduced sentence reflected the not-for-profit nature of the club, Dakta Green's political motivation, and the manner in which cannabis was being sold. The sentencing judge noted that "the proceeds […] were not being directed towards commercial profits, but rather towards a cause" and "[the offending] was to some extent committed in a responsible manner in the sense that young persons were not served and the cannabis was consumed on-site" (NZ Court of Appeal, 2011). However, the sentence was increased to one year and 11 months on appeal, with the appeal judge considering Dakta Green's political motivation irrelevant, disagreeing with the claimed "non-commercial" nature of the offending (i.e. cannabis was supplied "at a price") and stressing the "sustained" nature of offending with "breaches spanning 14 months" (Hopkins, 2011a; NZ Court of Appeal, 2011).

Cannabis vending machine and Daktory closure

While Green was serving the sentence, the club continued to operate. In January 2012 a cannabis vending machine (selling 1 gram cannabis bags for $20NZD) was installed at the premises, a move that attracted attention from international media (Chapman, 2012; Huffington Post, 2012). NZ-NORML, who funded the machine, hoped it would serve as a method of distributing cannabis without anyone being culpable for dealing. However, further police raids were executed in March 2012 and subsequently in June 2012, ultimately leading to the permanent closure of Auckland Daktory in June 2012 (Andrew, 2020; NZ Herald, 2012).

Another attempt at the Daktory club in regional New Zealand

Although the country-wide network of cannabis clubs envisioned by Dakta Green has not eventuated, a few other attempts to run CSCs followed the closure of the Auckland Daktory. In 2016, a group of activists led by another cannabis campaigner (Brian Borland, also involved in the Auckland Daktory) opened a cannabis club in Whangarei, a town in the upper North Island. Known as 'Whangarei Daktory', the club rules envisioned there would be

> a garden and members will each own a (cannabis) plant, this plant will have their name on it; when after 14 weeks this plant is harvested and dried, the member will receive a portion and their name will go on another plant. Members will in effect get their membership fees [$200NZD per year] back.
>
> (Newlove, 2016)

The club was vocal about its political cause, hosting regular anti-prohibition events and openly speaking to local and national media. The New Year's Eve Party hosted at the club featured as a story in the mainstream 6pm national television news program (Newshub, 2016). The club was closed following a police raid on 11 January 2017, after a local resident raised concerns in the local paper and with police (Hoyle, 2017; NZ Herald, 2017b). Two club members were arrested, with Borland subsequently sentenced to imprisonment for four years and nine months; the severe penalty was due to his previous offending (including cannabis supply) (Lambly, 2017; NZ Herald, 2017a). The judge did not accept the defense argument about the not-for-profit nature of offending, noting his involvement in the wholesale of cannabis to the club (Lambly, 2017). Borland served part of his sentence in prison and in 2020 was released on parole, with subsequent reports of his recall to prison due to non-compliance with parole conditions (consumption of cannabis) (Green, 2021).

Daktory 2.0 in the capital city Wellington

More recently, in anticipation of possible legalization of cannabis via the 2020 national referendum, Dakta Green opened another Daktory club in central Wellington (the capital of New Zealand). Within two months of opening (which took place on 11 April 2019), the club had an estimated 700 members (Manch, 2019). Like the Auckland Daktory, the Wellington club membership was restricted to adults (with a membership fee $20NZD per month or $200 per year). The club organized community events (including live music) and there was an 'arts and crafts section' at the premises for members' use. Members could bring their own cannabis or purchase it from the club in quantities of up to 5 grams (Manch, 2019), with products including dried cannabis flowers, oils, and edibles. No alcohol or tobacco use was allowed on the premises and members were provided with bongs and a vaporizer as a harm-reduction measure. Following the arrest of Dakta Green and two police raids in 2019, the club transitioned to a BYO only ('bring your own') consumption space, with club operations now suspended (as of late 2020) (Fonseka, 2019; Sadler, 2019).

Barriers to CSCs under prohibition in New Zealand

Law and police enforcement

The prohibition of cannabis has undoubtedly been the greatest barrier to the establishment and survival of CSCs in New Zealand. Despite the liberalization of some aspects of drug policy in recent years, New Zealand legislation does not allow for any personal cannabis cultivation limit, and personal possession of cannabis is not formally decriminalized (as of March 2021). The history of Daktory clubs and cannabis activism in New Zealand shows that a certain degree of tolerance from police allowed the clubs to exist for extended period of times when there were no public complaints. Dakta Green has been outspoken about the clubs (including in the media) and described the early police attitude as tolerant (personal communication with Dakta Green, 14 August 2020). Media reports of Green's 'Cannabus' tour around the country also stated that some local police departments did not approach the campaigners, "unless [they] received a complaint about the bus and any activities being carried out there" (Dinsdale, 2010). However, once concerns from the public or media were voiced, the police executed search warrants and arrests – given that there are no laws accommodating shared consumption or growing of cannabis for personal use.

Media publicity and promotion

The original Auckland Daktory and subsequent clubs in Whangarei and Wellington have attracted significant media attention and publicity, featuring in local, national, and even international news. The extent of publicity around the Daktory clubs has attracted some criticism, even from within the cannabis community and organizations supporting cannabis law reform. For example, the director of the New Zealand Drug Foundation, a drug and alcohol NGO that lobbied for a 'yes' vote in the 2020 cannabis law reform referendum, has described Green's most recent club in Wellington as a form of "unlawful disobedience which might have unintended consequences", including the potential to "upset people to vote negatively in a referendum" (Manch, 2019). Green's response to such criticism has always been that his goal is to "expose the law for what it is", with a focus on the injustice of criminalising cannabis users (personal communication with Dakta Green, 14 August 2020). He has explained he is led by political activism and sees no point in running a CSC that is quiet about its existence.

Maintaining neighbor and community acquiescence

The operation of the Daktory clubs was dependent on the tacit acquiescence of neighbor and the wider community. Managing significant numbers of patrons proved challenging at times, as evidenced in the restructuring of the Auckland Daktory and reduction of its opening hours in the early stage of club operations. While the club was able to negotiate some issues of concern raised by neighbors (e.g., by changing their opening hours), ongoing community acquiescence has been difficult to sustain in the long run. This perhaps reflects popularized negative societal attitudes towards cannabis. For example, recent opinion polls in New Zealand indicated mixed support for recreational cannabis law reform (Newshub, 2020), with some sectors of society opposing any relaxation of laws. In contrast, illegal compassionate supply of cannabis to medicinal users has attracted much broader social support, perhaps in part reflecting the public image of so-called 'green fairies' (i.e., suppliers of illicit cannabis products focused on medical patients), with media reports often featuring female 'green fairies' and focused on the compassionate nature of supply (Spinoff, 2020).

Availability of cannabis via other sources of supply

Although we are not aware of other public examples of CSCs, it is quite likely that groups of friends in New Zealand informally combine their expertise and resources to grow cannabis to distribute among themselves for personal use. New Zealand's moderate climate and many isolated rural areas make it particularly favorable for outdoor clandestine cannabis growing (Wilkins et al., 2018) and 11% of current cannabis users have reported growing at least some of their cannabis themselves (NZ Drug Trends Survey 2020, unpublished data). This may indicate that more informal social supply arrangements are commonly used to provide cannabis supply rather than the more public formal social clubs.

Prospects for CSCs and other regulated community supply options in New Zealand

The not-for-profit and social character of CSCs makes the model an attractive 'middle-ground' option for cannabis law reform (Caulkins & Kilmer, 2016) that avoids the harmful aspects of a commercial cannabis industry, in particular the financial incentive to expand use, while capturing the potential benefits of providing legal access to cannabis for existing users. While CSCs have proven very popular in Spain, a lack of formal regulatory frameworks has inhibited the sustainability of individual clubs and their development of harm-minimization characteristics (Decorte & Pardal, 2020). Only one country, Uruguay, has established a legislated framework and enforceable rules for CSCs to date (Queirolo et al., 2016).

New Zealand's proposed CLCB, which was the subject of the national referendum in October 2020, did not include specific provisions for the establishment of CSCs (e.g., rules around membership criteria or size of allowed communal crop cultivation). Therefore, it appeared the 'classic' CSC models from Spain, Uruguay, or Belgium (involving communal growing and sharing to a closed circuit of adults) would not have been permitted under the CLCB. Indeed, the CLCB aimed to establish a largely commercial market with production and sale by private entities, albeit operating in a highly regulated environment (e.g., limits on maximum annual production, a ban on advertising, and centrally-monitored licensing system) (Wilkins & Rychert, 2020a, 2020b). The CLCB provisions did allow home cultivation for personal use (up to two plants per person) and social sharing of up to 14 grams of cannabis with others, but restricted home cultivation to a maximum of four plants per household (with unlicensed growing of ten or more cannabis plants a criminal offence), seemingly preventing the larger communal crops required for a CSC (Wilkins & Rychert, 2020a).

However, under social equity principles, the Bill contained provisions that aimed to prioritize community-oriented and not-for-profit operators in the licensing process, potentially allowing for CSC-like entities to operate under this regime. The additional criteria for assessing cultivation and micro-cultivation licenses included: (1) "representing or partnering with communities disproportionately affected by harm from cannabis, including Māori and people from economically deprived areas"; (2) "the generation of social benefit and building of community partnerships by engagement with individuals, whānau [families] and communities in the design and deliveries of their activities"; and (3) "the promotion of employment opportunities and career pathways in the cannabis industry for Māori and those from economically deprived areas" (CLCB, 2020a). The additional criteria for assessing distribution (retail) licenses include "prioritizing, where practicable, not-for-profit applicants that [sic] can demonstrate the commitment to delivering social benefit to the community or communities in which the applicant intends to operate" (CLCB, 2020b).

These provisions could potentially have provided a pathway for social enterprise, community-oriented, and not-for-profit operators. However, they would need to comply with essential regulatory, testing, and security requirements that applied to other commercial applicants, which may be beyond the expertise and financial resources of a typical group of cannabis users (Wilkins & Rychert, 2020a). The extent of the priority to be given to not-for-profit and social enterprise operators also remained unclear, and there was a risk that the CLCB's social equity criteria would merely encourage the inclusion of corporate social responsibility into the business plans of for-profit commercial companies. The balancing of profit-seeking and social objectives by cannabis social enterprises could have been enhanced with additional regulatory detail in the CLCB specifying the minimum required commitment to delivering social and community benefit (e.g., a requirement to distribute a defined minimum percentage of profits to social and community causes including harm reduction or cannabis club events) (Rychert & Wilkins, 2020).

The CLCB also prevented vertical integration of licensed operators by prohibiting the same licensee from holding both production (cultivation) and distribution (retail) licenses. This suggests the need for some type of partnership between a not-for-profit retailer (e.g., a not-for-profit CSC-like retail network) and a community-oriented grower (e.g., micro-cultivators that could involve small-scale growers from the cannabis community).

The CLCB's emphasis on prioritizing licensees with links to indigenous Māori communities, particularly in the production space, is notable. Māori have been shown to be three times more likely to be arrested and convicted for cannabis offences under the current prohibition regime (Fergusson et al., 2003). Cannabis law reform has been promoted as a means of addressing the bias in policing and the wider criminal justice system, as well as an opportunity for economic development and employment in economically depressed rural regions with high proportions of Māori (Hindmarsh, 2020). Attempts to include indigenous actors in the legal cannabis space in other countries have had mixed results to date (Adinoff & Reiman, 2019; Kilmer & Neel, 2020) and the extent to which the CLCB 'social equity' provisions would genuinely benefit Māori communities remains unclear. There is an established precedent of one high-profile New Zealand medicinal cannabis company creating employment in a Māori community (Rua Bioscience, 2020).

New Zealand has a rich tradition of community-based and social enterprise organizations that provide working examples of 'middle-ground' models for the legal cannabis regime. For example, Dakta Green's envisioned network of cannabis clubs around the country was inspired by an existing community organization – the Royal New Zealand Returned and Services' Association (NZ-RSA) (personal communication with Dakta Green, 14 August 2020). The NZ-RSA (established in 1916 by soldiers returning from Europe after World War I) is a not-for-profit organization that provides support for veterans and their families, including by organising charitable events. RSA clubs also provide alcohol, food, and social events for their members. The RSA network currently involves 182 local RSA 'clubs', each an entity in its own right and managed by its own executive committee.

In the lead up to the 2020 referendum, a number of other not-for-profit and community-oriented 'middle-ground' cannabis law reform options were envisioned for New Zealand (Decorte, 2018; Rychert & Wilkins, 2019; Wilkins, 2018). Wilkins (2018), inspired by a system for gaming machine gambling societies in New Zealand, developed a not-for-profit cannabis reform model where incorporated cannabis 'societies' would distribute 40% of their profits back to local community needs, including for drug treatment and harm-reduction services in the regions. Rychert and Wilkins (2019), drawing on the example of New Zealand's alcohol licensing trusts, proposed a democratically managed 'community enterprise' model under which geographically defined communities (defined by local council area boundaries) would elect community trustees to run cannabis retail outlets, with profits owned by the community and a portion re-distributed annually to local community and social causes.

Following the announcement of the referendum results, and despite the closeness of the outcome, the government has rejected suggestions of any legislative changes to the status of recreational cannabis in the foreseeable future (including *de jure* decriminalization) (Rychert & Wilkins, 2021). Instead, they have committed to implementation of the 2019 amendment to the Misuse of Drugs Act, which instructs the police not to prosecute personal drug possession unless it is required 'in the public interest'. While this will dampen the prospects for reform, cannabis activists are likely to continue to pressure political actors for some type of law change. It is also possible further reforms could potentially occur via refinements to the recently enacted Medicinal Cannabis Scheme (e.g., via a legislated limited allowance for home-growing cannabis for medicinal uses).

Conclusions

New Zealand has a rich history of cannabis activism, with a number of high-profile attempts to establish and run CSCs during the past decade or so. The prohibition of the use, possession, and supply of cannabis under the Misuse of Drugs Act has prevented the clubs from surviving in the long term. Their high profile, popularity, and visibility in the media ultimately drew the attention of law enforcement, with subsequent closures and arrests of key activists. The extent of less formalized social supply of cannabis in New Zealand appears significant, with two in three current users reporting the purchase of cannabis from "friends or family members", and one in five receiving all their cannabis supply for "free" (NZ Drug Trends Survey 2020, unpublished data).

The not-for-profit and social character of the CSC model makes it an attractive 'middle-ground' option for cannabis law reform. While the government's proposed CLCB did not include specific provisions for CSCs, the 'social equity' provisions for community-oriented and not-for-profit operators could have been utilized to operate CSCs-like entities. However, it remains uncertain to what extent these cannabis social enterprises would be able to operate like a CSC in an otherwise largely commercial environment. Due to the ban on vertical integration of licensed cannabis operators under the CLCB, a CSC-like model would require a partnership between a not-for-profit retailer (e.g., licensed club-like retail network resembling the RSA model) and a community-oriented grower (e.g., licensed micro-cultivators, which could involve small-scale growers from the cannabis community). The lack of attention to CSCs in the CLCB may have proved a significant barrier in the effort to encourage illegal cannabis users and growers to transition to the legal market.

Acknowledgements

We would like to thank Dakta Green, who agreed to be interviewed for the purpose of this chapter. The analysis was supported by a grant from the Marsden Royal Society of New Zealand (MFP-MAU1813).

Note

1 'Tinny houses' or drug houses are residential properties converted for the retail sale of cannabis and other illicit drugs in New Zealand.

References

Adinoff, B., & Reiman, A. (2019). Implementing social justice in the transition from illicit to legal cannabis. *The American Journal of Drug and Alcohol Abuse*, 45(6), 673–688. doi:10.1080/00952990.2019.1674862.

Andrew, M. (27 September 2020). Remembering The Daktory – West Auckland's legendary cannabis club. *The Spinoff*. Retrieved from: https://thespinoff.co.nz/business/27-09-2020/remembering-the-daktory-west-aucklands-legendary-cannabis-club/ (last accessed 27 September 2020).

Barriuso, M. (2011). Cannabis social clubs in Spain: A normalizing alternative underway. *Series on Legislative Reform of Drug Policies*, 9, 1–8. Retrieved from: https://www.tni.org/en/node/943/field_publication_series/drug-law-reform-series-25 (last accessed 11 March 2022).

Belackova, V., Tomkova, A., & Zabransky, T. (2016). Qualitative research in Spanish cannabis social clubs: "The moment you enter the door, you are minimising the risks". *International Journal of Drug Policy*, 34, 49–57. doi:10.1016/j.drugpo.2016.04.009.

Caulkins, J., & Kilmer, B. (2016). Considering marijuana legalization carefully: Insights for other jurisdictions from analysis for Vermont. *Addiction*, 111(12), 2082–2089. doi:10.1111/add.13289.

Chapman, P. (22 March 2012). Cannabis vending machine opens in New Zealand. *The Telegraph*. Retrieved from: https://www.telegraph.co.uk/news/worldnews/australiaandthepacific/newzealand/9159536/Cannabis-vending-machine-opens-in-New-Zealand.html. (last accessed 23 September 2021).

CLCB. (2020a). Cannabis Legalisation and Control Bill. Exposure draft for the referendum. Cl 85(2). Retrieved from: https://at.govt.nz/media/1983067/cannabis-att-6-cannabis-legalisation-and-control-bill-exposure-draft-for-referendum-004.pdf (last accessed 24 March 2022).

CLCB. (2020b). Cannabis Legalisation and Control Bill. Exposure draft for the referendum. Cl 88(a). Retrieved from: https://at.govt.nz/media/1983067/cannabis-att-6-cannabis-legalisation-and-control-bill-exposure-draft-for-referendum-004.pdf (last accessed 24 March 2022).

Decorte, T. (2018). *Regulating cannabis. A detailed scenario for a nonprofit Cannabis Market*. Bloomington IN: Archway Publishing.

Decorte, T., & Pardal, M. (2020). Insights for the design of Cannabis Social Club regulation. In T. Decorte, S. Lenton, & C. Wilkins (Eds.), *Legalizing cannabis: experiences, lessons and scenarios* (pp. 409–426). Abingdon: Routledge.

Decorte, T., Pardal, M., Queirolo, R., Boidi, M. F., Sánchez Avilés, C., & Parés, Ò. (2017). Regulating Cannabis Social Clubs: A comparative analysis of legal and self-regulatory practices in Spain, Belgium and Uruguay. *International Journal of Drug Policy*, 43, 44–56. doi:10.1016/j.drugpo.2016.12.020.

Dinsdale, M. (15 August 2010). Vehicle for cannabis law change runs out of puff. *nzherald.co.nz*. Retrieved from: https://www.nzherald.co.nz/northern-advocate/news/article.cfm?c_id=1503450&objectid=11000280 (last accessed 23 September 2021).

Edge, K. (12 January 2010). Cannabis clubs planned for NorthJanuary. *nzherald.co.nz*. Retrieved from: https://www.nzherald.co.nz/northern-advocate/news/cannabis-clubs-planned-for-north/NHQDTQHVRPMO5J6ACJD53X35BU/ (last accessed 23 September 2021).

ENCOD. (9 December 2011). *European Coalition for Just and Effective Drug Policies - Code of Conduct for European Cannabis Social Clubs.* Encod. Retrieved from: https://encod.org/en/cannabis-social-club/how-to-create-a-cannabis-social-club/code-of-conduct-for-european-cannabis-social-clubs/ (last accessed 11 March 2022).

Fergusson, D. M., Swain-Campbell, N. R., & Horwood, L. J. (2003). Arrests and convictions for cannabis related offences in a New Zealand birth cohort. *Drug and Alcohol Dependence*, 70(1), 53–63. doi:10.1016/S0376-8716(02)00336–00338.

Fisher, D. (12 April 2009). Cannabis club tilts at the law. *nzherald.co.nz*. Retrieved from: https://www.nzherald.co.nz/nz/news/article.cfm?c_id=1&objectid=10566272 (last accessed 23 September 2021).

Fonseka, D. (24 August 2019). Cops raid cannabis club in Wellington. *Stuff*. Retrieved from: https://www.stuff.co.nz/national/115252996/cops-raid-cannabis-club-in-wellington (last accessed 23 September 2021).Green, D. (10 August 2010a). Cannabis Armistice Tour Kicks Off. *Scoop*. Retrieved from: https://www.scoop.co.nz/stories/PO1008/S00118/cannabis-armistice-tour-kicks-off.htm (last accessed 23 September 2021).

Green, D. (23 August 2010b). Cannabis Club Set Up in Whangarei. *Scoop* Retrieved from: https://www.scoop.co.nz/stories/AK1008/S00369/cannabis-club-set-up-in-whangarei.htm?from-mobile=bottom-link-01 (last accessed 23 September 2021).

Green, D [@daktagreen]. (29 January 2021). *Dakta Green's TwitterJanuary.* Retrieved from: https://twitter.com/daktagreen/status/1354985792393728008?s=19&fbclid=IwAR2hJp6YqjuBFaBtZcrsYAslq24p5IdoQjEoXz6rVIRvt8977iq21asQ_GY (last accessed 23 September 2021).

Hindmarsh, N. (7 August 2020). Cannabis referendum: how NZ's ex-illicit growers are poised to transform the proposed legal market. *Stuff*. Retrieved from: https://www.stuff.co.nz/national/cannabis-referendum/122197081/cannabis-referendum-how-nzs-exillicit-growers-are-poised-to-transform-the-proposed-legal-market (last accessed 23 September 2021).

Hopkins, S. (2011a). Cannabis club founder's sentence doubled (31 October 2011). *Stuff*. Retrieved from: http://www.stuff.co.nz/national/crime/5879467/Cannabis-club-founders-sentence-doubled (last accessed 23 September 2021).

Hopkins, S. (2011b). Pot clubs go nationwide (11 January 2011). *Stuff*. Retrieved from: http://www.stuff.co.nz/national/3218470/Pot-clubs-go-nationwide (last accessed 23 September 2021)

Hoyle, C. (11 January 2017). *Police arrest two at Whangarei Daktory cannabis club after neighbour speaks out*. Retrieved from: https://www.stuff.co.nz/national/88294739/whangarei-resident-appalled-by-lack-of-action-against-daktory-cannabis-club. (last accessed 23 September 2021)

Huffington Post. (22 March 2012). Cannabis Vending Machine Proves Popular In New Zealand Club. *Huffington Post*. Retrieved from: https://www.huffingtonpost.co.uk/2012/03/22/cannabis-vending-machine-popular-in-new-zealand-club_n_1372064.html?guccounter=1 (last accessed 23 September 2021).

Karauria, M. (22 March 2008). Cannabus comes to town. *Whanganui Chronicle*. Retrieved from: https://www.nzherald.co.nz/whanganui-chronicle/news/cannabus-comes-to-town/IDTWUEDUH7EB5GGRCN4V6NXJFM/ (last accessed 23 September 2021).

Kilmer, B., & Neel, E. (2020). Being thoughtful about cannabis legalization and social equity. *World psychiatry: Official journal of the World Psychiatric Association (WPA)*, 19(2), 194–195. doi:10.1002/wps.20741.

Lambly, A. (10 November 2017). Jail for Daktory cannabis founderNovember. *Stuff*. Retrieved from: https://www.stuff.co.nz/auckland/local-news/northland/98764492/jail-for-daktory-cannabis-founder (last accessed 23 September 2021).

Manch, T. (4 June 2019). Cannabis campaigner Dakta Green opens cannabis club in Wellington, claiming 700 members. *Stuff*. Retrieved from: https://www.stuff.co.nz/national/113212281/cannabis-campaigner-dakta-green-opens-cannabis-club-in-wellington-claiming-700-members (last accessed 23 September 2021).

MOJ. (2020). *Ministry of Justice Data tables – Cannabis offences*. Justice.govt.nz. Retrieved from: https://www.justice.govt.nz/justice-sector-policy/research-data/justice-statistics/data-tables/ (last accessed 4 November 2021).

Newlove, A. (5 May 2016). Whangarei in line for cannabis club. *NZHerald.co.nz*. Retrieved from: https://www.nzherald.co.nz/nz/news/article.cfm?c_id=1&objectid=11634115 (last accessed 23 September 2021).

Newshub. (31 December 2016). Cannabis lovers gather at Whangarei Daktory for happy end to 2016. *Newshub*. Retrieved from: https://www.newshub.co.nz/home/new-zealand/2016/12/cannabis-lovers-gather-at-whangarei-daktory-for-happy-end-to-2016.html (last accessed 23 September 2021).

Newshub. (30 August 2020). Support for legalising cannabis burning out. *Newshub*. Retrieved from: https://www.newshub.co.nz/home/new-zealand/2020/08/support-for-legalising-cannabis-burning-out-survey.html (last accessed 23 September 2021).

NZ Court of Appeal. (30 September 2011). *R v Green [2011] NZCA* 507. Court of appeal of New Zealand. Retrieved from: http://www.nzlii.org/cgi-bin/sinodisp/nz/cases/NZCA/2011/507.html?query=%22situation%20could%20not%20be%20likened%20to%20a%20tinnie%20house%22 (last accessed 23 September 2021).

NZ Health Survey. (2020). *Annual data explorer (2018/19 data) – Cannabis use in the past 12 months*. Ministry of health. Retrieved from: https://minhealthnz.shinyapps.io/nz-health-survey-2018-19-annual-data-explorer/_w_dfde97f7/#!/explore-topics (last accessed 23 September 2021).

NZ Herald. (2012). Three arrested during raid at Auckland's 'Daktory'. *nzherald.co.nz*. Retrieved from: https://www.nzherald.co.nz/nz/news/article.cfm?c_id=1&objectid=10814707 (last accessed 23 September 2021).

NZ Herald. (2017a). Daktory members found guilty of drug-offences. *nzherald.co.nz*. Retrieved from: https://www.nzherald.co.nz/nz/news/article.cfm?c_id=1&objectid=11932021&ref=rss (last accessed 23 September 2021).

NZ Herald. (2017b). Whangarei police raid Daktory cannabis club after concerns from local resident. *nzherald.co.nz*. Retrieved from: https://www.nzherald.co.nz/nz/news/article.cfm?c_id=1&objectid=11780216 (last accessed 23 September 2021).

Pardal, M. (2018). An analysis of Belgian Cannabis Social Clubs' supply practices: A shapeshifting model? *International Journal of Drug Policy*, 57, 32–41. doi:10.1016/j.drugpo.2018.03.027.

Pardal, M., Decorte, T., Bone, M., Parés, Ò., & Johansson, J. (2020). Mapping Cannabis Social Clubs in Europe. *European Journal of Criminology*, 1–24. doi:10.1177/1477370820941392. Queirolo, R., Boidi, M. F., & Cruz, J. M. (2016). Cannabis clubs in Uruguay: The challenges of regulation. *International Journal of Drug Policy*, 34, 41–48. doi:10.1016/j.drugpo.2016.05.015.

Rowe, D. (7 August 2019). The “most significant drug reform in 40 years” is about to become law. *The spinoff*. Retrieved from: https://thespinoff.co.nz/politics/07-08-2019/the-most-significant-drug-reform-in-40-years-is-about-to-become-law/ (last accessed 23 September 2021).

Rua Bioscience. (2020). Indigenous innovation for global health. Rua bioscience. Retrieved from: https://www.ruabio.com/our-story (last accessed 23 September 2021).

Rychert, M., & Wilkins, C. (2019). A ‘community enterprise’ model for recreational cannabis: Lessons from alcohol licensing trusts in New Zealand. *International Journal of Drug Policy*, 67, 72–78. doi:10.1016/j.drugpo.2019.03.007.

Rychert, M., & Wilkins, C. (2020). “You have to make some money before you can do some good”: Balancing the commercial, social and public health objectives in a “community enterprise” regulatory model for alcohol and cannabis. *International Journal of Drug Policy*, 77, 102689. doi:10.1016/j.drugpo.2020.102689.

Rychert, M., & Wilkins, C. (2021). Why did New Zealand’s referendum to legalise recreational cannabis fail? *Drug and Alcohol Review*, 4, 877–881. doi:10.1111/dar.13254.

Rychert, M., Wilkins, C., Parker, K., & Graydon-Guy, T. (2020). Exploring medicinal use of cannabis in a time of policy change in New Zealand. *New Zealand Medical Journal*, 133(1515), 54–69. Sadler, R. (20 December 2019). Wellington cannabis club the Daktory raided by police, one arrested. *Newshub*. Retrieved from: https://www.newshub.co.nz/home/new-zealand/2019/12/wellington-cannabis-club-the-daktory-raided-by-police-one-arrested.html. (last accessed 23 September 2021)

Spinoff. (6 August 2020). The green fairies at the forefront of New Zealand’s fight to legalise cannabis. *Spinoff*. Retrieved from: https://thespinoff.co.nz/society/06-08-2020/the-green-fairies-at-the-forefront-of-new-zealands-fight-to-legalise-cannabis/?fbclid=IwAR2k60YB84rU5NkLW6kav6OQoDrOa-0NVahv1JE-m0Hh3VWB2eVTPfRPDrg. (last accessed 23 September 2021)

Wikipedia. (3 June 2020). Daktory. *Wikipedia, The Free Encyclopedia*. Retrieved from: https://en.wikipedia.org/w/index.php?title=Daktory&oldid=960462047. (last accessed 17 August 2020)

Wilkins, C. (2018). A “not-for-profit” regulatory model for legal recreational cannabis: Insights from the regulation of gaming machine gambling in New Zealand. *International Journal of Drug Policy*, 53, 115–122. doi:10.1016/j.drugpo.2017.12.002.

Wilkins, C., & Rychert, M. (2020a). Assessing New Zealand’s Cannabis Legalization and Control Bill: prospects and challenges. *Addiction*, 116(2), 222–230. doi:10.1111/add.15144.

Wilkins, C., & Rychert, M. (2020b). The Government’s proposal to legalise cannabis in New Zealand: 10 key questions. *New Zealand Medical Journal*, 133(1515), 9–15.

Wilkins, C., & Sweetsur, P. (2012). Criminal justice outcomes for cannabis use offences in New Zealand, 1991–2008. *International Journal of Drug Policy*, 23(6), 505–511. doi:10.1016/j.drugpo.2012.03.002. Wilkins, C., Sznitman, S., Decorte, T., Hakkarainen, P., & Lenton, S. (2018). Characteristics of cannabis cultivation in New Zealand and Israel. *Drugs and Alcohol Today*, 18(2), 90–98. doi:10.1108/DAT-03-2018-0010.

5 The Spanish Social Club

What's in a name?

Isidro Marín-Gutiérrez and Mónica Hinojosa-Becerra

Introduction

Cannabis Social Clubs (CSCs) are non-profit organizations in which typically cannabis is grown and consumed collectively. To become a member of a CSC, it is usually necessary to be of legal age and have the endorsement of a current member (Belackova, et al., 2016; Muñoz Sánchez, 2017; Parés et al., 2019). As a result, a closed circuit between producers and consumers is established (Bone & de Hoedt, 2018; Decorte et al., 2017). Since its inception, the CSC model seems to have relied on and motivated different forms of social interaction.

A brief summary of the history of CSCs in Spain[1]

CSCs have a long and rich history in Spain, rooted in the cannabis movement which began with the youth counterculture of the 1960s and 1970s (Romaní, 2004). In 1992, the Corcuera Law acted as a precipitating factor for the emergence of the associative movement more directly involved with the creation of CSCs in Spain (Marks, 2019). Under this law, the public consumption and possession of cannabis received administrative sanctions, generating great discontent among cannabis users (Marín-Gutiérrez, 2008). Around that time, the Asociación Ramón Santos de Estudios Sobre el Cannabis (ARSEC) was created – and soon after, the first experiment with collective cannabis cultivation within the framework of a cannabis association took place in Spain, as we discuss in more detail in the next sections.

In the years after the creation of ARSEC, in particular between 1994 and 1997, many other similar associations – self-described as oriented towards the 'study of cannabis' – were established across the country (including: AMEC in Madrid; KALAMUDIA in Bilbao; ACAC in La Coruña; SECA in Zaragoza; AECA in Huelva – see Figure 5.1; AMA in Albacete; AECA in Asturias; Amigos de María in León; AlaCannabis in Alicante; Bena Riamba in Valencia; AMIC in Mallorca – see Marín-Gutiérrez, 2008; Marín-Gutiérrez & Hinojosa-Becerra, 2017). In 2001, the first association explicitly adopting the denomination of 'Cannabis Social Club' was created (Arana & Parés, 2020). It

DOI: 10.4324/9781003055679-5

Figure 5.1 A party organized by AECA in Huelva (1999)

was the Barcelona Cannabis Tasters Club (CCCB) (Márkez, 2002). During the first decade of the 21st century, CSCs appeared with special incidence in the Basque Country, Catalonia, and Andalusia (Blickman, 2014).

Most of these early CSCs were integrated into the Federation of Cannabis Associations (FAC) (Arana & Parés, 2020; Marín-Gutiérrez, 2011) – Figure 5.2 depicts a meeting leading to the establishment of this Federation. A CSC Federation is a supra-organization that represents the affiliated CSCs, developing codes of conduct for the functioning of CSCs and representing the CSCs in other lobbying and advocacy work (Jansseune et al., 2019). Today multiple Federations play an active role in this field (Belackova & Wilkins, 2018; Decorte et al., 2017). Between 2011 and 2014, there was a massive opening of CSCs in

Figure 5.2 Meeting prior to the creation of the FAC at the AMEC headquarters in Madrid (2002)

Barcelona, although only a few of these new CSCs followed the FAC operating standards or codes of conduct (Arana & Parés, 2020; Belackova & Wilkins, 2018; Jansseune et al., 2019). For instance, during this period of expansion, a commercial version of the CSC model emerged alongside the non-profit CSC model. These commercial CSCs sought to maximize their profits by producing cannabis outside the CSC, actively attracting tourists, and enrolling a large membership base (Martínez Oró, 2015; Parés & Bouso, 2015).

While it is impossible to estimate with certainty the exact number of CSCs active in Spain today, it is likely that there are between 600 and 700 CSCs, of which 350 are located in Catalonia and 75 in the Basque Country (Blickman, 2014, Martínez Oró, 2015). Despite multiple attempts to regulate the model, particularly by autonomous communities (e.g. Basque Country, Catalonia, Navarra) and even at the municipal level, no legislation has been introduced nationwide, and as a result CSCs remain exploiting the particularities of the Spanish legal framework (Arana & Parés, 2020; Decorte & Pardal, 2020). While according to Arana & Parés (2020), most court rulings involving CSC members between the mid-1990s until early 2015 had a favorable outcome for them, more recent cases have resulted in the conviction of CSC members. CSCs, also known as the 'Spanish model' due to the historical roots of these associations in the country, therefore continue to face important legal challenges.

Goal of this chapter

Many CSCs in Spain and elsewhere operate as quasi cannabis dispensers (even if non-profit) without any or nearly any activism or other forms of engagement beyond the supply of cannabis to their members (Pardal, 2018; Pardal et al., 2019). For those CSCs, the organization of social activities or other events for their members is secondary or absent. Earlier research in Spain suggests that the CSCs that are affiliated with a CSC Federation tend to organize more social activities and have a more public profile (Belackova & Wilkins, 2018; Jansseune et al., 2019). Nevertheless, historically, CSCs have been 'social clubs', providing other services apart from distributing cannabis, and relying on different forms of collective action to create links between people and connect them (even with regards to the production of the substance). In this chapter, we focus precisely on the breadth of activities organized by CSCs in Spain over time, considering what has made them 'social clubs'.

Methods

Our goal is to explore the extent to which Spanish CSCs have played a social role for their members and the broader community. For that purpose, we draw on different data sources. Firstly, we rely on a review of the literature focusing on CSCs in Spain. This allows us to document CSC practices as identified across different research projects. In addition, and primarily, our analysis builds on data collected in the context of earlier research by the authors. Namely, the first author conducted an extensive study of the cannabis movement in Spain between 1991 and 2007, with a particular focus on CSCs as central actors of that movement (Marín-Gutiérrez, 2008). This was a mixed methods study that involved: 1) participant observation in different events of the cannabis movement (e.g. protests, social events, cannabis 'cups'), between 2000 and 2007; 2) surveys among growers (n=265), 'grow shops' clients, and owners (n=80 and n=26, respectively), in 2006; 3) semi-structured and in-depth interviews with key individuals of the movement and representatives of cannabis associations (n=25 and n=14, respectively), between 2002 and 2007; 4) review of multiple documentary sources (e.g. media) (Marín-Gutiérrez, 2008; Marín-Gutiérrez & Hinojosa-Becerra, 2017). Furthermore, in this analysis we also rely on previously unpublished data from participant observations at meetings among CSCs and other associations in the south of Spain, which took place in 2011, as well as field notes from a court case involving a CSC member-grower in 2006. Between 1999 and 2011, the first author has also taken photographs during the course of his ethnographic research, which document some of the key activities developed by the Spanish CSCs. All the included photographs were taken without arranging the scene or asking participants to pose, as the researcher sought to avoid disrupting the activities. These are included in our analysis as they visually support the discussion of CSCs as 'social clubs'.

The focus of this chapter lies on identifying different key ways in which CSCs in Spain have acted as 'social clubs'. However, we do not claim that these social aspects have been integrated by all or most CSCs. Indeed, the available evidence has shown a diversity of views and practices among CSCs in Spain and elsewhere (Bone et al., this volume; Jansseune et al., 2019; Pardal, 2018). There may also be other social aspects that may have remained undocumented. Here we pay particular attention to the early period of development of the CSC model in Spain (since the late 1990s), and over time, which allows us to offer a historical perspective of the issues at stake.

Results

CSCs' functioning as social clubs is manifested across a number of areas. In our analysis we focus on instances in which CSCs have focused on being 'social' in relation to their affiliated members, growers, as well as with other CSCs and other actors of the broader cannabis movement.

General social and cultural activities

A first general aspect related to CSCs' social function relates to the actual physical space of these associations. CSC members are generally able to meet and spend time at the premises of the CSCs, as depicted in Figure 5.3. The venues are not public and typically only registered members are allowed entry (Belackova & Wilkins, 2018). The use of cannabis is generally allowed either in the main social space of the CSCs or in specific dedicated areas in the clubs

Figure 5.3 A party of the ARSECSE association in Seville (2002)

(Decorte et al., 2017; Jansseune et al., 2019). Some CSCs provide entertainment activities and/or materials to their members as well, such as the loan of gaming consoles, hosting DJ sessions or showing soccer games on television, organizing movie sessions, talks, or book presentations, keeping a photo gallery, or hosting theater performances, art exhibitions or other events at the premises of the CSCs (Jansseune et al., 2019; Martínez Oró, 2015). Parties and other social events for members are also organized by the CSCs (Figures 5.1 and 5.3).

Another important event is the celebration of Saint Canuto, which is a holiday as well as a day for activism. Saint Canuto was an 11th-century Danish monarch turned saint whose feast day is January 19. During Saint Canuto day, activists take to the streets to meet and make themselves visible. The Saint's relationship with the world of cannabis is explained by the name given in Spanish to a cannabis joint (in Spanish: *canuto*). This holiday arose spontaneously in university circles during the 1990s as a way to vindicate the use of cannabis. The feast of Saint Canuto is a protest act, it is a day when people go out to the streets. Live performances, live music or training workshops on cultivation topics are often organized as well. In the region of Galicia, one of the best-known Saint Canuto festivals is the one celebrated in the city of Vigo, organized by the Vigo Association for Cannabis Studies (AVE María) – see Figure 5.4, where a collective smoke moment has taken place for years in the Plaza de la Constitución.

Collective plantations

Another aspect where CSCs engage in social or collective action relates to the way cannabis cultivation tends to be organized within CSCs. Indeed, since the

Figure 5.4 Celebration of Saint Canuto in Vigo (2008)

very beginning, these associations have drawn on the idea of 'collective' and to some extent 'cooperative' cultivation of cannabis, in the sense that the CSCs organize one or multiple plantations where cannabis is produced – often relying on the assistance of growers and others who are members of the association – for the members of the collective (as opposed to individual home growing or individual plantations) (Alvarez et al., 2016; Belackova & Wilkins, 2018). It was back in 1993 that the first known collective plantation was carried out by the ARSEC association (Herer, 1999; Decorte et al., 2017; Madera, 2017; Matthews, 2002). In a letter to the anti-drug prosecutor of Catalonia (dated June 15, 1992), ARSEC informed him of their intention of carrying out a collective cultivation. In 1993, the General Assembly of ARSEC members indeed decided to develop a collective plantation (Marks, 2019). Each of the signing members committed to planting and caring for two cannabis plants each (Montañés Sánchez, 2017). The plantation was located in Montbrió del Camp (Tarragona, Catalonia), but it was not harvested given that the Civil Guard seized it. Four members of the association were accused of a drug-trafficking crime for growing cannabis. The Tarragona Audience Court acquitted them as it considered that the crop was for their own consumption and not meant for traffic. Nevertheless this decision was appealed by the Public Prosecutor. Eventually, the Supreme Court sentenced them (on November 17, 1997) to four months and one day in prison (as a suspended sentence) and to pay a fine of €3,000 for a crime of "abstract danger" (Barriuso, 2001; Kilmer et al., 2013; Matthews, 2002).[2]

The negative outcome of the ruling involving ARSEC was a step back for the movement, but in 1997 another attempt was made by another cannabis association. In the Basque Country, the Kalamudia association cultivated

1,500 square meters with about 600 cannabis plants (Barriuso, 1997b). Also in this case, the police found the plantation and confiscated the plants. Barriuso, a former president of the Kalamudia association, was called to testify as accused of a crime against public health. The judge ruled that there was no crime and the drug prosecutor did not appeal in this instance (Herer, 1999). The economic participation of each member-grower towards the collective plantation was of €6 – to pay for rented land, discreet and away from towns, fenced and with a padlocked gate. Individualized signed declarations were made recognizing the ownership of the plants by each member of the association (Barriuso, 1997a). The association Kalamudia once again carried out a publicly announced collective plantation in 2000. The ultimate goal was to demonstrate that collective cultivation was a valid alternative to the illicit market. The group reported the cultivation to the prosecution office. The cultivation was publicized in the press, radio, and television and gathered the support of artists, intellectuals, and politicians (Barriuso 2000). In 2001, they organized a subsequent collective cannabis plantation without experiencing any legal problems (Novoa, 2004).

Starting from 2002 and following these earlier initiatives, several associations were created and carried out collective cultivations as well (Barriuso, 2005; Madera, 2017). Barriuso highlighted some of the advantages of these collective cultivations, noting that it would allow those who sign up for the collective crops – who "either due to lack of means or time or due to health problems cannot cultivate on their own, to delegate agricultural tasks to the association and thus avoid having to resort to the black market" (Barriuso, 2005, p. 165). Additionally, there is a potential for job creation in relation to these collective cultivations, as although some crops can be taken care of jointly among the participants/members themselves, others could be managed by people hired by the association, such as gardeners, guards or administrators (Barriuso, 2005).

Growers' contests: the 'Cannabis Cups'

Further interaction among cannabis growers and with CSC members takes place also within the context of the so-called 'Cannabis Cups'. This is one of the forms of meetings that takes place within CSCs, where growers bring forward their produce and compete with one another to find out who produced 'the best' cannabis.

These so-called 'cannabis cups' are developed in private premises where only members are granted access and growers compete in a personal capacity. In order to compete or enter the venues where these 'cups' are held, one must be a member of an association or CSC (ACCV, 2004, p. 11) – see Figure 5.5 for an example. Most associations and CSCs celebrate their own 'cannabis cups'. Up to 100 growers can compete, and around 1,000 people may participate in the event. Parallel to the contests, there are usually also talks on topics related to cannabis: such as on legality, cultivation, history or health (Marín-Gutiérrez, 2008).

In order to compete, apart from growing cannabis, one needs to be a member of a CSC. This encourages associativism among growers. Growers participating in the cup need to provide a minimum amount of grams of cannabis to enter the

Figure 5.5 A 'Cannabis Cup' of the Bellaflor in Málaga (2002)

competition. The contest judges do not know to whom each sample belongs to so that their vote is impartial. These judges are a mix of invited people (e.g. magazine editors, artists) and general cannabis consumers. Most of these contests occur several months after harvest, between November and December, once the plants are dry – Figure 5.6 shows the different samples competing in a 'cannabis cup' in Seville.

The meeting place where these contests are held is known a few months in advance and it is often published in the different cannabis magazines as well as online (Mota, 1999).

The associations celebrate their 'cannabis cups' as a festive meeting between cannabis growers and consumers, with the underlying purpose of stimulating the further development of a 'cannabis culture' in Spain. With these activities, the CSCs also seek to claim the right to grow cannabis as a valid alternative for the consumer who wants to avoid the illicit market. These 'cups' can be seen as the expression of what the CSCs and the movement

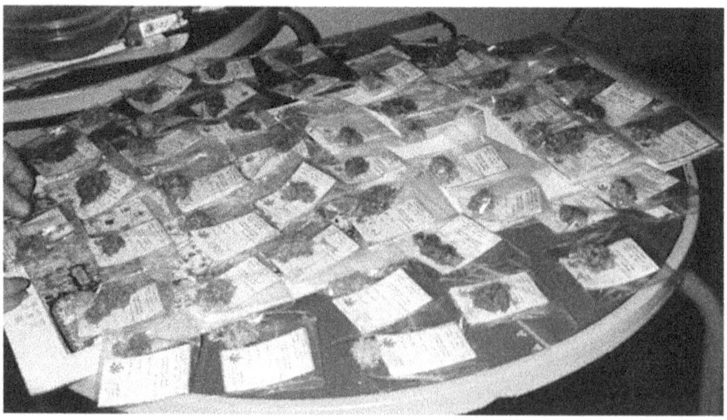

Figure 5.6 Cannabis varieties presented to the ARSECSE Cup in Seville (2003)

describe as the right to cultivate, while simultaneously giving growers the opportunity to taste the cannabis produced by others in a festive atmosphere.

Study meetings, discussion, and Expocannabis

The CSCs' social engagement is also outward-looking. While the CSCs have organized entertainment, educational, and social events which are exclusive for members, some of their activities are also meant for and open to a broader public. These are also often organized in collaboration with other actors from the broader social movement. For instance, the CSCs have organized talks, round tables, seminars, and symposia (Tschorne, et al., 1990) – see Figure 5.7. Most of them last several days and deal with issues related to cannabis and of importance to the associations and to cannabis consumers more broadly. The topics of the talks in these conferences have focused on: CSCs – their situation and the possible strategies to follow; the history of cannabis consumption, cultivation issues; on the therapeutic properties of the plant; legal issues related to its consumption and on how to appeal fines. There are often also workshops on cultivation, on culinary recipes using cannabis, music workshops, as well as audiovisual and photographic exhibitions.

In addition, CSCs have also been involved in the organization and/or participated in Expocannabis. These particular events started in 1999 and continue to take place today – Figure 5.8 below was taken at Expocannabis in Córdoba. This event is usually held in large Spanish cities (e.g. Madrid, Barcelona, Málaga, or Bilbao). The number of visitors to these Expocannabis events exceeds tens of thousands of people today. Currently, the Expocannabis organization continues to support cannabis associations and CSCs, for instance by offering several free tickets per organization and a place for their meetings and talks.

Figure 5.7 CannabisSur Conference in Málaga (2001)
Note: One of the speakers was the President of ARSECA Fernanda de la Figuera

Figure 5.8 Expocannabis in the city of Córdoba (1999)
Note: The President of ARSEC, Felipe Borrallo (with sunglasses), and Moisés López (with glasses), founder of *Cáñamo* magazine, appear in the picture

In Expocannabis the whole sector of cannabis is represented: in them one finds exhibitors from both Spanish and foreign companies. These include vendors and representatives from seed banks, industry representatives involved in the supply of grow materials, hemp craft beers, hemp fabrics, therapeutic products, vaporizers, light and temperature controllers, among others. Conventional and specialized media (e.g. *Cáñamo, Yerba* and *Cannabis Magazine*) are typically present, as illustrated in Figure 5.9. From the late 1990s onwards, the role of these magazines has been fundamental for the cannabis movement as they give a voice and platform to CSCs, which then appear in newsstands across different neighborhoods within Spanish cities. As a result they contribute to the normalization of cannabis consumption and to making CSCs something less underground or hidden. Some of these specialized cannabis magazines have been present in multiple events and calls from CSCs from their inception to the present day, having a trajectory of more than 20 years (Marín-Gutiérrez & Hinojosa-Becerra, 2017).

But also the associative community and CSCs take part in Expocananbis. The program of the event usually includes conferences that revolve around the therapeutic and recreational properties of cannabis, debates on its legalization, and on current legal problems associated with prohibition.

Demonstrations

The main objective of a demonstration is to influence the actors with power, the government, and the authorities, on whose action the inclusion of the protesters'

Figure 5.9 Expocannabis in Barcelona (2004)
Note: The director of the magazine *Yerba*, Luis Ruiz (Wismy), appears in the picture

interests in the decision-making process may depend (Jiménez Sánchez, 2003). The organization of demonstrations by the cannabis community was considered of such importance that *Cáñamo* magazine actually published articles on how to legally organize a demonstration (Ramos Rodríguez, 2003). The demonstrations have indeed in most cases been legally organized and communicated to the public authorities. The convening organizations have primarily been cannabis-related associations and CSCs. Their engagement with this type of protest action could be seen as another example of their 'social' side, as they join and/or collaborate with other actors of the broader cannabis movement and cannabis users to voice their discontent for current cannabis policies.

In Spain, these demonstrations generally take place in the spring (typically between May and June). The duration of these demonstrations can be relatively long (e.g. more than three hours) and often continue with night parties where the protesters celebrate with music and dancing. The associative movement in favor of cannabis has relatively weak, small, and unstable organizations but it has managed to mobilize support to carry out large demonstrations, thanks to magazines and especially through online mobilization (Marín-Gutiérrez, 2008).

In these demonstrations a series of routes through the cities, slogans (e.g. "no to prohibition" as included in AMEC's banner in Figure 5.10 or "legalization is the solution"), symbols (e.g. various representations of the cannabis plant/ leaves – see Figure 5.11), and a regular order of march are repeatedly present.

The first demonstrations in the late 1990s only managed to gather relatively few people, around 300 protesters. For instance, the mobilizations and demonstrations organized by AMEC were isolated and their convening power mainly reached activists from Madrid (Figures 5.10 and 5.11).

Figure 5.10 Demonstration in Madrid in favor of the legalization of cannabis (2002)

Figure 5.11 Demonstration in favor of cannabis in Madrid (2001)

There have also been criticisms in relation to the attention given to these protests, even by members of the cannabis associativism, and especially in comparison with other types of events (such as Expocannabis): "the fact is that for a long time the most numerous public events around cannabis have not been popular demonstrations or smokes, but trade fairs" (Barriuso, 2006, p. 28). Some of the more general problems identified in relation to the cannabis movement include insufficient training in political strategy, the cult of the personality of its leaders, legal insecurity, social stigma, lack of recognition among the authorities, lack of self-criticism, authoritarian behaviors, little use of participatory methodologies in the elaboration of proposals, internal disputes, and under-representation of female activists in the associations (Montañés Sánchez, 2017).

The latest Global Marijuana March in Spain was held in Madrid on May 11, 2019. Associations and groups, along with civil society, demanded the legalization and regulation of cannabis during the protest journey, which included a march from the Puerta del Sol to Plaza de España. Various sources claim that there were thousands of participants (Cáñamo, 2019; CuartoPoder, 2019).

Meetings among CSCs and other cannabis associations: notes from the 2011 Andalusian CSC meetings

The CSC movement in Spain is characterized by some division and a multiplicity of views – reflected for instance in the creation of different CSC Federations, with their own separate code of conducts and strategies (Belackova & Wilkins, 2018; Decorte et al., 2017; Montañés Sánchez, 2017). At the same time, several CSCs have also developed social, collaborative ties and discussed common approaches with other CSCs and associations. Typically, every year several cannabis associations and CSCs come together to discuss their strategies and activities, both on an informal basis as well as within the framework of the CSC Federations they are affiliated with (Jansseune et al., 2019). During 2011, we made participant observations at some of these meetings in the south of Spain (Andalusia).

A meeting at the Astarté Club Social de Cannabis in September 2011 gathered representatives from 14 CSCs. At this meeting, it was proposed that the associations and CSCs of Andalusia work together for a regulation on the cultivation of cannabis. Several more specific aspects related to the functioning of CSCs were discussed as well. For instance, having hired professional staff at CSCs was a topic of debate during the meeting. Members' engagement in the life of the associations was also considered, and the attendees at the meeting thought about activities that could motivate them to engage more, so that members could get to know each other, such as hosting cannabis tasting events, participating in radio programs, organizing conferences, parties, offering training in cultivation, organizing demonstrations, and other events.

The participants at the meeting also considered different ways for future collaboration among CSCs and other associations, including: making a request for audience in the Andalusian Parliament as an united, organized and strong collective force; responding collectively in case the police intervened at the cultivation sites of any association or club; holding regular meetings between associations and CSCs to get to know each other better and try to create an environment conducive to further mutual collaboration.

We had the opportunity to attend another meeting of the FAC-Sur (see Figure 5.12), hosted by the CSCs of Andalusia and Extremadura in the town of Lucena (Córdoba) (in October 2011). FAC-Sur is a regional subdivision of the national FAC Federation of CSCs, which emerged in 2011. This meeting began with a debate coordinated by the president of the ADEUC association, who made an introduction to the current situation of the association. Throughout the discussion, the lack of organization within the associative cannabis movement was highlighted. Also here, the CSC representatives participating in the meeting talked about organizing activities aimed at promoting the cannabis associative movement (e.g. the organization of demonstrations and protests, information channels and recreational activities, such as concerts, therapeutic workshops, and meetings with the Andalusian Ombudsman). It was hoped that these would help project a positive image of CSCs. The associations and CSCs voiced also their intention to extend their collaboration to grow shops, as a way to better organize themselves and make shared proposals. It was stressed that it is necessary for the associative movement to unite in a strong lobby force.

Legal defense of CSC growers

Finally, another aspect worth highlighting when thinking of CSCs as 'social clubs' has to do with their somewhat vulnerable legal position, and the support the CSCs as institutions tend to offer to those affiliated with the associations who may run a higher personal risk because of their direct involvement in cannabis supply-related CSC activities. Indeed, CSCs and cannabis growers frequently have been confronted with police interventions and subsequent legal action.

One of the other 'social'/solidary manifestations of cannabis associations and CSCs in particular has been to defend their members when they face legal issues.

Figure 5.12 Meeting of the FAC-Sur in Lucena, Córdoba (October 19, 2011)
Note: One of those gathered was the President of ARSECA Fernanda de la Figuera

While several CSCs have cultivated cannabis and some of those have been intercepted by the police, in the next paragraphs we focus on a specific case which we have been able to observe first-hand, as the trial unfolded, and which illustrates well the criminal process and the role that associations and CSCs play in the defense of their members. This case related to a plantation in Huelva, for which a cannabis grower, member of ARSECSE, was arrested and prosecuted.

On July 2006, the trial of a member of ARSECSE took place in the court of Huelva. This ARSECSE member – also a cannabis user, was judged in relation to the cultivation of 24 cannabis plants. Earlier on, two policemen had appeared at his property, having received a tip-off from a relative of his neighbor. They handcuffed him and took him to the police station to testify, but he was later released.

During the trial, the defendant talked about how he began to use cannabis and explained that his current use was both recreational and therapeutic (e.g. to aid his lower back pain problems from having worked in the mines). The defendant indicated that the plantation belonged to ARSECSE, and that the seeds and tools for the plantation were bought by the association. Furthermore, he mentioned that other members of the association came every weekend to help him maintain the plantation.

The president of ARSECSE appeared as a witness during the trial. He explained that ARSECSE was an association of consumers and cannabis growers created in 2001, and that they were dedicated to the study of cannabis. He mentioned the size of the association (at the time: 40–50 members), the requirements for membership, and other general features of the association.

With regards to cultivation, ARSECSE's president explained that in 2003 the association decided, at their General Assembly meeting, to grow cannabis collectively. He noted that the farm of the accused CSC member was used to grow the plants, although these remained property of the association. The prosecutor did not ask the President of ARSECSE any questions. Another member of ARSECSE (and friend of the defendant) later appeared as a witness as well. He was aware of the collective cultivation of the association at the defendant's farm, and declared having participated in the cultivation of the crops. The lawyer asked him if his friend had ever sold or donated cannabis; the witness denied it. The next witness was another member of the association who corroborated that the set-up of this collective cultivation was decided at an ARSECSE General Assembly meeting. The lawyer asked the witness if the defendant had sold cannabis, to which he replied "no". He explained that they organized a collective cultivation because not everyone had land to cultivate nor the skills to do it individually.

In the concluding remarks, the Prosecutor indicated that she was on the brink of requesting the conviction of all the defense witnesses for affirming before a trial that not only they were cannabis consumers, but that they were cannabis growers. She noted that the association to which the accused belonged could not have as a goal the cultivation and consumption of cannabis because that would go against the applicable norms. She went on to argue that if the cannabis cultivated was not for the accused's consumption but for the members of this association, then that would constitute a crime of donation (typified in article 368 of the Spanish Penal Code) (Marks, 2019). She affirmed that it was a crime for people to promote and/or favor the consumption of psychoactive substances.

The defense attorney stated that the association did formally exist and that it was legally constituted. By then, ARSECSE had been organizing activities of all kinds for five years. The attorney concluded that this collective cultivation belonged to the association and not to the accused. The lawyer also stated that he wanted there to be a change in jurisprudence. He noted that while it is true that Spanish legislation prohibits the cultivation of cannabis, for it to be punishable, an intent of trafficking is required – which, in his view, was absent in this case. This cultivation had been organized so that people from an association could have access to cannabis and did not have to buy it on the illicit market. It was about a group of consumers – who came to defend the accused, who set up a collective plantation to be self-sufficient, he noted. The lawyer asked for an acquittal of his client, which finally was granted.

This case shows how both the CSC – in the figure of his president, and the several individual members, rallied to the defense of the CSC grower/member who was facing accusation. In this case, the association also paid the lawyer's expenses. In Spain, there are law firms which have specialized in the creation of CSCs and in the legal defense around crimes against public health and involving psychoactive substances. It is very common for associations to rely on this legal expertise in these matters.

The underlying legal problem persists nevertheless, as no law specifies what might be the maximum amount tolerated for self-consumption, and therefore each judge may apply his/her own criteria. Within Spanish jurisprudence, the different judgments of the Spanish courts on CSCs have been very ambiguous regarding what constitutes 'personal consumption' (Marks, 2019; Ramos, 2017).

Discussion and conclusions

In Spain, the cannabis associative movement created the Cannabis Social Clubs, with their bylaws specifying shared/collective cannabis cultivation. Throughout these 30 years of cannabis associativism, CSCs in Spain have engaged in different ways with the idea of being 'social clubs', not only in relation to collective cannabis cultivation.

In this chapter we have focused on shedding light into the different ways in which CSCs have acted as social spaces throughout the last decades. Perhaps the most obvious one has to do with how the CSCs provide a physical space for cannabis users to gather, use the substance together, or participate in different events hosted at the premises of these associations. These are spaces open to members only, and that allow peer-to-peer contact and support (Belackova et al., 2016; Belackova & Wilkins, 2018). CSCs have also used different forms of collective action to create links between their members and generate interaction among them. They have put in practice what can be described as known forms of collective action (e.g. demonstrations in the streets as the most classic example, or the defense of their members/affiliated cannabis growers in court), but have also introduced more playful innovations (e.g. cannabis cups, parties).

CSCs are also a model for the supply of cannabis. Within CSCs, some form of socialization occurs in the organization of collective cannabis plantations. This activity has gathered much media attention, as many CSCs have not hidden the organization of collective plantations but rather put it forward as a demand of the movement. Also in organizing competitions among growers, CSCs promote close contact between producers and users of the substance distributed within those associations.

In other instances, CSCs have shown to be 'social' *extra muros*, i.e. engaging with the broader cannabis movement and the communities in which the CSCs are based more broadly. The feast of San Canuto is another example of socialization among the broader community. During San Canuto, activists and cannabis users take to the streets of their cities to meet and make themselves visible to society. The feast of San Canuto is a vindictive and playful act, it is a day when people go out to demand to be able to consume cannabis. CSCs have also organized talks, round tables, seminars, and symposia (e.g. about cannabis consumption, cannabis cultivation, therapeutic properties of the plant, legal issues). These are an opportunity for different members of different associations and CSCs to meet each other. Individuals who do not belong to the core social movement circles but who are interested in the topics addressed at these events are also able to participate. Expocannabis and the demonstrations in which CSCs participate are other examples of CSCs' engagement with the broader cannabis movement, and these are the events that tend to gather the largest concentration of participants.

In conclusion, this historic overview of CSCs as 'social clubs' revealed that since its origin, and the initiative taken by the ARSEC association with a view to cultivate cannabis for their members, the CSCs have incorporated a range of social aspects into their practice. CSCs offer a private and safe space for consumption. But they also have tools to inform and advise on different issues such as legal matters, on cultivation-related queries, they organize and/or are involved in demonstrations, parties and other festivities (Saint Canuto), conferences, and other events (e.g. Expocannabis). As such, the Spanish CSCs have been more than just a space for safe consumption, but have also become places for organization, meeting – where people connect and engage in the cannabis social movement. Currently it is impossible to know how many CSCs are active in Spain, due to the lack of a legal framework to regulate their activities. While there is some (mixed) evidence in this regard (Belackova et al., 2016; Jansseune et al., 2019), the question remains of whether and how today CSCs in Spain have preserved, expanded, or reduced their 'sociality'.

Notes

1 For a more detailed overview of different aspects related to the development of CSCs and the broader cannabis movement in Spain, please see, for instance, Martínez Oró (2017).

2 In article 368 of the Spanish Penal Code, an abstract danger crime is defined as "dangerous conduct according to general experience and that is punishable without the need to specifically endanger the protected legal asset". In the Sentence of the Supreme Court November 17, 1997 we refer to above it is considered that "the cultivation of plants that produce raw material for trafficking is a characteristically dangerous act for public health, despite the fact that in the case a danger has not been produced in concrete".

References

ACCV (Asociación de la Cultura Cannábica de Valencia) (2004). II Copa de la Barraca de María. *Cáñamo*, (73), 11–12.

Alvarez, A., Gamella, J. F., & Parra, I. (2016). Cannabis cultivation in Spain: a profile of plantations, growers and production systems. *International Journal of Drug Policy*, 37, 70–81.

Arana, X., & Parés, Ò. (2020). Cannabis social clubs in Spain: recent legal developments. In: Decorte, T., Lenton, S., & Wilkins, C. (Eds.), *Legalizing cannabis: experiences, lessons and scenarios*, 307–322. London: Routledge. Barriuso, M. (1997a). La brecha vasca. Y Kalamudia nació y se plantó. *Cáñamo*, (1). 6–7.

Barriuso, M. (1997b). Euskadi. Cosecha histórica. *Cáñamo*, (3), 10–12.

Barriuso, M. (2000). La brecha vasca se abre de nuevo. *Cáñamo*, (32), 22–23.

Barriuso, M. (2001). El camino a la libertad no pasa por el Congreso. *Cáñamo*, (45). 12–13.

Barriuso, M. (2005). Adiós al ghetto: el discreto encanto de la normalidad. *Revista Española de Drogodependencias*, (1–2), 206–211.

Barriuso, M. (2006). Lo cannábico no es alternativo. *Yerba*, (58), 9–11.

Belackova, V., & Wilkins, C. (2018). Consumer agency in cannabis supply – exploring auto-regulatory documents of the cannabis social clubs in Spain. *International Journal of Drug Policy*, 54, 26–34. doi:10.1016/j.drugpo.2017.12.018.

Belackova, V., Tomkova, A., & Zabransky, T. (2016). Qualitative research in Spanish cannabis social clubs: "The moment you enter the door, you are minimising the risks". *International Journal of Drug Policy*, 34, 49–57. doi:10.1016/j.drugpo.2016.04.009.

Blickman, T. (2014). Cannabis policy reform in Europe. Bottom up rather than top down. *Series on Legislative Reform of Drug Policies*, 28, 1–24. doi:10.13140/2.1.2977.3603.

Bone, M., & de Hoedt, G. (2018). Being the change: charting Greg de Hoedt's cannabis journey. *Drugs and Alcohol Today*, 18 (29), 126–136. doi:10.1108/DAT-01-2018-0001.

Cáñamo (2019). Éxito de la Marcha mundial de la marihuana de Madrid 2019. *Cañamo*. Retrieved from: https://canamo.net/noticias/espana/exito-de-la-marcha-mundial-de-la-marihuana-de-madrid-2019 (last accessed September 24, 2021).

CuartoPoder (11 May 2019). Sol se tiñe de verde por la marcha mundial de la marihuana 2019. *Cuartopoder*. Retrieved from: https://www.cuartopoder.es/espana/2019/05/11/sol-se-tine-de-verde-por-la-marcha-mundial-de-la-marihuana-2019/ (last accessed September 24, 2021).

Decorte, T., & Pardal, M. (2020). Insights for the design of Cannabis Social Club regulation. In: Decorte, T., Lenton, S., & Wilkins, C. (Eds.), *Legalizing cannabis: experiences, lessons and scenarios*, 409–426. London: Routledge.

Decorte, T., Pardal, M., Queirolo, R., Boidi, M. F., Avilés, C. S., & Franquero, Ò. P. (2017). Regulating Cannabis Social Clubs: a comparative analysis of legal and self-regulatory practices in Spain, Belgium and Uruguay. *International Journal of Drug Policy*, 43, 44–56. doi:10.1016/j.drugpo.2016.12.020.

Herer, J. (1999). *El emperador está desnudo.* Castellar de la Frontera, Spain: Castellarte.

Jansseune, L., Pardal, M., Decorte, T., & Parés, Ò. (2019). Revisiting the birthplace of the Cannabis Social Club model and the role played by Cannabis Social Club Federations. *Journal of Drug Issues*, 49 (2), 338–354. doi:10.1177/0022042618815690.

Jiménez Sánchez, M. (2003). El estudio de las organizaciones y la estructura de los movimientos sociales. El caso del movimiento ecologista en España. In Funes Rivas, M., & Adell Argilés, R. (Eds.), *Movimientos sociales: cambio social y participación*. Madrid: UNED Ediciones.

Kilmer, B., Kruithof, K., Pardal, M., Caulkins, J. P., & Rubin, J. (2013). *Multinational overview of cannabis production regimes.* Santa Monica, CA: RAND Corporation.

Madera, H. (2017). Autocultivo y autocultivadores de cannabis. Desarrollo del movimiento y peritaciones de consumos y cultivos In: Martínez Oró, D. P. (Ed.), *Las sendas de la regulación del cannabis en España*, 177–190. Martorell, Spain: Bellaterra.

Marín Gutiérrez, I. (2008). La cultura "cannábica" en España (1991–2007): análisis socioantropológico de un nuevo tipo de movimiento social [Doctoral thesis, Universidad de Granada].

Marín-Gutiérrez, I. (2010). *Cannabis: el movimiento cannábico en España.* Madrid: Popular.

Marín-Gutiérrez, I. (2011). *La Cultura Del Cannabis en España.* Saarbrücken, Germany: Editorial Académica Española (EAE).

Marín-Gutiérrez, I. (2016). *Historia General del Cannabis*, Madrid: Amargord.

Marín-Gutiérrez, I. & Hinojosa-Becerra, M. (2017). Veinticinco años del movimiento cannábico español. In: Martínez Oró, D. P. (Ed.), *Las sendas de la regulación del cannabis en España*, 123–135. Martorell, Spain: Bellaterra.

Márkez, I. (2002). *Cannabis: de la salud y del derecho. Acerca de los usos, normativa, estudios e iniciativas para su normalización, 6.* Vitoria-Gasteiz, Spain: Observatorio Vasco de Drogodependencias.

Marks, A. (2019). Defining 'personal consumption' in legal instruments on drug control and Spanish Cannabis Clubs. *International and Comparative Law Quarterly*, 68 (1). 193–223. doi:10.1017/S0020589318000404.

Martínez Oró, D. P. (2015). Clubs sociales de cannabis: normalización, neoliberalismo, oportunidades políticas y prohibicionismo. *Clivatge. Estudis i testimonis sobre el conflicte i el canvi socials* (3). 92–112. Retrieved from: https://revistes.ub.edu/index.php/clivatge/article/view/11985 (last accessed March 11, 2022).

Martínez Oró, D. P. (Ed.) (2017). *Las sendas de la regulación del cannabis en España.* Martorell, Spain: Bellaterra.

Matthews, P. (2002). *La cultura del cannabis.* Madrid: Alianza Ensayo.

Montañés Sánchez, V. (2017). Evolución del activismo cannábico en España. In: Martínez Oró, D. P. (Ed.), *Las sendas de la regulación del cannabis en España*, 145–158. Martorell, Spain: Bellaterra.

Mota, J. (1999). Cogollos de campeonato. Cómo montarse un concurso sin perder los papeles. *Cáñamo*, (24), 50–53.

Muñoz Sánchez, J. (2017). La relevancia penal de los clubes sociales de cannabis. Análisis jurisprudencial. In: Martínez Oró, D. P. (Ed.), *Las sendas de la regulación del cannabis en España*, 361–385. Martorell, Spain: Bellaterra.

Novoa, J. (2004). Martín Barriuso: premio al activista del año. *La María de Soft Secrets*, (4), 3–4.

Pardal, M. (2018). An analysis of Belgian Cannabis Social Clubs' supply practices: a shapeshifting model? *International Journal of Drug Policy*, 57, 32–41. doi:10.1016/j.drugpo.2018.03.027.

Pardal, M., Queirolo, R., Álvarez, E. y Repetto, L. (2019). Uruguayan Cannabis Social Clubs: From activism to dispensaries? *International Journal of Drug Policy*, 73, 49–57. doi:10.1016/j.drugpo.2019.06.022.

Parés, Ò., & Bouso, J. (2015). *Innovation born of necessity: pioneering drug policy in Catalonia*. New York: Open Society Foundations.

Parés, Ò., Jubert-Cortiella, X., Olivares-Gálvez, S., Díaz-Castellano, A., Jiménez-Garrido, D. F., & Bouso, J. C. (2019). Use and habits of the protagonists of the story: Cannabis Social Clubs in Barcelona. *Journal of Drug Issues*, 49(4), 607–624. doi:10.1177/0022042619852780.

Ramos, R. (2017). La defensa de los Clubs Sociales de Cannabis en la prática. In: Martínez Oró, D. P., *Las sendas de la regulación del cannabis en España*, 435–447. Martorell, Spain: Bellaterra.

Ramos Rodríguez, R. (2003). Las reuniones y manifestaciones. *Cáñamo*, (63), 14–15.

Romaní, O. (2004). *Las drogas. Sueños y razones*. Barcelona: Ariel.

Tschorne, P., Mas, C. y Regojo, J.L. (1990). *Guía para la gestión de asociaciones*. Madrid: Popular.

6 Legal or not

A comparative analysis of Belgian and Uruguayan Cannabis Social Club members' profile and policy preferences

Eliana Álvarez, Rosario Queirolo, Lorena Repetto and Mafalda Pardal

Introduction

Recent research and media reports have pointed to the presence of Cannabis Social Clubs (CSCs) in at least 13 European countries (Pardal et al., 2020b), New Zealand (see Rychert and Wilkins, this volume), South Africa (Business Tech, 2020), Costa Rica (Garza, 2020), Chile (Arica Mia, 2016), and Uruguay (Queirolo, et al., 2016). This cannabis supply model has the particularity of being non-profit – at least in its original design, but it can take different forms (Caulkins et al., 2015; Decorte et al., 2017; Pardal, 2018a). There is a growing body of literature focusing on the origins, organization, and vision(s) of CSCs around the world (Arana & Montañés, 2011; Arnoso & Elgorriaga, 2016; Barriuso, 2011; Belackova & Wilkins, 2018; Belackova et al., 2016; Marín, 2009; Oró, 2015; Pardal et al., 2020b; Parés & Bouso, 2015). However, less is known about the CSC members: their sociodemographic characteristics, the reasons why they choose to obtain cannabis via CSCs rather than through other supply channels, or their preferences regarding cannabis policies. In fact, only a few studies relying on CSC members' self-reports have been carried to date, more specifically in Belgium and Spain (Arnoso & Elgorriaga, 2016; Marín, 2008, 2009; Pardal & Decorte, 2018, Parés et al., 2019).

This chapter adds to this literature by drawing a comparison between members of CSCs in Belgium and Uruguay. We rely on data from two online surveys carried out in these two countries using the same questionnaire, and with a very similar recruitment procedure. Our goals are to describe the sociodemographic profile as well as the patterns of use and the policy preferences of CSC members in the two countries. By comparing Belgium and Uruguay, we have an opportunity to analyze the extent to which CSC membership (e.g., the profile and use patterns of users affiliated with CSCs) varies across settings with a different legal framework for CSCs (i.e., no regulation in Belgium vs. a comprehensive legal framework in Uruguay). It allows for a discussion of whether this cannabis supply model might be attractive for the same type of users – regardless of the legal and regulatory context or, on the

DOI: 10.4324/9781003055679-6

contrary, whether having legal CSCs, as it is the case in Uruguay, might make the model more attractive for a wider variety of users. Furthermore, in Uruguay users can choose[1] to legally acquire cannabis through different channels: CSCs, pharmacies or home cultivation. Our analysis will also bring new insights as to whether having these other legal alternatives to the CSC model might have an effect on CSC membership profile.

Cannabis Social Clubs in Belgium and Uruguay: some highlights

Belgium and Uruguay are different countries in many ways, and the legal context in which CSCs operate is not an exception. At the time of writing, the only jurisdiction where the CSC model has been introduced as part of a national cannabis regulation is Uruguay. Uruguay was also the first country in the world to introduce a nationwide legal framework for the supply of cannabis for non-medical purposes: from production to distribution. That law – Law 19.172, included the CSC model as one of the three legal supply models, with the other two being sales at pharmacies and home growing (Decorte et al., 2017; Queirolo, et al., 2016). Very differently, Belgian CSCs, as in other countries in Europe, Latin America, and in other regions of the world, function at the margins or in breach of what are the applicable domestic legal frameworks. Typically, they do so by taking advantage of grey zones in their respective legislations, but their functioning is not necessarily seen as legal, and in fact many CSCs have closed following police action, and their representatives have faced legal consequences, including fines and prison time (Decorte el al., 2017; Pardal, 2016; Pardal & Decorte, 2018).

Partially as a result of these divergent legal contexts, the origin, and trajectories of CSCs in both countries also differ. Belgian clubs started to operate in 2006 as the result of the action of a group of cannabis activists who were aware of Spanish CSCs and sought to replicate that experience (Decorte, 2015; Pardal, 2018b). They initiated their activities by arguing that a 2005 ministerial guideline – which attributed the lowest priority to the prosecution of cases involving the possession of one cannabis plant or up to 3 grams of cannabis (in the absence of other aggravating factors), could also be applied to their activities. Their reasoning was that if they were to cultivate one cannabis plant for each member that lower-level prioritization should also be extended to these collectives. This interpretation has nevertheless been explicitly rejected by the College of Public Prosecutors in 2017. More recent developments, with further CSCs brought to court (including the oldest and largest CSC in the country) have meant that hardly any CSCs in Belgium remain active today (Lefelon, 2020).

However, at the time the survey was conducted in Belgium (February–September 2017) at least seven active CSCs had been identified (Pardal, 2018b). Even in the absence of a regulatory framework, most Belgian CSCs completed formal registration as associations with a non-profit statute. They developed their own set of (self-regulatory) rules: in relation to how one could become a CSC member (typically this involved a minimum age threshold, residency/nationality, and having used cannabis prior to enrolment at the CSC), the maximum number of members admitted (the largest CSC had 400 members circa 2016–2017), on the quantity of cannabis members could obtain (this varied with CSCs reporting a maximum quantity of 15–60 grams per month), the distribution methods (e.g. individually or during so-called 'exchange fairs') (Pardal, 2018b). The specific self-regulatory frameworks developed by the Belgian CSCs were the result of the clubs' cumulated experiences, and of what they perceived as being the legal limits. The clubs tended to rely on volunteers to run their operations, but the cannabis growers (who are also members of the CSCs) received a payment to cover their costs and compensate them for their efforts. The CSCs were cultivating different cannabis strains and occasionally tested the potency and quality of their produce (Pardal, 2018a).

In the case of Uruguay, CSCs were not a reality before 2013 when the Law 19.172 introduced them as one of the three regulated cannabis supply models. Furthermore, the first draft of the law did not include CSCs. At the time, Uruguayan cannabis activists, who were familiar with the European Coalition for Just and Effective Drug Policies (ENCOD), joined efforts with international activists, and successfully pushed for the incorporation of the CSC model in the final version of the law (Musto, 2018; Musto, this volume). Despite this somewhat timid beginning, the number of legal CSCs in Uruguay has been increasing rapidly since October 2014, when the implementation of the regulation commenced in practice. In 2015, when IRCCA,[2] the public institution in charge of overseeing the implementation of the cannabis regulation, started to review applications for CSCs, 15 CSCs were authorized and could start operating. Initially, the CSCs experienced a variety of problems: financial, bureaucratic, organizational (Queirolo et al., 2016). Nevertheless, by 2021 there were over 171 legal CSCs operating throughout the country, mostly concentrated in three departments: 75 located in the capital Montevideo, 34 in Canelones, and 25 in Maldonado (IRCCA, 2021).[3] Also, these three departments and Rocha have the highest rates of CSCs per adult population.[4]

According to the applicable legal requirements, CSCs in Uruguay can cultivate up to 99 female plants in the location of the club. Each CSC can have between 15 and 45 members and is allowed to distribute up to 40 grams per member on a monthly basis. Any surplus cannabis must be destroyed, and this is one of the aspects audited in IRCCA's visits. The CSC premises are inspected by the IRCCA: the CSCs can be penalized or even asked to close if they do not follow the regulations (Pardal et al., 2019; Queirolo et al., 2016). The CSCs can decide on the varieties of cannabis they cultivate, and there are no legal limits to the percentage of THC of the cannabis produced in that context (in contrast with cannabis acquired through pharmacies). Although several CSCs report testing some of the cannabis produced, this practice is not mandatory by law.

It is also worth noting that activism was an important driver for some of the first CSCs in Uruguay. Those clubs were highly connected with the cannabis movement and took an active role in promoting the model by sharing their knowledge on how to build a CSC with interested users. The passage of time and the expansion of the CSC model in the country seems to have brought a new type of club, less committed to activist-driven action or in promoting a social agenda, but instead more pragmatically focused on simply supplying cannabis and, as a result, looking very similar to a (non-profit) dispensary model (Pardal et al., 2019).

Reaching CSC members: our research approach

The analysis draws on quantitative data collected through online surveys in two countries: Belgium and Uruguay. The survey was first conducted in Belgium, between February and September of 2017, and later on in Uruguay, between September of 2018 and March of 2019. The survey initially carried out in Belgium by Pardal & Decorte (2018) was adapted to the Uruguayan context. Both surveys included questions about the sociodemographic characteristics of CSC members, their cannabis use, the relationship with the CSC, including the activities organized by the club and the members' engagement, and explored respondents' policy preferences by including a set of questions about their views on cannabis legalization and specifically on the Uruguayan regulatory approach.

At the time of data collection in Belgium, the number of CSC members in the country (based on the accounts from the CSC directors participating in the study) was estimated at about 676 individuals, and the survey was answered by 190 members, which corresponds to 27% of the total number of CSC members.[5] In Uruguay, we had 135 respondents from a total of – at that time – 2.831 registered CSC members (IRCCA, 2018),[6] which represents 4.7% of the total number of registered CSC members.[7] Both surveys were non-representative samples because respondents were self-selected.

In both surveys, as shown in Table 6.1, the eligibility criteria were the same: i.e., respondents were adults above 18 years old, who were current members of CSCs at the time the survey was launched. In order to protect participants' privacy and anonymity, the CSC members were reached indirectly through their CSC directors. The research team was already in contact with many CSC directors and staff from previous phases of the respective research projects (namely from interviews conducted with CSC representatives), so they were crucial in promoting the survey, both in Belgium and in Uruguay. In Uruguay, we also had IRCCA's institutional support: that institute sent out an email to all CSC directors endorsing the survey and encouraging participation. In both countries, the surveys were also disseminated on social media and other online platforms, and the research team distributed flyers at cannabis events and at grow shops.

We encountered different obstacles in Belgium and Uruguay with regards to ensuring CSC members' participation in the online surveys. In Uruguay, where the CSC model is regulated, all clubs are registered in a national database. This meant that the research team was able to identify all the legal CSCs and their names, but no other contact information (such as the exact

Table 6.1 Key features of the online surveys for Belgian and Uruguayan CSC members

	Belgium	*Uruguay*
Survey period	February–September 2017	September 2018–March 2019
Recruitment	Contact with CSC directors	Contact with CSC directors IRCCA shared our invitation to the registered CSCs
Eligibility criteria	Adults, current members of CSCs	Adults, current members of CSCs
Dissemination	Flyers, posters and QR cards; Facebook page and website; emails and direct messages to stakeholders and participants in previous research	Flyers, posters and QR cards; Facebook page and Twitter; Emails and direct messages to stakeholders and participants in previous research
Sample coverage (100% responses)	190 members (27%)	135 members (4.7%)

Source: Online survey of CSC members in Uruguay (n=135) and Belgium (n=152) conducted by authors.

location or another mean of contact of these associations) is publicly available. Furthermore, any kind of advertisement by the CSCs is prohibited by law. So, even though we knew the total number and names of all the existing CSCs, we didn't have a direct way to contact them. In this sense, IRCCA's assistance in reaching out to the CSCs was important to disseminate the study among the registered CSCs. In the case of Belgium, no such central register is available as the CSC model is not a legal nor regulated supply option. But differently than in Uruguay, and despite the abovementioned legal constraints, the Belgian CSCs had a more visible presence on social media and online platforms as well as through the traditional media (Pardal & Tieberghien, 2018). The Belgian study included also a period of fieldwork and observations at the CSCs which facilitated the building of a positive rapport with the study participants (Pardal, 2018a).

Considering the different legal backgrounds for CSCs in the two countries, one could perhaps expect to have a higher response rate among CSC members in Uruguay than in Belgium. However, this was not the case and the difference in response rates is puzzling. One possible explanation to the higher response rate among Belgian CSC members could be related to the perceived incentives for participation. In Uruguay, where cannabis is legal, and CSCs and other cannabis supply models are already regulated, potential respondents may perceive little to no incentive in participating in surveys/research (Pardal et al., 2020a). Although legality might ensure safety to CSC members and thus increase willingness to participate, as it is the case with other hard-to-reach populations, they might not perceive a strong advantage in taking part in research (Barratt et al., 2007; Ellard-Gray et al., 2015). On the contrary, in Belgium, even if CSC members might be more afraid to complete the survey, they may also be driven by an activist motivation to participate in the study, as this could also be a channel to express their views and policy preferences. An alternative hypothesis[8] could be that potential respondents from the legal CSCs in Uruguay may avoid filling the survey for being suspicious about the true purposes of the research, particularly as IRCCA, the institution in charge of overseeing implementation of the regulation, endorsed the project. In other words, the trusting relationships with CSCs already established in Belgium may have been a more positive factor contributing to a higher response rate, compared to what the research team was able to generate on the basis of the institutional support of IRCCA in Uruguay. We discuss these and other challenges encountered during CSC research in a separate publication (Pardal et al., 2020a).

Finally, and more generally, as the respondents were self-selected, it is possible that they are different in some ways than those who did not participate. It is reasonable to expect that the more committed and/or activist CSC members might have been keener to complete the surveys, which affects the representativeness of the overall sample and it is therefore a limitation of our study.

Results

CSC members' profile

Based on our survey data, CSC members in Belgium and Uruguay show some similarity in terms of sociodemographic features. The typical CSC member in both countries seems to be a male cannabis user, with middle-class status and, to some extent, with completed university studies (44% among Belgian CSC respondents; 38% among Uruguayan CSC respondents). On average, the Belgian participants are older than the Uruguayan CSC members: 42.3 and 34.1 years old, respectively (see Table 6.2). In Uruguay,

Table 6.2 CSCs members' sociodemographic characteristics by country

	Belgian CSC members	*Uruguayan CSC members*
Male	76%	72%
University educated	44%	38%
Income**	€1.000 to under €1.500	€986 to under €1.101
Age*	42.3	34.1

Source: Online survey of CSCs members in Belgium (n=163 to n=190) and Uruguay (n=135) conducted by authors

Notes:
*Average value
**A scale in local currency was used for income. The exchange rate used was the average for the survey period (1 Euro = 39.04 Uruguayan pesos).

according to nationwide data from IRCCA, CSC members are mainly men (76%), with an average age of 33 years old (IRCCA, 2019).

The Belgian and Uruguayan CSC members appeared similar also in terms of frequency and amounts of cannabis used (see Table 6.3). Almost all participants had used cannabis in the last 30 days (98% among Uruguayan CSC members and 93% among Belgian CSC members) and, on average, used it for more than 20 days in the last month. Most of them used 1 gram or less in the days of use (81% among Belgian respondents and 82% among Uruguayan respondents).[9]

Almost seven out of ten Uruguayan respondents and six out ten Belgian respondents declared knowing the THC level of the cannabis they receive from their CSC. Among those who reported having that knowledge, the Belgian CSC members estimated that the cannabis they obtain from their CSC had 15% THC, while Uruguayan CSC members reported an average of 22% THC. In the case of Uruguay, this constitutes an interesting difference between CSCs and the other legal supply models, especially with regards to pharmacy sales where the cannabis distributed can have a maximum potency of 9% THC, according to the legal requirements. As noted earlier, no such threshold has been introduced by the legislator with regards to the cannabis supplied via CSCs. Nevertheless, readers should note that these estimations are based on respondents' own perceptions about the quality and potency of

Table 6.3 Cannabis use and self-reported knowledge about cannabis content by country

	Belgian CSC members	*Uruguayan CSC members*
Used in the last 30 days	93%	98%
Knowledge about THC content of the cannabis received from the CSC*	57%	67%
Estimated % of THC**	15%	22%
Knowledge about CBD content of the cannabis received from the CSC***	37%	48%
Estimated % of CBD**	6%	15%

Source: Online survey of CSC members in Belgium (n=170 to n=42) and Uruguay (n=137 to n=59) conducted by authors.

Notes:
*In both countries, the question was asked in the following way: "THC is the main psychoactive ingredient in cannabis plants. Now we want to talk about the type of cannabis you most typically obtain from your Cannabis Social Club. Do you know the amount of THC of that type of cannabis you obtain from your Cannabis Social Club?"
**For Belgium we report on the most frequent percentage indicated and for Uruguay the average value.
***In both countries, the question was asked in the following way: "CBD is the abbreviated name for cannabidiol, a compound in cannabis plants that counters the psychoactive effects of THC. Now we want to talk about the type of cannabis you most typically obtain from your Cannabis Social Club. Do you know the amount of CBD of that type of cannabis?"

the cannabis they receive at their CSCs. The CSCs in Uruguay are not obliged to test and/or inform members about THC or CBD percentages of the cannabis they produce. As a result, CSC members do not necessarily have information coming from lab testing. Even so, these estimates are in line with the statements made by CSC representatives in a previous study in Uruguay. Indeed, one of the distinctive features of CSCs as cannabis suppliers in Uruguay (in comparison with the other two alternative supply models) relates to the perceived quality and potency of the cannabis produced by those collectives (Pardal et al., 2019). Obtaining a 'quality product' was also the main reason reported by the Uruguayan respondents (29%) to join a CSC, and in a subsequent question in our survey most respondents declared being satisfied (21%) or very satisfied (68%) with the quality of the cannabis they received from their CSC.

In general, CSC members were less familiar with the CBD content of the cannabis produced by their CSCs (vis-à-vis the self-reported THC knowledge). Among the two country samples, less Belgian CSC members indicated being aware of the CBD content of the cannabis they obtained from their CSC (37%), compared to Uruguayan respondents (48%) (see Table 6.3). Uruguayan CSC members estimate, on average, a CBD content of 15%, while Belgian CSC members point to a 6% CBD percentage. Overall, Uruguayan CSC members reported being more informed about the substance they receive from their CSCs and tend to obtain a higher THC potency cannabis than respondents from our Belgian sample, although also with a higher CBD percentage. It could be argued that having a legal framework that protects the functioning of CSCs might leave CSCs in a more comfortable position to share this type of information with their members. However, these indicators of THC and CBD are an estimate from users and might not be accurate depictions. Other types of data, such as analytical testing of cannabis samples, would help improve our knowledge of this matter.

The survey responses regarding use of cannabis in the last 30 days as well as the estimates of THC content shown in Table 6.3 could be seen as an indicator of heavy cannabis use among CSC members (i.e., a near daily or daily use combined with a high potency product). In the surveys, we also enquired about CSC members' self-perception of use before and after joining a club. There was some variation between the samples from the two countries (see Figure 6.1). The majority of Belgian respondents reported using the same amount now than before joining the CSC, and 20% declared that their use "fluctuates". This is not the case for Uruguayan CSC members. Almost three out of ten reported using "more" or "much more" cannabis after joining the CSC, and about the same proportion said that their use is variable.

These estimations do not allow us to make causal claims about the relationship between joining a CSC and an increase in cannabis use. Even so, we can put forward some tentative hypotheses. First, one possibility is that as some Uruguayan CSCs rely on monthly deliveries of 40 grams per member, this might be influencing users to consume more than they would usually do

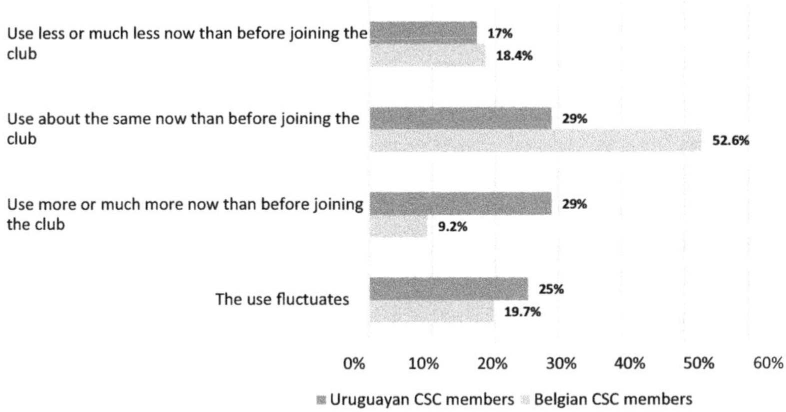

Figure 6.1 CSC members' self-reported cannabis use evolution by country
Source: Online survey of CSC members in Uruguay (n=135) and Belgium (n=152) conducted by authors

(Pardal et al., 2019). Second, legalization and regulation of the cannabis market in Uruguay could have normalized cannabis use, making people more open to talk about their consumption. Third, the high-potency cannabis that members are obtaining might contribute to an increase in use over time as individuals build up tolerance. In any case, more research is needed in order to better understand how CSC membership might be affecting quantities used by consumers.

CSCs in both countries seem able to fulfill users' demand of cannabis. Most participants declared that the CSCs were their only source of cannabis: 72% among Belgian respondents and 85% among Uruguayan CSC members. Before joining a CSC, respondents from both countries reported acquiring cannabis from a different source. In Belgium, Dutch coffeeshops (n=125), dealers (n=92), and friends (n=69) were the most mentioned former suppliers. In Uruguay, the most popular sources used before joining a CSC were dealers (n=53), friends (n=31), and home growing (n=31).[10] This reported transition from relying on dealers to now obtaining cannabis from CSCs is particularly interesting as it suggests that CSCs (legal, in the Uruguayan context) might be keeping users away from illicit sources. This seems to also be the case in Belgium, although in that context a significant group of CSC members indicated previously purchasing cannabis at coffeeshops in a neighboring country (i.e., the Netherlands). However, since 2012, a number of restrictions to coffeeshop sales of cannabis to non-Dutch nationals were introduced which limited access to Belgian users and may help explain the transition to domestic CSCs (Pardal, 2018b).

In Uruguay, although 85% of the respondents reported obtaining cannabis exclusively from their CSC, it is interesting to note that 15% declared that they also have some other means of access to cannabis. Given that in

Uruguay the three legal cannabis supply models are mutually exclusive (i.e. users have to choose whether they obtain cannabis via pharmacies, CSCs or by growing it themselves, and can rely on one model only at a time), this seems to indicate that a small percentage of CSC members is still obtaining cannabis from the illegal market or the new grey market (corresponding mainly to social supply from friends or from dealers).[11] What is more, we also asked participants in Uruguay about whether they shared the costs of CSC membership and/or the cannabis they received with other (non-registered) users – these could be other indicators of 'grey market' dynamics. Most CSC members in Uruguay did not seem to split the costs associated with CSC membership with others (55% vs. 40% who did split the costs, typically with one other person). With regards to the cannabis received from their CSC, 60% declared they shared it with other users (about 29% kept the cannabis received for their own personal consumption only) – typically with several other users. In the case of Belgium, the CSC members who reported continuing to acquire cannabis from other sources indicated mainly cultivating cannabis at home (n=18), buying cannabis from dealers (n=15), and also from Dutch coffeeshops (n=14).[12]

CSCs' harm reduction role: activities organized by the clubs and members' engagement

Considering that CSC members' main contact with the substance is through their CSCs, these organizations are in a position where they can have an important role in raising awareness of possible harms from cannabis use and about how to manage those. In theory, one of the distinctive features of CSCs in relation to other supply models has to do with their potential role in terms of harm reduction. This can be achieved in very different ways: by organizing workshops, lectures or meetings with experts, by sharing information about cannabis among the members, by encouraging CSC members' participation in research projects, or by creating a network of peer-to-peer support, among other activities (Belackova, et al., 2016).

In general, Belgian CSCs tend to organize more activities than the Uruguayan clubs. The legal framework in Uruguay might have had an (unintended) impact here. For instance, non-CSC members are not allowed to enter the CSC premises and, as a result, the CSCs cannot invite speakers who are not members of the club, nor organize events with people not affiliated with the club (Pardal et al., 2019). Asked about whether their CSC had ever organized or been part of four different activities (i.e., general assembly meetings, meetings with other CSCs, research projects, and workshops), fewer Uruguayan respondents reported that their CSC had done so, in contrast with the results for the Belgian CSCs (see Figure 6.2). This is true even in the case of assemblies, which are legally mandatory for Uruguayan CSCs.[13]

Overall, most CSC members reported engaging with the activities we enquired about (see Figure 6. 3).[14] More than half of the Uruguayan respondents reported participation in assembly meetings, research projects, and workshops. In Belgium,

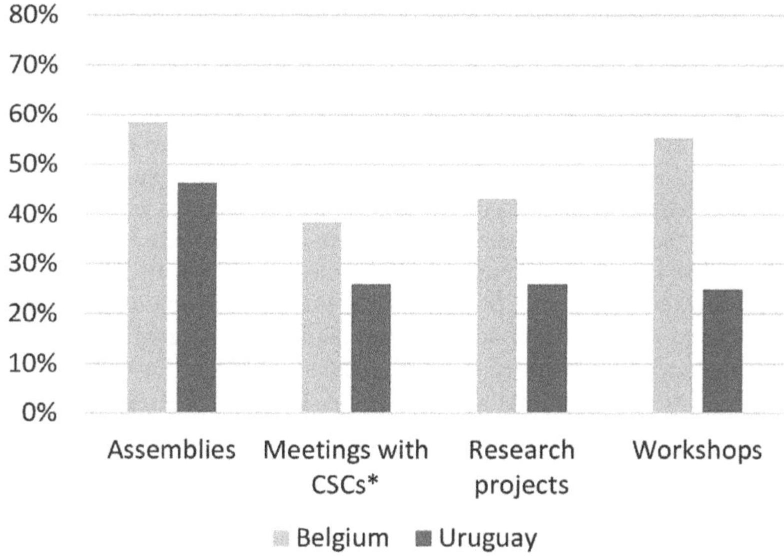

Figure 6.2 Organization of activities by CSCs by country
*In Belgium this might include meetings with other kinds of organizations working in the field of cannabis.
Source: Online survey of CSCs members in Belgium (n=190) Uruguay (n=177) conducted by authors

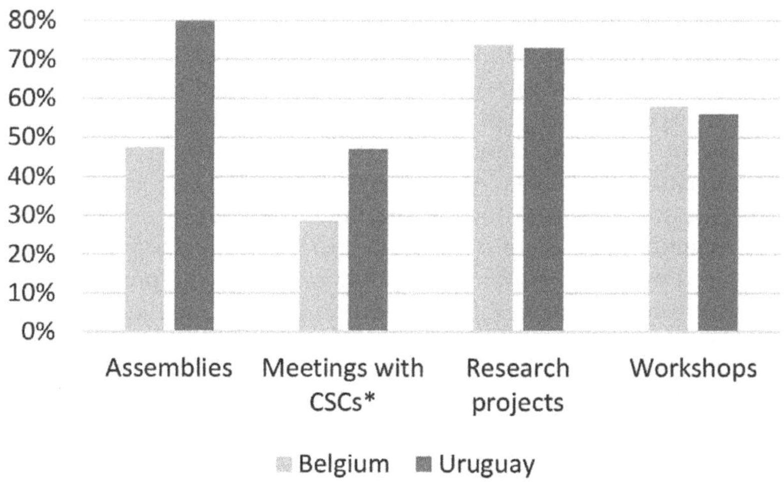

Figure 6.3 CSC members' participation in activities by country
*In Belgium this figure might include meetings with other kinds of organizations working in the field of cannabis
Source: Online survey of CSCs members in Belgium (n=99 to n=100) Uruguay (n=82 to n=43) conducted by authors

that was only true with regards to participation in research projects and workshops. Participation in assemblies and meetings with other CSCs seems to be more popular among Uruguayan CSC members. In the case of Uruguay, it is worth bearing in mind that organizing assemblies is mandatory for clubs, as they are registered as civil associations. In Belgium, while there is no legal framework supporting and regulating the CSC model, those CSCs that have formally registered as non-profit associations ought to meet at least once or even twice a year (according to their bylaws), but in practice not all CSCs were organizing these assemblies. The interactions among CSCs in Uruguay might be the result of the ongoing efforts to develop a CSC Federation (Musto, this volume), an umbrella organization to represent and advocate for the interest of legal CSCs, in particular with regards to discussions with the public authorities (Pardal et al., 2019). In the case of research projects and workshops, Belgian and Uruguayan respondents do not differ in the level of participation, despite the challenges that Uruguayan legislation itself seems to impose on the organization of this type of activities.

Opinions towards the Uruguayan regulatory approach

In our surveys, the Uruguayan and Belgian CSC members were also asked about their opinions on the legalization of cannabis markets or of the CSC model specifically. In general, almost all participants from both countries indicated being in favor of the legalization of cannabis (see Figure 6.4). In Belgium, 93% were in favor of the regulation of CSCs for recreational and medical purposes, and 7% only for medical use. Meanwhile, in Uruguay 92% of participants strongly agreed or agreed with the domestic cannabis policy.

In addition, participants in both countries were asked about their opinions regarding the specific rules that the Uruguayan regulation imposes for CSCs, focusing on the following aspects: CSC membership restricted to adults and Uruguayan citizens/residents only, selection of only one cannabis supply model per person at a time (out of the three possible), registration as CSC member, quantity limit of up to 40 grams per month for each member, CSC membership restricted to between 15 and 45 members, and prohibition of any type of advertising by the CSC. The creation of a national agency dedicated to policy implementation and enforcement (IRCCA) was also included in this question. Figure 6.5 shows the results for both countries.

Membership restriction on the basis of citizenship or residency is the least popular feature among Belgian participants (31%) and one of the least favorites among Uruguayans (31%). Belgian CSC members may have had an experience related to this kind of requirement: as we noted earlier, many local counties in the Netherlands have prohibited foreign citizens from buying cannabis at coffeeshops. This policy switch was negatively perceived by Belgian consumers that used to buy at coffeeshops and could explain why they do not favor this requirement when thinking of a CSC legal framework. In the case of Uruguay, CSC members' opposition is consistent with a repeated

BELGIUM[1]

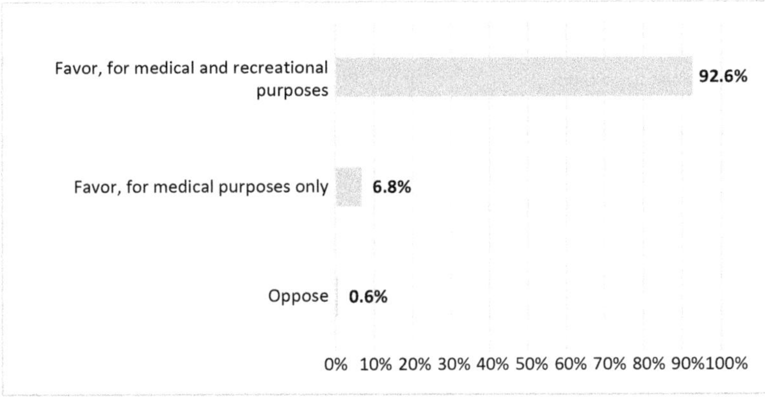

URUGUAY[2]

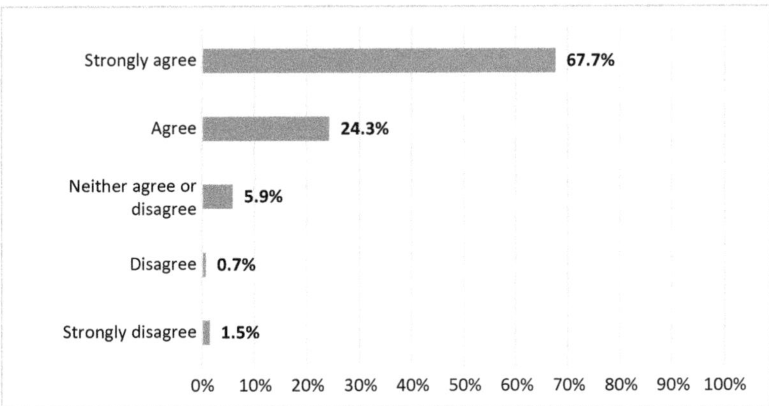

Figure 6.4 Agreement with regulations by country*
* This question was formulated differently in each country: see footnotes for more

[1] In Belgium, the question was asked in the following way: "Do you favor or oppose the introduction of legislation formally allowing and regulating the Cannabis Social Club model in Belgium?"

[2] In Uruguay, the question was asked in the following way: "In Uruguay, the marijuana market is decriminalized and regulated by the government. Do you strongly agree, agree, disagree, or strongly disagree with this measure?"

criticism coming from cannabis entrepreneurs, users, and even some authorities who argue that this requirement has curbed the development of a cannabis industry in the country (El Observador, 2020; El País, 2018; Gold, 2017). On the contrary, the restriction of access to minors is the most consensual regulatory aspect, both among Uruguayans (93%) and Belgians (86%).

The introduction of a legal limit to the number of members a CSC can enroll, the mandatory registration system, and the selection of only one legal

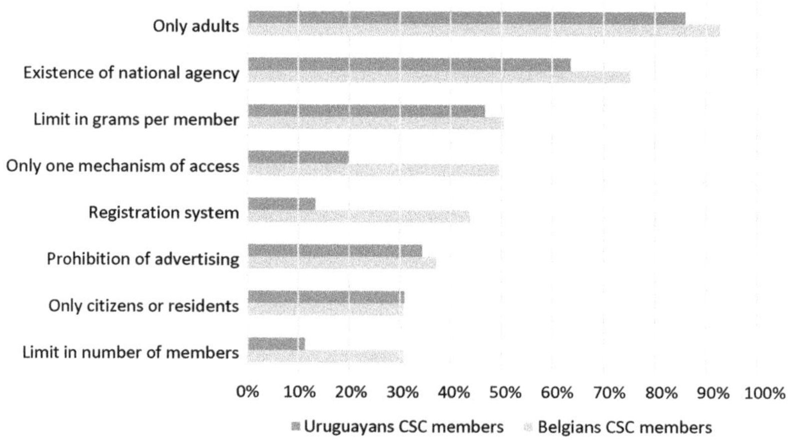

Figure 6.5 CSC members' agreement with Uruguayan rules for CSCs by country
Source: Online survey of CSCs members in Belgium (n=158 to n=143) and Uruguay (n=138 to n=137) conducted by authors

supply model are the least approved legal features among Uruguayan CSC members (11%, 13%, and 20% respectively). However, Belgians do not perceive these aspects so negatively (31%, 44%, and 50% respectively). The concern with and debate about the maximum number of CSC members is an old one, and one that has had important consequences in terms of CSCs' finances as well (Queirolo et al., 2016). The main difference between the stated preferences of CSC members in the two countries relates to the registration system implemented in Uruguay. Its approval is higher among Belgian respondents than among Uruguayan participants. The inclusion of a registration system was one of the most controversial measures when the bill was discussed in Uruguay. Questions concerning the confidentiality of the information collected in this central register, as well as to whom would be allowed access the information and its security were raised. Although there have been no known problems with the registration system to date, and privacy of registered users has been guaranteed by the government, some of the initial fears might still be present among Uruguayan CSC members. At the same time, the need to register the CSC as a civil association and to register each member of the CSC imply a bureaucratic process that might be perceived as an extra burden and increase the disapproval of this measure among Uruguayan respondents.

Overall, differences in the approval levels of these key aspects of the Uruguayan regulatory approach among Belgian and Uruguayan CSC members may be related to the very different experiences in the two countries. In cases where CSCs are already legal, as in Uruguay, members may perhaps be more critical of the actual implementation of the policy based on their experience. Differently, members of CSCs that still operate within an illegal framework, or within a grey legal zone, are usually still advocating for the introduction of legislation that regulates their operations, and might be more optimistic about having one, regardless of the specific characteristics of that policy.

Discussion

In this chapter, we explore some key features characterizing membership of CSCs in Belgium and in Uruguay. One country has a relatively strict drug prohibition policy, where activist groups and CSCs have demanded a different regulatory approach for years (Decorte, 2015; Pardal, 2018b). The other is the first country in the world to regulate its cannabis market in 2013, after a top-down initiative from the government (Queirolo et al., 2019). Comparing how the CSC model has developed in these two very different drug policy contexts can generate important insights, especially seeing as not much is known about the individuals who decide to become CSC members and their experiences as such. Following Pardal & Decorte (2018) and Parés et al., (2019), this chapter aims to further contribute to that knowledge, comparing these two cases.

Results from our two online surveys among CSC members in Belgium and in Uruguay show similarities in members' profile, characteristics of the substance being provided by the CSCs, and clubs' role – despite the very different legal framework in which the CSCs are functioning in these two settings. The general sociodemographic features of participants in our surveys (i.e., mainly male, middle-class, educated users) are also consistent with earlier findings from surveys among CSC members in Spain (where CSCs remain unregulated) (Marín, 2008; Parés et al., 2019). This is perhaps surprising: one could have expected that in Uruguay, where being a CSC member does not necessarily imply a risky behavior or being close to/part of the cannabis underground culture, CSC membership would be more diverse. One possible explanation might be that the way in which CSCs are organized and regulated in Uruguay may narrow the diversity of users that might be interested in selecting this supply model (e.g., it might be better suited to middle- and high-income class users, who can afford a fixed monthly fee and higher prices per gram in comparison to the alternative legal supply models). Also, in unregulated contexts, CSCs' typical procedures regarding enrolment, planned consumption, and membership fees might form a relatively "high threshold" for access (Belackova & Wilkins, 2018).

In general, CSC members in our sample can be described as being regular, heavy cannabis users – both in terms of frequency (near daily or daily use), intensity of use (1 gram or less per day of use), and of the potency of the substance consumed. Parés et al. (2019) did not enquire about the THC content of the cannabis supplied by CSCs in Barcelona, but that study revealed a similar frequency of use among the majority of the 155 CSC members who completed that survey: i.e. 96% reported having used cannabis in the last month, and most were daily cannabis users (68%). The reported quantity of cannabis used per day of use by CSC members in our sample seems to be somewhat lower than what has been reported among daily users in the US. Across three different online surveys in that country, the median quantity for day of use was 1.5 grams (Caulkins, et al., 2020). Furthermore, looking beyond frequency and intensity of use, based on respondents' self-assessment, regulated CSCs in Uruguay may be delivering cannabis with more than 20% THC on average, well above the 9% THC cannabis offered at pharmacies in that country. The Uruguayan legal framework has not incorporated guidelines nor limitations to the potency and quality of the substance produced by CSCs. In an unregulated context in Belgium, CSCs may have been supplying cannabis with 15% THC (circa 2017). Based on data collected across the European Union, it has been found that the potency of herbal cannabis has been increasing in that region over the decade 2006–16, with THC content estimated to be at about 10% in 2016 (Freeman et al., 2019). While we should be cautious in interpreting the subjective perception of THC (and CBD) content reported by our survey participants, the availability of high-potency cannabis within CSCs raises important public health implications, as research in this area has identified a range of adverse outcomes associated with the consumption of higher THC products, particularly if over a period of years (Di Forti et al., 2009; Hall & Degenhardt, 2009).

At the same time, future cannabis policies might want to take into account that if CSC members are mainly heavy users and have the CSC as their preferred choice, the CSC model could be a safeguard for those users from more commercial outlets which might try to promote consumption even further by reducing prices or applying quantity discounts, or by promoting a variety of products such as dabs, edibles, topicals, or vapes, and advertising sales and bargains (Smart et al., 2017). On the other hand, drawing on the results of this study, one could also question whether the CSCs are able to fulfill that safeguard function in practice. Of course, from a harm reduction perspective the focus does not necessarily lie on eliminating or even reducing use. Nonetheless, it would be interesting to understand whether CSCs might be contributing to increased consumption or, at the very least, to the maintenance of regular/heavy consumption patterns (which can bring increased harms for users). In order to keep track of these possible effects, it will be important to draw on longitudinal surveys.

Albeit not relying on longitudinal data, in our study we tried to zoom in on this issue as well. For instance, we asked participants if their CSCs were organizing any activities and if they have participated in those. Having events or meetings can be a strategy to promote bonding among members and to identify potentially harmful use. In general, more Belgian respondents reported that their club organized assemblies, meetings with other CSCs, workshops, and participated in research projects. As many of these activities are conceived to advocate for legalization, something that is perhaps no longer a central incentive for Uruguayan CSCs, that could explain the more intense engagement by the Belgian CSCs.

An interesting finding is that in both countries the majority of CSC members declared that the club is their only cannabis supplier. As a result, the risks associated with being in contact with criminal groups might therefore be mitigated. This has positive implications for both illegal and legal contexts, but especially for the latter because it could mean that the legal supply models might be replacing the illegal ones. Regarding policy preferences, CSC members from Belgium seem to have a more positive view of the Uruguayan regulation than Uruguayans themselves. Although it is not completely clear why, we put forward two tentative explanations. First, direct contact with the regulation gives Uruguayan CSC members more information on how the system works in practice. Belgian CSC members, on the other hand, are far away from what it means to operate in a regulated context, so their evaluation might have been more idealistic. Second, the actual experience of living in a country with a legalized cannabis market – or not – might have effects on users' expectations. From a comparative perspective, Uruguayan respondents have achieved important advances in terms of cannabis policy compared to CSC members around the world. As a result, it could be expected that the Uruguayan regulatory model is perceived as a positive reference frame for CSC members elsewhere. Details about registration and thresholds may not seem as important as having that legalization framework itself. However, for Uruguayan CSC members, cannabis legalization is a reality. Therefore, their expectations about the more specific aspects of that regulation and how it is being implemented might perhaps be higher, which might lead towards more negative or critical opinions about it.

There are important limitations to this analysis. Low response rates and self-selection bias limit the representativeness of our results. At the same time, the difficulties that reaching this population represent for researchers should be noted (Pardal et al., 2020a). Even though our results are modest, they nevertheless represent one of the first attempts at comparing this supply model across illegal and legal contexts. In addition, it is the first study to quantitatively describe the characteristics of CSC members in Uruguay.

Final remarks

The data presented here shows that the 'same spirit' seems to prevail among CSC members of the two countries. Those who decide to become members of a CSC in Belgium or in Uruguay had a lot in common: sociodemographic features, the cannabis they use and how often they use it, and how they interact with these collectives. Our findings also shed light into some of the challenges and opportunities for the CSC model. First, there seems to still be room for improvement in terms of the way CSCs embrace a harm reduction role. Although an important group of members declared that their use has not increased since joining a CSC, others do consume more, and report receiving a relatively strong potency product. In the Uruguayan CSC regulation, there is no maximum potency limit for the cannabis produced by those collectives. Differently, Uruguayan pharmacies are only allowed to sell cannabis with a maximum of 9% THC. Regulating the potency of the cannabis produced by CSCs could be a protective measure from a public health standpoint. Nevertheless, it could also make the model less attractive for this group of users, as one of the reasons to join a CSC (versus purchasing cannabis at pharmacies, for instance) is precisely related to the possibility of having access to a greater variety of strains and to cannabis with a higher potency. In addition, our results show that organizing activities and engaging members is relatively common in CSCs in the two countries. We lack information about the topics and issues addressed in those activities. In any case, these events – among others that CSCs might implement – could be opportunities to raise awareness about cannabis use and potential associated harms. Most members declared that the clubs were their only supplier, which gives CSCs an opportunity to take on a harm-reduction role.

Finally, the fact that most CSC members reported that they no longer acquired cannabis through dealers or other illicit suppliers represents an important positive contribution of the model. In a more obvious way in the case of Uruguay, as it implies a competition between the new licit market and the illicit market, and the gradual achievement of one of the main goals of the legal reform in that country. For jurisdictions that have not yet legalized cannabis, including Belgium, this information suggests that CSCs might help reduce contact between cannabis users and the illicit market – at least among this particular type of cannabis users.

Acknowledgements

Álvarez, Repetto and Queirolo thank the support of OSF Grant OR2016-27307 to conduct this project in Uruguay.

Notes

1 According to Law 19.172, cannabis users must select and complete registration for one of the three legal supply models (i.e. home cultivation, CSC, pharmacy sales). Registered users can change their preference through time (e.g. stop their registration as home growers and register to join a CSC), but at one given moment, they can only legally obtain cannabis through one of the three available supply models.
2 *Instituto de Regulación y Control del Cannabis* [Cannabis Regulation and Control Agency].
3 There might be differences in the total number due to updates in IRCCA's website.
4 Maldonado has the highest rate (2.11 CSCs every 10.000 adult residents), followed by Rocha (1.82), Canelones (0.91) and Montevideo (0.74).
5 Twenty-seven per cent of the total known CSC members in Belgium (n=676) (Pardal & Decorte, 2018).
6 We have 177 answers if we consider 42 incomplete responses that can still be considered for some specific questions (6.2% of the CSCs members).
7 In Uruguay, there is a national register of cannabis users run by IRCCA. As a result, it is possible to know the total amount of CSC members at the time the survey was collected.
8 We thank one of the anonymous reviewers for suggesting this alternative hypothesis.

9 A picture with a reference to 0.5 gram was used as a visual aid in the Uruguayan survey. No visual aids were used in the Belgian survey, and we refer here to the data reported for 'typical day of use'.

10 This issue was addressed with different questions in each country. In Belgium, each respondent could select all the sources they used before (multiple choice), while in Uruguay respondents were asked to identify the "main source" before joining the CSC. As a result, in the Belgian sample the N for this question is higher than the actual number of participants.

11 This last is a new intersection between legal and illegal markets in which registered users sell and/or share with non-registered users (Pardal et al., 2019).

12 This issue was addressed with different questions in each country. In Belgium, each respondent could select all the additional suppliers (multiple choice), while in Uruguay respondents were asked to identify the "main additional supplier". As a result, in the Belgian sample the N for this question is higher than the actual number of participants.

13 In Uruguay, CSCs are legally registered as civil associations. This means that they have to adhere to civil associations' regulations, which include having members assemblies on a regular basis.

14 Only in the cases when CSCs actually organized the activities, members were asked about their engagement in them.

References

Arana, X., & Montañés, V. (2011). Cannabis cultivation in Spain – the case of Cannabis Social Clubs. In: Decorte, T., Potter, G. R., & Bouchard, M. (Eds.), *World Wide Weed: Global trends in cannabis cultivation and its control*, 163–177. Farnham, Surrey: Ashgate.

Arica Mia (31 August 2016). Lanzan en Arica el primer club cannábico medicinal de Chile. *Arica Mia*. Retrieved from: https://www.aricamia.cl/lanzan-en-arica-el-primer-club-cannabico-medicinal-de-chile/ (last accessed 22 March 2021).

Arnoso, A., & Elgorriaga, E. (2016). *Estudio de las pautas de consumo de cannabis en los Clubes Sociales de Cannabis y Evaluación de su eficacia*. San Sebastian, Spain: Fundación Renovatio.

Barratt, M. J., Norman, J. S., & Fry, C. L. (2007). Positive and negative aspects of participation in illicit drug research: Implications for recruitment and ethical conduct. *International Journal of Drug Policy*, 18(3), 235–238. doi:0.1016/j.drugpo.2006.07.001.

Barriuso, M. (2011). Cannabis Social Clubs in Spain: a normalizing alternative underway. *Series on Legislative Reform of Drug Policies*, 9, 1–8.

Belackova, V., Tomkova, A., & Zabransky, T. (2016). Qualitative research in Spanish cannabis social clubs: "The moment you enter the door, you are minimising the risks". *International Journal of Drug Policy*, 34, 49–57. doi:10.1016/j.drugpo.2016.04.009.

Belackova, V., & Wilkins, C. (2018). Consumer agency in cannabis supply – Exploring auto-regulatory documents of the cannabis social clubs in Spain. *International Journal of Drug Policy*, 54, 26–34. doi:10.1016/j.drugpo.2017.12.018.

Business Tech (18 September 2020). South Africans are setting up 'cannabis clubs' across the country – are they legal? *Business Tech*. Retrieved from: https://businesstech.co.za/news/lifestyle/434401/south-africans-are-setting-up-cannabis-clubs-across-the-country-are-they-legal/ (last accessed 17 December 2020).

Caulkins, J. P., Kilmer, B., Kleiman, M., MacCoun, R. J., Midgette, G., Oglesby, P., Pacula, R. L., & Reuter, P. H. (2015). *Considering marijuana legalization: Insights for Vermont and other jurisdictions*. Santa Monica, CA: RAND Corporation.

Caulkins, J. P., Pardo, B. & Kilmer, B. (2020). Intensity of cannabis use: Findings from three online surveys. *International Journal of Drug Policy*, 79, 102740.
Decorte, T. (2015). Cannabis social clubs in Belgium: Organizational strengths and weaknesses, and threats to the model. *International Journal of Drug Policy*, 26(2), 122–130.
Decorte, T., Pardal, M., Queirolo, R., Boidi, M. F., Avilés, C. S., & Franquero, Ò. P. (2017). Regulating Cannabis Social Clubs: A comparative analysis of legal and self-regulatory practices in Spain, Belgium and Uruguay. *International Journal of Drug Policy*, 43, 44–56. Di Forti, M., Morgan, C., Dazzan, P., Pariante, C., Mondelli, V., Marques, T. R., Handley, R., Luzi, S., Russo, M., Paparelli, A., Butt, A., Stilo, S. A., Wiffen, B., Powell, J., & Murray, R. M. (2009). High-potency cannabis and the risk of psychosis. *The British Journal of Psychiatry*, 195(6), 488–491. doi:10.1192/bjp.bp.109.064220.
Ellard-Gray, A., Jeffrey, N. K., Choubak, M., & Crann, S. E. (2015). Finding the hidden participant: solutions for recruiting hidden, hard-to-reach, and vulnerable populations. *International Journal of Qualitative Methods*, 1–10. doi:10.1177/1609406915621420.
El Observador (10 March 2020). Ministro de Turismo abre la puerta a la venta de marihuana para turistas. *El observador*. Retrieved from: https://www.elobservador.com.uy/nota/ministro-de-turismo-abre-la-puerta-a-venta-de-marihuana-para-turistas-2020310112014 (last accessed 22 March 2021).
El País (24 March 2018). Recomiendan abrir venta de marihuana a turistas. *El Pais*. Retrieved from: https://www.elpais.com.uy/informacion/sociedad/recomiendan-abrir-venta-marihuana-turistas.html (last accessed 22 March 2021).Freeman, T. P., Groshkova, T., Cunningham, A., Sedefov, R., Griffiths, P., & Lynskey, M. T. (2019). Increasing potency and price of cannabis in Europe, 2006–16. *Addiction*, 114(6), 1015–1023. doi:10.1111/add.14525.
Garza, J. (10 December 2020). Nace el primer club social de consumidores de cannabis en Costa Rica. *La Republica.net*. Retrieved from: https://www.larepublica.net/noticia/nace-el-primer-club-social-de-consumidores-de-cannabis-en-costa-rica (last accessed 22 March 2021).
Gold, N. (30 April 2017). Cannabis para turistas: una trampa en la ley. *El Observador*. Retrieved from: https://www.elobservador.com.uy/nota/cannabis-para-turistas-una-trampa-en-la-ley-2017430500 (last accessed 22 March 2021).
Hall, W., & Degenhardt, L. (2009). Adverse health effects of non-medical cannabis use. *The Lancet*, 374(9698), 1383–1391. doi:10.1016/S0140-6736(09)61037–0.
IRCCA. (2021). Clubes de Membresía con habilitación vigente. IRCCA. Retrieved from: https://www.ircca.gub.uy/clubesaprobados/ (last accessed 10 May 2021).
IRCCA. (December 2019). Monitoreo y evaluación de ley 19.172: principales indicadores del Mercado de cannabis en Uruguay. IRCCA. Retrieved from: https://www.ircca.gub.uy/wp-content/uploads/2020/02/Indicadores-cannabis-dic2019.pdf (last accessed 22 March 2021).
IRCCA. (30 September 2018). Mercado regulado de cannabis. Informe al 31/09/2018. IRCCA. Retrieved from: https://www.ircca.gub.uy/wp-content/uploads/2018/11/InformeMercadoReguladoCannabis-30set2018.pdf (last accessed 22 March 2021).
Lefelon, P. (2 April 2020). Oudste cannabisclub van het land legt de boeken neer. *Het Laatste Nieuws*. Retrieved from: https://www.hln.be/antwerpen/oudste-cannabisclub-van-het-land-legt-de-boeken-neer~a115f09f/ (last accessed 22 March 2021).

Marín, I. (2008). La cultura "cannábica" en España (1991–2007). Análisis socio-antropológico de un nuevo tipo de movimiento social [Doctoral dissertation, Universidad de Granada].

Marín, I. (2009). *Cannabis: el movimiento cannábico en España*. Madrid: Editorial Popular. Musto, C. (2018). *Regulating Cannabis Markets. The construction of an innovative drug policy in Uruguay* [Doctoral dissertation, University of Kent, Utrecht University].

Oró, D. P. M. (2015). Clubs sociales de cannabis: normalización, neoliberalismo, oportunidades políticas y prohibicionismo. *Estudis i testimonis sobre el conflicte i el canvi socials*, (3), 92–112.

Pardal, M. (2016). Cannabis Social Clubs in Belgium: growing in a legal haze? In: de Maillard, J., Groenmeyer, A., Ponsaers, P., Shapland, J., & Vianello, F. (Eds.), *Crime and order, criminal justice experiences and desistance* (4th ed.) (pp. 13–30). Antwerp: Maklu.

Pardal, M. (2018a). An analysis of Belgian Cannabis Social Clubs' supply practices: a shapeshifting model? *International Journal of Drug Policy*, 57, 32–41. doi:10.1016/j.drugpo.2018.03.027.

Pardal, M. (2018b). The Belgian Cannabis Social Club landscape. *Drugs and Alcohol Today*, 18(2), 80–89doi:10.1108/DAT-09-2017-0051.

Pardal, M., Bone, M., Decorte, T., Queirolo, R., Parés, Ò., Johansson, J., Alvarez, E. & Repetto, L. (2020a). Hidden and uninterested populations: Methodological insights and unresolved issues from the study of Cannabis Social Clubs. *Methodological Innovations*, 13(3), 1–12. doi:10.1177/2059799120976963.

Pardal, M., & Decorte, T. (2018). Cannabis use and supply patterns among Belgian Cannabis Social Club members. *Journal of Drug Issues*, 48(4), 689–709. doi:10.1177/0022042618791295.

Pardal, M., Decorte, T., Bone, M., Parés, Ò., & Johansson, J. (2020b). Mapping Cannabis Social Clubs in Europe. *European Journal of Criminology*. doi:10.1177/1477370820941392.

Pardal, M., Queirolo, R., Álvarez, E., & Repetto, L. (2019). Uruguayan cannabis social clubs: from activism to dispensaries? *International Journal of Drug Policy*, 73, 49–57.

Pardal, M., & Tieberghien, J. (2018). Cannabis Social Clubs on YouTube: a qualitative content analysis. In: Korf, D., Fountain, J., & Potter, G. (Eds.), *Place, space and time in European drug use, markets and policy*, 81–95. Lengerich, Germany: Pabst Science Publishers.

Parés, Ò., & Bouso, J. C. (2015). *Cannabis Social Clubs Innovation born of necessity. Pioneering drug policy in Catalonia*. New York: Open Society Foundations. Parés, Ò., Jubert-Cortiella, X., Olivares-Gálvez, S., Díaz-Castellano, A., Jiménez-Garrido, D. F., & Bouso, J. C. (2019). Use and habits of the protagonists of the story: Cannabis Social Clubs in Barcelona. *Journal of Drug Issues*, 49(4), 607–624. doi:10.1177/0022042619852780.

Queirolo, R., Boidi, M. F., & Cruz, J. M. (2016). Cannabis clubs in Uruguay: the challenges of regulation. *International Journal of Drug Policy*, 34, 41–48. doi:10.1016/j.drugpo.2016.05.015. Queirolo, R., Rossel, C., Álvarez, E., & Repetto, L. (2019). Why Uruguay legalized marijuana? The open window of public insecurity. *Addiction*, 114 (7), 1313–1321. doi:10.1111/add.14523.

Smart, R., Caulkins, J. P., Kilmer, B., Davenport, S., & Midgette, G. (2017). Variation in cannabis potency and prices in a newly legal market: evidence from 30 million cannabis sales in Washington state. *Addiction*, 112(12), 2167–2177. doi:10.1111/add.13886.

Part II

7 Bringing Foucault to Cannabis Social Clubs (through the notion of counter-conduct)

Pieter Rondelez and Mafalda Pardal

Cannabis Social Clubs and social movements studies

Cannabis Social Clubs (CSCs) are associations formed by adult cannabis users who collectively cultivate and distribute cannabis among themselves, usually without commercial intent (Decorte, 2015; Pardal, 2016b). The first known CSCs were created in Spain during the 1990s, in a prohibitionist context where the supply of cannabis was and continues to be prohibited (Arana & Montañés, 2011; Arana & Parés, 2020; Kilmer et al., 2013). Many of these associations and some of their representatives or members have been subject to law enforcement interventions and legal sanctions (Arana & Montañés, 2011; Arana & Parés, 2020; Pardal, 2016a). Nevertheless, those grassroots experiments first tried out in Spain have continued to grow in that country (although accurate figures are lacking, some estimate a total number of CSCs ranging between 800 and 1000: see, for instance: Decorte et al., 2017) and have also appeared in many other countries (Blickman, 2014; Bone & de Hoedt, 2018; Bone et al., this volume; Decorte & Pardal, 2017; Pardal et al., 2020b). With the exception of Uruguay though (Queirolo et al., 2016), no other national jurisdiction has passed legislation allowing and regulating the functioning of these associations, so their cannabis supply activities remain, albeit to different degrees (i.e. depending on local policies and law enforcement priorities), in a sphere of illegality.

Research in this area has explored different aspects in relation to CSCs. Some of the studies have, for instance, tried to document CSCs' practices as cannabis suppliers or discussed the potential or shortcomings of CSCs as an alternative way to organize the supply of cannabis, in an attempt to inform public policies (Belackova et al., 2016; Caulkins et al., 2015; Decorte, 2015; Jansseune et al., 2019; Pardal, 2018a). Others have focused on the individual agency of users, or the particular roles of other actors playing key roles within the life of those associations, such as cannabis growers or CSC leaders (Belackova & Wilkins, 2018; Pardal, 2018c, 2019). Of particular relevance to our analysis is the CSC research strand which has considered the appearance of CSCs within a larger movement or protest by cannabis users, the so-called 'cannabis movement' or the 'activist movement of people using cannabis'

DOI: 10.4324/9781003055679-7

(Arana & Montañés, 2011, p. 168; Marín & Hinojosa, 2017). This research has mainly tried to understand how and why CSCs have emerged as well as their contribution to the broader cannabis movement (which seeks to overturn the current prohibitionist regime).

For instance, Aguiar & Musto (2015) and Martínez (2015) pointed to openings in the political opportunities structure, respectively, in Uruguay and in Spain to explain the emergence or local developments of the movement.[1] Many authors have also explored the role played by the different mobilizing structures within that cannabis movement, considering a range of formal and informal actors (including also grow shops, other lobbying groups, etc.). In this regard, the CSCs were described as important social movement organizations, and their repertoire of action has been identified and analyzed – noting, for instance, other activities organized by the associations that are not related to the supply of cannabis (Arana & Montañés, 2011; Castro, 2014; Marín, 2009; Montañés, 2017; Pardal et al., 2020; Pettitt-Schieber, 2012).[2] Finally, the framing processes adopted by cannabis activists in Uruguay or CSCs in Belgium to advance their goals have also been subject to analysis (Aguiar & Musto, 2015; Castro, 2014; Pardal & Tieberghien, 2017, 2018). In doing so, this body of literature has engaged with social movement theories in the study of CSCs.

In our view, this connection to social movement studies invites a reflection. Social movements are often seen as actors questioning the status quo and as facilitators of social change. The mobilization of a social movements' perspective is typically driven by a need to understand the way these movements seek to induce social change. A key effect of the introduction of social movement perspectives in the study of CSCs or other drug user initiatives is thus making their social change agenda visible, tangible, and thinkable, rather than focusing exclusively on the legal nature of (some of) its actions.

Second, given the theoretical pluralism in the field of social movement studies, what does it mean to apply a social movement perspective? Although the classical paradigm among social movement scholars has gradually lost its central position throughout the 21st century, it is still a useful perspective (van Stekelenburg & Roggeband, 2013). Accordingly, in order to study the emergence and development of social movements, the classical approach combines three elements: political opportunity structures – to consider "the structure of political opportunities and constraints confronting the movement", mobilizing structures – "the forms of organization (informal as well as formal) available to the insurgents", and the framing processes – "the collective processes of interpretation, attribution, and social construction that mediate between opportunity and action" (McAdam et al., 1996, p. 2). The integration of these three lenses provides us with a comprehensive understanding of the origins and development of social movements.[3] As noted above, previous studies looking at the emergence of CSCs in Spain and Uruguay seem to have also relied on at least one of these three lenses that (used to) form the 'classical paradigm' when applying a social movement perspective.

Our goal and approach

In this chapter we seek to go beyond the 'classical perspective' in social movement studies. We do this by relying on the work of Michel Foucault, who was/is a major influence to the study of criminology, social movements, protest, and contentious politics. The aim of this chapter is to reflect on the use of a counter-conduct approach in the study of contentious politics in general, and to elaborate on its relevance in understanding and questioning the practices of CSCs in particular. Herein we focus on the meaning(s) of CSCs' practices, rather than on questions around how CSCs emerged and/or how they develop their action. We rely on earlier research conducted on the topic by the second author (e.g. Pardal, 2018c, 2018b) and on a broader review of the literature (related to CSC research as well as to Foucault studies) for this analysis. We argue that considering CSCs from the prism of counter-conducts has mainly two advantages. Using this approach, we can benefit from an understanding of the role of CSCs (and other actors) in (I) the destabilization of the power/resistance binary; and in (II) the destabilization of truth regimes.

Foucault's study of power and resistance[4]

Relying upon the work of Foucault, Carl Death proposed a counter-conduct approach to study protest, social movements, and contentious politics (Death, 2010, 2016).[5] The notion of counter-conduct was introduced by Foucault in the lecture series of 1977–1978, *Security, territory, population*, in particular in the eighth session (on 1 March 1978). Foucault tried to find a notion that could be used to designate the type of revolts or resistance to forms of power that do not exercise sovereignty and do not exploit, but 'conduct' (Foucault, 2007a). These forms of power that 'conduct' are studied by Foucault through his notion of government and governmentality (Gordon, 1991). However, questions could be raised about whether (and how) the notion of governmentality and counter-conduct could be used outside of the context of Foucault's thought (Dean, 2010). According to Dean, one should be careful in allowing the terms (and in particularly governmentality) to transform into a kind of dogma or to become a mere social science methodology.

Governmentality is first and foremost understood as a specific historical phenomenon or regime of power (Senellart et al., 2007). It is the name for the regime of power deployed in the 18th century which had "the population as its target, political economy as its major form of knowledge and apparatuses of security as its essential technical instrument" (Foucault, 2007b, p. 108; Senellart, 2007). The introduction of this concept should be understood in the context of Foucault's intellectual journey of understanding power beyond the notion of the law (Davidson, 2003). In his examination of how power evolved through time, he observed two other forms of power: 1) disciplinary power which developed in the 17th and 18th centuries; 2) biopolitics, which emerged in the second half of the 18th century, and which was not focused on the individual but on the population as a whole (Foucault, 1976). These two powers should be considered as two parts of the same coin called biopower defined as power over life or the power that replaced "the ancient right to take life or let live by a power to foster life or disallow it to the point of death" (Foucault, 1976, p. 138).

Nevertheless, support for using both notions of governmentality and counter-conduct beyond the context of Foucault's thought can be found in Foucault's work itself. First, because of its intrinsic genealogical character, it is quite legitimate to bring Foucault's notions to the analysis of current forms of power and its contestation. Although Foucault introduced his concept of governmentality as a specific historical phenomenon or regime of power (Senellart et al., 2007), he exceeded this by focusing on the history (and evolution through time) of governmentality itself. What he tried to do was to establish a 'genealogy for biopower', and for this reason he developed and used the notion of governmentality (Fontana & Bertani, 2003). It is impossible to detach the notion of governmentality from genealogy, both in its historical version and more abstract meaning (see below) (Senellart, 2007). Because the notion of counter-conduct is linked with the notion of governmentality, counter-conduct is also genealogical in character and constantly evolving. Foucault's notion of governmentality is situated in the study of power-relationships in which the exercise of power entails a complex interplay with the condition of freedom (Foucault, 1994a).[6] Contestations always emerge within (and against) the notion of governmentality because of the intrinsic relationship between power and freedom, or as result of the encounter between technologies of power and technologies of the self (which Foucault defined as governmentality) (Foucault, 1994b).[7] Senellart (2007) asserts that for Foucault "the analysis of types of governmentality is inseparable from the analysis of corresponding forms of resistance or counter-conducts" (pp. 389–391). Foucault asserted that the notion of counter-conduct refers to the struggle "against the processes implemented for conducting others" (Foucault, 2007a, pp. 200–201).

A second reason relates to the shift in Foucault's own work of the notion of governmentality to a more general and abstract meaning (Valverde, 2017; Senellart, 2007). From 1979 onwards, Foucault no longer uses this notion to grasp a particular (political) regime of power but as an analytical tool for studying power relations in general (Senellart, 2007). Government could also be defined as 'conduct of conduct' in a wider sense, thereby referring to different ways of directing the conduct of individuals and groups: the government of children, souls, communities, families, the sick (and not only governmental practices as political government) (Foucault, 1994a, 2008; Gordon, 1991). Instead of speaking in terms of government, Foucault used the notion of governmentality (or rationality of government) which he equated with "art of government" (Gordon, 1991). The latter notion indicates that Foucault was not interested in studying the development of real governmental practices (the particular context, problems, tactics, instruments) (Foucault, 2008). The art of governing points to "the reasoned way of governing best and, at the same time, the best possible way of governing" (Gordon, 1991).[8] Using the notion of governmentality entails that the exercise of power is intrinsically linked to the notion of knowledge (as we will see further).

The question remains of whether the notion of counter-conduct can be used separately? Again, we find answers in the work of Foucault. In *Subject and Power* Foucault suggests to study power by "taking the forms of resistance against different forms of power as a starting point" (Foucault, 1994a, pp. 128–129). The idea thus is to study power not "from the point of view of its internal rationality, but by means of analyzing power relations through the antagonisms of strategy". It is therefore key to start from the actors of counter-conduct, and how that reflects on itself and on its self-proclaimed "art of governing" (Rondelez, 2021).

The relevance of Foucault's notion of counter-conduct to the study of CSCs

In contrast to Dean's argument, Carl Death takes the notion of counter-conduct/governmentality out of the context of Foucault's thinking and tries to apply it to the analysis of movements, protests, and contentious politics. Death explicitly states that "what I term here a 'counter-conducts approach' differs in some crucial ways however, from how Foucault deployed the term in these lectures" (Death, 2016, p. 210). Death proposed 'a more modest claim': he sought to approach certain identifiable acts of the 21st century (i.e. occupation in South Africa) through a counter-conduct approach – hoping that it would result in raising different questions and different understandings of the phenomena under investigation. In a similar vein, in this section we reflect upon the application of the notion of counter-conduct to the study of CSCs, thereby focusing on two aspects: the destabilization of the power/resistance binary, and the contingency, and destabilization of truth regimes (or truth games).

(I) The destabilization of the power/resistance binary

Much of the social movement literature has tended to conceptualize resistance as the act of opposing power (Death, 2010). The problems of such a perspective are manifold: 1) movements/protestors themselves are categorized as either revolutionaries or collaborators (or co-opted); 2) it does not grasp the complexity of power and contestation which exceeds this simplistic binary; 3) it does not provide a systematic approach to analyze this complexity. In a nutshell, it is impossible to draw a clear distinction between power and resistance. Resistance is coextensive and absolutely contemporaneous to power (Davidson, 2011). Foucault emphasized in *The Will to Knowledge* that resistance is not in a position of exteriority with respect to power. We should think of resistance as existing in a strategic field of relations of power, and relations of power themselves only exist relative to a multiplicity of points of resistance. This led Foucault to note that: "where there is power, there is resistance".

In *Security, territory, population*, Foucault highlighted the non-exteriority, the immanent relation, of conduct and counter-conduct (Davidson, 2011). This is not a denial of power asymmetries but it goes to point out that the opposition between those who govern and those who are governed should not be framed as a simple binary relation (Valverde, 2017). This destabilization of the conventional binary between power and resistance using the notion of counter-conduct (as part of a larger governmentality approach) brings us to the mutually constitutive relationship between power and resistance (Death, 2010). According to Death, a counter-conduct approach complicates our understanding of resistance, because it focuses on the concrete interaction between power and resistance (Death, 2016, p. 202):

> It can draw attention to modes of protest which form in parallel to techniques of governmentality; are deeply interpenetrated with the power relations they oppose; and which facilitate or enable the production and performance of alternative subjectivities through processes of ethical self-reflection of not being like that.

This destabilization makes us aware of the fact that forms of contestation have the potential to reinforce dominant forms of governance, but also could undermine and challenge them (Death, 2010). According to Cadman, governmental counter-conducts are not merely additional or reactive, but are wholly immanent and necessary to the formation and development of governmentality (Cadman, 2010). Also subordinate groups exert power towards not only the powers that be, but also in relation to their own members and to other groups (Valverde, 2017). In addition, it is also useful to apply Cadman's pre-emptive stance towards counter-conduct in order to go beyond a mere understanding of counter-conduct as a *post hoc* reaction or response to so-called governmental regimes of truth. Another important point raised by Death is that studies relying on a power/resistance binary run the danger of ignoring certain phenomena because of their irrelevance or its politically compromised character (Death, 2016). This is the direct result of its focus on movements or actors that actually or explicitly challenge dominant power relations.

If we consider what has been documented with regards to CSCs' practices, it becomes clear that they oppose the current prohibitionist regime with regards to cannabis and would like to see a policy change in that area – such that would allow for the regulation of the model they advocate for: the CSC (Jansseune et al., 2019; Marín, 2009; Pardal, 2018b; Pardal et al., 2020b). Some CSC representatives have described the creation of these associations as "an active way of calling for regulation of cannabis" (Pardal et al., 2020b, p.

14), other CSCs have engaged in legislative proposals (Jansseune et al., 2019; Pardal, 2018b; Val, 2017), and/or organized protests and demonstrations (Bone & de Hoedt, 2018; Marín & Hinojosa, 2017; Pardal et al., 2020b). However, and although these might be the more visible or clear acts of opposition, CSCs' resistance includes other – perhaps more diffuse – elements. Engaging with the notion of counter-conducts in the study of CSCs allows us to extend our gaze to practices that would otherwise be dismissed, either because a too strictly legalistic view might lose sight of other aspects of resistance; or because social movement perspectives may otherwise over-focus on episodes of protest, and as such not pay enough attention to other CSC practices and their meanings.

Other forms of resistance can thus be identified, and as Hayward & Schuilenburg (2014) asserted resistance integrates also a positive and creative process. For instance, many CSCs actually are constituted as formal associations (i.e. they have undertaken the steps that any other association would be expected to take and completed a local or national registration) – while at the same time explicitly referring to the supply of cannabis as part of the goals or activities of the association in those same bylaws (Barriuso, 2011; Decorte & Pardal, 2017; Jansseune et al., 2019; Pardal, 2018a). Similarly, the collective cultivation of cannabis by CSCs can be seen as another element of counter-conduct and resistance. This element has actually been picked up in previous research, which considered it as "an innovation in the repertoire of non-violent collective actions by militants in a new social movement" (Alvarez et al., 2016, p. 78; Marín & Hinojosa, 2017). Indeed, many of the active CSCs have in fact already developed their own model of production and distribution of cannabis for adults' personal use, even if risking legal sanctions (Decorte et al., 2017; Jansseune et al., 2019; Pardal, 2018a; Pardal, et al., 2020). As Hunt et al. (2010) suggested, CSCs constitute a 'user-driven market intervention'.

While social movements tend to be conceptualized as a conflict or battle against something, the perspective of counter-conducts considers not just an opposition to the status quo (which is part of what the CSCs are about) – the resistance, but also looks at what are the practices which they construct and implement. Such practices, albeit perhaps constituting "small acts of resistance", have the "potential for blowing little holes in the daily practice of the social order" (Ferrell, 2019, p. 3). In this regard, it is worth highlighting that the CSCs have indeed built a comprehensive model or way of working that goes beyond their protest or opposition practices and which is based, in most instances, in self-regulatory efforts (Belackova & Wilkins, 2018; Bone & de Hoedt, 2018; Decorte, 2015; Decorte et al., 2017; Jansseune et al., 2019; Pardal, 2018b).

Furthermore, a counter-conducts approach implies an understanding of power and resistance as being intertwined. CSC practices offer an example of this complex relationship. Indeed, and as discussed, the CSCs oppose the way they are 'being conducted' by the powers that be. At the same time, some of their practices seem to suggest some degree of compliance (or even act to reinforce) those powers or conducts. For example, the so-called 'Catalan breach' (i.e. a milestone of the CSC movement in Spain connected with the first collective cultivation experience put forward by an association of cannabis users) happened after the cannabis association ARSEC enquired the public prosecutor about the legality of cultivating and sharing cannabis among their members (Arana & Montañés, 2011; Marín & Hinojosa, 2017; Montañés, 2017). While the initiative was somewhat provocative and entailed some risk (in fact, the police intervened and confiscated the crops) (Jansseune et al., 2019; Kilmer et al., 2013), there was also an attempt by those involved to reach out to the authorities and to adhere to their view on the matter.

In Belgium, we find another example of how these groups have tried to re-interpret – while adhering as much as possible to – the applicable legal texts and policies. In concrete, the first Belgian association was created by cannabis activists in 2006 - following the passage of a Ministerial Guideline that suggested the lowest priority for the prosecution of cases involving the possession of one cannabis plant or of three grams of cannabis (Pardal, 2018b). Since then, the working of CSCs – although defying and arguing for a more substantive legal change in the country, has continued to be defined in adherence to the threshold defined by that Ministerial Guideline (Decorte, 2015; Pardal, 2018b, 2018a). Indeed, the Belgian CSCs have created a collective production system in which one cannabis plant is produced for each of the users affiliated with the association. While this is not a guarantee of legality (many CSC representatives have been brought to court on charges of illicit production, possession, and/or supply of cannabis), it has been an explicit and continuous choice of the activists involved – in what could be described as an attempt to challenge the dominant power by subverting what are perceived as its own conduct limits (of one plant or three grams per person). We find a similar example from CSCs in the UK, which have also adhered to a threshold put forward in the official sentencing guidelines (Bone & de Hoedt, 2018). More generally, in the Spanish context, several authors have highlighted the impact of a legal analysis by Muñoz & Soto (2000) which was very informative for the way CSCs developed their practices (Montañés, 2017). While this apparent will to comply might be, at least in part, due to strategic and even survival reasons (i.e. reducing the risk of sanctions or the potential severity of penalties), it nonetheless goes to show the complexities of resistance and its relation to power.

Furthermore, a counter-conducts perspective acknowledges that resistance may not be a uniform reaction, there may be multiple views, practices, and tactics used in resisting power. Such complexity can also be found with regards to CSCs. At a first level, not all the individuals affiliated with the movement share the same view in terms of what would be the ideal regulatory framework or supply model they would like to see implemented – in other words, there are different positionings with regards to the core claim(s) being pursued (Belackova & Wilkins, 2018; Bone & de Hoedt, 2018; Bone et al., this volume; Pardal, 2018a). For some, the CSC model – in particular with adherence to the ideals of non-profitability and cooperative cultivation – is seen as the ideal and final supply model which should be legalized and regulated; others seem to perceive the CSC model as more of a transitory experiment that might lead the way to the legalization of other models of supply for cannabis (for instance, including also commercial policy designs) (Parés, 2018).

Not only are there different visions, but we can also observe different power dynamics, even among the 'subordinated' groups. As such, one could question whether in fact even within this notion of counter-conduct (*in casu*, CSCs' general 'resistant' action), there are underlying conduct-counter-conduct dynamics present as well. For instance, particularly in Spain, research has noted that several CSCs have sought to create coordinating organizations, the so-called CSC Federations (Belackova & Wilkins, 2018; Jansseune et al., 2019). These umbrella organizations have been a way for CSCs to join efforts and share practices, but can also be seen as an attempt to conduct the movement – each CSC Federation typically issues their own code of conduct (the expectation being that the affiliated CSCs will adhere to it) as well as their own advocacy and social agendas (Belackova & Wilkins, 2018; Jansseune et al., 2019; Montañés, 2017; Val, 2017). For instance, Greg de Hoedt – one of the founders of the UKCSC association explained that they: "created a really detailed Operations Manual which covers everything including: the UKCSC's constitution, detailed models for growing and selling cannabis at fair trade prices, harm reduction measures, and standardized posters designed to inform the police of the model" (p. 9). In his view "having many growing [cannabis] under the same model, as opposed to many growing under no model shows some respect for regulation" (p. 9).

Nevertheless, these conduct efforts (within counter-conduct) have also been met with resistance: multiple CSC Federations have been created and many (if not most) CSCs remain operating independently of those (Belackova & Wilkins, 2018; Jansseune et al., 2019; Montañés, 2017; Parés, 2018). What is more, this dynamic of conduct and counter-conduct and of complex power relations is also found among CSCs. Earlier research into CSCs has indeed noted the existence of cliques and disputes between and within CSCs (Pardal, 2018c; Pardal et al., 2020). Beyond the different expressions of counter-conducts we already noted, this idea of conduct-counter-conduct within the sphere of counter-conduct can also illustrated by the position of some the leading figures of the CSC movement who have often drew a line (arguably also as a deviance management strategy) between their own action and that of others who they see as the 'real' deviants, the 'real' criminals (Pardal, 2019) – which again goes to show that the relationship or interaction between power and contesting actors is a rather complex one (and is also indicative of how CSCs enter the truth games, which we discuss in more depth below).

(II) The contingency and destabilization of truth regimes (or truth games)

In *What is Critique*, Foucault links the notion of critique immediately as an attitude or practice of the actors of counter-conduct who are driven by the question: "how not to be governed like that, by that, in the name of those principles, with such and such an objective in mind and by means of such procedures, not like that, nor for that, not by them" (Foucault, 2007d, p. 44). As a result, critique entails 'resistance' against the governing power (Karskens, 2012). But as we already mentioned above, counter-conduct is more than just resistance to power. Foucault argues that the core of critique is not only focused on power as such, but on the relationship between power, truth, and subject (Foucault 2007d, p. 47). In his analysis of power, Foucault wanted to go beyond its mere repressive character as that is a narrow interpretation of power. It neglects the fact that what makes power to hold is what makes it accepted, by producing things, knowledge, discourse, etc. In other words: knowledge is power and vice versa. The way knowledge is produced is not simply a top-down process in Foucault's thinking. An implicit assumption that is central in Foucault's approach on governmentality and is related to the constant interplay between discourses and practices is the condition of contingency. This brings us back to the notion of genealogy to which governmentality is clearly linked.

The manner in which genealogy is embedded in Foucault's notion of governmentality could best be understood as his endeavor to indicate that moment or the process through which a particular set of discourses and practices are linked with each other (Foucault, 2008). A discourse that "on the one hand constitutes these practices as set bound together by an intelligible connection and on the other hand legislates and can legislate on these practices in terms of true and false" (Foucault, 2008, pp. 18–19). Foucault conceptualizes this as a regime of truth. The struggle for power is also a struggle for truth, since truth is not outside power and vice versa (Foucault, 1994c). In 1976, Foucault explained that by truth he did not mean the ensemble of truths to be discovered and accepted, but rather the ensemble of rules according to which the true and the false are separated. Therefore, we should not think in terms of a battle on behalf of the truth, but about the status of truth. What Foucault sought to do was to show how a set of practices and regime(s) of truth evolve and become linked together in order to form an apparatus of knowledge power "that marks out in reality that which does not exist and at the same time legitimately submits it to the division between true and false" (Foucault, 2008, pp. 18–19).

By using a genealogical approach, Foucault does not see the emergence of a regime of truth/power as inevitable (Foucault, 2008; Lemke, 2001). The notion of governmentality (in combination with the method of genealogy) starts from the recognition of an interplay between discourses and practices thereby accepting the notion of change and contingency. The way how rationalities evolve and change make visible that the government of men is a practice which is not simply imposed by those who govern upon those who are governed (Cadman, 2010; Foucault, 2008). A regime is not imposed by either one side or the other, not globally nor totally but by transaction: by a series of conflicts, crises, agreements, disagreements, discussions, concessions.

Therefore, a governmental 'regime of truth' is never fully established. For Foucault, the analysis of governmentality is inseparable from analyzing the corresponding modes of counter-conducts (Senellart, 2007).

The constant interaction between actors of conduct and counter-conduct is reflected in the way how both are involved in the process of constructing and deconstructing the regimes of truth and what is 'appropriate conduct'. The consideration of what constitutes 'appropriate conduct' and is legally sanctioned as such with regards to the use and/or supply of psychoactive substances has evolved through time (Berridge, 2013). Scholars in this field have traced the 'history' of those representations (and of the power relations involved). For instance, Seddon (2016) discussed the historical contingency of the 'drug' concept and argued how it has become a regulatory construct, i.e. a way to govern populations. With regards to cannabis, currently the dominant view is connected to the prohibition of production and distribution, and an attempt to reduce its consumption. This has been enshrined in the international treaties and various national legal texts. Nevertheless, cannabis policy is in a state of flux. Several jurisdictions have passed laws that legalize and regulate the supply of cannabis for medical and/or non-medical purposes (Kilmer & Pacula, 2016; Lancione et al., 2020; Seddon et al., 2020), and the United Nations Commission on Narcotic Drugs has decided to remove cannabis and cannabis resin from Schedule IV of the 1961 Convention (while remaining on schedule I of the same Convention) thus recognizing some therapeutic value for that substance (United Nations Office on Drugs and Crime, 2020).

With regards to CSCs in particular, several examples can be brought forward of how 'appropriate conduct' has been defined and, in some cases, redefined. As noted earlier, in Belgium, the CSCs interpreted a 2005 Ministerial Guideline as enacting some degree of tolerance/acceptance towards the cultivation and/or possession of cannabis for personal consumption. Nevertheless, in 2017 the College of Public Prosecutors clarified that that earlier Ministerial Guideline could not be extended to instances of collective cultivation and/or possession within associations (such as it was the case with CSCs). Furthermore, law enforcement policy across different Belgian regions seems to be inconsistent (Decorte et al., 2014), contributing to a further lack of clarity concerning the interpretation of domestic laws, and of what might be deemed 'appropriate conduct'. In Spain, Arana and Parés (2020) have also observed how two conflicting approaches with regards to CSCs seem to have developed in recent years (particularly between 2013 and 2018). The authors noted that, on the one hand, there have been several initiatives at the municipal and regional levels to regulate the model (and thus validate the appropriateness of that conduct). On the other hand, there are also several indications that the powers that be do not condone CSCs – for instance, in 2013 the Attorney General's Office issued an order that introduced changes to how CSC leaders/directors could be prosecuted: not only as committing a crime against public health but also of being part of a criminal organization (which would result in an increase in the length of prison sentence). Nevertheless, in previous years (from the mid-1990s until early 2015), the majority of the court rulings involving CSC members did not consider their activities to be illegal (Arana & Parés, 2020).

At the same time, the CSC model has been brought forward in recent legislative proposals at national and/or regional level (e.g. Belgium, Mexico, Portugal, Spain, Uruguay) (Decorte & Pardal, 2020). While most of these attempts to change the set of rules have been unsuccessful, they nevertheless mark a departure from the prohibitionist discourse. In the case of Uruguay, CSCs have become one of the legal, regulated models for the supply of cannabis in the country. The specific inclusion of the model was the result of negotiation and compromise between different actors. In fact, the Uruguayan case is insightful as to how policy-makers and CSC advocates (or cannabis activists more broadly) were involved in the construction (and maintenance) of a new truth regime (Musto, 2018; Queirolo et al., 2018; Repetto, 2014; von Hoffmann, 2016) – as well as of the tensions characterizing that (ongoing) process (Musto, this volume).

The CSCs (and cannabis activists more broadly) have entered the 'truth games' as well. They actively question the governmental 'regime of truth' and try to influence it or change it. Underlying their proposal for a supply model for cannabis lays a different interpretation of what is 'appropriate conduct' with regards to the use of cannabis and its supply within a closed circuit of members of the CSC and on a non-profit basis (or other views that they may hold in this regard – Bone et al., this volume). They take a critical stance and try to destabilize the current regime of truth in a myriad of ways: through protest, by implementing their supply model of choice, by entering in debate with governmental and non-governmental actors, participating in research, and publicly voicing their views on the media (Pardal et al., 2020; Pardal & Tieberghien, 2017, 2018). The CSCs' discourse is complex and heterogeneous, and it seems to be informed by different (and at times competing) visions or ideologies: a focus on the use of cannabis for medical reasons and the provision of a service to people who are ill; on promoting 'responsible use'; on human rights; on harm reduction; on being an alternative to the criminal market or even to the cannabis industry; on being 'cannactivists', 'consumers', etc. (Belackova et al., 2016; Bone et al., this volume; Pardal, 2019; Pardal & Tieberghien, 2018).

At the same time, it could be argued that groups of resistance, and in this case CSCs, can contribute (consciously or not) to reproduce or reinforcing that what constitutes the 'appropriate conduct' and its corresponding regime of truth. For instance, by focusing on the idea of 'responsible use' (in contrast with 'excessive' or uncontrolled drug use) or distancing themselves from the 'real' (criminal) dealers,[9] CSCs may be perpetuating a narrative that incorporates elements of prohibitionism and, for instance, is oblivious of the idea of pleasure (O'Malley & Valverde, 2004). We find some critique to this positioning from the actors of counter-conduct themselves (Montañés, 2017; Val,

2017). Montañés (2017), reflecting on the recent evolution of the cannabis movement in Spain noted that: "we identified common patterns between the prohibition movement and cannabis activism" (p. 157, own translation), referring for instance to a "tacit prohibition of dissent", which tends to characterize both movements, and to difficulties for self-criticism among the actors involved. In a study of legal CSCs in Uruguay, one CSC representative questioned whether the regulation of the CSC model actually constitutes a progress from prohibition, stating that:

> the idea of a club resembles the idea of a sect. It's about prejudice, it's a model that reflects prohibitionism. Cannabis [...] can be a substance as controlled as alcohol. [...] The club model continues to see the cannabis user as a drug addict, as a person outside of society who needs to be placed in clubs, sects, in order to access a quality product.
>
> (Pardal et al., 2019, p. 54)

CSCs' dealings with the current regime(s) of truth is therefore complex, and reflective of different visions, strategies, and aspirations about what should be deemed 'appropriate conduct'.

Concluding thoughts

Applying Foucault's perspective of counter-conduct to the study of a phenomenon such as CSCs is perhaps not an obvious choice. Nevertheless, it allowed us to better understand and situate CSCs' actions and their meanings – particularly in relation to two elements of Foucault's work: 1) the destabilization of power – resistance binary; and 2) the destabilization of truth regimes/games. By considering CSCs' actions through this prism, we were able to tap into their complex relationship with regards to power and resistance: it becomes apparent that CSCs are not only a manifestation of rule-breaking, not just opposition, not just protest. As we have noted, even within counter-conduct we found different views, different tactics to relate to power, and to exert critique towards the status of truth. Additional dynamics resembling conduct and counter-conduct could be found within counter-conduct as well. Furthermore, we identified a number of instances in which the CSCs seem to have taken part and tried to influence the truth regime: by seeking co-construction, by putting forward a particular (and often challenging or destabilizing) set of practices and discourses. But we can also question whether in some instances, CSCs' practices and critique in fact may contribute to the maintenance of the regime of truth they seek to destabilize. In our view, future CSC research could benefit from drawing on these notions, especially as an opportunity to capture the more nuanced positioning of the different actors and their complex relation to one another and to power. For instance, it could be of interest to analyze the arguments mobilized in criminal cases involving CSCs and their representatives, and how the 'truth games' play out in that setting. More broadly, drug policy research – for instance, focusing on harm reduction practices (which intertwine compliance and resistance) could also be further informed by this approach.

Notes

1 Martínez (2015) noted some opening at the regional and municipal levels to debate and to introduce legislation that would regulate CSCs (especially in the Basque Country, Catalonia, and Navarra).
2 This is not to say that the cultivation of cannabis falls outside CSCs' activities of protest or resistance, as we discuss later in this chapter.
3 A study of CSCs in Belgium by the second author applied also this approach (Pardal, 2018a).
4 This section is based on an article written by one of the authors: Rondelez, 2021.
5 Other examples of authors who use the notion of counter-conduct in their study or reflect on it more deeply are: Bulley (2016); Cadman (2010); Odysseos et al. (2016); Rossdale & Stierl (2016).
6 In the *Subject and Power*, Foucault (1994a, p. 139) argues that: "At the very heart of the power relationship, and constantly provoking it, are the recalcitrance of the will and the intransigence of freedom. Rather than speaking of an essential antagonism, it would be better to speak of an "agonism" – of a relationship that is at the same time mutual incitement and struggle; less of a face-to-face confrontation that paralyzes both sides than a permanent provocation".
7 Government as the conduct of conduct also ranges from governing others to governing the self (Lemke, 2001). In *Technologies of the Self*, Foucault (1994b) defines this encounter between these two forms of technologies as governmentality. According to Foucault (1994b, 2007c) "governing" has always been "a versatile equilibrium", in which there is a conflictual and complementary relationship between techniques or technologies of power (that determine the conduct of subjects or the conduct of others) and techniques or technologies of the self (that permit subjects – in particularly individuals – to self-conduct or to construct and modify the self: body, mind, soul).
8 Gordon (1991): "a rationality of government will thus mean a way or system of thinking about the nature of the practice of government (who can govern, what governing is; what or who is governed), capable of making some form of that activity thinkable and practicable both to tis practitioners and to those upon whom it was practiced" (p. 3).
9 Although, and as noted by one of us elsewhere (Pardal, 2019), some of this discourse can also be part of a "deviance management strategy" (Lindblom & Jacobsson, 2014) or a "micro-politics" of normalization (Pennay & Moore, 2010).

References

Aguiar, S., & Musto, C. (2015). El rayo verde: regulación de la marijuana en Uruguay. In Labate, B. C., & Rodrigues, T. (Eds.), *Drogas, política y sociedad en América Latina y el Caribe* (pp. 297–316). Mexico City: CIDE.

Alvarez, A., Gamella, J. F., & Parra, I. (2016). Cannabis cultivation in Spain: A profile of plantations, growers and production systems. *International Journal of Drug Policy*, 37, 70–81. doi:10.1016/j.drugpo.2016.08.003.

Arana, X., & Montañés, V. (2011). Cannabis cultivation in Spain – the case of Cannabis Social Clubs. In Decorte, T., Potter, G. R., & Bouchard, M. (Eds.), *World wide weed:*

global trends in cannabis cultivation and its control (pp. 163–177). Farnham, Surrey: Ashgate.

Arana, X., & Parés, Ò. (2020). Cannabis social clubs in Spain: recent legal developments. In Decorte, T., Lenton, S., & Wilkins, C. (Eds.), *Legalizing cannabis. Experiences, lessons and scenarios* (pp. 307–322). New York: Routledge.

Barriuso, M. (2011). Los Clubes Sociales de Cannabis en España. *Serie Reforma Legislativa En Materia de Drogas*, 9, 1–8.

Belackova, V, Tomkova, A., & Zabransky, T. (2016). Qualitative research in Spanish Cannabis Social Clubs: "the moment you enter the door, you are minimising the risks." *International Journal of Drug Policy*, 34, 49–57. doi:10.1016/j.drugpo.2016.04.009.

Belackova, V, & Wilkins, C. (2018). Consumer agency in cannabis supply – exploring auto-regulatory documents of the cannabis social clubs in Spain. *International Journal of Drug Policy*, 54, 26–34. doi:10.1016/j.drugpo.2017.12.018.

Berridge, V. (2013). *Demons: our changing attitudes to alcohol, tobacco, & drugs.* Oxford: Oxford University Press.

Blickman, T. (2014). Cannabis policy reform in Europe: bottom up rather than top down. *Transnational Institute: Series on Legislative Reform of Drug Policies*, 28, 1–24.

Bone, M., & de Hoedt, G. (2018). Being the change: charting Greg de Hoedt's cannabis journey. *Drugs and Alcohol Today*, 18(2), 126–136.

Bulley, D. (2016). Occupy differently: Space, community and urban counter-conduct. *Global society*, 30(2), 238–257. doi:10.1080/13600826.2015.1133567.

Cadman, L. (2010). How (not) to be governed: Foucault, critique, and the political. *Environment and Planning D: Society and Space*, 28(3), 539–556. doi:10.1068/d4509.

Castro, G. (2014). From punishment to markets: social movements, the state, and legal marijuana in Uruguay. *Edisciplinas. Usp.Br*, 7–10. Retrieved from: http://www.equipos.com.uy/noticias_despliegue.php?i=135 (last accessed 25 October 2021).

Caulkins, J. P., Kilmer, B., Kleiman, M., MacCoun, R., Midgette, G., Oglesby, P., Pacula, R., & Reuter, P. (2015). *Considering marijuana legalization: insights for Vermont and other jurisdictions.* Santa Monica, CA: RAND Corporation.

Davidson, A. I. (2003). Introduction (D. Macey, Trans.). In Ewald, F. Fontana, A., & Davidson, A. I. (Eds.), *Society Must Be Defended. Lectures at the Collège de France, 1975–1976* (pp. xv–xxii). London: Picador.

Davidson, A. I. (2011). In praise of counter-conduct. *History of the Human Sciences*, 24(4), 25–41. doi:10.1177/0952695111411625.

Dean, M. (2010). *Governmentality: power and rule in modern society* (2nd ed.). London; Thousand Oaks, CA; New Dehli: SAGE Publications.

Death, C. (2010). Counter-conducts: a foucauldian analytics of protest. *Social Movement Studies*, 9(3), 235–251. doi:10.1080/14742837.2010.493655.

Death, C. (2016). Counter-conducts as a mode of resistance: Ways of "Not being like that" in South Africa. *Global Society*, 30(2), 201–217. doi:10.1080/13600826.2015.1133566.

Decorte, T. (2015). Cannabis social clubs in Belgium: organizational strengths and weaknesses, and threats to the model. *International Journal of Drug Policy*, 26(2), 122–130. doi:10.1016/j.drugpo.2014.07.016.

Decorte, T., & Pardal, M. (2017). Cannabis Social Clubs in Europe: prospects and limits. In Colson, R., & Bergeron, H. (Eds.), *European drug policies: the ways of reform* (pp. 285–299). Oxfordshire: Routledge.

Decorte, T., Pardal, M. (2020). Insights for the design of Cannabis Social Club regulation. In Decorte, T., Lenton, S., & Wilkins, C. (Eds.), *Legalizing cannabis: experiences, lessons and scenarios*, 409–426. London: Routledge.

Decorte, T., Pardal, M., Queirolo, R., Boidi, M. F., Sánchez Avilés, C., & Parés Franquero, Ò. (2017). Regulating Cannabis Social Clubs: a comparative analysis of legal and self-regulatory practices in Spain, Belgium and Uruguay. *International Journal of Drug Policy*, 43, 44–56. doi:10.1016/j.drugpo.2016.12.020.

Decorte, T., Paoli, L., Kersten, L., Heyde, J., Dun, E. V., & Vlaemynck, M. (2014). *Cannabis production in Belgium: assessment of the nature and harms, and implications for priority setting*. Ghent, Belgium: Academia Press.

Ferrell, J. (2019). In defense of resistance. *Critical Criminology*, 1–17. doi:10.1007/s10612-019-09456-6.

Fontana, A., & Bertani, M. (2003). Situating the lectures: Alessandro Fontana and Mauro Bertani. In Ewald, F., Fontana, A., & Davidson, A. I. (Eds.), *Society must be defended. Lectures at the Collège de France. 1975–1976* (pp. 273–294). New York: Picador.

Foucault, M. (1976). Part five. Right of death and power over life. (R. Hurley, Trans.). In Foucault, M. (Ed.), *The will to knowledge. The history of sexuality*, vol. 1 (pp. 133–160). London: Penguin Books.

Foucault, M. (1994a). The subject and power. In Rabinow, P., & Rose, N. (Eds.), *The essential Foucault. Selections from the essential works of Foucault, 1954–1984* (pp. 126–144). New York; London: The New Press.

Foucault, M. (1994b). Technologies of the self. In Rabinow, P., & Rose, N. (Eds.), *The essential Foucault. Selections from the essential works of Foucault, 1954–1984* (pp. 145–169). New York; London: The New Press.

Foucault, M. (1994c). Truth and power. In Rabinow, P., & Rose, N. (Eds.), *The essential Foucault. Selections from the essential works of Foucault, 1954–1984* (pp. 300–318). New York; London: The New Press.

Foucault, M. (2003). Eleven. 17 March 1976 (D. Macey, Trans.). In Ewald, F., Fontana, A., & Davidson, A. I. (Eds.), *Society must be defended. Lectures at the Collège de France. 1975–1976* (pp. 239–263). New York: Picador.

Foucault, M. (2007a). Eight. 1 March 1978. (G. Burchell, Trans.). In Senellart, M., Ewald, F.Fontana, A., & Davidson, A. I. (Eds.), *Security, territory, population. Lectures at the Collège de France. 1977–1978* (pp. 191–226). New York: Picador Palgrave Macmillan.

Foucault, M. (2007b). Four. 1 February 1978 (G. Burchell, Trans.). In Senellart, M., Ewald, F.Fontana, A., & Davidson, A. I. (Eds.), *Security, territory, population. Lectures at the Collège de France, 1977–1978* (pp. 87–114). New York: Picador Palgrave Macmillan.

Foucault, M. (2007c). Subjectivity and truth. In Lotringer, S. (Ed.), *The politics of truth* (pp. 147–168). South Pasadena, CA: Semiotext(e).

Foucault, M. (2007d). What is critique? In Lotringer, S. (Ed.), *The politics of truth* (pp. 41–82). South Pasadena, CA: Semiotext(e).

Foucault, M. (2008). One. 10 January 1979. (G. Burchell, Trans.). In Senellart, M., Ewald, F.Fontana, A., & Davidson, A. I. (Eds.), *The birth of biopolitics. Lectures at the Collège de France. 1978–1979* (pp. 1–26). New York: Picador Palgrave Macmillan.

Gordon, C. (1991). Governmental Rationality: An Introduction. In Burchell, G., Gordon, C., & Miller, P. (Eds.), *The Foucault effect. Studies in governmentality. With two lectures by and an interview with Michel Foucault* (pp. 1–52). Chicago: University of Chicago Press.

Hayward, K., & Schuilenburg, M. (2014). To resist = to create? Some thoughts on the concept of resistance in cultural criminology. *Tijdschrift over Cultuur & Criminaliteit*, 1(1), 22–36.

Hunt, N., Albert, E., & Montañés Sánchez, V. (2010). User involvement and user organising in harm reduction. In Rhodes, T, & Hedrich, D. *(Eds.), Harm reduction: evidence, impacts and challenges* (pp. 333–354). Lisbon: EMCDDA.

Jansseune, L., Pardal, M., Decorte, T., & Parés Franquero, Ò. (2019). Revisiting the birthplace of the Cannabis Social Club model and the role played by Cannabis Social Club Federations. *Journal of Drug Issues*, 49(2). doi:10.1177/0022042618815690.

Karskens, M. (2012). Hoofdstuk 2. Waarheid. In Karskens, M. (Ed.), *Foucault* (pp. 46–77). Amsterdam: Uitgeverij Boom.

Kilmer, B., Kruithof, K., Pardal, M., Caulkins, J. P., & Rubin, J. (2013). *Multinational overview of cannabis production regimes*. Santa Monica, CA: RAND Corporation.

Kilmer, B., & Pacula, R. L. (2016). Understanding and learning from the diversification of cannabis supply laws. *Addiction*, 112, 1128–1135. doi:10.1111/add.13623.

Lancione, S., Wade, K., Windle, S. B., Filion, K. B., Thombs, B. D., & Eisenberg, M. J. (2020). Non-medical cannabis in North America: an overview of regulatory approaches. *Public Health*, 178, 7–14. doi:10.1016/j.puhe.2019.08.018.

Lemke, T. (2001). "The birth of bio-politics": Michel Foucault's lecture at the Collège de France on neo-liberal governmentality. *Economy and Society*, 30(2), 190–207. doi:10.1080/03085140120042271.

Lindblom, J., & Jacobsson, K. (2014). A deviance perspective on social movements: the case of animal rights activism. *Deviant Behavior*, 35(2), 133–151. doi:10.1080/01639625.2013.834751.

Marín, I. (2009). *Cannabis: el movimiento cannábico en España*. Madrid: Editorial Popular.

Marín, I., & Hinojosa, M. (2017). Veinticinco años del movimiento cannábico español. In Martínez, D. P. (Ed.), *Las sendas de la regulación del cannabis en España* (pp. 123–135). Barcelona: Edicions Bellaterra.

Martínez, D P. (2015). Clubs sociales de cannabis: normalizacion, neoliberalismo, oportunidades politicas y prohibicionismo. *CLIVATGE*, 3, 92–112.

McAdam, D., McCarthy, J. D., & Zald, M. N. (1996). Introduction: opportunities, mobilizing structures, and framing processes – towards a synthetic, comparative perspective on social movements. In McCarthy, J. D., & Zald, M. N. (Eds.), *Comparative perspectives on social movements*. Cambridge: Cambridge University Press.

Montañés, V. (2017). Evolución del activismo cannábico en España. In Martínez, D. P. (Ed.), *Las sendas de la regulación del cannabis en España* (pp. 145–176). Barcelona: Edicions Bellaterra.

Muñoz, J., & Soto, S. (2000). Uso terapéutico del cannabis y creación de establecimientos para su adquisición y consumo: viabilidad legal. *Boletín Criminológico*, 47, 1–4.

Musto, C. (2018). Cannabis market regulation in Uruguay: the construction of an innovative drug policy. [Doctoral thesis, University of Kent, Utrecht University].

Odysseos, L., Death, C., & Malmvig, H. (2016). Interrogating Michel Foucault's counter-conduct: theorising the subjects and practices of resistance in global politics. *Global Society*, 30(2), 151–156. doi:10.1080/13600826.2016.1144568.

O'Malley, P., & Valverde, M. (2004). Pleasure, freedom and drugs: the uses of "pleasure" in liberal governance of drug and alcohol consumption. *Sociology*, 38(1), 25–42 doi:10.1177/0038038504039359.

Pardal, M. (2016a). Cannabis Social Clubs in Belgium: growing in a legal haze? In de Maillard, J., Groenmeyer, A., Ponsaers, P., Shapland, J., & Viannello, F. (Eds.), *Crime and order, criminal justice experiences and desistance* (pp. 13–30). Antwerp: Maklu.

Pardal, M. (2016b). Cannabis Social Clubs through the lens of the drug user movement. *Tijdschrift over Cultuur & Criminaliteit*, 6(2), 47–58. Pardal, M. (2018a). An analysis of Belgian Cannabis Social Clubs' supply practices: a shapeshifting model? *International Journal of Drug Policy*, 57, 32–41. doi:10.1016/j.drugpo.2018.03.027.

Pardal, M. (2018b). The Belgian Cannabis Social Club landscape. *Drugs and Alcohol Today*, 18(2), 80–89. doi:10.1108/DAT-09-2017-0051.

Pardal, M. (2018c). "The difference is in the tomato at the end": understanding the motivations and practices of cannabis growers operating within Belgian Cannabis Social Clubs. *International Journal of Drug Policy*, 56, 21–29. doi:10.1016/j.drugpo.2018.02.016.

Pardal, M. (2018d). "The difference is in the tomato at the end": understanding the motivations and practices of cannabis growers operating within Belgian Cannabis Social Clubs. *International Journal of Drug Policy*, 56, 21–29. doi:10.1016/j.drugpo.2018.02.016.

Pardal, M. (2019). Een inkijk in het leiderschap van Cannabis Social Clubs in België: criminelen, activisten, modelburgers? *Tijdschrift over Cultuur & Criminaliteit*, 8(3), 7–24. doi:10.5553/tcc/221195072018008003002.

Pardal, M., Bone, M., Decorte, T., Queirolo, R., Parés, Ò., Johansson, J., Álvarez, E., & Repetto, L. (2020a). Hidden and uninterested populations: methodological insights and unresolved issues from the study of Cannabis Social Clubs. *Methodological Innovations*, 13(3), 205979912097696. doi:10.1177/2059799120976963.

Pardal, M., Decorte, T., Bone, M., Parés, Ò., & Johansson, J. (2020b). Mapping Cannabis Social Clubs in Europe. *European Journal of Criminology*, 147737082094139. doi:10.1177/1477370820941392.

Pardal, M., Queirolo, R., Álvarez, E., & Repetto, L. (2019). Uruguayan Cannabis Social Clubs: From activism to dispensaries? *International Journal of Drug Policy*, 73, 49–57. doi:10.1016/j.drugpo.2019.06.022.

Pardal, M., & Tieberghien, J. (2017). An analysis of media framing of and by Cannabis Social Clubs in Belgium: making the news? *Drugs: Education, Prevention and Policy*, 24(4), 348–358. doi:10.1080/09687637.2017.1336509.

Pardal, M., & Tieberghien, J. (2018). Cannabis Social Clubs on YouTube: a qualitative content analysis. In Korf, D., Fountain, J., & Potter, G. (Eds.), *Place, space and time in European drug use, markets and policy* (pp. 81–95). Lengerich, Germany: Pabst Science Publishers. Parés, Ò. (2018). Epifanía cannábica, segundo y tercer movimiento, allegro ma non troppo. Barcelona 2010–14. In Salomao Shecaira, S., Arana, X., Silva Cardoso, F., & Macedo de Miranda, B. (Eds.), *Drogas, desafios contemporâneos*. Belo Horizonte, Brazil: Editora D'Plácido.

Pennay, A., & Moore, D. (2010). Exploring the micro-politics of normalisation: narratives of pleasure, self-control and desire in a sample of young Australian "party drug" users. *Addiction Research and Theory*, 18(5), 557–571. doi:10.3109/16066350903308415.

Pettitt-Schieber, B. (2012). *El "Amenecer Verde": la legalización de la marihuana en Uruguay en el contexto del movimiento regional contra la prohibición*. Independent Study Project Collection, Paper 1399.

Repetto, L. (2014). Regulación del cannabis: un asunto de seguridad? Entrada y mantenimiento en agenda de un problema de política pública. *Revista Uruguaya de Ciencia Política*, 23, 119–141.

Rondelez, P. (2021). How to decenter neoliberalism in the analysis of contestation and change? Reflections on the usefulness of Foucault's (extended) governmentality approach. *SN Social Sciences*, 1, 55. doi:10.1007/s43545-021-00062-4.

Rossdale, C., & Stierl, M. (2016). Everything is dangerous: conduct and counter-conduct in the occupy movement. *Global Society*, 30(2), 157–178. doi:10.1080/13600826.2015.1133569.

Queirolo, R., Boidi, M. F., & Cruz, J. M. (2016). Cannabis clubs in Uruguay: the challenges of regulation. *International Journal of Drug Policy*, 34, 41–48. doi:10.1016/j.drugpo.2016.05.015.

Queirolo, R., Rossel, C., Álvarez, E., & Repetto, L. (2018). Why Uruguay legalized marijuana? The open window of public insecurity. *Addiction*, 114(7), 1313–1321.

Seddon, T. (2016). Inventing Drugs: A Genealogy of a Regulatory Concept. *Journal of Law and Society*, 43(3), 393–415. doi:10.1111/j.1467-6478.2016.00760.x.

Seddon, T., & Floodgate, W. (2020). A global review of cannabis regulation models. In Seddon, T., & Floodgate, W., *Regulating Cannabis* (pp. 15–83). Cham, Switzerland: Springer International Publishing. doi:10.1007/978-3-030-52927-7_2. Senellart, M. (2007). Course context (G. Burchell, Trans.). In Senellart, M., Ewald, F.Fontana, A., & Davidson, A. I. (Eds.), *Security, territory, population. Lectures at the Collège de France. 1977–1978* (pp. 369–402). New York: Picador Palgrave Macmillan.

Senellart, M., Ewald, F., Fontana, A., & Davidson, A. I. (2007). *Michel Foucault. Security, territory, population. Lectures at the Collège de France 1977–1978*. New York: Picador Palgrave Macmillan.

United Nations Office on Drugs and Crime. (2020). CND Votes on Recommendations for Cannabis and Cannabis-Related Substances. Retrieved from: https://www.unodc.org/unodc/en/frontpage/2020/December/cnd-votes-on-recommendations-for-cannabis-and-cannabis-related-substances.html (last accessed 25 October 2021).

Val, I. (2017). Evolución y actualidad de los clubes sociales de cannabis en Euskadi, una mirada retrospectiva de los últimos veinte años. In Martínez, D. P. (Ed.), *Las sendas de la regulación del cannabis en España* (pp. 160–176). Barcelona: Edicions Bellaterra.

Valverde, M. (2017). *Michel Foucault*. New York: Routledge.

van Stekelenburg, J., & Roggeband, C. (2013). Introduction: the changing dynamics of contention. In van Stekelenburg, J., & Roggeband, C., & Klandermans, B. (Eds.), *The future of social movement research: dynamics, mechanisms, and processes*. Minneapolis: University of Minnesota Press.

von Hoffmann, J. (2016). The international dimension of drug policy reform in Uruguay. *International Journal of Drug Policy*, 34, 27–33. doi:10.1016/j.drugpo.2016.04.015.

Warf, B. (2014). High points: an historical geography of Cannabis. *Geographical Review*, 104(4), 414–438. doi:10.1111/j.1931-0846.2014.12038.x.

8 CSC + 2

Can the Cannabis Social Club model be a buffer against market distortions?

Davide Fortin

Introduction

Scholars have discussed a number of advantages associated with the Cannabis Social Club (CSC) model such as the potential to curb the illicit market and to play a harm-reduction role. Yet, its positioning when competing with other supply alternatives has not been investigated yet (Queirolo et al., 2016). Accordingly, the goal of this theoretical exercise is to analyze the potential role of CSCs in a hypothetical post-prohibition regime which would include both commercial outlets for adult users and pharmacies for patients with physician's prescription.[1] Overall, the chapter considers the European welfare model and investigates whether and how the presence of CSCs could improve market segmentation[2] by appealing to those daily users who either are not willing to pay the price at retail stores, or who use cannabis for medical purposes but do not have a physician's prescription.

The inclusion of the CSC as an additional supply option would lower what economists call 'market distortions', phenomena generated by the multi-purpose nature of cannabis and the different price based on its purpose. In most US states, advocates have succeeded in having medical cannabis exempt from cannabis specific taxes. Although a lower monetary cost for individuals using cannabis medically may seem justified, it may also interfere with the behavior of some consumers. In practice, it leads to a deviation between the market price of cannabis and its marginal social costs in two scenarios: first, when a non-medical consumer purchases cannabis at a price that was set only for individuals using it for medical purposes; and second, when a medical user pays a sin tax on its purchase.[3]

The theoretical model introduced in this chapter provides a description of the potential dimensions of attractiveness of the various supply channels to four archetypes of cannabis users. The model generates a number of testable predictions concerning demand characteristics. While we could not fully test this model in real-life settings, we draw on data gathered by Pardal and colleagues to explore and reflect on the validity of the hypotheses put forward. In particular, in the context of that study, the author carried out field observations and interviews with CSC directors, cannabis growers operating within

DOI: 10.4324/9781003055679-8

CSCs and other stakeholders; ran an online survey among Belgian CSC members (n=190) (Pardal & Decorte, 2018); and gathered other private and public documentary sources concerning the development of the model in that country (Pardal & Tieberghien, 2017). Further below, we introduce the Belgian context and the presence of CSC model in the country, and discuss their features in light of the proposed theoretical framework.

Issues concerning legal supply models for cannabis

Shortcomings of the commercial model for recreational use

Once the decision of legalizing cannabis supply is taken, policymakers face another critical choice: deciding on what kinds of organizations should be allowed to participate in the market. Thus far, most jurisdictions have proposed a for-profit model, perhaps – at least in part, for the fear of losing consensus by introducing hybrid or other lesser known models which may be more difficult to explain to voters (Caulkins et al., 2016). Nevertheless, scholars have become concerned that the commercial interests driving this supply model will promote daily use. This consideration stems from three assumptions: 1) daily users account for the largest proportion of the cannabis consumed in a given market and may abuse it (Caulkins, 2019); 2) an industry prioritizes profits over consumer protection, eventually targeting the minority of users "whose consumption is, on balance and at the margin, damaging rather than beneficial to themselves" (Kleiman et al., 2014, p. 79); and 3) the influence of the industry on politicians might eventually also favor producers' interests over consumers' interests (Caulkins & Kilmer, 2016).

Interrelation between the medical and recreational markets

The supply of cannabis for medical use is a complex and controversial issue. In terms of access, the jurisdictions that have attempted to regulate cannabis supply to patients have introduced significantly different conditions under which the provision of cannabis for medical use is allowed, the type of product that is supplied, the distribution mechanisms, as well as the extent of domestic supply (Kilmer & Pacula, 2017). The regulatory scheme significantly affects the extent to which medical cannabis is purchased via that legal channel, but accessibility has to also be balanced with another policy objective, such as the minimization of diversion of cannabis (meant for medical use) to recreational users. In fact, cannabis products can be consumed for both medical and recreational purposes and this complicates – and likely delays – a wide(r) provision of cannabis for medical reasons. Indeed, most European countries impose significant restrictions both on eligible medical conditions and on the type of cannabis products available for those (EMCDDA, 2018). In Belgium, the majority of CSC members declaring to use cannabis for medical reasons did not have a written recommendation from a healthcare professional, and herbal preparations are not available in pharmacies (Pardal & Decorte, 2018). Currently, only these EU member states allow herbal preparations: Denmark (within a pilot program), Czech Republic, Italy, Netherlands, Portugal, and Germany. Furthermore, Italy and the Netherlands only permit access to irradiated herbal cannabis.[4] At the same time, in a growing number of European countries, treatment costs are covered by the health system for certain patients.[5]

Thus far, a regulatory model that maximizes access to cannabis for medical use has been primarily implemented in North America. In Canada and in several American states, cannabis (for medical use) is distributed through dispensaries without there being restrictions to specific types of cannabis products. Patients with a valid recommendation from a medical professional can buy cannabis from these specialized outlets, which provide a range of (cannabis) products, therefore virtually addressing any segment of patients' demand. The problem with this distribution approach is that it is relatively easy for a recreational user to obtain a medical card/recommendation.

In general, there seems to be a blurred line between medical and recreational use. Sznitman (2017) examined the differences by distinguishing between people who use cannabis for recreational purposes, unlicensed and licensed medical users in Israel. She found more variables distinguishing unlicensed from licensed medical users than there were distinguishing features between unlicensed medical users and recreational users. Mode and patterns of use represented the most meaningful differences: recreational users were more likely to be male, to use cannabis frequently, and less likely to eat it than unlicensed medical users. Other research has found an interrelation between medical and recreational users not only within jurisdictions allowing only medical cannabis sales (i.e. California), but also in supply architectures which separate the medical and recreational markets (MacCoun, 2013; Pacula et al., 2016).

In Colorado, the direct consequence of this distortion is that the state collects tax revenues below the social optimum due to the lower taxation for medical cannabis; to a degree, the recreational market serves out of state tourists, while in-state residents can generally obtain a medical card regardless of their actual state of health. Nevertheless, such a distortion could become a major issue in a welfare state framework. Indeed, when considering that European countries tend to cover patient costs, there would be a real risk that public funding would be subsidizing recreational use of cannabis – if recipients were to acquire and use the substance outside of its intended medical scope. However, if there is a distinct group of patients who use it exclusively for medical reasons, governments may want to guarantee that this group can obtain cannabis products at a reasonable price. Another approach was taken in Canada to reduce the economic incentive for recreational users to purchase their cannabis in medical outlets. There, policymakers have set the same tax rate on medical and recreational cannabis, de facto applying (after the regulation of non-medical use) a sin tax on its medical use (Kane, 2018).

Competition from the illicit market

The replacement of the illicit cannabis market with legal supply appears to be a longer process than previously thought. For example, one year after retail stores opened in Canada, most consumers were being supplied cannabis flowers by the illicit market (Wadsworth et al., 2021). Three years after retail stores opened in Washington, it was estimated that about 40% of the cannabis consumed was still being supplied by the illicit market (Caulkins et al., 2019). As a solution, the authors suggest that, during the transition period, law enforcement ought to chase out the residual illicit market more aggressively.

Nevertheless, the high price per unit in the legal market as well as the limited inclusion of illicit suppliers in the legal market might be playing an important role as well. Excessive taxation may be one of the factors contributing to the survival of the illicit market. Unlike Colorado, Washington State implemented a uniform taxation scheme which in practice demands that medical users pay a sin tax for cannabis products, and may also deter those consumers who are more sensitive to price (or less willing to pay more for the product) from the legal market.

Another important issue that could be limiting the ability to reduce the presence of an illicit market relates to the relational embeddedness between consumers and their illicit cannabis dealers. This plays a significant role in enhancing customer loyalty, especially when both sides are part of the same social network and altruistic values are involved (Sandberg, 2012). Buyers' preference for small-scale dealers with whom they also have non-commercial ties suggests the existence of some degree of monopoly (Kennally, 2001).[6] Accordingly, illicit suppliers will continue to operate in the illicit business so long as they can make profits through their existing network of clients or are embedded in social supply networks. A seemingly simple yet controversial solution would be to try to engage these individuals in the legal market – together with their existing customers. The critique to this view points out that participation in a newly regulated industry will depend on a high degree of voluntary cooperation and adherence to rules. Accordingly, those who have previously engaged in illicit activities and are not accustomed to comply with business regulations, may not be ideal candidates to enter this new industry. Differently, those advocating for that approach – especially from a social equity perspective, note that the entrance of individuals previously involved in the illicit market in the new legal market remains de facto limited by a number of legal and economic barriers. For instance, in many jurisdictions, legal market operators are not allowed to employ those individuals with a criminal record. In other places, there are high entry barriers to obtain a commercial license which deters most cannabis dealers who are not able to ensure proper compliance.[7]

Our conceptual framework

The theoretical model we put forward is conceptualized to maximize segmentation between medical and recreational markets by reducing consumption distortions. It integrates the commercial model adopted in the US for the recreational market with the European approach of integration of medical cannabis within the healthcare system.[8]

Its major aim is to limit the arbitrage between these markets by creating a buffer for those consumers who would not fit within the supply channel designed for their use. Two groups of consumers/segments of the market in particular come to mind: the first is represented by those medical users who would decide to avoid buying from pharmacies (i.e. for the lack of their favorite product typology or for privacy reasons); and those who were refused a valid prescription/recommendation from a medical professional. The second group of users is represented by daily non-medical users whose reservation price[9] is below the price per unit of retail stores.

The CSC model is included as a complementary supply channel which could be attractive to these two groups and therefore would enhance a user-controlled discrimination scheme, i.e. a scheme where cannabis users would select themselves into one of the three supply channels: pharmacies (i.e. through the healthcare system), specialized commercial outlets (i.e. retail stores) and CSCs. This self-selection approach would exploit the heterogeneity of cannabis market participants in three dimensions: price, transaction costs, and volume purchased.[10]

A taxonomy of cannabis users and their supply channels

Cannabis remains a contested substance. As such, those who have never used it before may find it difficult to ask for advice on its use from physicians – even though they might be suffering from a condition for which it might be effective (Pardal & Bawin, 2018). This is particularly problematic in the chronic pain field where training for physicians (on pain management) tends to be limited and where those with high level of "perceived knowledge" were found to have a lower intention to prescribe cannabis (Zolotov et al., 2019). In spite of this, as regulation evolves and more doctors are aware of the potential therapeutic properties of cannabis products, it is likely that a growing number of individuals is able to initiate its use for strictly medical reasons.

Apart from this segment of users, being able to accurately distinguishing whether someone is using cannabis for medical vs. recreational reasons is challenging. In a regulated system allowing different legal supply models for recreational and medical users, users' choice on which market to resort to would likely depend on:

- The decision to use cannabis in a medical context. This will mainly depend on the user's belief on the effectiveness of self-medication, the perception that medical-grade cannabis is of higher quality and the health benefits of cannabis. Another factor involved in the choice of the cannabis user is an intuitive cost–benefit analysis depending on the trade-off

between the monetary cost of the product and the patients' entry barriers (i.e. privacy concerns, stigmatization, and ethical concerns: for instance, if this user does not have a medical condition);
- The willingness/capacity of healthcare professionals to prescribe or recommend a less conventional type of therapy for a certain condition (which in turn may depend on the medical evidence supporting the utility of cannabis for a given condition, and on the availability of effective, evidence-based therapeutic alternatives);
- The physician's ability to distinguish medical users from recreational ones, which in turn stems from their knowledge of medical cannabis, their monetary incentives, and beliefs about the harms of cannabis use, as well as the penalties for an incorrect prescription.

We contextualize our model within an European welfare state. In doing so, we will adopt the simplifying assumption that the market for medical cannabis is in equilibrium and is fully integrated within the healthcare system. In other words, there is full (or partial) coverage of the treatment. Accordingly, the price per unit of product in a pharmacy is assumed to be always cheaper than at any other supply alternative, regardless of their cost-structure. In this scenario, it is reasonable to believe that there will be cases of users who attempt to obtain cannabis from the healthcare system to save money. The aim of the model we put forward is to encourage users to self-select their supply channel in a way that minimizes this consumption distortion, while incentivizing risky users towards a supply channel which may offer more opportunities for harm-reduction support.

Overall, we distinguish four consumer segments, which we argue will be attracted to particular supply models. The first two user segments represent non-medical consumers which differ only on their intensity of use and on their demand elasticity. Indeed, given their higher price-sensitivity, daily non-medical users are assumed to be majorly responsible for the *over-consumption* of medical cannabis when the substance is cheaper than if purchased in retail stores (Collins et al., 2014; Pacula & Lundberg, 2013). Therefore, the introduction of the CSC model in our hypothesized scenario is mainly aimed at attracting this segment and lower their incentive to participate in the medical market. Accordingly, from the perspective of this type of user, CSCs must be more competitive not only with regards to the retail outlets, but also vis-à-vis the healthcare system.

The other user segments represent those suffering from a medical condition for which cannabis appears to be effective. They differ on two aspects: the accuracy of the signal they reveal to physicians and inclusion of their medical condition in a pre-defined list of pathologies where there is evidence around the effects of cannabis. Members of the first group (medical patients) suffer from a condition which is medically verifiable, and where clinical trials on humans have been performed proving the efficacy of cannabis such as multiple sclerosis and certain types of epilepsy. Conversely, the second group (therapeutic patients) include all other patients who seek to use cannabis for a variety of other conditions or complaints but for which the evidence on cannabis benefits is lacking, making it challenging to verify its real medical purpose by physicians such as anxiety, difficulty sleeping, and pain (which, incidentally, account for the great majority of conditions cited by medical card applicants in some jurisdictions).[11] Both groups would likely obtain a recommendation from a medical professional in the North-American context and would therefore end up effectively paying the same price, with no or reduced cannabis specific excise tax. Nevertheless, the price would be quite different within a welfare state framework as 1) it would likely be more difficult to obtain a valid prescription/recommendation for the therapeutic patients; 2) some established systems discriminate (in an economic sense) against therapeutic patients in terms of both access and treatment costs.[12]

While medical patients would have access to the healthcare system, therapeutic patients could benefit from the existence of CSCs when they are unable to obtain a valid prescription/recommendation from a medical professional. Indeed, while the CSC model has primarily attracted non-medical users consuming the product on a daily or near daily basis (Pardal & Decorte, 2018; Parés-Franquero et al., 2019), we argue that some medical users could join a CSC to accommodate their needs. That could happen in at least four scenarios. First, if access to the legal supply of cannabis for medical purposes is restricted to verifiable conditions. Second, if the costs for the pharmaceutical-grade product is considered too high for non-subsidized patients.[13] Third, if a segment of individuals using cannabis for medical purposes is concerned about privacy and lacks trust in the confidentiality of a government-controlled database. Fourth, when medical users believe in the efficacy of a specific product (or cannabis variety) and cannot find such product within the supply system for medical use.[14]

In this context, we assume that occasional users (and tourists) would acquire cannabis through retail stores. The low quantity consumed makes their demand more inelastic than that of regular users (Pacula & Lundberg, 2013), and an entry cost – such as a membership fee – would counterbalance the lower cost per unit associated with CSC membership. Overall, it appears unlikely that this group of users would give away their private information without an economic gain. Any additional commitment mechanism, such as a minimum consumption quota (i.e. some CSCs in Uruguay have set a minimum quantity threshold of 10–25 grams that members must acquire monthly – see Pardal et al., 2019) would be a strong deterrent for them, and could be a strong incentive for these users to satisfy their needs in retail stores.

Taken together, according to this self-selection discrimination scheme, CSCs would attract primarily: 1) daily non-medical consumers who would be willing to spend time being enlisted into these clubs; as well as 2) therapeutic patients whose request for a prescription/recommendation was refused by their medical professional, or that have a preference on purchasing through CSCs due to their product offerings, and/or their privacy policy. This assumed supply/demand relation is shown in Table 8.1.

Table 8.1 Supply and demand assumed relationship

Type of Consumers	*Legal Supplier*
Medical Patients	Healthcare
Therapeutic Patients	Healthcare or CSCs
Recreational Regular Users	Retail Stores or CSCs
Tourists & Occasional Users	Retail Stores

The model

This model taps into the heterogeneity of consumers in terms of intensity of consumption (or volume purchased). Regardless of the purpose of use for cannabis, two major factors would influence the consumer's choice in term of supply: the actual price of the product, and the transaction costs needed to access the product (i.e. annual membership fee, costs of obtaining a prescription, privacy costs associated with registration in a state-controlled database). For simplicity, income is not included in the model.

We assume that M is a composite good whose price is set to 1, and cannabis is a homogenous good with q being the quantity purchased by a consumer.[15] $\bar{U}$ is the initial and minimum level of utility which must be guarantee to each consumer. There are three pricing schemes available to purchase cannabis depending on the chosen supply channel: E_{LP} which is the linear pricing with per-unit price p_{RET} (applied at retail stores); E_{2PT} scheme is a two-parts tariffs where p_{CSC} is the per-unit price and T_{CSC} is the fixed fee (applied at CSCs); E_{FT} is a scheme with a fixed tariff T_{PHA}, and is not dependent on the quantity consumed (applied within the healthcare system with full reimbursement of medication costs). The illicit market is omitted from the model as it is assumed that the legal market would attract the most skilled labour outcompeting the illicit market on price and product diversity in the long term, assuming reasonable taxation levels.

Consumer problem with linear pricing:

$$\min_q E_{LP} = M + p_{RET}q \tag{1}$$

$$s.t.\bar{U} = M + U(q) \tag{2}$$

Which can be rewritten:

$$\min_q E_{LP} = \bar{U} - U(q) + p_{RET}q \tag{3}$$

Consumer problem with two-parts tariffs:

$$\min_q E_{2PT} = M + p_{CSC}q + T_{CSC} \tag{4}$$

$$s.t.\bar{U} = M + U(q) \tag{5}$$

Which can be rewritten:

$$\min_q E_{2PT} = \bar{U} - U(q) + p_{CSC}q + T_{CSC} \tag{6}$$

Consumer problem with fixed tariff:

$$\min_q E_{FT} = M + T_{PHA} \tag{7}$$

$$s.t. \bar{U} = M + U(q) \tag{8}$$

Which can be rewritten:

$$\min_q E_{FT} = \bar{U} - U(q) + T_{PHA} \tag{9}$$

For a given $\bar{U}$, the consumer will choose the two-parts tariff if:

$E_{2PT} < E_{LP}$ and $E_{2PT} < E_{FT}$ i.e. if

$$\bar{U} - U(q) + p_{CSC}q + T_{CSC} < \bar{U} - U(q) + p_{RET}q \text{ and} \tag{10}$$

$$\bar{U} - U(q) + p_{CSC}q + T_{CSC} < \bar{U} - U(q) + T_{PHA} \tag{11}$$

Which can be rewritten:

$$q_1 = \frac{T_{CSC}}{p_{RET} - p_{CSC}} < q < \frac{T_{PHA} - T_{CSC}}{p_{CSC}} = q_2 \tag{12}$$

These quantities are also denoted as q_1 and q_2 in Figure 8.1. Accordingly, the chosen scheme will depend on the quantity consumed, the price per unit, and the access fees across the different supply channels. To show how the choice would change across consumer types, we assume the following pricing schemes: the per-gram price in retail stores and CSCs is €8 (p_{RET}=8) and €6 (p_{CSC}=6) respectively. The annual membership of the CSC is set at €40 (T_{CSC}=40), so q1 = 20 grams per year, or less than one joint per week, whereas the transaction cost to obtain a prescription for a patient is set at to €300 (T_{PHA}=300) which makes q2 = 43 grams per year.

In the model, there are two types of consumers (medical and recreational) for three supply channels. The choice for non-medical cannabis users will depend on q_1. If they consume *more*, they may decide to buy cannabis

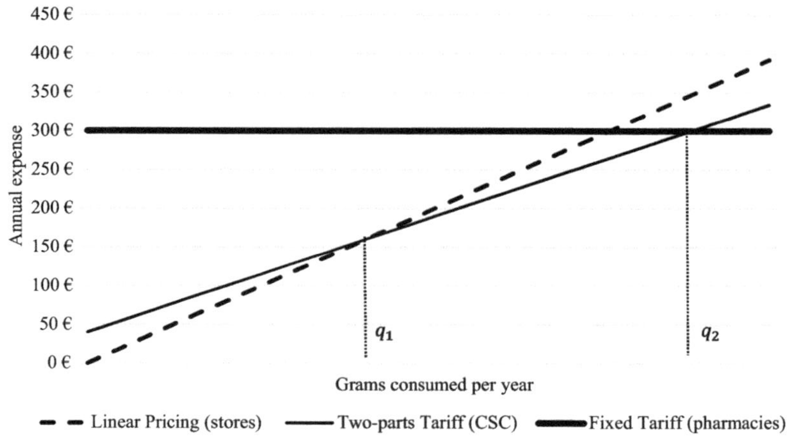

Figure 8.1 Pricing across supply channels

through the *CSCs.* If they consume, *less than* q_1, they will buy through *stores.* In parallel, the choice for those using cannabis for medical purposes will depend on q_2. If they consume *more* than q_2, they will decide to buy cannabis *through the healthcare system.* If they buy *below* q_2, they are more likely to buy *through CSCs* (and those with high privacy costs and very low quantity consumed may even buy cannabis in stores).

In other words, occasional consumers would prefer to buy in stores rather than in CSCs. In parallel, regular users would not have an interest in buying in stores as they would lower their total cost by purchasing at CSCs or through pharmacies. Note that not all those with a demand above q_2 will purchase in pharmacies. Many regular users may not be able to obtain the prescription/recommendation from their medical professional, or they may perceive that the privacy costs of enlisting in a government-run database may overcome their economic benefits.

Transaction costs and price

We consider the access fee to be the sum of the transaction costs necessary to have access to the specific supply market. For instance, T_{PHA} differs across type of cannabis consumers based on the purpose of use and the effort necessary to obtain a prescription/recommendation. To put it simply, at the two extreme lie individuals suffering from a (verifiable) condition for which there is strong evidence of efficacy for cannabis (e.g. epileptics) *and* those whose only purpose of use is to *get high.* For the former group of users, it is possible that their own physician/medical professional prescribes a cannabis product – i.e. given its approval from major health agencies worldwide for this condition, de facto minimizing the transaction costs. Conversely, it may be more challenging for users who are not suffering for any medical conditions to convince a physician to get a prescription and sometimes incur an ethical cost in reducing the budget available to patients (when treatment costs are reimbursed). There is also a privacy cost linked with being registered in a centralized database which varies on the employment of the consumer and the stigmatization of the substance within a given community.

For the model to be able to increase the segmentation within the cannabis market, the transaction costs of CSCs would need to be perceived to be lower compared to those requested by the healthcare system. At the same time, the retail stores would need to have the lowest level of transaction costs to purchase cannabis among the available supply channels. In this setting, the model would satisfy the following condition:

$$T_{RET} < T_{CSC} < T_{PHA}$$

In the US, the CSC model has not been implemented, but this condition has been validated in the medical and recreational market. Indeed, patients need to undergo an annual physical examination to obtain a prescription/recommendation, pay a fixed annual cost to the authorities, as well as being registered in a centralized database, whereas any adult can buy at retail stores without any preliminary obligation (CDPHE, n.d.).

In relation to the final price paid by consumers, in this scenario, the CSC model would need to satisfy a second condition:

$$p_{PHA} < p_{CSC} < p_{RET}$$

Ideally, in a CSC the price for a unit of cannabis (i.e. for 1 gram of herbal material or oil) would need to lie between the price paid by patients through a medical model and the cost for consumers who would buy it in retail outlets. This second condition is motivated by political economy reasons as well as to minimize market distortions. Even assuming similar production costs in the three settings, the higher price in CSCs and retail stores could be achieved through taxation, as a form of sin tax is considered appropriate for the non-medical use of harmful goods. Optimally, the level of taxation would be set in proportion with the degree of self-control of users, but in practice this is not feasible as the personal level of consumption is not observable by tax authorities (Haavio & Kotakorpi, 2011). In practice, tax rates are also determined by the relative political power of the various special interest groups. Alternatively, and as noted above, the solution adopted by US authorities for the cannabis market has been to apply a uniform tax.

In this model, we propose a different approach which combined sin tax and sin licenses.[16] CSC members would pay a lower tax rate for cannabis compared with what customers would pay at retail stores. This might seem counterintuitive given that, within our theoretical scenario, we expect the average consumption of a CSC member to be higher compared to retail stores' customers.[17] What we apply is a second-degree price discrimination where high-demand consumers (i.e. CSC members) pay a low price per unit, whereas low-demand consumers (i.e. occasional users or tourists) pay a high price per unit.[18] The choice of abandoning the purely sin tax approach for a model which combines sin taxes and sin licenses can be explained by the two characteristics of the cannabis market: first, high prices are unlikely the best way to target problematic users (Williams, 2016); second, cannabis can be cultivated domestically for a relatively low cost (Potter, 2008).[19] As a consequence, above a certain threshold of price per unit daily consumers' choice in term of quantity consumed may remain virtually unaffected by price increase for some users who may decide either to begin a domestic cultivation, or to increase the size of their crop, to supplement or replace their reliance on the illegal market (Potter et al., 2015). Accordingly, a sin tax is unlikely to neither distort nor correct their consumption behavior. In conclusion, the price in CSCs would thus need to be lower compared to retail stores in order to attract daily users with higher price-sensitivity.[20]

Retail outlets would mostly attract occasional users and out-of-state visitors/ tourists who are unwilling (or incapable) to incur in the transaction costs demanded to a CSC member given their occasional consumption behavior. With regards to the medical market, patients would obtain a cheaper product either without paying any tax, or by obtaining coverage through private insurance or by the national health system.

Discussion

Having clarified the model, it is important to discuss how realistic its assumptions are. The closest real-world examples to our theoretical model can be found in Belgium and Uruguay (Pardal, 2018a; Queirolo et al., 2016). In Uruguay, consumers can (legally) opt between joining CSCs, acquiring cannabis in pharmacies (not necessarily for medical reasons) or produce it themselves. In Belgium, although no legal regime for the supply of cannabis has been introduced to date, users have resorted to the existing CSCs in the country and, given the proximity with the Netherlands, may also purchase cannabis through Dutch coffeeshops.[21] Although neither the case of Uruguay nor Belgium fully matches our hypothetical scenario, we discuss it in light of the Belgian experience, seeing as Dutch coffeeshops are considered more commercial than pharmacies in Uruguay.[22]

We turn to the exploratory validation of the two conditions in our hypothetical regulatory framework. The first is the existence of an entry cost for consumers to access CSCs, in order to deter occasional users. In Belgium, the model only partially fits with this condition, as the possibility of obtaining cannabis through a CSC is limited by a number of entry barriers.[23] At the same time, it can be argued that, for most users, the transaction costs are still lower than visiting a physician to obtain a prescription. This is assuming that, in terms of privacy costs, the list of patients is available at the national level in a centralized government-controlled database, while the list of members may be kept by the clubs individually. However, this scheme was not chosen in Uruguay where also CSC members have to register in a centralized government-controlled database.[24] Nevertheless, it must be recognized that the physical distance of coffeeshops from Belgian consumers increases the transaction costs involved with their access, and some may perceive it to be of the same magnitude (or even greater) than those involved with becoming members of CSC or obtaining a prescription.

The second condition relates to the per-unit price of cannabis in the CSCs – which, according to our framework, should be lower than in the retail stores. This would depend both on the production efficiency of growers and on the taxation applied at the various channels. In the current CSC framework in Belgium, the amount of cannabis cultivated is based on the number of members as well as their predicted level of consumption. Given its unregulated nature, it appears to be difficult to implement a large-scale system of production (Pardal, 2018b). At the time of that research, the Belgian CSCs applied a price per gram ranging between €6.5–9, and did not apply quantity discounts (Pardal, 2018a). That value is lower than the average price per gram at a Dutch coffeeshop, which was estimated at €11.82 based on 2016–2017 data (Rigter & Niesink, 2017). While this would appear to show that the condition related to the per-unit price between CSC and retail stores is currently validated, it must also be recognized that cannabis production has not been legalized neither in the Netherlands, nor in Belgium.

It is fair to note that our analysis can say little about the details of how a CSC would compete with the commercial model in practice. We discuss the Belgian experience which is likely to be most similar, but perhaps we would need to examine this model in other contexts for further validation. Still, it is difficult to conceptualize other supply model formulations with the same potential to increase market segmentation. Home cultivation could be considered as another potential buffer to reduce the participation of non-medical users in the medical market. Nevertheless, the transaction costs involved with this model are arguably larger than those involved with getting a prescription in the medical market, and would make its adoption more limited than with CSCs. It would also incentivize a grey market when regular users do not have the resources (e.g. space, skills) to grow it themselves as they would have to obtain it from other domestic growers. Moreover, home growing cannot be considered a harm-reduction model as there would be no nudging to avoid an increase in consumption patterns.

The conceptual schema proposed herein aims to contribute to the discussion about the relative advantages and limitations of a hypothetical co-existence of three different supply models for cannabis. Having explained this theoretical scenario, we should remember that the main objective of drug policy is to find the equilibrium between economic efficiency and harm minimization (Kopp, 2004). In terms of harm minimization, a number of scholars (Belackova et al., 2016) argue that CSCs can simultaneously promote a number of public health objectives and that its non-profit nature could help prevent the most problematic uncertainties of legalization (Kleiman et al., 2014).

First, CSCs have the potential to reduce the perverse relation between daily users and the profit-oriented recreational industry (Caulkins, 2019) without the need to ban retail outlets. Indeed, the commercial model could serve the vast majority of the market participants since they buy cannabis occasionally only.[25] The retail stores could become the preferred option for those who do *not* want to commit towards daily or near daily cannabis consumption by becoming CSC members.[26] Overall, the supply architecture outlined in this chapter may provide incentives to the commercial model towards the maximization of consumer health. Retail stores may have an interest in avoiding their clients' escalation in consumption as they would become more price-sensitive, and eventually could shift towards CSCs for a lower cost per intoxication.

Second, the 'supply-follows-demand' philosophy of CSCs would be a form of nudging which may improve the decision-making of cannabis users and lower their risk of abuse (Thaler & Sunstein, 2008). Scholars argue that policymakers should design the choice architecture of consumers so their decision is more in line with their goals and less with their instinct by establishing a personal quota to limit their consumption (Kleiman et al., 2014).[27] While these control mechanisms do not guarantee a lower absolute consumption level among members, they are likely to deter escalation by monitoring user consumption. Indeed, there are two conditions which must be satisfied for a shop owner to counsel customers when they buy a much larger quota than usual: either, when there is a non-profit incentive for the supplier (i.e. CSCs); or when the for-profit supplier knows that the escalation of consumption may incentivize the client towards a competing supply channel. The current evidence from CSC experiences is mixed though (Álvarez et al., this volume; Parés-Franquero et al., 2019). In Belgium and Spain, the portion of members declaring to have lowered the intensity of consumption after joining the CSC is greater than the fraction who declare to have increased it.[28] Conversely, the contrary is true in Uruguay, perhaps in view of the different institutional framework. All in all, however, the majority of members reported using about the same amount of cannabis than before joining the CSC.

Third, the lower tax rate on CSCs will keep a larger fraction of daily users in the legal sphere, therefore improving the average quality consumed by them. Indeed, those daily users who are neither willing to buy in retail stores, nor able to obtain a prescription/recommendation from a medical professional could resort to the illicit market to satisfy their demand. In that case they would be acquiring a product which they have no control of in terms of its quality, purity, and potency. While most CSCs are not testing their production (Belackova et al., 2016; Pardal & Bawin, 2018), members often contribute to the cultivation process as CSCs tend to rely on in-house members/growers, which de facto reduces the asymmetric information exchange between consumers and growers.[29]

Limitations

The major limitation of the model presented here relates to the assumed homogenous nature of cannabis-derived products which may be considered overly simplistic. The plant can indeed be cultivated and processed to generate a wide range of products with very different combinations of active principles. In certain medical cannabis markets, regulators restrict the type of products available allowing standardized drugs containing a mix of isolated cannabinoids.[30] This type of medication would provide a consistent dose of active ingredients for patients. Individuals with compromised immune systems would clearly have a preference to receive such products, if available. Nevertheless, access to the market of these cannabis-based pharmaceuticals depends on the interest of companies to apply for their marketing authorization through clinical trials on safety, quality, and efficacy which are currently very costly (DiMasi et al., 2003). The limited number of conditions for which there is evidence of effectiveness for cannabinoid-based products along with the high cost of these medications have persuaded regulators to allow herbal cannabis, mostly through special-access schemes and even reimburse its costs in certain cases. One may speculate that there will be cannabis-based drugs authorized for most conditions where it may be beneficial. However, the technical and economic barriers for demonstrating its efficacy and in protecting patents may extend their approval times by decades (Fortin & Massin, 2020). Even with a significant expansion of cannabinoid-based pharmaceuticals, it is unlikely that patients using herbal cannabis will switch to these standardized medicines, if they believe in the superiority of the entourage effect (Russo, 2019).[31] Unless it will be proven that botanical drugs are less efficacious than their isolated components, there will thus still be patients using herbal cannabis. As this is the most common form of cannabis used recreationally, we consider our assumption of homogenous product to be reasonable for the time being.

Another significant limitation relates to the very limited applicability of the model in the US context in view of the specific nature of its medical cannabis market. The transaction costs to become a patient is much lower there as its historical use has lowered the stigma and prescription practices for narcotics seem to be looser than in other countries (i.e. opioid crisis). Compared to a prescription, physicians' responsibility deriving from the misuses of the recommended treatment is much lower and there are clear economic incentives for physicians to close an eye on non-medical users 'faking an ache'. While the model may provide good insights to European countries and other jurisdictions with a welfare system having the characteristics presumed in the framing, it may not adequately fit other markets with health approaches similar to the US.

Other limitations stem from the risk of over-regulating CSCs and the potential unsustainability of the model (Belackova & Wilkins, 2018). Setting, for instance, extremely low thresholds to the number of members, the number of plants per CSC or the member's quantity supplied might in turn cause other distortions such as an increased diversion of the product outside the closed-circle[32] or even deter cannabis users from CSC membership. Yet, unless the CSCs are regulated through an unreasonable layer of bureaucracy, their introduction will likely encourage economic efficiency in a harm-reduction context.

Finally, one may argue that if daily or near daily users indeed join CSCs, then the size of the private industry would become much smaller. While this is possible, the great majority of cannabis users are occasional and could potentially be interested in purchasing in retail stores (Caulkins et al., 2016). Besides for occasional users, in certain countries, tourists may represent another group of users who could source their product through the private industry. Among regular users, some may be interested in buying it in recreational stores for privacy reason or because the CSC is located too far from where they are located. Even CSC members may purchase something in stores if it will not be available in CSCs. Together, taxation is likely to be a major factor behind the size of the legal cannabis market and its ability to reduce the illicit trade.

Conclusion

The first commercial markets for cannabis have demonstrated that commercialization conflicts with public-health-oriented policy goals (Pacula, 2017; Subritzky et al., 2016) and market segmentation between medical and recreational users (Pacula et al., 2016). Canadian regulators have decided to apply the same taxation level to cannabis regardless on the purpose of use of the product. Government officials declared having taken this decision in view of the shortcomings of Amendment 64 in Colorado which is argued to have allowed significant market distortions of non-medical users using the medical channel to save money by avoiding taxes. It also recognizes the reality that there is in fact little difference between the 'medical' product and the 'recreational' product (Cash et al., 2020).

This chapter suggests that there are design options that can represent an improvement vis-à-vis the sole implementation of a commercial model especially within the European model. Kilmer (2019) identified 14 choices concerning the introduction of cannabis legalization – the 14 Ps. Among the different design choices, Kilmer includes a consideration of the profit motive and the price – which are aspects that are critical for the correct functioning of our proposed model as well. Our analysis suggests an additional important (P) choice: plurality, in the sense that jurisdictions may want to consider the introduction of multiple supply models in light of the different segments of users in a given jurisdiction.

In particular, we argue that the CSC model has the potential to complement the commercial and medical models. If a jurisdiction has an established reimbursement policy for medication, the co-existence of the CSC model could help reducing the number of cannabis users procuring cannabis from the national health system. If the CSC charges lower prices than the private industry, it would also be an attractive model for daily or near daily users, who would thus be supplied by a non-commercial model in a harm-minimization setting.

In practice, supply models can potentially compete with each other when they are designed to supply different demand segments. The difference should not be limited to the effective price paid, but should consider the overall transaction costs in order to limit as much as possible eventual market distortions. These transaction costs in turn should not be limited to an annual fee, but should reflect other aspects, such as an ideological choice to avoid being registered on a centralized government-control database.

In conclusion, an indirectly positive effect of the co-existence of different supply channels is limiting the empowerment of a cannabis industry. The special interest of CSCs could counterbalance the industry power, permitting greater regulatory controls.

Notes

1 Other types of suppliers can be considered in contexts where patients do not access medical cannabis through pharmacies (i.e. American patients access medical cannabis in medical marijuana centers).

2 We describe market segmentation as the process of slicing the demand for a product, consisting of existing, and potential users, into sub-groups of consumers (known as segments). Each market segment represents a group of potential customers with common characteristics who perceive the value of a product differently. This technique is normally designed to identify the most profitable segments and focus their limited resources with tailor branding. In our paper, we discuss market segmentation with a view to minimize the risk that a target group (i.e. non-medical cannabis users) ends up buying in a supply channel designed for another target group (i.e. patients). To better satisfy the needs and purchase motivations of the different segments, supply options need to be developped in a way that resonates with the selected target market and is attractive to the group of consumers.

3 A sin tax is used on activities that are considered socially undesirable to increase their price in an effort to lower their use. Besides for drugs such as alcohol and tobacco, these taxes have be levied on sugar, vehicles emitting excessive pollutants, etc.

4 Gamma irradiation minimizes the content of potentially harmful microbes by exposing the herbal material to packets of light that damage their DNA strands.

5 In Germany, health insurers reportedly accept two-third of requests for reimbursement (Economist, 2018). In Italy, the national system covers the costs of cannabis for medical use to patients with specific conditions "when other available medications have proven to be ineffective or inadequate to the therapeutic needs of the patient" (Bifulco & Pisanti, 2015; Zaami et al., 2018). In the Netherlands, most Dutch health insurance companies provide some form of reimbursement (Hazekamp & Pappas, 2014). Canada's reimbursement policy established a limit of 3 grams per day to Veterans (Veterans Affairs Canada, 2017).

6 This may be also due to the preferences for a specific cannabis variety or preparation.

7 See Kilmer (2019) for details on the relationship between regulation and social equity.

8 These two supply models have been chosen not only because they have been the most adopted so far, but as they appear to be the most political feasible to policymakers in Western societies given their resemblance to existing models for alcohol and prescription drugs respectively.

9 A reservation price on the demand side is the highest price that a buyer is willing to pay for a product/service.

10 Transaction costs are anything that contribute to the cost of something being purchased other than the cost of the production (i.e. preference for privacy, entry fees).

11 For instance, chronic pain or mental health-related issues.

12 For example, in Italy medical cannabis is prescribed at the expense of the National Health Service if the prescription is based on a treatment plan drawn up by the medical specialist for patients with specific diseases (severe spasticity spinal cord

injury, etc.) who have not previously responded to recommended treatment. Note that there is great heterogeneity across European countries in term of reimbursement regulation (Zaami et al., 2018).

13 In the near future, the occurrence of the first two scenarios (limitation in the eligible conditions and lack of reimbursement) is far from unlikely. Indeed, a substantial number of clinical trials need to still be performed for the health system to recognize cannabis as a medicine *and* to cover the treatment costs for the pathologies it is currently alleged to be effective for. Furthermore, there are technical and economic barriers to demonstrating the efficacy of medical cannabis (Fortin & Massin, 2020). Its multi-compounds nature lowers the incentive to perform clinical trials (in particular on its herbal form) as pharmaceutical companies need to secure a patent to make the research investment profitable. These patents rely on the ability to identify an active principle to be effective in a specific condition. Accordingly, there is little financial incentive for the pharmaceutical industry to explore a medication whose most common form (i.e. herbal preparation) is characterized by multiple active ingredients. Even patent combination therapies containing two or more isolated cannabis compounds would be difficult to protect in term of intellectual property as 1) they would lack the entourage effect; 2) the cost for efficacy testing is very high; and 3) limited protection is granted on patent concerning a combination without chemical reaction.

14 In virtually every European country with a medical cannabis program there are up to 14 varieties available (Schlag, 2020).

15 Economic models are often characterized by a higher degree of abstraction. The reality of the cannabis market is that there is an explosion in product types and forms with legalization. See the discussion the contextualization of the assumption of homogeneity in the model.

16 O'Donoghue & Rabin (2003) first considered sin licensees as a way to enable those with self-control problems to commit to a future consumption. Haavio & Kotakorpi (2016) demonstrated that a system imposing a maximum quota of sin goods that can be purchased at a lower price would be the favorite type of non-linear personalized scheme for individuals with self-control problems.

17 On the contrary, if the level of taxation is set in proportion with the degree of self-control problem of users, CSC members should pay a higher taxation given that we assume they are daily cannabis users.

18 Second-degree price discrimination, also known as non-linear pricing, means that the price per unit only depends on how much you buy. It is commonly used by public utilities as well as by other industries which apply bulk discounts for large purchases.

19 Small-scale cultivation for personal use or 'social supply' has some minimal requirements of space, time, and skill, although domestic growers can (and often do) use specialist equipment, and more advanced growing techniques are easily learnt from online sources (Potter, 2010).

20 In addition, the production costs for CSCs are likely to be higher than for large-scale commercial businesses.

21 The Dutch government's decision to introduce a 'weed pass' to deter foreigners to buy cannabis in the coffeeshops of cities at the border may have decreased this purchase behavior. Yet, the great majority of observations on CSCs are collected from Flanders, a region at the border with the Netherlands only few hours away from Amsterdam where any adult can purchase cannabis at coffeeshops.

22 In Uruguay, aside from CSCs, cannabis can also be purchased through licensed pharmacies at a price set by the government, which in turn acquire the product through two monopoly producers. The limitation of both Uruguayan and Belgian models is that they lack a medical distributor, although in practice it is possible for Belgian medical users to obtain their medical cannabis from Dutch pharmacies.

23 See Álvarez et al. (this volume) for details.
24 While registration information would be likely privacy-protected, Boidi et al. (2016) show that 40 percent of frequent users in Uruguay would not register mostly for lack of trust in the registry or as they reject the idea of being registered as cannabis users.
25 Other advantages stemming from the existence of the commercial model include the provision of a constant stream of revenues, the reduction of the illicit market, the implementation of quality control (MacCoun, 2013), and an incentive to product innovation with positive externalities for consumers. This can in turn raise the health burden on the increase of sales of high THC products and other relatively more dangerous products (Smart et al., 2017; Carlini, 2017).
26 The commercial model would also supply those who want to purchase cannabis legally but are fearful of any type of registration scheme.
27 Behavioural economics have demonstrated that individual decision-making deviates from rationality in certain circumstances (Laibson, 1997). Problematic drug us can then be considered a problem of impaired will. A change in the conditions under which choices are made – for instance, by respecting the consumption quota of CSCs – can help to reduce its consumption.
28 Note that in Spain other three key patterns of use after joining a CSC were identified: those who have stopped and started using cannabis again many times; those whose consumption has changed over the years; and those whose consumption gradually increased until it reached a peak and then decreased (Parés-Franquero et al., 2019).
29 In fact, there is a natural incentive towards quality when growers will consume the output themselves.
30 Whereas it may be difficult to standardize the content of an herbal product, it is an easier task to use formulated pharmaceuticals based on phytocannabinoids and/or synthetic cannabinoids.
31 The concept of herbal synergy assumes a combinatorial activity of endocannabinoids via 'the entourage effect' of active and inactive metabolites. In other words, the entourage hypothesis postulates that there are greater benefits for a patient when the whole plant is used compared to using single extracts of cannabinoids (such as in the cannabis-based pharmaceuticals who have received marketing approval thus far). See Russo (2019) for a review of cannabis synergy.
32 For instance, a member may ask for a greater amount of product than s/he needs and sell the surplus to other consumers.

References

Belackova, V., Tomkova, A., & Zabransky, T. (2016). Qualitative research in Spanish cannabis social clubs: "the moment you enter the door, you are minimising the risks". *International Journal of Drug Policy*, 34, 49–47. doi:10.1016/j.drugpo.2016.04.009.

Belackova, V., & Wilkins, C. (2018). Consumer agency in cannabis supply – exploring auto-regulatory documents of the cannabis social clubs in Spain. *International Journal of Drug Policy*, 54, 26–34. doi:10.1016/j.drugpo.2017.12.018.

Bifulco, M., & Pisanti, S. (2015). Medicinal use of cannabis in Europe: the fact that more countries legalize the medicinal use of cannabis should not become an argument for unfettered and uncontrolled use. *EMBO Reports, 16*(2), 130–132. doi:10.15252/embr.201439742.

Boidi, M. F., Queirolo, R., & Cruz, J. M. (2016). Cannabis consumption patterns among frequent consumers in Uruguay. *International Journal of Drug Policy*, 34, 34–40. doi:10.1016/j.drugpo.2016.05.008.

Carlini, B. H. (2017). Potency increase, product development and marijuana marketing in times of legalization. *Addiction*, 112(12), 2178–2179. doi:10.1111/add.13945.

Cash, M. C., Cunnane, K., Fan, C., & Romero-Sandoval, E. A. (2020). Mapping cannabis potency in medical and recreational programs in the United States. *PloS one*, 15(3), doi:10.1371/journal.pone.0230167. Caulkins, J. P. (2019). Legalising drugs prudently: The importance of incentives and values. *Journal of Illicit Economies and Development*, 1(3), 279–287.

Caulkins, J. P., Davenport, S., Doanvo, A., Furlong, K., Siddique, A., Turner, M., & Kilmer, B. (2019). Triangulating web & general population surveys: do results match legal cannabis market sales? *International Journal of Drug Policy*, 73, 293–300. doi:10.1016/j.drugpo.2019.06.010.

Caulkins, J. P., & Kilmer, B. (2016). Considering marijuana legalization carefully: insights for other jurisdictions from analysis for Vermont. *Addiction*, 111(12), 2082–2089. doi:10.1111/add.13289.

Caulkins, J. P., Kilmer, B., & Kleiman, M. A. (2016). *Marijuana legalization: what everyone needs to know®*. Oxford: Oxford University Press.

CDPHE. (n.d.). Laws and policies – Medical Marijuana Registry. Retrieved from: https://www.colorado.gov/pacific/cdphe/laws-and-policies-medical-marijuana-registry (last accessed 25 October 2021).

Collins, R. L., Vincent, P. C., Yu, J., Liu, L., & Epstein, L. H. (2014). A behavioral economic approach to assessing demand for marijuana. *Experimental and Clinical Psychopharmacology, 22*(3). doi:10.1037/a0035318.

DiMasi, J. A., Hansen, R. W., & Grabowski, H. G. (2003). The price of innovation: new estimates of drug development costs. *Journal of health economics*, 22(2), 151–185. doi:10.1016/S0167-6296(02)00126–00121.

Economist. (1 February 2018). Drugs policy in Germany is a mess. *The Economist*. Retrieved from: http://media.economist.com/news/europe/21736184-despite-legalisation-medicinal- cannabis-often-unavailable-german-patients-drugs-policy (last accessed 27 September 2021).

EMCDDA (European Monitoring Centre for Drugs and Drug Addiction) (2018). *Medical use of cannabis and cannabinoids: Questions and answers for policymaking*. Luxembourg: Publications Office of the European Union.

Fortin, D., & Massin, S. (2020). Medical cannabis: thinking out of the box of the healthcare system. *Journal de gestion et d'économie de la santé*, 2, 110–118. doi:10.3917/jges.202.0110.

Haavio, M., & Kotakorpi, K. (2011). The political economy of sin taxes. *European Economic Review*, 55(4), 575–594. doi:10.1016/j.euroecorev.2010.06.002.

Haavio, M., & Kotakorpi, K. (2016). Sin licenses revisited. *Journal of Public Economics*, 144, 40–51. doi:10.1016/j.jpubeco.2016.09.006.

Hazekamp, A., & Pappas, G. (2014). Self-medication with cannabis. In: Pertwee, R. G. (Ed.), *Handbook of cannabis*. New York: Oxford University Press.

Kane, L. (2018). 'There is a difference' between medical and recreational marijuana, patients say. CTV News. Retrieved from: https://www.ctvnews.ca/health/there-is-a-difference-between-medical-and-recreational-marijuana-patients-say-1.3798663 (last accessed 25 October 2021).

Kennally, G. (2001). Regulating the trade in recreational drugs. *European Journal of Law and Economics, 11*(1), 69–82. doi:10.1023/A:1008765813086.

Kilmer, B. (2019). How will cannabis legalization affect health, safety, and social equity outcomes? It largely depends on the 14 Ps. *The American Journal of Drug and Alcohol Abuse, 45*(6), 664–672. doi:10.1080/00952990.2019.1611841.

Kilmer, B., & Pacula, R. L. (2017). Understanding and learning from the diversification of cannabis supply laws. *Addiction*, 112(7), 1128–1135. doi:10.1111/add.13623.

Kleiman, M. A., Ziskind, J., & Collins, J. (2014). Lawful access to cannabis: gains, losses and design criteria. LSE Expert Group on the Economics of Drug Policy (Ed.), *Ending the drug wars*, 77–82.

Kopp, P. (2004). *Political economy of illegal drugs*. London: Routledge.

Laibson, D. (1997). Golden eggs and hyperbolic discounting. *The Quarterly Journal of Economics*, 112(2), 443–478.

MacCoun, R. J. (2013). *The paths not (yet) taken. Something's in the air: race, crime, and the legalization of marijuana*. Hoboken, NJ: Taylor & Francis, 40–53.

O'Donoghue, T., & Rabin, M. (2003). Studying optimal paternalism, illustrated by a model of sin taxes. *American Economic Review*, 93(2), 186–191. doi:10.1257/000282803321947029.

Pacula, R. L. (2017). *Regulating medical marijuana markets: Insights from scientific evaluations of state experiments*. Testimony presented before the florida house of representatives health & human services committee, subcommittee on health quality on 25 January 2017. Santa Monica, CA: RAND Corporation.

Pacula, R. L., Jacobson, M., & Maksabedian, E. J. (2016). In the weeds: a baseline view of marijuana use among legalizing states and their neighbours. *Addiction*, 111 (6), 973–980. doi:10.1111/add.13282.

Pacula, R. L., & Lundberg, R. (2013). Why changes in price matter when thinking about marijuana policy: A review of the literature on the elasticity of demand. *Public Health Reviews*, 35(2), 2. doi:10.1007/BF03391701. Pardal, M. (2018a). An analysis of Belgian Cannabis Social Clubs' supply practices: a shapeshifting model? *International Journal of Drug Policy*, 57, 32–41. doi:10.1080/09687637.2017.1336509.

Pardal, M. (2018b). "The difference is in the tomato at the end": understanding the motivations and practices of cannabis growers operating within Belgian Cannabis Social Clubs. *International Journal of Drug Policy*, 56, 21–29. doi:10.1016/j.drugpo.2018.02.016.

Pardal, M., & Bawin, F. (2018). The supply of cannabis for medical use through Cannabis Social Clubs in Belgium. *Contemporary Drug Problems*. doi:10.1177/0091450918768545.

Pardal, M., & Decorte, T. (2018). Cannabis use and supply patterns among Belgian Cannabis Social Club members. *Journal of Drug Issues*, 48(4), 689–709. doi:10.1177/0022042618791295.

Pardal, M., Queirolo, R., Álvarez, E., & Repetto, L. (2019). Uruguayan cannabis social clubs: from activism to dispensaries?. *International Journal of Drug Policy*, 73, 49–57. doi:10.1016/j.drugpo.2019.06.022.

Pardal, M., & Tieberghien, J. (2017). An analysis of media framing of and by Cannabis Social Clubs in Belgium: making the news? *Drugs: Education, Prevention and Policy*, 24(4), 348–358doi:10.1080/09687637.2017.1336509.

Parés-Franquero, Ò., Jubert-Cortiella, X., Olivares-Gálvez, S., Díaz-Castellano, A., Jiménez-Garrido, D. F., & Bouso, J. C. (2019). Use and habits of the protagonists of the story: Cannabis Social Clubs in Barcelona. *Journal of Drug Issues*, 49(4), 607–624. doi:10.1177/0022042619852780.

Potter, G. R. (2010) *Weed, need and greed: a study of domestic cannabis cultivation*. London: Free Association Books.

Potter, G. R. (2008). The growth of cannabis cultivation: explanations for import substitution in the UK. In: Korf, D. J. (Ed.), *Cannabis in Europe: dynamics in perception, policy and markets* (pp. 87–105). Lengerich, Germany: Pabst Science Publishers.

Potter, G. R., Barratt, M. J., Malm, A., Bouchard, M., Blok, T., Christensen, A.-S., Decorte, T., Frank, V. A., Hakkarainen, P., Klein, A., Lenton, S., Perälä, J., Werse, B., & Wouters, M. (2015). Global patterns of domestic cannabis cultivation: Sample characteristics and patterns of growing across eleven countries. *International Journal of Drug Policy*, 26(3), 226–237.

Queirolo, R., Boidi, M. F., & Cruz, J. M. (2016). Cannabis clubs in Uruguay: the challenges of regulation. *International Journal of Drug Policy*, 34, 41–48. doi:10.1016/j.drugpo.2016.05.015.

Rigter, S., & Niesink, R. (2017). *THC-concentraties in wiet, nederwiet en hasj in Nederlandse coffeeshops (2016–2017)*. Utrecht: Trimbos-Instituut.

Russo, E. B. (2019). The case for the entourage effect and conventional breeding of clinical cannabis: no "strain," no gain. *Frontiers in Plant Science*, 9, 1969.

Sandberg, S. (2012). The importance of culture for cannabis markets: Towards an economic sociology of illegal drug markets. *British Journal of Criminology*, 52(6), 1133–1151. doi:10.1093/bjc/azs031.

Schlag, A. K. (2020). An evaluation of regulatory regimes of medical cannabis: what lessons can be learned for the UK? *Medical Cannabis and Cannabinoids*, 3(1), 27–34. doi:10.1159/000505028.

Smart, R., Caulkins, J. P., Kilmer, B., Davenport, S., & Midgette, G. (2017). Variation in cannabis potency and prices in a newly-legal market: Evidence from 30 million cannabis sales in Washington State. *Addiction*, 112(12), 2167–2177. doi:10.1111/add.13886.

Subritzky, T., Pettigrew, S., & Lenton, S. (2016). Issues in the implementation and evolution of the commercial recreational cannabis market in Colorado. *International Journal of Drug Policy*, 27, 1–12. doi:10.1016/j.drugpo.2015.12.001.

Sznitman, S. R. (2017). Do recreational cannabis users, unlicensed and licensed medical cannabis users form distinct groups?. *International Journal of Drug Policy*, 42, 15–21. doi:10.1016/j.drugpo.2016.11.010.

Thaler, R. H., & Sunstein, C. R. (2008). *Nudge: improving decisions about health, wealth, and happiness.* New Haven & London: Yale University Press.

Veterans Affairs Canada. (2017). Cannabis for medical purposes: new reimbursement policy. Retrieved from: http://www.veterans.gc.ca/eng/help/faq/cannabis-medical-purposes#a01(last accessed 27 September 2021).

Wadsworth, E., Driezen, P., & Hammond, D. (2021). Retail availability and legal purchases of dried flower in Canada post-legalization. *Drug and Alcohol Dependence*, 108794. doi:10.1016/j.drugalcdep.2021.108794.

Williams, J. (2016). Economic insights on market structure and competition. *Addiction*, 111(12), 2094–2095. doi:10.1111/add.13458.

Zaami, S., Di Luca, A., Di Luca, N. M., & Vergallo, G. M. (2018). Medical use of cannabis: Italian and European legislation. *European Review for Medical and Pharmacological Sciences*, 22, 1161–1167. doi:10.26355/eurrev_201802_14405.

Zolotov, Y., Vulfsons, S., & Sznitman, S. (2019). Predicting physicians' intentions to recommend medical Cannabis. *Journal of Pain and Symptom Management, 58*(3), 400–407. doi:10.1016/j.jpainsymman.2019.05.010.

9 Cannabis legalization in Washington

Policy evolution and emerging evidence from the first nine years

Julia Dilley, Caislin Firth and Beau Kilmer

Introduction

Since the early 1970s, an increasing number of states and localities in the U.S. have liberalized laws prohibiting cannabis. The early movers decriminalized or deprioritized cannabis possession arrests and in 1996 California became the first state to allow cannabis to be used for medical purposes. Over the next 15 years, several other states changed laws with respect to medical cannabis, although qualifying conditions and methods of supply varied across jurisdictions (Pacula et al., 2015). Cannabis possession and supply remain illegal under federal law and federal agencies did enforce these laws against some patients and suppliers, but these legal changes smoothed the transition for states to legalize cannabis supply and possession for adults for nonmedical purposes (Kilmer & MacCoun, 2017).

Jurisdictions considering alternatives to prohibiting cannabis supply have several options, ranging from only allowing home production to licensing large companies to produce, sell, and advertise cannabis to adults (Caulkins et al., 2015). There are multiple middle-ground supply options as well (e.g., cooperatives, state stores), but these approaches seem to generate more interest outside of the U.S (Cerdá & Kilmer, 2017; Decorte, 2018).

In November 2012, voters in the U.S. states of Colorado and Washington passed ballot initiatives to remove the prohibition on cannabis and allow for-profit companies to produce, distribute, and sell cannabis to adults ages 21 and older. While the Dutch coffeeshop model and Spanish coops (known as Cannabis Social Clubs) had been operating for decades (Pardal, this volume), these changes were noteworthy because they explicitly allowed cannabis to be produced and sold via state-licensed businesses. Since cannabis is prohibited by the U.S. government, it was unclear how federal authorities would react to these state-level changes. In August 2013, the U.S. Department of Justice released a memorandum indicating that the enforcement of federal law against these activities would not be a priority as long as certain guidelines were followed (Cole, 2013). While this memorandum was rescinded by the Trump Administration in 2018 (U. S. Department of Justice, 2018) for all intents and purposes, the federal approach to these state legalization regimes did not change. The federal government neither interfered with state regulatory efforts nor revenue collection from licensing fees and taxes.

DOI: 10.4324/9781003055679-9

As of early 2021, more than 40 percent of the U.S. population lives in 18 states that have passed laws to legalize the commercial supply and sales of cannabis to adults for nonmedical purposes.[1] There is an emerging research literature evaluating the effects of these changes; however, many of these analyses use a simple binary measure to classify legalization and non-legalization states. Lumping all legalization states together can compromise inferences as there are important differences in how legalization has been implemented and how regulations have changed in states that have repealed cannabis prohibition (e.g., differences in tax rates, testing protocols). There is also important local variation (e.g., local bans on cannabis businesses) that can create challenges for analyses that use state-level outcome measures, especially those that may not be based on state-representative data.

This chapter begins with a detailed description of the implementation and evolution of commercial cannabis legalization in one of the first states to pass such a law: Washington.[2] We do not attempt to rigorously compare Washington's regime to those implemented in other states; for some comparisons on various dimensions see publications by Darnell and Bitney (2017), Pacula et al. (2021), Pardo (2014), and Transform Drug Policy Foundation (2020). The chapter then reviews the emerging evidence about changes in cannabis consumption and various public health and safety outcomes in Washington. These sections include some trend data (which do not allow for causal inferences on their own) as well as summaries of studies that include comparison groups and attempt to rule out alternative explanations. We conclude with some thoughts about how the cannabis landscape could change in Washington, especially if the federal government decides to remove the prohibition on cannabis and starts regulating and taxing state-legal cannabis sales.

Evolution of cannabis laws and policies in Washington

Most states that have passed cannabis legalization for nonmedical purposes had already decriminalized cannabis possession and made allowances for medical cannabis supply. While some U.S. states make it easy for individuals to obtain a medical recommendation and access cannabis for medical purposes, others are much more restrictive (Williams et al., 2016). Understanding these medical regimes is critical for determining how much legalization for nonmedical purposes really changed the cannabis landscape in the state. To this end, this section starts with a description of Washington's legal context and medical cannabis policies before highlighting the transition to nonmedical legalization and how it has evolved.

Legalization of medical cannabis

Washington was one of the first states in the U.S. to legalize possession of limited amounts of cannabis for medical purposes. In November 1998, Washington's Medical Use of Marijuana Act (I-692) passed via ballot initiative with 59 percent support (Washington State Department of Health, 2021b). Although I-692 allowed for providers to recommend cannabis for "debilitating illnesses" and offered examples of such, there was no state regulatory system established to oversee the activity of cannabis collectives, medical cannabis authorizers, or patients. In 2011, Washington lawmakers acted to establish a system of regulation for medical cannabis use, with a primary focus on provider allowances for recommending medical cannabis. However, no centralized registry of medical cannabis patients was established. A partial veto by the state's governor that eliminated legalization of dispensaries as well as the medical cannabis industry's interpretation of ambiguities in the law (Washington State Senate, 2009), led to hundreds of medical cannabis collective gardens effectively operating as storefronts for personal access without oversight (Dilley et al., n.d.a).

Decriminalization

Unlike many other states, Washington did not pass a statewide decriminalization law for possessing cannabis (i.e., making possession a civil offense instead of a criminal one) prior to legalizing medical or nonmedical cannabis. However, some local entities in the state placed a lower priority on enforcement of cannabis possession laws. For example, the City Attorney for Seattle - which accounts for about 10 percent of the state's population – announced a departmental policy to not enforce small cannabis possession offenses in 2010, although this did not eliminate all possession arrests (Heffter, 2010).

Legalization of nonmedical cannabis

In November 2012, 55.7 percent of Washington voters supported Initiative 502 (I-502) which legalized possession for adults and created a regulatory framework for commercial cannabis production and sales (Office of Program Research, 2012). Effective 6 December 2012, Washington allowed adults ages 21 years and older to legally possess up to 1oz of flower, 16oz solid infused, 72oz liquid infused, or 7g concentrate cannabis for personal use (Office of Program Research, 2012). Possession of quantities by adults above these limits remains illegal in Washington as does any possession by minors. Public consumption of cannabis and opening cannabis packaging in public remains prohibited (a civil infraction with a maximum fine of $50) as does using cannabis while in a motor vehicle, even if not driving (Darnell & Bitney, 2017).

In addition to state-level changes, some local jurisdictions implemented measures to further curb criminal penalties associated with cannabis. For example, in 2018, the City of Seattle filed a motion to remove misdemeanor possession convictions that occurred prior to legalization from criminal records dating back to 1997 (Beekman & Clarridge, 2018).

Washington's Liquor and Cannabis Board (LCB, formerly known as the Liquor Control Board), the state government agency already providing oversight of alcohol and tobacco markets, was charged with developing rules for licensing and oversight of the for-profit cannabis market. Based on alcohol market regulatory models intended to support checks and balances for product and tax management, a 'three-tiered' system was developed for independent regulation and licensing for producers (who grow cannabis), processors (who receive plant materials from growers and prepare different products for sale), and retailers (who sell cannabis to individual consumers). The LCB assigned a maximum number of cannabis retail sales licenses that would be allowed in each city or county area, based on projected demand and with an original statewide maximum ('retail cap') of 334 licenses (Washington State Liquor and Cannabis Board, 2014). Nonmedical retail sales started on 8 July 2014.

Integration of nonmedical and medical markets

Implementation of I-502 was also associated with developing a stronger statewide system to regulate the previously 'loose' medical market which operated on a for-profit basis. The 2015 Cannabis Patient Protection Act required existing medical dispensaries to close by 1 July 2016 (Washington State Senate, 2015). The state increased the cap for retail cannabis sales outlets to 556 to accommodate integration of the prior medical market (Washington State Liquor and Cannabis Board, 2015). In this integrated market, sales of medical cannabis products to qualifying patients and designated caregivers were allowed in nonmedical cannabis stores with a medical endorsement.

Stores with a medical cannabis endorsement can sell *"medically compliant"* cannabis products that may be higher in THC (medical patients can purchase tinctures and other cannabis products with up to 500mg THC compared to 100mg among non-medical consumers) (Washington State Department of Health, 2016; Washington State Liquor and Cannabis Board, 2019) and must meet higher quality standards for pesticides, heavy metals, and mold contamination. LCB reports indicate that 66 percent (288 of 434) of state-licensed cannabis retailers have medical endorsements as of September 2021 (Washington State Department of Health, 2016; Washington State Liquor and Cannabis Board, 2021a and 2021b). However, a report of the state's Department of Health (DOH) indicated in April 2021 that only 157 medically endorsed stores were 'active', meaning that the store has a certified medical consultant on staff who is registered in the state database (Washington State Department of Health, 2021a). Certification is managed by the DOH, and requires individuals to be age 21 or older, have completed a 20-hour training program, and complete CPR training (Washington State Department of Health, 2021c). Certified consultants are limited in their allowed activities and may not provide medical advice or diagnose conditions.

In addition to sales through cannabis retail outlets with medical endorsements, the new regulatory system provided patient access to cannabis for medical uses through newly created 'cannabis cooperatives' which were similar in concept but had much more regulatory oversight than the unregulated 'collective gardens'; however, in practice these new cooperatives have played a very small role in post-legalization cannabis access (see Table 9.1).

Table 9.1 Cannabis collective gardens and cooperatives in Washington

	Cannabis Collective Gardens	*Cannabis Cooperatives*
Establishing regulation	• WA Senate Bill 5073 (passed 2011) authorized providers to recommend cannabis, but not sales. Collective gardens emerged as storefront medical dispensaries/sales outlets due to legal ambiguities. They were not required to operate on a non-profit basis.	• WA Senate Bill (SB) 5052 (passed April 2015) replaced unregulated collective gardens with small patient cooperatives. There was no provision for the sale of cannabis from these cooperatives.
Dates of activity	• 2011–2016: Collectives were required by WA Senate Bill 5052 to close by June 30, 2016, unless they had a new retail license from the LCB.	• 2015 to present.
Numbers of outlets	• No list of licensees existed; however, one 2014 study indicated that about 262 medical sales access points were operating statewide.[9]	• LCB's FY20 annual report indicates 14 cooperatives statewide.[28]
Oversight and requirements for operation	• No oversight framework. • Up to 10 medical marijuana patients could work together to harvest up to 45 plants used by members of the collective. • "Membership" was not well defined; outlets could serve many people by issuing "temporary membership" to store patrons for the length of their transaction. • Collective garden "members" should have a provider recommendation for medical marijuana use issued on tamper-proof paper. • Some entities had multiple collective gardens under the same roof.	• Cooperatives must be licensed with the LCB.[29] LCB conducts random compliance checks. • Up to 4 members per cooperative allowed. Total plants cannot exceed 60 (up to 15 per member). • Members must be over age 21 and in the WA cannabis patient registry. • Cooperatives must be located at one member's home. If grow is outdoors, it must be out of public view and enclosed by an 8-foot fence.
Restrictions	• n/a	• Individuals can only be a member of one cooperative, and cannot grow plants elsewhere. • Cooperatives may not be located within 1 mile of licensed retailer, within 1,000 feet of specified youth facilities (e.g., schools, others); where prohibited by local law.

Simultaneous with these changes in 2016, the DOH also launched a medical cannabis authorization database (Washington State Department of Health, 2021d). A person who has a qualifying condition can obtain a medical authorization from their provider and then be voluntarily entered into the database at a medically endorsed retail cannabis store. Joining the database exempts the individual from paying excise tax, increases purchase limits, and allows for home growing of up to six cannabis plants (up to 15 plants if specifically authorized by their provider). A person who has a medical authorization, but who is not included in the DOH database, is legally allowed to grow four cannabis plants, but otherwise is subject to usual limits on purchasing and still pays tax on purchase of cannabis products.

To prevent oversupply of cannabis products, the state initially placed a cap on the total canopy for cannabis growing at 2 million square feet (Washington State Liquor and Cannabis Board, 2013), and limited licensed producers to only operate at 70 percent of total licensed production capacity. Limits were later modified to allow for addition of medical cannabis producers (Washington State Legislature, 2021).

Some medical cannabis advocates, including dispensary owners, were initially unsatisfied with this integration of medical cannabis sources following legalization of adult use cannabis markets, arguing that patient access was reduced and that the existing medical dispensaries were not protected and assured a place in the new market (Coughlin-Bogue, 2016; Joint Blog, 2015). However, in the seven years since retail marketplaces were opened there has not been any strong movement to separate or otherwise redesign the medical marketplace.

Local regulatory control

As state laws around cannabis were evolving, the legal authority of local government (e.g., city, county) entities was also clarified. Cities can apply specific regulations within their municipal boundaries, and counties can apply specific regulations in unincorporated areas (e.g., excluding municipal areas). Local entities are allowed to regulate time, place, and manner of cannabis business operations as long as they are not less restrictive than the state (e.g., hours of sale, land use policies, requiring siting 'buffers' from other operations), including completely banning these businesses. Local entities in Washington cannot apply excise taxes to cannabis; however, they can collect usual business and occupational taxes and sales taxes (Dilley et al., 2017).

Tribal regulatory control

Washington has 29 federally recognized American Indian tribes, which are sovereign governments within the state's geographic boundaries. Washington's changes in cannabis laws did not automatically apply on tribal land; federal law applies by default, and any changes in tribal law are under the control of each tribe. In 2015, Washington's governor was authorized by the state legislature to enter into agreements with tribes concerning cannabis legalization and markets, including tax collection. Several have acted to do so (Native Business Staff, 2020).

Unique factors in Washington's current cannabis laws and policies

Washington's approach to regulating cannabis differs from that applied in most states in a few significant ways. First, Washington's 'cap' on retail cannabis licenses has not yet been applied in other states. As a result, among the first states to legalize cannabis sales and that have established markets (Colorado, Oregon, Alaska), Washington has a significantly lower number of retailers per capita statewide (Dilley et al. (n.d.d)). Second, Washington is the only state to completely ban home growing of cannabis plants for nonmedical purposes, although plants can be grown for state-authorized medical patients. Third, particularly in comparison to nearby states that have legal markets (Oregon; California), Washington applies relatively greater restrictions on cannabis advertising. Additional restrictions applied in 2017 to state rules limited storefront marketing (e.g., only two signs of restricted size and which must be attached to the storefront are allowed, no 'moving' ads or 'sign-wavers') and restricted outdoor marketing content (e.g., billboards) (Washington State Senate, 2017). Finally, Washington applied some relatively restrictive specific packaging requirements on cannabis edibles for the purpose of preventing accidental ingestion by children. These include requiring that each edible 'dose' be separately packaged for most products: a candy bar or cookie must have individually wrapped servings within the packages, not just 'scoring' for each piece; capsules, lozenges, and mints may be packaged loosely within a resealing outer package if approved by the LCB on a case-by-case basis. Edibles packaging must include an LCB-developed 'not for kids' warning symbol that includes the Washington Poison Control center telephone number (Washington State Liquor and Cannabis Board, n.d.a).

Another issue to keep in mind when analyzing outcomes associated with legalization in Washington is that there was a major change to alcohol policy that occurred around the same time. This has implications given the possibility of substitution/complementarity. Prior to June 2012, off-premises liquor was only sold in state-controlled stores. But with the passage of a ballot initiative in 2011 (Initiative 1183), liquor sales were privatized and spirits could be purchased at grocery stores and other outlets. As a result, the number of stores selling liquor in the state increased from 328 to more than 1,600 by 2019 (Dilley et al., 2019; Northwest Prevention Technology Transfer Center, 2021). The prevalence of alcohol use (including liquor consumption specifically) increased among adults following the change in law and increases in some alcohol-related harms were documented (e.g., alcohol-related traffic crashes, emergency department visits, and dependence treatment among youth; increases in some crimes that are associated with alcohol use). Privatization was also associated with increased liquor prices, on average 15.5 percent for 750mL size packages and 5 percent for 1.75mL over the first two years and an additional 4 percent and 7 percent in the next two years, which may have suppressed some purchasing and what could otherwise have been even greater increases in consumption and harms (Kerr et al., 2015; Williams et al., 2020). Long-term studies will be needed to determine whether risky drinking behaviors that had increased after liquor privatization were reduced following cannabis legalization, or whether these environmental changes had synergistic effects.[3]

Cannabis markets after legalization

This section highlights the available information on licensees, sales, tax revenues, prices, and advertising. Information about the size of the illegal market is provided in the Other Public Safety Outcomes section.

Producers and other non-retail licensees

The LCB is responsible for distributing licenses to cannabis related entities ranging from producers to processors to retail outlets. The LCB's fiscal year 2020 report notes that there were more than 1,800 active cannabis licenses in the state, with nearly three-quarters going to those who produce and/or process cannabis (Figure 9.1).[4]

Retail outlets

Access to outlets for nonmedical cannabis purchasing grew steadily from July 2014, when the market opened, to late 2018 (Figure 9.2). Since mid-2018, the number of licensees has been relatively stable at around 435 stores.[5]

In a study comparing Washington's 'grey market' of unregulated medical cannabis outlets (i.e., collective gardens) prior to legalization with the legal market, researchers identified 224 'grey market' outlets operating in early 2014, and 433 state-licensed cannabis outlets in December 2018 (Dilley et al., n.d.a). Unregulated markets were not evenly dispersed in the state as they were subject to the limitation of whether they could operate with tacit approval from their communities. In comparison to unregulated grey market outlets, state-licensed cannabis stores in Washington were significantly more likely to be located in census tracts with greater percentages of residents under age 21 (e.g., areas with college campuses), more likely to be located in communities that were rural, have a greater percentage of people in poverty, and have a greater percentage of White residents (Dilley et al., n.d.c; Tabb et al., 2018). These findings have

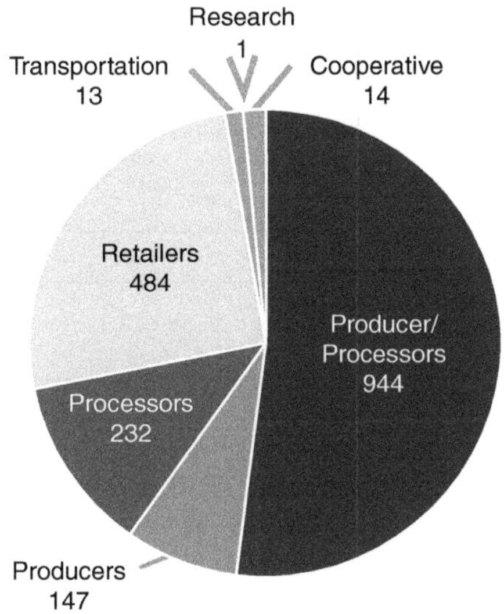

Figure 9.1 Active cannabis licenses in Washington in fiscal year 2020
Note: Retailers includes all businesses that are licensed by the LCB but some licensed retailers are not allowed to operate due to local restrictions
Source: Washington State Liquor and Cannabis Board (2020)

implications for how the market may affect different populations, as exposure to retail outlets can affect consumption.

Because Washington applied area-specific caps on the number of retail outlets that can be licensed, market growth is limited to some extent and dispersion of businesses is not entirely market-driven. Immediately following legalization, many communities in Washington acted to temporarily or permanently ban cannabis businesses. Two years following the opening of the state's cannabis retail markets about 30 percent of Washington's population lived in communities where retail sales were banned (Dilley et al., 2017). By 2018, some communities had relaxed their policies so that only 22 percent of the population were living in communities where cannabis retail businesses were banned (Dilley et al., n.d.c). Some communities acted to restrict the location or number of businesses in addition to state requirements, for example by implementing policies to require greater minimum distances between cannabis licensees and specified sites (e.g., substance use treatment facilities, parks, residential zones). Some tribal governments also exerted their authority to negotiate compacts with Washington's state government and enter the cannabis market: at the end of 2020 six of Washington's 29 federally recognized tribes had at least one cannabis business licensed within their boundaries (500 Nations, 2019).

As policies have relaxed over time and the number of retailers has grown, Washington residents statewide have been increasingly exposed to retail outlets (see Figure 9.3) (Everson et al., 2019).

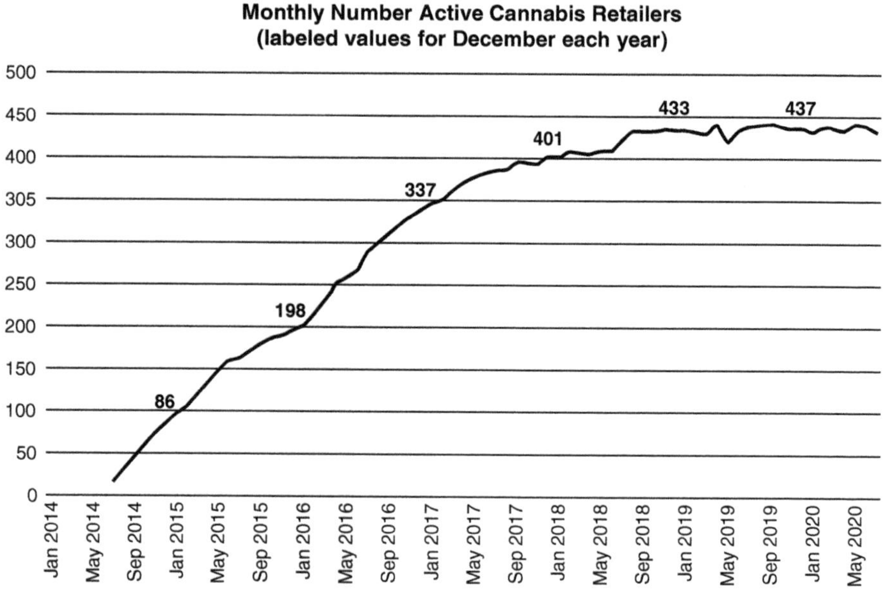

Figure 9.2 Monthly number of cannabis retailers making sales* in Washington
Note: *Fewer retailers are actively selling cannabis in comparison to the total number that are licensed, as shown in Figure 9.1, due to local restrictions such as bans that prevent operation
Source: Washington State Liquor and Cannabis Board (LCB) cannabis market tracking system. Numbers are shown for December of each calendar year

Cannabis sales and tax revenues

Washington's LCB tracks cannabis plants and products from 'seed-to-sale', including amounts and type of products sold. Several analyses have documented that legal sales increased over time (Firth et al., 2020a; Davenport, 2021; Caulkins et al., 2018; Smart et al., 2017). A recent summary of Washington's total pre-tax cannabis retail sales showed that there is some seasonal variation, but sales have continued to steadily increase over time. Sales increased at an even greater than expected rate during the COVID-19 pandemic, following initial 'stay at home' orders in the state during March 2020, and reaching an all-time monthly high of $129 million in total retail sales during May 2020 (Figure 9.4) (Dilley et al., n.d.d; Schauer et al, 2021).

The products sold within this cannabis market are also evolving. Washington's data show the legal cannabis market has trended toward flower products with delta-9-tetrahydrocannabinol (THC) concentration over 20 percent and extract products with over 60 percent THC (Smart et al., 2017). While flower dominates legal sales in WA, the fastest growing segment is extracts for inhalation which includes high-potency oils and concentrates (Figure 9.5) (Firth et al., 2020a). Discussions regarding the regulation of potency typically concern the concentrations of THC and/or cannabidiol (CBD), and the state

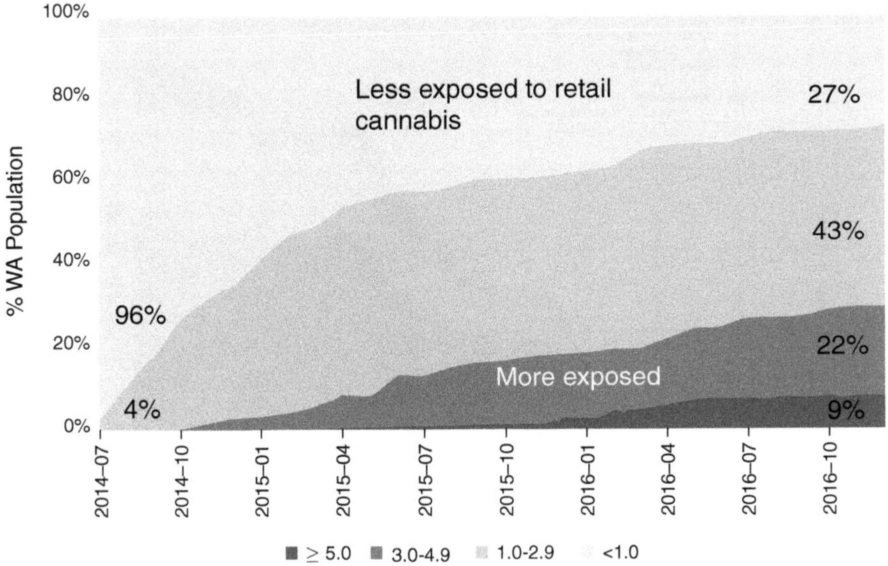

Figure 9.3 Percentage of WA residents in communities with different levels of cannabis retailer density (access density, quartiles), 2014–2016
Source: Reproduced from Everson et al. (2019)

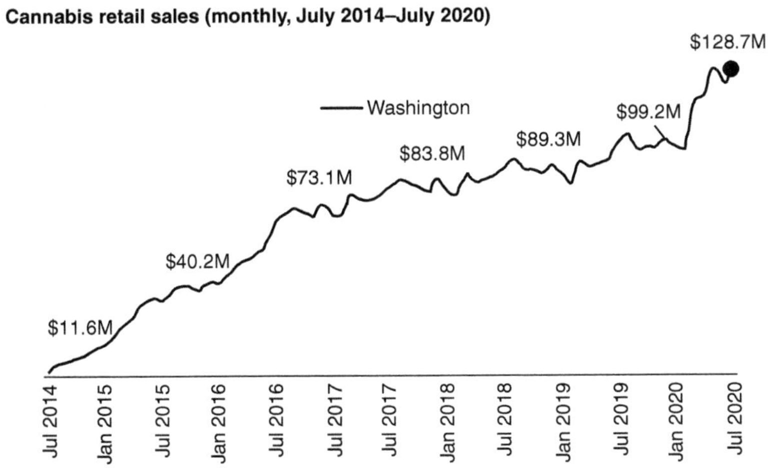

Figure 9.4 Monthly cannabis retail sales in Washington, July 2014–July 2020
Source: (Dilley et al., n.d.d.)

recently convened a workgroup on cannabis product potency to inform ongoing considerations by policymakers about whether to apply restrictions on products by potency (Carlini et al., 2020; Washington State Liquor and

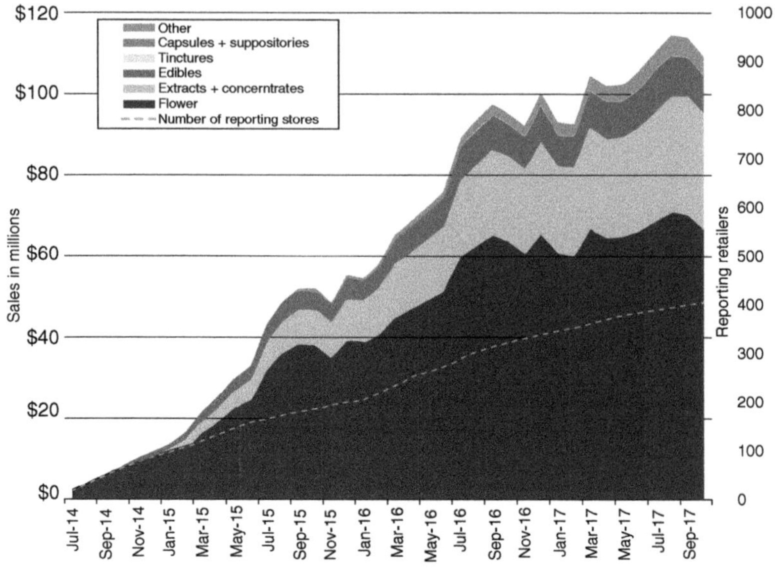

Figure 9.5 Monthly sales of cannabis by product type in Washington, July 2014–October 2017
Source: Reproduced from Firth et al. (2020a)

Cannabis Board, n.d.b). The state does not currently provide data that can allow for separation of designated medical products from other products.

I-502 initially specified a 25 percent tax applied at each of the 'three-tier system' levels (producer, processor, retail). In July 2015, as a result of tax reforms defined by the state legislature (Washington State Legislature), and revised Washington rules (Washington State Legislature, 2021), these were consolidated to a single excise tax applied as 37 percent of all retail sales. In fiscal year 2019, Washington generated nearly $400 million in cannabis taxes and licensing fees, which works out to about $50 per person and is similar to the per capita rate collected in Colorado (Kilmer, 2020). Most of these revenues were dedicated to basic health care and the state's general fund. Some tax revenues were also used to support prevention, treatment, enforcement, and research (Washington State Treasurer; Northwest Prevention Technology Transfer Center, 2020).

Retail prices

Because of a change in the 'seed-to-sale' tracking system, the most reliable retail price series for cannabis in Washington goes through October 2017. All cannabis products have seen a large reduction in price since the market opened (Figure 9.6), with one analysis finding:

> In October 2017, price per 10mg THC was roughly $3 among edibles, 70 cents among extract cartridges, and 30–40 cents for other flower and

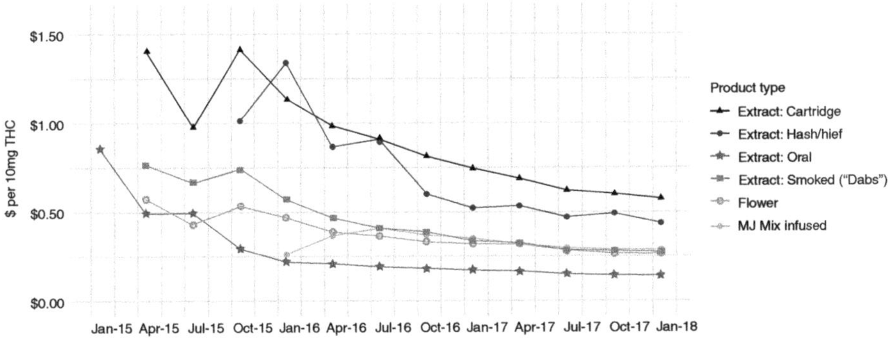

Figure 9.6 Regression-based estimates for price per 10 mg THC by product/subtype over time in Washington

Note: These regressions included fixed effects for the lab that conducted the test

Source: Reproduced from Davenport (2021)

> other extracts; solid concentrates offered the lowest priced THC among extract products. Price declines continue but have slowed.
>
> (Davenport, 2021, p. 1)

Advertising

There are concerns that advertising may normalize and increase cannabis use, including potentially problematic use (e.g., frequent use and use of high potency products). In response to complaints from stakeholders and concerns of legislators, the state acted in 2017 to restrict cannabis advertising, limiting billboard content and street marketing (e.g., 'sign-wavers' and mechanized displays).[39] An analysis of cannabis marketing violations issued by the LCB immediately following the opening of the adult use commercial market (October 2014 to September 2015), and again from May 2017 to July 2019, obtained 328 violations filed against 183 cannabis businesses (over both periods). The most common advertisement violations were storefront and online advertisements that included banned content (e.g. including cartoons that are appealing to minors) or were related to size or location of the advertisement (e.g., sandwich boards on public sidewalks) (Carlini et al., 2022). Unfortunately, we are not aware of any efforts to systematically measure exposure to marketing in Washington state, although some other states (e.g., Oregon) have assessed this using adult or youth surveys and found a majority of people report seeing cannabis advertising in their communities (Fiala et al., 2018, 2020).

Cannabis use

This section highlights what is known about cannabis availability and use in Washington and how it has changed since the passage of I-502. It distinguishes between youth and adults and reviews the available evidence on total cannabis consumption in the state. We remind readers that they should not draw causal inferences from the trend data reported in this or other sections. One must also acknowledge that people may be more honest about reporting cannabis use when there is less stigma around the drug after legalization; however, we are unaware of any research documenting this.

Youth

The effects of cannabis legalization specifically on youth, and youth growing up in a legalized context, are still unclear. Experience with tobacco and alcohol regulation indicates that youth access and perceived acceptability will be sensitive to regulatory environments that influence availability, price, enforcement, and advertising (Pacula et al., 2014). However, while the regulated market was opening up in Washington, efforts were being made to curb the unregulated medical market. School-based surveys find that the

Table 9.2 Self-reported youth cannabis use prevalence and accessibility, 2010–2018

Percentage of youth with outcome, within grade (±margin of error)						
		2010	2012	2014*	2016	2018
Any cannabis use in past 30 days	6th grade	1.6% ±0.4	1.2% ±0.4	1.3% ±0.4	0.8% ±0.2	1.3% ±0.3
	8th grade	9.5% ±1.1	9.4% ±1.0	7.3% ±1.0	6.4% ±1.1	7.2% ±1.0
	10th grade	20.0% ±1.8	19.3% ±1.6	18.1% ±1.6	17.2% ±1.6	17.9% ±1.6
	12th grade	26.3% ±2.0	26.7% ±1.4	26.7% ±2.2	26.5% ±1.8	26.2% ±2.1
Using cannabis 10+ of past 30 days	6th grade	0.3% ±0.1	0.1% ±0.1	0.3% ±0.1	0.2% ±0.1	0.2% ±0.1
	8th grade	2.5% ±0.5	2.6% ±0.3	2.3% ±0.5	1.9% ±0.4	1.8% ±0.4
	10th grade	6.2% ±0.8	6.4% ±1.0	5.9% ±0.9	5.5% ±0.8	5.1% ±0.9
	12th grade	9.9% ±1.4	9.4% ±1.1	10.3% ±1.3	10.5% ±1.3	9.3% ±1.1
Perceive cannabis would be "very easy" to get	6th grade	4.3% ±0.6	3.6% ±0.7	3.5% ±0.6	2.7% ±0.4	3.3% ±0.5
	8th grade	12.9% ±1.5	14.2% ±1.8	10.9% ±1.6	10.1% ±1.4	10.6% ±1.3
	10th grade	33.1% ±2.6	31.4% ±2.5	32.4% ±2.5	27.1% ±2.2	27.3% ±2.3
	12th grade	42.8% ±2.3	42.2% ±2.5	42.1% ±2.5	40.8% ±1.9	37.8% ±2.7

Source: Washington State Healthy Youth Survey (HYS), 2010–2018

percentage of youth in Washington who said it would be "not very hard" or would be "easy" to get cannabis declined after cannabis legalization in the state (see Table 9.2). The prevalence of both current use (on one or more of the past 30 days) and frequent use (ten or more days in the past 30 days) of cannabis declined or remained stable among 6th, 8th, 10th, and 12th grade youth in Washington State in 2014–2018 (after legalization) compared to 2010–2012 (see Table 9.2) (Washington State Liquor and Cannabis Board, 2020).

An early study that used national Monitoring the Future (MTF) data reported increased cannabis use for 8th and 10th grade students in WA after legalization (Cerdá et al., 2017). A study using Washington's much larger and state-representative school-based survey found statewide decreases (Dilley et al., 2019), as had been reported in the state's reports (see Table 9.1); however, this latter study did not include data from comparison states. Both studies documented no change in cannabis use among 12th graders. Each of these surveys is well-established and of high quality; differences in findings may be related to design and sampling.[6]

There may be important differences in effects of cannabis legalization among different types of youth. Gender and age may be contributing factors: among the first four states to legalize retail cannabis (Washington, Colorado, Oregon, Alaska), state-based youth surveys identified a consistent pattern of post-legalization increases in cannabis use among older girls (11–12th grades), in comparison to younger girls (8–10th grade) and all ages of boys (Dilley et al., n.d.b). Another study of Washington youth documented increases in cannabis use among youth who work in part-time jobs, with a pronounced effect by age (greater risk among older youth) and number of hours worked per week (Graves et al., 2019).

Adults

Cannabis use among adults has increased in Washington post-legalization: results from an interrupted time series analysis found adult current use (on one or more of the past 30 days) grew significantly between 2009 and 2016, not significantly changing immediately after legalization, but increasing after commercial retail markets opened in 2014 (Figure 9.7) (Everson et al., 2019). Further analysis using multilevel longitudinal models to control for within-state changes that may have contributed to changes in cannabis use found that the effects of legalization on cannabis use patterns was most pronounced among adults in areas with greater access to cannabis retailers. For example, by the end of 2016 current use significantly increased among adults living near a retailer (e.g., within 0.8 miles: odds ratio [OR]=1.45; 95% confidence interval [CI]=1.24, 1.69). Odds for frequent use (defined as using 20 or more days in the past 30) also increased among adults living within 0.8 miles of a retailer (OR=1.43; 95% CI=1.15, 1.77).[7]

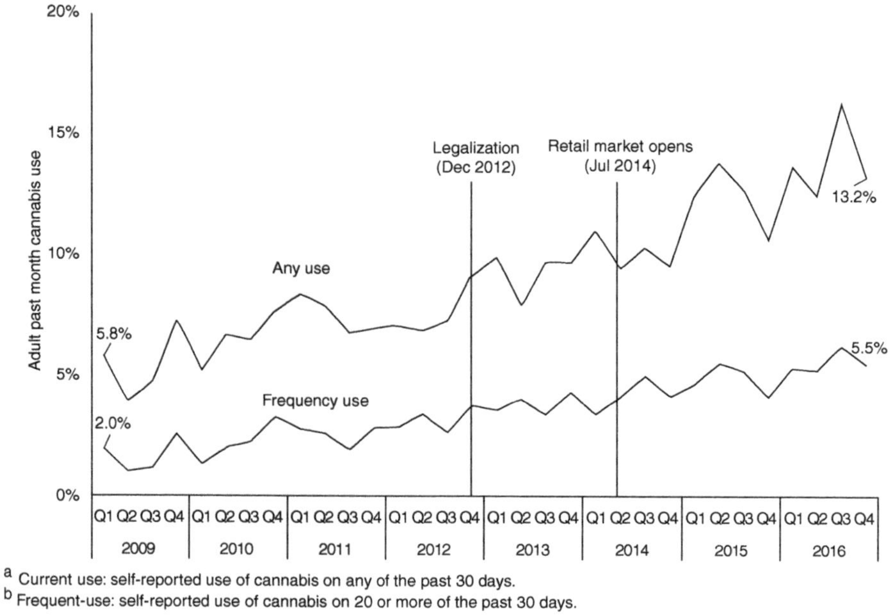

Figure 9.7 Adult cannabis current use and frequent-use prevalence, by quarter, Behavioral Risk Factor Surveillance System, Washington, 2009–2016
Source: Reproduced from Everson et al. (2019)

Total consumption

An analysis based on general population survey data (National Survey on Drug Use and Health [NSDUH]) and insights from a web survey of people who use cannabis estimated that in 2013 – the year before retail stores opened – Washington residents consumed 175 metric tons (MT) of cannabis, with a plausible range of 135 to 225 MT (Kilmer et al., 2013). RAND researchers conducted a follow-up analysis focused on the three years after the stores opened and noted:

> The analysis presented here for Washington State is similar enough to what was done previously (Kilmer et al., 2013) that it allows for crude comparisons over time in terms of flower equivalents. For 2013, our best estimate for total cannabis consumed by Washington residents was 175 MT (135–225). Our rounded FY 2017 estimate of 250 MT (200–300) is roughly 40-percent larger, but the wide and overlapping uncertainty bands surrounding these figures suggest that one should be careful about making strong claims about the precise magnitude of the increase.
>
> (Kilmer et al., 2019, p. 37)

Another study attempted to gain insight about changes in total cannabis consumption using wastewater analysis. While this approach is common in

Europe and increasingly used in other parts of the world, it is relatively rare in the United States. Focusing on 1 December 2013 to 31 December 2016, Burgard and colleagues report that wastewater estimates for THC-COOH (a THC metabolite) suggest a doubling in cannabis consumption over this three-year period (Burgard et al., 2019). However, the authors caution that:

> For the purposes of this study, we assume an unknown but constant excretion rate. However, as the market matures and the WA cannabis market shifts towards more edibles and extracts this excretion rate will probably also shift. More work is needed to understand more clearly THC excretion factors and in-sewer degradation/conversion of THC-COOH.
>
> (p. 1588)

Other public health outcomes

This section highlights the available evidence on adverse health events and substance use treatment admissions in Washington. The previous caveat about the possibility of people being more honest about cannabis use post-legalization applies to this section as well. This section is focused on harms as we are not aware of any research examining how legalization has influenced the medical use of cannabis and the extent to which this has produced health benefits in Washington. Of course, absence of evidence is not the same as evidence of absence.

Adverse health events

In an analysis of trends in emergency department visits among Medicaid enrollees for 2006–2015, researchers with the state agency that manages public-paid healthcare systems found that cannabis-related emergency department visits (i.e., visits with codes for cannabis abuse or dependence) had increased generally during the period, with the biggest increases in 2014–2015 (Hong, 2018).

Cannabis-related exposures reported to the Washington Poison Center are a sentinel indicator for underlying adverse health experiences. While reported exposures for cannabis in Washington are not common, there have been notable increases, particularly beginning in 2014 (see Figure 9.8) (Dilley, 2020).[3] Two specific elements of these trends are notable from a public health perspective. First, reported exposures have continued to increase for all age groups and specifically among children under the age of 12, which may indicate accidental exposures. A qualitative examination of all cannabis-related exposures in 2016 that were reported to the Washington Poison Center for children under age 12 (n=50) indicated that most children exposed were very young (88 percent under age 6), all were unintentional, and among those with source information 90 percent of cannabis involved in the exposure was from a parent or grandparent (Close et al., 2020).

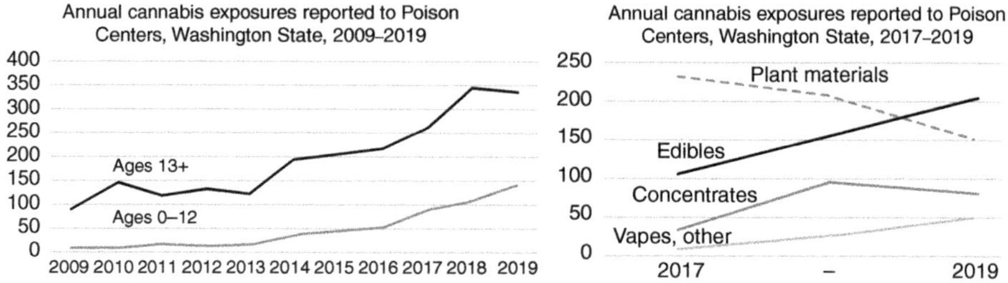

Figure 9.8 Annual number of cannabis-related exposures reported to Poison Centers, Washington State, 2009–2019
Source: Analysis of data used in Dilley et al. (2021) and Firth (2021)

Further, cannabis-related exposures for plant materials (e.g., flower) are declining, but exposures from manufactured products (e.g., edibles, concentrates, vapes), which may contain higher levels of THC than plant materials, are increasing (Dilley et al., 2019; Firth, 2021). An analysis of national data indicated that both of these trends are more common in states that have legalized retail cannabis in comparison to those that have not (Dilley et al., 2019; Whitehill et al., 2019).[7]

Treatment admissions

Based on data from the state's publicly funded substance use treatment systems, the annual number of admissions for cannabis-involved treatment services increased steadily from 2002 to 2009 but declined steadily from 2009 to 2015. These declines in recent years were specifically observed for treatment where cannabis was the first-listed treatment goal and for treatment services that were not mandated by criminal justice system involvement (Pacula et al., 2021).

A separate study of Washington State Medicaid enrollees evaluated the association between local access to legalized cannabis and utilization and publicly funded substance use disorder (SUD) treatment related to cannabis (Hong et al., in preparation). Results indicated that residents living in closer proximity to cannabis retail stores were admitted to SUD treatment at a higher rate than those living in communities when there was less or no access to retail cannabis.

Cannabis-related arrests and convictions

Cannabis-specific crimes

Statewide, adult legalization of cannabis has drastically reduced the number of people arrested and convicted for cannabis-related crimes, yet the effect of legalization on arrest rates varied by population group. Overall, the number of criminal incidents involving cannabis and reported to the FBI by law enforcement in Washington state decreased by 63 percent three years after legalization, from 6,336 in 2012 to 2,313 in 2015 (Firth et al., 2019).

The rate of arrest among adults at least 21 years old for cannabis crimes dropped by 87 percent after legalization (Firth et al., 2019). For underage adults ages 18 to 20 years, arrest rates for cannabis crimes decreased, but not as dramatically as among older adults who can legally possess cannabis (Firth et al., 2019). For people convicted under the age of 21, misdemeanor possession of cannabis declined in the first year after legalization by 29 percent from 1,015 in the first quarter of 2012 to 722 in the first quarter of 2013 (Pacula et al., 2021). One national study found that state legalization of cannabis for adults, including in Washington, had no effect on cannabis possession arrests among person under the age of 18 (Plunk et al., 2019). However, Washington's neighbor, Oregon, saw the number of cannabis allegations increase by 28 percent – allegations that include possession offenses – for persons under the age of 18 following adult legalization (Firth et al., 2019).

Racial disparities in cannabis-related arrests

Prior to I-502, Washington had a history of disproportionately arresting people of color for cannabis and other drug-related crimes (Beckett et al., 2005; Task Force On Race and the Criminal Justice System, 2012). People of color represented roughly 30 percent of Washington state's population in 2019: Latinx is the largest community of color and accounts for 13 percent of the state's population; 9 percent are Asian, and 4 percent are Black (Washington State Office of Financial Management, 2020). Despite documented overrepresentation of Latinx adults in Washington state's criminal justice system (Beckett et al., 2005; Vera institute of Justice, 2019), law enforcement are not required to report Latinx ethnicity of people involved in criminal incidents to the FBI (Criminal Justice Information Services Division, 2018). Therefore, disparity analyses of cannabis legalization typically compare Black and white arrest rates. Using an interrupted time series approach to examine the impacts of legalization on racial disparities in arrest, Black adults ages 21 and older in Washington were 2.5 times more likely to be arrested for cannabis crimes than whites prior to adult legalization (Firth et al., 2019). Arrest rates for Black adults dropped after legalization of possession in Washington, but the *relative* disparity between Black and white arrest rates grew to five times higher after the retail market opened in 2014 (Firth et al., 2019). The disparity in arrest rates between Black and white underage adults, persons 18 to 20 years of age, did not change after legalization in Washington; Black underage adults remained 70 percent more likely to be arrested for cannabis crimes (Firth et al., 2019).[8] Practices such as over-policing in low-income neighborhoods and racial profiling (Washington State Office of Financial Management, 2020) may have mitigated some of the potential positive impacts of I-502.

Other public safety outcomes

This section extends the previous criminal justice discussion, focusing on the available evidence about how legalization has influenced traffic safety, non-drug specific criminal activity, and the size of the illegal cannabis market in Washington.

Traffic safety

A 2020 study from Washington found that the share of drivers in fatal crashes who had THC in their blood had nearly doubled since December 2012 (Tefft & Arnold, 2020). While concerning, this does not tell us how legalization has influenced overall traffic safety in the state. One must not only account for the fact that legalization could influence other types of impaired driving accidents, but without a comparison group it is difficult to attribute any changes to legalization versus other factors. In addition, just because someone has cannabis in their system does not mean that consumption played a role in the crash (Compton, 2017).

Another report focused exclusively on driving under the influence (DUI) in Washington concluded:

> we documented an increase in the proportion of DUI cases involving THC and an increase in the level of THC in cases from 2005–2014 among cases tested by toxicology, excluding those positive for alcohol, however there was no additional increase related to the passage of I-502 in 2012.
>
> (Banta-Green et al., 2016, p. 3)

Most of the peer-reviewed studies examining this question have lumped the legalization states together and compared them with non-legalization states; making it hard to isolate the effect in Washington. Early studies which examine the period immediately after the laws passed found no effect on traffic fatalities (Aydelotte et al., 2017; Hansen et al., 2020), but those including additional years which captured time after the retail stores opened found a small, positive, and possibly temporary increase in traffic fatalities (Aydelotte et al., 2019; Lane & Hall, 2019). A more recent study which focused on Colorado and Washington separately found that legalization was associated with increased traffic fatalities in the former, but not the latter (Santaella-Tenorio et al., 2020).

Washington's DUI arrests do not distinguish between cannabis and other drugs, and when alcohol is also involved, the arrest record may only indicate alcohol use since it is easier to measure. However, examining trends in drug-only DUI arrests may be useful. After declining from 2011 to 2015, the number of non-alcohol-involved DUI arrests in Washington has increased annually during the past several years, from 1,222 in 2015 to a new record high of 2,029 in 2018 (Forecasting and Research Division, 2019). Washington requires that drivers who are killed in traffic crashes must have blood tested for drugs, and many surviving drivers involved in fatal traffic crashes are also tested. Among those drivers that were tested, the percentage who tested positive for Delta-9 THC was 8–10 percent per year in 2008–2013, but increased to 22 percent in 2014 – the year that Washington's retail cannabis market opened – and then has increased steadily each year to reach a new high of 26 percent in 2017 (Forecasting and Research Division, 2019). For the same period, the percentage of these drivers who also tested positive for alcohol or other drugs has declined gradually. However, as previously noted, presence of cannabis in blood does not necessarily mean that consumption played a role in the crash (Compton, 2017).

Non-drug specific criminal activity

So far, there does not appear to be much evidence that cannabis legalization in Washington has affected non-drug specific crimes. Using an interrupted time series approach focused on Colorado and Washington, Lu et al. (2019) concluded:

> Our results suggest that marijuana legalization and sales have had minimal to no effect on major crimes in Colorado or Washington. We observed no statistically significant long-term effects of recreational cannabis laws or the initiation of retail sales on violent or property crime rates in these states.
>
> (p. 565)

However, one must be careful about drawing strong inferences from analyses that do not include information from states that did not legalize cannabis.

Using a similar methodology and focusing on a different outcome measure - clearance rate, which captures the share of reported crimes that result in an arrest – Makin et al. (2019) found no evidence that legalization of cannabis negatively affected clearance rates for violent and property crime in Colorado and Washington. In fact, they report that for some crimes the clearance rate actually improved, leading them to conclude:

> Moreover, in the absence of other compelling explanations, the current evidence suggests that legalization produced some demonstrable and persistent benefit in clearance rates, benefits we believe are associated with the marijuana legalization proponents' prediction that legalization would positively influence police performance.
>
> (Makin et al., 2019, p. 32)

However, another analysis which included additional years of data and incorporated data from all states found that legalization of cannabis did not affect clearance rates in Washington (Jorgensen & Harper, 2020).

A different analysis by Makin and colleagues examined calls for service to the police in two border cities: Pullman, Washington and Moscow, Idaho (Makin et al., 2020). They conclude:

> Our findings demonstrate that recreational sales were associated with an increase in calls for service for the Pullman Police Department, and no change in calls for service for the Moscow Police Department. Importantly, these results do not document changes in calls across any of what would be considered Part I index crimes. Rather, this increase in Pullman seems more associated with changes in calls associated with concerns for social welfare.
>
> (p. 9)

Size of the illegal cannabis market

When thinking about how legalization has affected the illegal cannabis market, it is important to make a distinction: the share of consumption by Washington residents that is coming from licensed vs. unlicensed sellers, and the amount of cannabis that is being illegally exported outside of Washington. The latter is very difficult to measure. Data from the Northwest High Intensity Drug Trafficking Area suggest the number of cannabis seizures outside of Washington involving cannabis originating from Washington decreased from 2010 to 2013, increased until 2015, and then fell again in 2016 (Figure 9.9); the size of these seizures was not reported.[9] One study examining discovered grow sites in national forests in Washington did not find a statistically significant change after legalization, but this does not tell us much about overall illegal activity.

Combining data from Washington's seed-to-sale tracking data, NSDUH, and a web survey fielded in 2018, Kilmer et al. conducted an analysis focused on the third year after the retail market was established in Washington. Not only did the

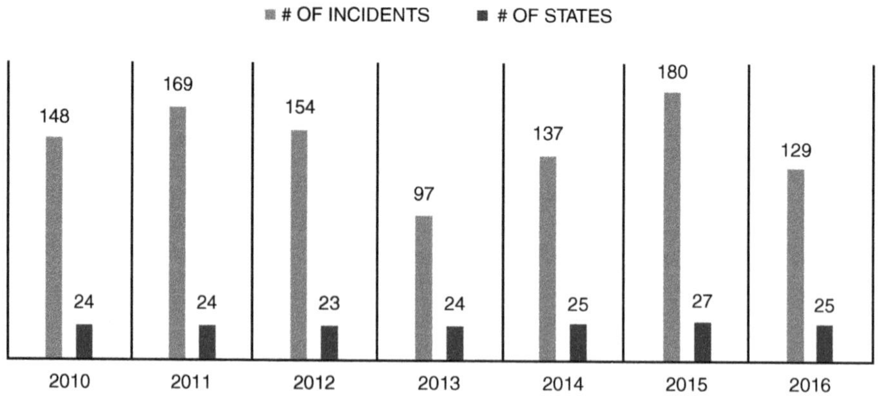

Figure 9.9 Cannabis originating from Washington that was seized in other states
Source: Chart from NWHIDTA, reproduced in Firth et al. (2019)
Notes: Reproduced with permission from NWHIDTA

authors estimate that total consumption had increased (discussed earlier), they found that between 40 percent to 60 percent of the THC obtained by Washington residents was purchased at state-licensed stores (Kilmer et al., 2019). We are unaware of more recent analyses which look beyond the first three years of legalization.

Concluding thoughts

It has been about nine years since Washington and Colorado passed legalization in 2012. Since that time, as of September 2021, 16 more states and Washington, DC, as well as the countries of Uruguay and Canada, have removed the prohibition on cannabis and allowed some form of supply to adults for nonmedical purposes. With an increasing number of jurisdictions in the U.S. (e.g., Pennsylvania) and elsewhere (e.g., Mexico) having serious conversations about legalizing sales, it seems very likely that more governments will head down this path. While there does not appear to be much appetite for non-profit cooperatives or other middle ground legalization approaches in the U.S., it will be interesting to see how this plays out in other countries.

This chapter provides a detailed examination of the evolution of cannabis laws and policies in Washington, including integration of Washington's previously unregulated medical market, and a review of the emerging evidence about how these changes may have affected health and safety outcomes. As more jurisdictions around the world contemplate cannabis legalization, many may turn to the first places to do so and ask "what will happen if we legalize?" However, the answers are not simple and may not be transferrable to other locations. While it has been almost nine years since Washington voters passed I-502, there is still much to learn. Given that retail stores did not open until July 2014 and there are significant data lags with many key datasets (as well as with publication in peer-reviewed journals), the overall effect is not a settled question. Even if there was a consensus on the short-run effects, the results may be very different in the long run. Further, whether one considers legalization a "success" or "failure" will likely be shaped by people's values and preferences for risk.

The longer-run consequences will also depend on actions taken by the state and localities (e.g., will potency limits or major changes in taxes be implemented?) as well as potential actions taken by the federal government. Federal legalization that allows cannabis products to be transported across state lines could dramatically affect the economic landscape of cannabis in Washington and other states. Indeed, with federal legalization, cannabis production could concentrate very quickly since all the cannabis consumed in the U.S. could be produced on a few dozen typical farms (Caulkins et al., 2016; Kilmer et al., 2021). And if Amazon and other large international companies are allowed to supply cannabis, this could have serious implications for retail prices as well as the viability of smaller cannabis businesses.[10]

By focusing on the experiences of Washington, we hope this chapter makes it clear that legalization is a complex and dynamic process that can be difficult to capture with a simple "yes" or "no" categorization. Understanding the consequences of alternatives to cannabis prohibition requires continued legal and policy surveillance and the acknowledgement that local variation may influence outcome evaluations.

Notes

1 Vermont implemented a "grow and give" model in 2018, but in October 2020 the governor signed the bill to create a commercial industry for nonmedical cannabis supply. This leaves Washington, DC as the only jurisdiction in the U.S. to legalize without creating a licensed commercial regime; however, there is a booming grey market in the District (Kaplan, 2019).

2 When this document refers to Washington, it refers to the state of Washington, not Washington, DC.

3 A new study focused on Washington finds that "legalizing cannabis leads to a 15 percent decrease in alcohol, mainly by liquor and wine, and 5 percent decrease in cigarette demand" (Miller & Seo, 2021, p. 107).

4 The LCB also reports that in FY 2020 it received more than over 1,000 change applications related to cannabis, mostly for changes in ownership and making alterations to the licensees' premises.

5 The LCB, which also regulates alcohol licenses, reported that in the same year there were over 18,000 alcohol retail licenses (and another 8,000 non-retail licenses).

6 MTF collects Washington-specific data as part of a U.S. region sample, rather than to provide generalizable information for the state. MTF also oversamples rural areas, where other Washington studies documented increases in cannabis outlets after legalization (Dilley et al., n.d.a).

7 Findings were replicated in a separate study that also found increases in cannabis use and frequency of use by Washington adults, with concentrated effects in rural communities (Ambrose et al., 2021).

8 Statewide evaluations of I-502 on cannabis crimes provide an overview or 'average effect' of legalization. This approach does not consider how the effects of legalization vary within the state and whether local policies, as discussed in a previous section, have different effects on cannabis crime outcomes. Examining trends in cannabis crimes within specific law enforcement agencies is informative because new cannabis crimes were created in response to legalization. For example, violations for public consumption of cannabis cannot be directly queried from state criminal justice datasets; however, the Seattle Police Department found a disproportionate number of citations for public consumption of cannabis were issued to Black people in Seattle during 2015 (Vera Institute of Justice, 2019).

9 For additional insights about cannabis seizures in Washington see Darnell et al. (2019), Appendix II.

10 What this would mean for Washington, at least in terms of tax revenue, is a bit unclear since Amazon is headquartered in Seattle.

References

500 Nations. (21 October 2019). Tribe opens cannabis retail store in Sequim. *500 Nations*. Retrieved from: https://www.500nations.com/Washington-Cannabis.asp (last accessed 25 October 2021).

Ambrose, C. A., Cowan, B. W., & Rosenman, R. E. (2021). Geographical access to recreational marijuana. *Contemporary Economic Policy*, 39(4), 778–807. doi:https://doi.org/10.1111/COEP.12518.

Aydelotte, J. D., Brown, L. H., Luftman, K. M., Mardock, A. L., Pedro, G. R., Texeira., Coopwood, B., & Brown, C. V. R. (2017). Crash fatality rates after recreational marijuana legalization in Washington and Colorado. *American Journal of Public Health*, 107(8), 1329–1331. doi:https://doi.org/10.2105/AJPH.2017.303848.

Aydelotte, J. D., Mardock, A. L., Mancheski, C. A., Quamar, S. M., Texeira, P. G., Brown, C. V. R., & Brown, L. H. (2019). Fatal crashes in the 5 years after recreational marijuana legalization in Colorado and Washington. *Accident Analysis & Prevention*, 132(105284). doi:https://doi.org/10.1016/j.aap.2019.105284.

Banta-Green, C. J., Rowhani-Rahbar, A., Ebel, B. E., Andris, L. M., & Qiu, Q. (2016). Cannabis use among drivers suspected of driving under the influence or involved in collisions: Analyses of Washington State Patrol data. Retrieved from: https://aaafoundation.org/wp-content/uploads/2017/12/CannabisUseAmongDriversInWashington.pdf (last accessed 29 September 2021).

Beckett, K., Nyrop, K., Pfingst, L., & Bowen, M. (2005). Drug use, drug possession arrests, and the question of race: Lessons from Seattle. *Social Problems*, 52(3), 419–441. doi:https://doi.org/10.1525/sp.2005.52.3.419.

Beekman, D., & Clarridge, C. (8 February 2018). Seattle to vacate hundreds of misdemeanor marijuana convictions, dismiss charges. *The Seatle Times*. Retrieved from: https://www.seattletimes.com/seattle-news/seattle-to-vacate-misdemeanor-marijuana-convictions-dismiss-charges/ (last accessed 27 September 2021).

Burgard, D. A., Williams, J., Westerman, D., Rushing, R., Carpenter, R., LaRock, A., Sadetsky, J., Clarke, J., Fryhle, H., Pellman, M., & Banta-Green, C. J. (2019). Using wastewater-based analysis to monitor the effects of legalized retail sales on cannabis consumption in Washington State, USA. *Addiction*, 114(9), 1582–1590. doi:https://doi.org/10.1111/ADD.14641.

Carlini, B., Barbosa-Leiker, C., Cuttler, C., Dilley, J., Firth, C., Haggerty, K., Kilmer, J., McDonell, M., Stella, N., Walker, D., & Willits, D. (2020). Cannabis concentration and health risks, a report for the Washington State Prevention Research Subcommittee. PRSC. Retrieved from: https://pttcnetwork.org/centers/northwest-pttc/news/cannabis-concentration-and-health-risks-report-washington-state (last accessed 25 October 2021).

Carlini, B. H., Garrett, S. B., Firth, C. L., & Pinsky, I. (2022). Cannabis industry marketing violations in Washington State, 2014–2019. *Journal of Studies on Alcohol and Drugs*, 83(1), 18–26.

Caulkins, J. P., Bao, Y., Davenport S, Fahli, I., Guo, Y., Kinnard, K., Najewicz, M., Renaud, L., & Kilmer, B. (2018). Big data on a big new market: Insights from Washington State's legal cannabis market. *The International Journal of Drug Policy*, 57, 86–94. doi:htpps://doi.org/10.1016/j.drugpo.2018.03.031.

Caulkins, J., Kilmer, B., & Kleiman, M. (2016). *Marijuana Legalization: What Everyone Needs to Know* (2nd edition). Oxford: Oxford University Press.

Caulkins, J. P., Kilmer, B., Kleiman, M., MacCoun, R. J., Midgette, G., Oglesby, P., Pacula, R. L., & Reuter, P. H. (2015) *Considering Marijuana Legalization: Insights for Vermont and Other Jurisdictions*. Santa Monica, CA: RAND Corporation.

Cerdá, M., & Kilmer, B. (2017). Uruguay's middle-ground approach to cannabis legalization. *International Journal of Drug Policy*, 42, 118–120. doi:https://doi.org/10.1016/j.drugpo.2017.02.007.

Cerdá, M., Wall, M., Feng, T., Keyes, M. K., Sarvet, A., Schulenberg, J., O'Malley, P. M., Pacula, L. R., Galea, S., & Hasin, S. D. (2017). Association of state recreational marijuana laws with adolescent marijuana use. *JAMA Pediatrics*, 171 (2), 142–149. doi:https://doi.org/10.1001/jamapediatrics.2016.3624.

Close, N. S., Baseman, J., & Dilley, J. A. (2020). *Cannabis Exposures among Children Reported to the Washington Poison Center after Legalization of Cannabis for Adult Use*. Research Society on Marijuana Annual Scientific Meeting (online).

Cole, J. M. (2013). *Guidance Regarding Marijuana Enforcement*. Washington, DC: Office of the Deputy Attorney General.

Compton, R. (2017). Marijuana-impaired driving – a report to Congress. (DOT HS 812 440). Washington DC. Retrieved from: https://www.nhtsa.gov/sites/nhtsa.gov/files/documents/812440-marijuana-impaired-driving-report-to-congress.pdf (last accessed 24 October 2021).

Coughlin-Bogue, T. (13 July 2016). How Washington State screwed over its medical marijuana dispensaries. *The Stranger*. Retrieved from: https://www.thestranger.com/news/2016/07/13/24332114/how-washington-state-screwed-over-its-medical-marijuana-dispensaries (last accessed 27 September 2021).

Criminal Justice Information Services Division. (n.d.) National incident-based reporting system. Retrieved from: https://ucr.fbi.gov/nibrs/2015/tables/data-tables (last accessed 14 June 2018).

Darnell, A. (2019). *Suppressing Illicit Cannabis Markets after State Marijuana Legalization*. Olympia: Washington State Institute for Public Policy. Retrieved from:https://www.wsipp.wa.gov/ReportFile/1708/Wsipp_Suppressing-Illicit-Cannabis-Markets-After-State-Marijuana-Legalization_Report.pdf(last accessed28 March 2022).

Darnell, A., & Bitney, K. (2017). I-502 Evaluation and benefit-cost analysis: Second required report. Olympia: Washington State Institute for Public Policy. Retrieved from: http://www.wsipp.wa.gov/ReportFile/1670/Wsipp_I-502-Evaluation-and-Benefit-Cost-Analysis-Second-Required-Report_Report.pdf (last accessed 27 September 2021)

Davenport, S. (2021). Price and product variation in Washington's recreational cannabis market. *International Journal of Drug Policy*, 91, 102547. doi:https://doi.org/10.1016/j.drugpo.2019.08.004.

Decorte, T., (2018). *Regulating Cannabis: A Detailed Scenario for a Nonprofit Cannabis Market*. Bloomington, IN: Archway Publishing.

Dilley, J. A. (2019). Alcohol deregulation: Considering the hidden costs. *Amercian Journal of Public Health*, 109(6), 840–842. doi:htpps://doi.org/10.2105/AJPH.2019.305104.

Dilley, J. A. (2020). *Building best practices: Cannabis data monitoring for public health*. National Public Health and Marijuana Summit (Plenary Panel for Virtual Conference).

Dilley, J. A., et al. (n.d.a). From gray market to green: describing changes in cannabis outlet distribution between Washington State's unregulated medical market and legal retail market. [in preparation].

Dilley, J. A., et al. (n.d.b). Prevalence of youth cannabis use in the first four states to legalize [in preparation].

Dilley, J. A., et al. (n.d.c). State legalization, local choice [in preparation].

Dilley, J. A., et al. (n.d.d). Viewing cannabis sales from a public health lens: five states with legal cannabis markets [in preparation].

Dilley, J. A., Graves, J. M., Brooks-Russell, A., Whitehill, J. M., & Liebelt, E. L. (2021). Trends and characteristics of manufactured cannabis product and cannabis plant product exposures reported to US Poison Control Centers, 2017–2019. *JAMA Network Open*, 4(5). doi:https://doi.org/10.1001/JAMANETWORKOPEN.2021.10925.

Dilley, J. A., Hitchcock, L., McGroder, N., Greto, L.A., & Richardson, S. M. (2017). Community-level policy responses to state marijuana legalization in Washington State. *International Journal of Drug Policy*, 42, 102–108. doi:https://doi.org/10.1016/j.drugpo.2017.02.010.

Dilley, J. A., Richardson, S. M., Kilmer, B., Pacula, R. L., Segawa, M. B., & Cerdá, M. (2019). Prevalence of cannabis use in youths after legalization in Washington State. *JAMA Pediatrics*, 173(2), 192–193. doi:https://doi.org/10.1001/jamapediatrics.2018.4458.

Drug Policy Alliance. (2018). From prohibition to progress: A status report on marijuana legalization. Retrieved from: http://www.drugpolicy.org/sites/default/files/dpa_marijuana_legalization_report_feb14_2018_0.pdf (last accessed 29 September 2021).

Everson, E. M., Dilley, J. A., Maher, J. E., & Mack, C. E. (2019). post-legalization opening of retail cannabis stores and adult cannabis use in Washington State, 2009–2016. *American Journal of Public Health*, 109(9), 1294–1301. doi:htpps://doi.org/10.2105/AJPH.2019.305191.

Fiala, S. C., Dilley, J. A., Everson, E. M., Firth, C. L., & Maher, J. E. (2020). Youth exposure to marijuana advertising in oregon's legal retail marijuana market. *Preventing Chronic Disease*, 17. doi:https://doi.org/10.5888/PCD17.190206.

Fiala, S. C., Dilley, J. A., Firth, C. L., & Maher, J. E. (2018) Exposure to marijuana marketing after legalization of retail sales: Oregonians' experiences, 2015–2016. *American Journal of Public Health*, 108(1). doi:https://doi.org/10.2105/AJPH.2017.304136.

Firth, C. L. (2021). Calls to Washington Poison Center for intentional exposure to cannabis, 2017–2020. University of Washington addictions, drugs & alcohol. Retrieved from: https://www.learnaboutmarijuanawa.org/topics/health-effects/calls-to-wpc-2017-2020/ (last accessed 25 October 2021).

Firth, C. L., Davenport, S., Smart, R., & Dilley, J. A. (2020a). How high: Differences in the developments of cannabis markets in two legalized states. *International Journal of Drug Policy*, 75, 102611. doi:htpps://doi.org/10.1016/j.drugpo.2019.102611.

Firth, C. L., Hajat, A., Dilley, J. A., Braun, M., & Maher, J. E. (2020b). Implications of cannabis legalization on juvenile justice outcomes and racial disparities. *Amercian Journal of Preventive Medicine*, 58(4), 562–569. doi:https://doi.org/10.1016/j.amepre.2019.11.019.

Firth, C. L., Maher, J. E., Dilley, J. A., Darnell, A., & Lovrich, N.P. (2019). Did marijuana legalization in Washington State reduce racial disparities in adult marijuana arrests? *Substance Use and Misuse*, 0(0), 1–6. doi:https://doi.org/10.1080/10826084.2019.1593007.

Forecasting and Research Division. (2019). Monitoring impacts of recreational marijuana legalization: 2019 update report. Retrieved from: https://sac.ofm.wa.gov/sites/default/files/public/pdf/marijuana_impacts_update_2019.pdf (last accessed 24 October 2021).

Graves, J. M., Whitehill, J. M., Miller, M. E., Brooks-Russell, A., Richardson, S. M., & Dilley, J. A. (2019). Employment and marijuana use among Washington State adolescents before and after legalization of retail marijuana. *Journal of Adolescent Health*, 65(1), 39–45. doi:https://doi.org/10.1016/j.jadohealth.2018.12.027.

Hansen, B., Miller, K., & Weber, C. (2020). Early evidence on recreational marijuana legalization and traffic fatalities. *Economic Inquiry*, 58(2), 547–568. doi:https://doi.org/10.1111/ecin.12751.

Heffter, E. (15 January 2010). Seattle's new city attorney to dismiss cases of pot possession. *The Seattle Times*. Retrieved from: http://www.seattletimes.com/seattle-news/seattles-new-city-attorney-to-dismiss-cases-of-pot-possession/ (last accessed 27 September 2021).

Hong, G. (2018). *Cannabis-related emergency department visits among Medicaid enrollees before and after legalization of marijuana in Washington State*. Academy Health Annual Research Conference.

Hong, G., Lucenko, B., & Dilley, J. A. Trends in cannabis-related substance use treatment among Washington State Medicaid enrollees after legalization [in preparation].Jaeger, K. (17 July 2018). Legalizing marijuana helps police solve other crimes, new study shows. *Marijuana Moment*. Retrieved from: https://www.marijuanamoment.net/legalizing-marijuana-helps-police-solve-other-crimes-new-study-shows/ (last accessed 4 November 2021).

Joint blog. (9 February 2015). Washington bill to close dispensaries, reduce patients' rights, moves to full senate. *The Joint Blog*. Retrieved from: https://thejointblog.com/washington-bill-close-dispensaries-reduce-patients-rights-moves-full-senate/ (last accessed 27 September 2021).

Jorgensen, C., & Harper, A.J. (2020). Examining the effects of legalizing marijuana in Colorado and Washington on clearance rates: A quasi-experimental design. *Journal of Experimental Criminology*, 1–22. doi:https://doi.org/10.1007/s11292-020-09446-7.

Kaplan, J. (26 September 2019). People in D.C.'s increasingly dangerous marijuana gray market want change. *Washington Citypaper*. Retrieved from: https://washingtoncitypaper.com/article/178350/people-in-dcs-increasingly-dangerous-marijuana-gray-market-want-change/ (last accessed 4 November 2021).

Kerr, W. C., Williams, E., & Greenfield, T. K. (2015). Analysis of price changes in Washington following the 2012 liquor privatization. doi:https://doi.org/10.1093/alcalc/agv067.

Kilmer, B. (28 August 2020). Gov. Wolf's push to legalize marijuana is oversold as coronavirus relief | Opinion. *The Philadelphia Inquirer*. Retrieved from: https://www.inquirer.com/opinion/commentary/marijuana-legalization-tom-wolf-pennsylvania-revenue-coronavirus-20200828.html (last accessed 29 September 2021).

Kilmer, B. (2019). How will cannabis legalization affect health, safety, and social equity outcomes? It largely depends on the 14 Ps. *American Journal of Drug and Alcohol Abuse*, 45(6), 664–672. doi:https://doi.org/10.1080/00952990.2019.1611841.

Kilmer, B., Caulkins, J., Kilborn, M., Priest, M., & Warren, K. (2021). Cannabis legalization and social equity: Some opportunities, puzzles, and tradeoffs. *Boston University Law Review*, 101(3), 1003–1041.

Kilmer, B., Caulkins, J. P., Midgette, G., Dahlkemper, L., MacCoun, R. J., & Pacula, R. L. (2013). Before the grand opening measuring Washington State's marijuana market in the last year before legalized commercial sales. Retrieved from: https://www.rand.org/pubs/research_reports/RR466.html (last accessed 29 September 2021).

Kilmer, B., Davenport, S., Smart, R., Caulkins, J. P., & Midgette, G. (2019). After the grand opening: Assessing cannabis supply and demand in Washington State. Retrieved from: http://www.rand.org/giving/contribute (last accessed 4 August 2020).

Kilmer, B., & MacCoun, R. J. (2017). How medical marijuana smoothed the transition to marijuana legalization in the United States. *Annual Review of Law Social Science*, 13, 181–202. doi:https://doi.org/10.1146/annurev-lawsocsci-110615-084851.

Lane, T. J., & Hall, W. (2019). Traffic fatalities within US states that have legalized recreational cannabis sales and their neighbours. *Addiction*, 114(5), 847–856. doi: https://doi.org/10.1111/add.14536.

Lu, R., Willits, D., Stohr, M. K., Makin, D., Snyder, J., Lovrich, N., Meize, M., Stanton, D., Wu, G., & Hemmens, C. (2019). The cannabis effect on crime: Time-series analysis of crime in Colorado and Washington State. *Justice Quarterly*, 38(4), 565–595. doi:https://doi.org/10.1080/07418825.2019.1666903.

Makin, D. A., Meize, M. R., Willits, D. W., Stohr, M. K., Hemmens, C., Lowrich, N. P., Nordman, A., & Stanton, D. (2020). The impact of recreational marijuana sales on calls for service: an analysis of neighbouring cities. *Policing and Society*, 31(7), 848–862. doi:https://doi.org/10.1080/10439463.2020.1773461.

Makin, D. A., Willits, D. W., Wu, G., Dubois, K. O., Lu, R., Stohr, M. K., Koslicki, W., Stanton, D., Hemmens, C. Snyder, J., & Lovrich, N. P. (2019). Marijuana legalization and crime clearance rates: Testing proponent assertions in Colorado and Washington State. *Police Quarterly*, 22(1), 31–55. doi:https://doi.org/10.1177/1098611118786255.

Miller, K., & Seo, B. (2021). The effect of cannabis legalization on substance demand and tax revenues. *National Tax Journal*, 74(1), 107–145. doi:https://doi.org/10.1086/712915.

Native Business Staff (26 June2020). Washington tribes leverage the cannabis economy. *Native Business Magazine*. Retrieved from: https://www.nativebusinessmag.com/washington-tribes-leverage-the-cannabis-economy/ (last accessed 24 October 2021).

Northwest Prevention Technology Transfer Center. (2021). Alcohol regulatory systems: Integrating support for public health and safet *y*. Retrieved from: https://pttcnetwork.org/sites/default/files/2021-03/Alcohol-Regulatory-Policy-Guide-2021.-draft-3.-mfs.3.5.21_508.pdf 5 (last accessed 24 October 2021).

Northwest Prevention Technology Transfer Center. (2020). *HHS Region 10, State Cannabis Policies and Regulations: A Guidance Document for Northwest Substance Misuse Prevention Practitioners*. Retrieved from: https://pttcnetwork.org/sites/default/files/2020-09/Cannabis Guidance Document_508_0.pdf (last accessed 17 March 2022).

Office of Program Research. (2012). *Summary of Initiative 502*. Retrieved from: https://leg.wa.gov/House/Committees/OPRGeneral/Documents/2012/I-502%20summary.pdf (last accessed 24 October 2021).

Pacula, R. L., Blanchette, J. G., Lira, M. C., Smart, R., & Naimi, T. S. (2021). Current U.S. state cannabis sales limits allow large doses for use or diversion. *American Journal of Preventive Medicine*, 60(5), 701–705. doi:https://doi.org/10.1016/j.amepre.2020.11.005.

Pacula, R. L., Kilmer, B., Wagenaar, A. C., Chaloupka, F. J., & Caulkins, J. P. (2014). Developing public health regulations for marijuana: Lessons from alcohol and tobacco. *American Journal of Public Health*. doi:https://doi.org/10.2105/AJPH.2013.301766.

Pacula, R. L., Powell, D., Heaton, P., & Sevigny, E. L. (2015). Assessing the effects of medical marijuana laws on marijuana use: the devil is in the details. *Journal for Policy Analysis and Management*, 34(1), 7–31. doi:https://doi.org/10.1002/pam.21804.

Pardo, B. (2014). Cannabis policy reforms in the Americas: A comparative analysis of Colorado, Washington, and Uruguay. *International Journal of Drug Policy*, 25(4), 727–735. doi:https://doi.org/10.1016/j.drugpo.2014.05.010.

Plunk, A. D., Peglow, S. L., Harrell, P. T., & Grucza, R.A. (2019). Youth and adult arrests for cannabis possession after decriminalization and legalization of cannabis. *JAMA Pediatrics*, 173(8), 763–769. doi:https://doi.org/10.1001/jamapediatrics.2019.1539.

Santaella-Tenorio, J., Wheeler-Martin, K., Dimaggio, C. J., Castilo-Carniglia, A., Keyes, K. M., Hasin, D., & Cerda, M. (2020). Association of recreational cannabis laws in Colorado and Washington State with changes in traffic fatalities, 2005–2017. *JAMA Internal Medicine*, 180(8), 1061–1068. doi:https://doi.org/10.1001/jamainternmed.2020.1757.

Schauer, G., Dilley, J., Roehlerm, D., Sheehy, T. J., Filley, J. R., Broschart, S. C., Holland, M. K., Baldwin, G. T., Holmes-Chavez, A. K., & Hoots, B. E. (2021). Cannabis sales increases during COVID-19: Findings from Alaska, Colorado, Oregon, and Washington. *International Journal of Drug Policy*, 98, 103384. doi:https://doi.org/10.1016/j.drugpo.2021.103384.

Smart, R., Caulkins, J. P., Kilmer, B., Davenport, S., & Midgette, G. (2017). Variation in cannabis potency and prices in a newly legal market: Evidence from 30 million cannabis sales in Washington state. *Addiction*, 112(12), 2167–2177. doi:https://doi.org/10.1111/add.13886.

Tabb, L. P., Fillmore, C., & Melly, S. (2018). Location, location, location: Assessing the spatial patterning between marijuana licenses, alcohol outlets and neighborhood characteristics within Washington state. *Drug Alcohol Dependence*, 185, 214–218. doi:htpps://doi.org/10.1016/j.drugalcdep.2018.01.004.

Task Force on Race and the Criminal Justice System. (2012). *Preliminary Report on Race and Washington's Criminal Justice System*. Seattle: Seattle University School of Law.

Tefft, B. C., & Arnold, L. S. (2020). Cannabis use among drivers in fatal crashes in Washington State before and after legalization (research brief). Retrieved from: https://aaafoundation.org/cannabis-use-among-drivers-in-fatal-crashes-in-washington-state-before-and-after-legalization/ (last accessed 24 October 2021).

Transform Drug Policy Foundation. (2020). Altered states: Cannabis regulation in the US. Retrieved from: https://transformdrugs.org/publications/altered-states-cannabis-regulation-in-the-us (last accessed 17 March 2022).

U. S. Department of Justice. (2018). Justice Department issues memo on marijuana enforcement (2018). *Justice News.* Retrieved from: https://www.justice.gov/opa/pr/justice-department-issues-memo-marijuana-enforcement (last accessed 27 September 2021).

Vera Institute of Justice. (2019). Incarceration trends in Washington. Retrieved from: https://www.vera.org/downloads/pdfdownloads/state-incarceration-trends-washington.pdf (last accessed 24 October 2021).

Washington State Department of Health. (2016). Compliant marijuana products. Retrieved from: https://www.doh.wa.gov/Portals/1/Documents/Pubs/608011.pdf (last accessed 24 October 2021)

Washington State Department of Health. (2021a). Medical marijuana data and statistics. Retrieved from: https://www.doh.wa.gov/YouandYourFamily/Marijuana/MedicalMarijuana/AuthorizationDatabase/DataandStatistics (last accessed 24 October 2021).

Washington State Department of Health. (2021b). Medical marijuana history in Washington. Retrieved from: https://www.doh.wa.gov/YouandYourFamily/Marijuana/MedicalMarijuana/LawsandRules/HistoryinWashington (last accessed 21 January 2021)

Washington State Department of Health. (2021c) Medical marijuana certified consultant. Retrieved from: https://www.doh.wa.gov/YouandYourFamily/Marijuana/MedicalMarijuana/ConsultantCertificationProgram (last accessed 5 December 2021).
Washington State Department of Health. (2021d). *Medical Marijuana: Authorization Database*. Retrieved from: https://www.doh.wa.gov/YouandYourFamily/Marijuana/MedicalMarijuana/AuthorizationDatabase (last accessed 5 December 2021).
Washington State Legislature. (2021). Chapter 314–55 WAC, Marijuana licenses, application process, requirements, and reporting. Retrieved from: https://apps.leg.wa.gov/wac/default.aspx?cite=314-55 (last accessed 25 October 2021).
Washington State Legislature. (2015a). RCW 43.06.490: Marijuana agreements – Federally recognized Indian tribes – Tribal marijuana tax – Tax exemption. Retrieved from: https://app.leg.wa.gov/rcw/default.aspx?cite=43.06.490 (last accessed 24 October 2021).
Washington State Legislature. (2015b). HB 2136–2015–16. Retrieved from: https://app.leg.wa.gov/billsummary?BillNumber=2136&Year=2015 (last accessed 25 October 2021).
Washington State Liquor and Cannabis Board. (n.d.a). Not for kids warning symbol. Retrieved from: https://lcb.wa.gov/marj/warning-symbol-article#:~:text=The%20Washington%20State%20Liquor%20and,effective%20on%20February%2014%2C%202017.
Washington State Liquor and Cannabis Board. (n.d.b). Potency tax feasibility study. Retrieved from: https://lcb.wa.gov/marj/potency-tax-study. Washington State Liquor and Cannabis Board. (2013). Board approves filing of proposed rules to implement Initiative 502. Retrieved from: https://lcb.wa.gov/pressreleases/board-approves-filing-proposed-rules-implement-initiative-502#:~:text=Production Limits Sets the maximum amount of space,and 40 metric tons of production for concentrates.
Washington State Liquor and Cannabis Board. (2014). Liquor control board approves lottery process for retail marijuana stores. Retrieved from: https://lcb.wa.gov/pressreleases/liquor-control-board-approves-lottery-process-retail-marijuana-stores.
Washington State Liquor and Cannabis Board. (2015). Board to increase number of retail marijuana stores following analysis of marketplace. Retrieved from: https://lcb.wa.gov/pressreleases/lcb-to-increase-number-of-retail-mj-stores.
Washington State Liquor and Cannabis Board. (2016). What is a medical marijuana cooperative? Olympia. Retrieved from: https://lcb.wa.gov/publications/Marijuana/Cooperatives – FAQ 2 0.pdf.
Washington State Liquor and Cannabis Board. (2019). Packaging and labeling guide for medically compliant and recreational marijuana. Retrieved from: https://lcb.wa.gov/sites/default/files/publications/Marijuana/LIQ-1420-Packaging-and-Labeling-Guide-201912_FINAL2.pdf.
Washington State Liquor and Cannabis Board. (2020). *Annual Report Fiscal Year 2020*. Olympia. Retrieved from: https://lcb.wa.gov/sites/default/files/publications/annual_report/2020 annual-report-final-opt.pdf.
Washington State Liquor and Cannabis Board. (2021a). Frequently requested lists: Cannabis sales activity by license number – traceability contingency reporting. Retrieved from: https://lcb.wa.gov/records/frequently-requested-lists (last accessed 5 December 2021).
Washington State Liquor and Cannabis Board. (2021b). Frequently requested lists: Medical cannabis endorsements. Retrieved from: https://lcb.wa.gov/records/frequently-requested-lists (last accessed 5 December 2021).Washington State Office of

Financial Management. (2020). Estimates of April 1 population by age, sex, race and Hispanic origin. Retrieved from: https://www.ofm.wa.gov/washington-data-research/population-demographics/population-estimates/estimates-april-1-population-age-sex-race-and-hispanic-origin (last accessed 27 September 2021).

Washington State Senate. (2009). Senate Bill Report ESSB 5073. Retrieved from: https://apps.leg.wa.gov/documents/billdocs/2009-10/Pdf/Bill%20Reports/Senate/5073-S.E%20SBR%20FBR%2009.pdf (last accessed 24 October 2021)

Washington State Senate. (2015). Senate Bill (SB) 5052-2015-16. Establishing the cannabis patient protection act. Effective date 24 July 2015. Retrieved from: https://lawfilesext.leg.wa.gov/biennium/2015-16/Pdf/Amendments/House/5052-S2%20AMH%20ENGR%20H2596.E.pdf (last accessed 5 December 2021).

Washington State Senate. (2017). Senate Bill Report ESSB 5131 2017–2018. https://lawfilesext.leg.wa.gov/biennium/2017-18/Pdf/Bills/Session%20Laws/Senate/5131-S.SL.pdf (last accessed 5 December 2021). Also see Washington State Liquor and Cannabis Board Frequently asked quetsions about advertising (2021). Retrieved from: https://lcb.wa.gov/mj2015/faq_i502_advertising (last accessed 5 December 2021).

Washington State Treasurer. Washington marijuana revenues, and health. Retrieved from: https://tre.wa.gov/portfolio-item/washington-state-marijuana-revenues-and-health/ (last accessed 29 September 2021).

Whitehill, J. M., Dilley, J. A., Brooks-Russell, A., Terpak, L., & Graves, J. M. (2021). Edible cannabis exposures among children: 2017–2019. *Pediatrics*, 147(4). doi:https://doi.org/10.1542/PEDS.2020-019893/180775.

Williams, E., Kerr, W. C., & Barnett, S. B. L. (2020). Price changes in Washington following the 2012 liquor privatization: An update through 2016 with comparisons to California, Idaho, and Oregon. *Alcoholism Clinical and Experimental Research*, 44(2), 501–510. doi:htpps://doi.org/10.1111/ACER.14255.

Williams, A. R., Olfson, M., Kim, J. H., Martins, S. S., & Kleber, H. D. (2016). Older, less regulated medical marijuana programs have much greater enrollment rates than newer "medicalized" programs. *Health Affairs*, 35(3), 480–488. doi:https://doi.org/10.1377/hlthaff.2015.0528.

10 From compassion to commercial

What got left behind in the transition to legal cannabis in Canada

Rielle Capler and Daniel Bear

Introduction

When considering the significant changes in cannabis policy occurring across the world in the last decade, it might be easy to forget some of the initial efforts that challenged the dominant prohibitionist model. Canada's new-found paradigm for cannabis legalization came after years of advocacy, widespread civil disobedience, and two decades of legal medical cannabis access. Canada may be viewed as occupying the progressive end of cannabis policies, in part because of its early adoption of medical cannabis regulations. However, there have been various barriers to accessing Canada's medical cannabis program, which has been accessed by only a small percentage of self-reported medical cannabis users (Belle-Isle et al., 2014, Health Canada, 2021). In this gap, some Canadians dedicated themselves to providing cannabis to individuals in medical need.

For two decades before the legalization of recreational cannabis, Compassion Clubs, and other illegal storefronts called cannabis dispensaries, which sold cannabis for both medical and non-medical purposes, operated in the face of potential criminalization and imprisonment. Together, these renegades helped to bring down the prohibitionist approach to cannabis while engendering a keen sense of community among consumers, retailers, and cultivators. In that community setting, something beyond the simple combustion of vegetable matter and the mere transaction of money and goods took place. In that relational context, a body of knowledge of how to grow, consume, curate, and sell cannabis was co-created. As the nascent Canadian non-medical cannabis market struggles to capture consumers (Health Canada, 2021), the discussion in Canada often turns towards questions about the products available, number of retail outlets, or the price of cannabis. We assert that while those aspects are certainly impactful, a truly successful legal cannabis market must look towards the relationships that alternative distribution systems offer.

This chapter sets the stage by examining the legal milieu in which Compassion Clubs were born in Canada and the government's legal medical cannabis access program that ran parallel to them. We then explore the Compassion Club model, utilizing the BC Compassion Club as an example, and follow the

DOI: 10.4324/9781003055679-10

trajectory of medical and non-medical cannabis dispensaries that developed outside of a legal framework. We outline the organizing and advocacy Compassion Clubs and dispensaries engaged in, and the impact this had on the movement towards cannabis policy reform in Canada. Next, we identify shared components of Compassion Clubs and CSCs, focusing on their deliberate and innovative practices to meet the needs of their members and operate in an environment unfriendly to cannabis. We then discuss non-medical cannabis legalization in Canada and the challenges it is posing for the relationships between consumers, retailers, and cultivators. Finally, we propose that the values and relationships fostered by CSCs and Compassion Clubs must be enshrined in cannabis reform efforts for both medical and non-medical cannabis in Canada and around the world.

Methods

This chapter utilizes a comparative case method, examining the Compassion Clubs and dispensaries of Canada with the CSCs found in several other countries. It provides a case study of Canada's first Compassion Club, the British Columbia Compassion Club Society, to illustrate the Compassion Club model. The chapter draws on available literature, market data, and policy documents for relevant historical context and current market issues. The authors write from positions of direct experience with Compassion Clubs, dispensaries, and cannabis cooperatives. Dr. Capler helped lay the foundations for Canada's first Compassion Club, is a co-founder and advisor of Canada's national dispensary association, and has researched extensively on access to cannabis for medical purposes in Canada. Dr. Bear conducted ethnographic research with the Wo/Men's Alliance for Medical Marijuana (WAMM), a non-profit collective of medical cannabis patients in California. WAMM was the first federally legal medical cannabis growers' collective in the United States and served as an inspiration for the British Columbia Compassion Club Society. In addressing Compassion Clubs and dispensaries in Canada, this chapter focuses on physical storefronts where in-person interactions occur, as opposed to businesses that solely distribute by mail order.

Compassion Clubs and cannabis dispensaries in Canada

Legal context of Compassion Clubs

Cannabis became a controlled substance in Canada in 1923 and was later designated as a Schedule 2 substance in the federal Controlled Drugs and Substances Act (CDSA), which prohibited its possession, production, or distribution (Controlled Drugs and Substances Act, 1996). With this designation, special provisions were required for patients to gain legal access to cannabis for medical use. In 2000, the Ontario Court of Appeal ruled that there was a constitutional right to access cannabis for medical purposes (R. v.

Parker, 2000). It declared the sections of the CDSA that prohibited the possession and production of cannabis unconstitutional because they forced people to choose between their liberty and their health.

Faced with the eminent de-scheduling of cannabis from the CDSA, in 2001 the federal government established a regulatory framework for medical cannabis (Government of Canada, 2001). Through several iterations of regulations, patients were licensed to possess cannabis for medical purposes upon recommendation of a health care practitioner. The regulations also permitted patients or a designated person to grow cannabis, and provided the option of purchasing cannabis from the government's sole contracted supplier that was offering only one cultivar of dried cannabis. The program did not include any options for purchasing cannabis from retail storefronts, relying instead on the delivery of the cannabis via the Canadian postal service. The program was beset by problems that included issues regarding the cost and quality of the cannabis and the fact that many medical cannabis patients did not participate in the program (Belle-Isle et al., 2014).

In 2014, a new set of regulations included the addition of private commercial licensed producers as legal suppliers of medical cannabis (Government of Canada, 2013). By 2016, there was a new set of regulations (Government of Canada, 2016) and 24 licenses had been issued for the production of cannabis and sale to medical patients online and shipped through the mail or other registered courier services. This represented the beginning of a shift towards the commercialization of cannabis in Canada, an act that fundamentally shifted relationships from relational to transactional. A notable absence from all these regulations were retail storefronts, which had emerged outside the legal framework to provide access to cannabis for those in medical need.

The Compassion Club model: a case study

Even before the court rulings and before the Canadian government established its medical cannabis program, the British Columbia Compassion Club Society opened its doors in Vancouver, BC in 1997, as Canada's first storefront medical cannabis dispensary. It was created to fill an unmet healthcare need, to serve as a model for medical cannabis access in Canada, and to advocate for legal access to cannabis for medical purposes (Capler, 2010).

Providing cannabis for medical use amid cannabis prohibition, the BC Compassion Club took measures to establish trust, tolerance, and acceptance among patients they served, policy makers, and the broader community. Foremost, this entailed strict adherence to membership protocols. To access the BC Compassion Club, applicants were required to obtain documentation providing a diagnosis and a recommendation for their use of cannabis from an accredited health care provider. These membership requirements served both to incorporate cannabis into the member's traditional medical care, and to ensure due diligence for encounters with law enforcement and possible appearances in court. Membership was initially restricted to people with certain medical conditions or symptoms for which the BC Compassion Club considered there was sufficient evidence for cannabis's efficacy (including in the context of cancer treatment, HIV/AIDS, arthritis, Crohn's disease, multiple sclerosis, brain injury, nausea, and chronic pain). Over time, the BC Compassion club updated their list of qualifying conditions on the basis of available research. New research led not only to broader membership criteria, but also to greater support from health care providers. Membership grew steadily over the years, with the organization increasing its capacity to keep up with the demands of hundreds and, over time, thousands of members.

The products and services provided by the BC Compassion Club included a diverse menu of raw cannabis and other forms of cannabis medicines such as tinctures and topicals, and were provided both locally in their storefront as well as nation-wide through mail order for those who were unable to come in person due to disability or distance. There were monthly limits on the quantity of cannabis that members could purchase. Product quality was carefully assessed by BC Compassion Club staff with visual and tactile inspection, and lab testing was utilized where possible to ensure products were free from harmful heavy metals, pesticides, or microbiological contaminants. Obtaining cannabis produced organically was a priority. Since producing cannabis was prohibited, the cannabis sold at the BC Compassion Club came from illicit sources. Careful vetting of suppliers was necessary to ensure none had ties with organized crime. To this end, cannabis cultivators were contracted to produce cannabis exclusively for the BC Compassion Club. These cultivation contracts also stipulated standards to which producers were expected to adhere which enabled a level of quality and consistency upon which members could rely. Members of the BC Compassion Club, many of whom were using cannabis for the first time, or using it for medical purposes for the first time, were provided in-depth personalized intake and education sessions upon admission to learn about the various products and how to use them to best meet their needs.

As a model of cannabis access, the BC Compassion Club also embodied broader social values that it hoped to imbed in this new field it endeavored to help establish. For example, they viewed cannabis as one of many medicinal herbs with potentially greater effectiveness and fewer side-effects than pharmaceutical drugs. To that end, they used the sales of cannabis to subsidize access to other natural health care modalities, such as herbal medicine and counselling, which were not covered by provincial health insurance. The organization chose to operate with a non-hierarchical structure and consensus decision-making to embody a vision of democracy and inclusion. They also provided a space to consume cannabis, in consideration of those who were unable to use it in their homes. This on-site consumption, along with social and educational events, were meant to provide a sense of community to address the fact that many people were shunned for their use of medical cannabis in other areas of their life.

Increasing acceptability of medical cannabis and community-based access was also part of working towards their vision of widespread legal access to medical cannabis for those in need. To this end, the BC Compassion Club engaged in educational efforts directed at health care providers, students, and the wider community, and collaborated on research projects with academics. Importantly, they incorporated as a non-profit society, to reflect their altruistic motivation and commitment to being a member-driven organization. In their view, taking on the role of being a model of medical cannabis distribution in the context of cannabis criminalization necessitated being upstanding members of society, being meticulous in following protocols, and only breaking one law at a time. One of their mottos was based on a Bob Dylan lyric, "to live outside the law you must be honest" (Dylan, 1:50–1:55). To support others who wanted to open community-based dispensaries, the BC Compassion Club along with the Vancouver Island Compassion Society published operational guidelines outlining their practices (Capler & Lucas, 2006). While the BC Compassion Club model is not generalizable to all Compassion Clubs, many used their operational guidelines as a foundational document.

From Compassion Clubs to dispensaries

For about ten years, the BC Compassion Club was the only Compassion Club in Vancouver, one of a few in the province, and one of less than a dozen operating across Canada. Running a Compassion Club was a challenging endeavor, with operators risking their liberty. It also was not possible in most Canadian cities. Part of the BC Compassion Club's success was the tolerance it was afforded by officials in this progressive west coast city. Vancouver was also home to an organization known as the Vancouver Area Network of Drug Users. This organization empowered the collective voice of people who use drugs to help shape public policy to reduce the harms that the community faced (Kerr et al., 2006). Vancouver was also home to Canada's first Supervised Injection Site, Insite, which opened in 2003 (Small et al., 2012).

Where tolerance did exist for Compassion Clubs, it stemmed from empathy for patients, which counteracted the morality concerns otherwise encountered with recreational cannabis use. Tolerance was justified by the fact that patients had a constitutional right to cannabis for medical use, but this right was not fulfilled through the government program. Support was also voiced from the Canadian Senate, which in 2002 recommended decriminalization of cannabis and collaboration with Compassion Clubs (Senate of Canada, 2002). These Compassion Clubs, considered by some to be a quasi-legal source of medical cannabis, were much utilized, providing access to cannabis for tens of thousands of patients across Canada. The public outreach and relationship building they engaged in created a high level of acceptance and comfort in their communities (Penn, 2014). Likewise, some court cases involving Compassion Clubs had favorable outcomes, with judges recognizing the need for these services (*Hitzig v. Canada*, 2003; *R. v. Beren & Swallow*, 2009).

In response to the perceived reduction in legal risk and increase in tolerance concerning Compassion Clubs, a burgeoning number of illicit storefront cannabis dispensaries opened across the country. This phenomenon was also spurred by federal regulatory changes aiming to remove production licenses from patients and designated producers, who had invested in spaces and equipment to grow cannabis and were now propelled to create outlets for their products. Most of these dispensaries focused on catering to a non-medical clientele, without the explicit community-building, law reform and social justice goals of Compassion Clubs. While strict age requirements were imposed for purchase, dispensaries resembled a retail model rather than a membership model. Prior to cannabis legalization, there were an estimated 215 illegal cannabis storefronts (including Compassion Clubs and dispensaries) in Canada serving 100,000 to 200,00 people (Cain, 2016; Mahamad & Hammond, 2019). Faced with an ever-growing number of these shops popping up, several municipalities in British Columbia decided to provide licenses to address zoning issues, disregarding the issue of illegal cannabis sales that remained criminal offences in the Federal Criminal Code (City of Vancouver, 2015). In other provinces, the response was to use law enforcement to shut them down (BBC News, 2019; Kupferman, 2016).

Organizing, advocacy, and impact

All the early Compassion Clubs had some form of membership or access requirements for documentation attesting to a medical condition, though some were less strict than others. Unlike the BC Compassion Club, most other Compassion Clubs and medical dispensaries were not registered as non-profits, and most did not provide natural health care services, which was a logistically challenging endeavor that cut into profits and salaries. Some served fewer than 100 members and others served thousands. None besides the BC Compassion Club utilized a non-hierarchical management structure and consensus decision-making. Despite these ideological and operational differences, they communicated with each other regularly about areas of common interest, be they operational, legal, or political, and collaborated on their advocacy efforts towards a common vision of storefronts existing within the legal framework for medical cannabis.

To consolidate their advocacy efforts and other collaborative endeavors under one umbrella, in 2011, these geographically diverse Compassion Clubs and medical cannabis dispensaries formed the Canadian Association of Medical Cannabis Dispensaries (CAMCD) (Penn, 2014). Through this Association they were able to pool resources to engage in lobbying efforts and support policy-relevant research. Membership in the Association was also a way of differentiating themselves from dispensaries that were perceived as 'bad actors' (i.e., connected with organized crime, selling to minors, selling other substances, profiteering) and could detrimentally impact the progress of reform efforts. In the absence of the government regulation they desired, Association members used this platform to self-regulate. To this end, they developed and published operational standards detailing best practices which formed the basis of a certification program to support dispensaries to provide the highest quality of care. These operational standards were a useful advocacy tool, since they answered many of the questions policy makers had about how they operated, and provided a vision of how they could be incorporated into the legal framework (Capler et al., 2020). In anticipation of cannabis legalization, this dispensary association later expanded its membership criteria to include non-medical cannabis dispensaries.

Beyond their organized advocacy efforts, by existing in physical space, Compassion Clubs and cannabis dispensaries created a new reality in the place of what had previously been theoretical discussion. By existing, they provided not only a rallying point for their members, customers, and cultivators, but also the opportunity for those opposed to cannabis to pose real questions about how and why they were engaging in these practices. By existing, they changed the physical landscape of cities and towns across Canada. By existing in substantial numbers, they provoked concern, curiosity, and eventually comfort among the wider community; they instigated a need for licensing, which is a form of normalization and acceptance.

Although Compassion Clubs and dispensaries were vying to be included in the legal framework, by operating outside of the law they were afforded the freedom to expedite the natural experiment of cannabis provision through trial and error without regulatory hurdles; they were able to create a viable model of cannabis distribution. The model they created outside of regulatory obstacles and the lessons they learned informed the discussions that helped shape policy when it came time for legalization. When commercial licensed producers were introduced into the legal medical and non-medical cannabis markets in Canada, they sought the expertise and plant genetics from these Compassion Clubs and cannabis dispensaries and the cultivators that produced for them.

Cannabis Social Clubs and Compassion Clubs – cannabis cousins

At nearly the same time, in the late 1990s, both Compassion Clubs and CSCs emerged as new approaches by cannabis activists to create cannabis access pathways within existing constitutional limitations of their particular jurisdictions. In Canada, any amount of cannabis production, distribution, and possession were illegal at the time Compassion Clubs were created, however, medical use became constitutionally protected and provided some justification for these activities. Tolerance for cannabis-related activities differs between the countries where CSCs are located, and also provided some arguable spaces for their existence. In a world generally hostile to cannabis, CSCs, and Compassion Clubs both created distinct structures and practices in an attempt to inoculate themselves from prosecution, created self-regulating bodies, innovated methods of providing cannabis at the retail level, and engaged in activism and advocacy. They have also both developed variants of their respective models veering away from their non-commercial roots over time, and created communities encompassing cannabis consumers, and cultivators.

An important practice common to both Compassion Clubs and CSCs is following a membership model. In both systems, the exclusivity derived by requiring membership serves as a protective shield. CSCs' membership practices are designed to create a closed supply system that does not extend to public retail, and to ensure that only active adult cannabis consumers are brought into the club in order to avoid promoting consumption to new cannabis users and avoid access to tourists. In jurisdictions where the CSC model has not been regulated, membership may also keep law enforcement at bay by demonstrating adherence to rules on personal possession or sharing of cannabis (Decorte et al., 2017). For Compassion Clubs, membership ensured cannabis was provided only to legitimate medical patients, which furthered the message that their actions, though illegal, were being undertaken for altruistic rather than profit-related purposes, affording them a buffer from the strong arm of the law in regards to both enforcement and the judicial system. In part due to their strict membership practices, Compassion Clubs created a more tolerant atmosphere for the establishment of dispensaries that did not require membership nor focus on cannabis for medical purposes.

While supporting medical cannabis access was central to creation of Compassion Clubs, this motivation was not the main drive in the formation of CSCs in Spain and other European and South American counties that tolerated personal production and sharing, such as Belgium, Chile, Colombia, Argentina, the United Kingdom, and France (Belackova & Wilkins, 2018). However, there is recognition that cannabis is used by CSC members for both recreational and medical purposes, and accommodations may be made for medical users in terms of age of admittance, amounts that can be purchased and price (Decorte, 2015; Jansseune et al, 2019; Pardal & Bawin, 2018; Pardal et al., 2020). In some countries, including the UK, Belgium, New Zealand, Switzerland, and Italy, there are some CSCs focused specifically on cannabis for medical purposes (Decorte, 2015; Pardal & Bawin, 2018; Pardal et al., 2020).

Operating outside the law and without formal regulation is another common feature of these cannabis cousins. CSCs, though in many cases existing as registered entities in their respective countries (Decorte et al., 2017), are not formally regulated at the national level, with Uruguay as the sole exception (Queirolo et al., 2016). Similarly, although some Compassion Clubs and dispensaries were registered, they were not externally regulated. In this regulatory gap, both CSCs and Compassion Clubs developed self-regulatory bodies. The European Coalition for Just and Effective Drug Policies (ENCOD) has provided some suggested codes of practice for CSCs (ENCOD, 2011), and CSC Federations in Spain and elsewhere also provide their own codes for affiliated CSCs which are also not compulsory or enforceable (Belackova & Wilkins, 2018). Compassion Clubs and dispensaries, in their quest for official recognition also codified industry standards, which functioned as recommended best practices with a subset of required practices for membership in CAMCD. By codifying their practices, CSCs and Compassion Clubs both provided a framework for formal cannabis regulation. Having access to a larger network through their Federations and Associations also allowed them to share their experiences and collaborate on legal reform efforts. Of note, both CSC Federations in Spain and CAMCD in Canada attracted only a small proportion of cannabis providers in their respective jurisdictions (Pardal et al., 2020).

For both Compassion Clubs and CSCs, the lack of any formal governmental regulation or strict self-regulation meant having the flexibility to experiment and innovate, albeit within challenging legal circumstances. Indeed, given the century of prohibition that proceeded the introduction of these respective cannabis supply models, there was little precedent for how to successfully provide cannabis to consumers outside of traditional black-market drugs distribution networks, making experimentation and innovation necessary. In this open space, each CSC and Compassion Club or dispensary was able to chart their own course based on individual motivations, as well local and national circumstances resulting in variants of those models (Decorte et al., 2017). The variety of experiences and structures created by CSCs provide an excellent example of the variation possible in this informal and unregulated approach (Pardal et al., 2020). Each CSC and Compassion Club could thus be considered part of a larger experiment in cannabis distribution practices. However, this variability in what actually constitutes a Compassion Club or CSC has the potential to dilute the 'brand', introduce unwanted entrepreneurial activities, and weaken any existing legal protections afforded to those arguing that their limited non-compliance with cannabis regulations is protected.

Started by activists who were intent on providing an avenue of access to cannabis and changing the laws, and espousing non-profit motives, in-house production, and harm reduction practices, over time some of the newer CSCs deviated from these values (Jansseune et al., 2019). The number of these 'Cannabis Commercial Clubs' increased exponentially in the mid 2010s (Decorte et al., 2017; Pardal, 2018). A similar pattern was seen in Canada in relation to Compassion Clubs with the advent of dispensaries, which proliferated in the mid-2010s and also veered away from adherence to the non-profit model. Non-profit status is a route of enshrining the concept of membership and solidifying the central role of the relationships through participatory decision-making. This status connotes more palatable objectives based on social and compassionate motivations rather than financial ones. It also represents a middle ground between prohibition and commercialization (Alonso, 2011; Decorte et al., 2017). As noted by Jansseune et al. (2019), "This deviation from the original non-profit ethos characteristic of the CSC model should not be understated as it could potentially blur the distance between this and other commercial models" (p. 350). It can be argued that in Canada commercialization was the driving force of legalization, which notably left out the Compassion Club model in the new regulatory landscape. Instead, highly regulated commercial retailers have been licensed with many restrictions that hamper not only innovation but also relationships.

Examining the relationship between cannabis cultivators and consumers reveals a striking similarity between many CSCs and Compassion Clubs.

Connecting cultivators to consumers is a key piece of the overall structure employed by both models, ensuring consumers have "greater rights and decision-making capacity about their consumption than they would in a commercial relationship" (Alonso, 2011, p. 6). Though Compassion Clubs did not grow in-house in most cases, their relationship with local cultivators ensured the cannabis they sourced was what was needed for their members, not simply what was produced. Likewise, most CSCs rely on a closely connected network of cultivators, either from within the membership or closely tied to the club (Jansseune et al., 2019). The entwined nature of the CSCs and the 'caretakers' who grow their cannabis ensure ready feedback between all stakeholders in the community (Decorte, 2015).

Both CSCs and Compassion Clubs have limitations as cannabis distribution models. Some of these limitations are the result of cannabis prohibition and would not exist in a legal market. For example, operating outside the law means that both Compassion Clubs and CSCs are not party to any consumer protection laws. They may also have difficulty accessing the same level of quality control testing mandated to legal entities. Additionally, while Compassion Clubs and CSCs try to obtain cannabis either by growing it themselves or aligning with like-minded cultivators, this is not always possible; crop failures, theft, or confiscation by authorities may push these organizations to "deviate from the ideal [suppliers]" (Belackova & Wilkins, 2018, p. 31), and interact with criminal distribution networks. The membership requirements employed in both models may inherently limit their viability, even in a legalized environment (Belackova & Wilkins, 2018). As seen in legal Uruguayan CSCs, a membership requirement that formally discloses a person's cannabis consumption to authorities may dissuade participation (Boidi et al., 2016). Such lack of privacy is not encountered when purchasing cannabis from an illicit source. After a century of stigma against cannabis consumers, even legal permissibility may not be enough to overcome the hesitancy many feel about registering their cannabis consumption.

Cannabis legalization in Canada

The road to legalization

As far back as 1972, the Le Dain Commission of Inquiry into the Non-Medical Use of Drugs recommended Canadian political leaders adopt decriminalization (Le Dain, 1972), as did the Senate Special Committee on Illegal Drugs in 2002; however, no government had ever undertaken that charge. Nearly a century of inaction finally came to an end in 2015, when the center-left Liberal Party secured a comfortable victory in the national election, having put cannabis legalization prominently on their platform. Less than five months after coming to power, on 20 April, during the 2016 UNGASS, Canada announced its intention to legalize cannabis for recreational purposes.

As promised, regulations for cannabis legalization were on the table within one year of the announcement, and hearings began in the Canadian parliament. Among those invited to present at the parliamentary hearings were a number of cannabis reform advocates, including the Canadian Association of Medical Cannabis Dispensaries, which advocated for the inclusion of private storefronts for both medical and non-medical retail. They also sought regulations that would encompass the Compassion Club and dispensary model that was currently in place and preserve the relationships therein, enabling smaller cultivators, like those they had been working with, to participate in the new legal market. Many others who addressed the parliamentary hearings were also aspiring to be part of the new legal industry, including representatives of pharmaceutical alcohol, tobacco, and mining industries. These latter voices had been gaining strength, power, and money since 2014 when commercial licensed producers were introduced into the medical cannabis market in Canada.

The Cannabis Act: regulating the legal cannabis market

On 17 October 2018 Canada became only the second country to legalize cannabis for non-medical purposes. Legalization of cannabis was driven by two competing forces; public health and private enterprise. The architects of the bill looked for the right balance, with the goal of creating a safe, legal market for cannabis adults that pulled customers away from illicit sources. The legalization process was driven by public safety considerations, the bill was shepherded through Parliament by the Minister of Public Safety, a former police officer, and Chief of Police. With this background came a false view of the illicit cannabis market as solely the realm of organized criminal actors (Capler et al., 2016), creating a challenging context for policy makers to acknowledge the experience and expertise of the pre-existing non-profit and entrepreneurial cannabis community, and their valuable insights towards making legalization a success.

Legalization also had to address divisions of power between the federal and provincial/territorial levels of government (Bear, 2017). The tension between these forces is visible in the myriad of regulations put forth in the Cannabis Act and accompanying regulations which address cultivation, processing, analytic testing, sale, research, labelling, packaging, and promotion of cannabis (Cannabis Regulations, 2018). Of note, the Canadian legislators failed to adequately consult with Indigenous peoples, and the Act did not recognize the inherent rights of Indigenous communities to exercise jurisdiction over the regulation, sale, consumption, and taxation of cannabis in their communities, as required by UNDRIP as well as the Calls to Action of the Truth and Reconciliation Commission of Canada. In response, some Indigenous communities have asserted their rights to regulate and control cannabis within their territories (Koutouki & Lofts, 2018).

In its first iteration, The Cannabis Act allows for the possession of 30 grams of cannabis in public by individuals over the minimum age of 18, and for personal home production of up to four plants per household. The commercial production of cannabis is regulated at the federal level. Regulations for cultivation include three classes of production licenses: a license for standard cultivation, a license for micro-cultivation, and a license for nurseries. These are separate from processing licenses (e.g., for finished cannabis packaging, and manufacturing and packaging of cannabis-based products), which again followed micro-processing and standard processing subclasses. Production licenses are based on cultivation area, not plant numbers. Micro-cultivation licenses allow for up to 200 square meters of cannabis growing surface (depicted in government infographics as the size of half of the center-ice section on a standard size Canadian ice-hockey rink, a size most Canadians can easily picture), and micro-processing licenses allow for 600 kilograms of dried cannabis processing per calendar year. There are no limits for standard cultivators and processors. The costs associated with attaining these licenses, which include application, security clearance, and annual regularly fees, and the necessity for a production-ready facticity before even submitting an application, can be prohibitive.

After years of demonstrably successful operation and advocacy towards reforming cannabis policy, storefront cannabis retail was included in regulations legalizing non-medical cannabis. Both private and public (i.e., run by the provincial government) retail were permitted in the Cannabis Act, as were private and public wholesale and distribution, at the discretion of provinces. Some provinces chose to have only public or private retail sales, and other chose a mix of both. Most provinces, at least to start, implemented public wholesale and distribution. The provinces also can decide whether to allow federally licensed producers to own retail stores and whether to allow retail shops to sell online or only through a storefront. Consumption was also left the provinces to regulate; no province has yet allowed on-site consumption in retail spaces or cannabis lounges of any kind.

The Cannabis Act maintains a separate but interconnected medical cannabis system, subsuming the medical cannabis regulations. Despite the high levels of use and high preference ratings by patients for storefront medical cannabis access (Capler et al., 2017), this option is still not included in the regulations for medical cannabis. Although licensed cannabis producers are permitted to sell cannabis for non-medical use in retail storefronts, they still are required to offer medical patients access to cannabis through the mail-order process. Additionally, although many people who use cannabis for medical purposes are accessing cannabis from non-medical cannabis storefronts, these retailers are banned from engaging in discussions about the medical uses of cannabis and marketing cannabis as responding to any specific ailment. In some provinces, pharmacies with proper licensing under the Cannabis Act are permitted to sell cannabis directly to patients by mail order. Given the complexity and costs of this route, it has had little uptake with the exception of large national pharmacy chains (Canadian Press, 2018).

The federal excise tax that was created for non-medical cannabis was also applied to medical cannabis, increasing the cost for patients, many of whom were already struggling to pay for their medicine. Provincial public health insurance does not cover the cost of cannabis as it does for other medicines; however, costs are covered by some private health insurance and national plans for veterans. The Canadian Medical Association, which has historically expressed reservations about physician's role in prescribing or recommending cannabis for medical purposes, has suggested there is no need for a separate medical cannabis program now that patients can access cannabis through the legal non-medical cannabis market. Upcoming reviews of the Cannabis Act in 2021 and 2023 may have implications for the medical cannabis system, creating concern for medical patients and advocates about its continuation.

Implementation of commercialization

To jumpstart the new legal non-medical cannabis industry, the federal government turned to the numerous licensed medical cannabis producers to quickly transition to meet the expected demand of the non-medical market. In the lead-up to legalization, these licensed medical cannabis producers had begun stockpiling cannabis (Health Canada, 2019) and developed numerous brands under which to sell their cannabis to both the medical and non-medical markets. New companies were also started up specifically for the legal non-medical cannabis market, many led by executives with backgrounds in mining, tobacco, alcohol, and consumer packaged-goods industries (Lamers, 2019; Skerritt, 2018). Attesting to the sudden mainstreaming and acceptability of the new legal industry, some of the high-placed executives in these companies were formerly working in governments and criminal justice organizations that had been upholding and enforcing cannabis prohibition (DiMatteo, 2018).

Media discussions during the first years of legal cannabis often focused on the stock price of these publicly traded cannabis companies that were worth hundreds of millions of dollars. The stock market buzz, akin to the dot-com bubble, had everyone talking about cannabis. Despite soaring stock prices, companies reported annual losses in the billions of dollars, closed facilities, laid off substantial numbers of their employees – including temporary workers from other countries leaving them in precarious situations - and gave their CEOs and other executives huge salary increases (Deschamps, 2020; Eagland, 2020). Even companies not producing or selling anything had high valuations and were being bought up, with copious amounts of money changing hands and cash infusions buffeting up this fledgling industry.

Besides the stock market hype, there was also excitement about new facilities being built and new jobs coming into communities. Cannabis quickly became big business and was a boon to Canada's economy, with almost 250,000 full-time equivalent positions in Canada by the end of 2020 (Leafly, 2020). By July of 2020, legal cannabis was estimated to have added $3.96B CND to the economy (Statistics Canada, 2021a), and brought in $66M CND in federal taxes the second year of legalization (Tumilty, 2020). The Act, however, did not provide for Indigenous communities to fully participate in the economic opportunities occasioned by the legalization of cannabis, and First Nations were also excluded from sharing cannabis tax venues (Koutouki & Lofts, 2018).

By March 2021 there were more than 600 licensed producers and processors of cannabis in Canada producing vastly more cannabis than can be consumed by Canadians. At the time of writing, there is more than 1M kg of cannabis sitting in producers' warehouses while the legal market only sells about 30,000 kg per month (George-Cosh, 2021). This ongoing supply glut demonstrates that the industry's economic incentives are not in line with the actual market for their product. The rollout of retail stores, which required the provinces develop and implement their own regulations for cannabis distribution from scratch after legalization passed at the federal level, went slowly in some provinces. In Ontario, Canada's largest province, the first retail store did not open until April 2019, a full six months after legalization.

Legalization in Canada has had a stronger ability to dismantle and suppress the Compassion Club model than prohibition ever did. By removing the legal grey area, legalization either pushed Compassion Clubs fully inside a regulatory framework that excluded their core values, or it pushed them completely outside the zone of tolerance they had previously inhabited. Legalization also introduced regulated cultivators and retailers who could pressure governments to sanction their unregulated competitors. With cannabis legalization, the provinces and territories no longer tolerate Compassion Clubs and dispensaries operating without a license and selling unregulated product. Many Compassion Clubs and dispensaries opted to transition to the legal market, abandoning their previous models of operation; members became customers, and independent businesses partnered with larger corporate investors seeking profits. Licensed retail stores had to access cannabis from legal wholesalers, disrupting direct relationships they previously had with producers. Their Association, now called the Association of Canadian Cannabis Retailers, pivoted to support them through the transition to the legal market, with their advocacy efforts are focused on regulations that are hampering private retailers' ability to not only keep their heads above water, but also to create a meaningful customer experience. While some Indigenous individuals and communities have sought to seize the economic opportunities that legal cannabis presents by establishing dispensaries, some of these retail operations have been deemed illegal and have been raided by Canadian police forces (CBC/Radio Canada, 2021).

Consumer capture

While the regulatory framework for legalization in Canada rejected the Compassion Club model, it embraced the existing regulatory approach for alcohol and, to a lesser degree, tobacco. This may have seemed expedient to policy makers; however, these substances are quite different in terms of effects and use patterns, potential harms, and benefits related to use, as well as historical and economic roles in society. Legalization thus produced a commercialized system that was not specifically suited to cannabis and was aligned with the same for-profit motivations of alcohol and tobacco companies. This system was absent many of the key features that brought success to Compassion Clubs and dispensaries; without these features, the legal cannabis market stumbled in its launch.

Cannabis consumers have been slow to enter the legal market. Canada-wide data estimates that legal cannabis sales surpassed the illicit market for the first time in late 2020, two years after legalization (Statistics Canada, 2021b). In 2020, about 45 percent of cannabis consumers reported accessing at least some of their cannabis from the legal market, with only 37 percent reporting always obtaining their cannabis from a legal source (Health Canada, 2021). The trajectory of legal cannabis sales is in part reflective of its price. In a 2020 national survey, price was identified as the most important factor influencing from whom cannabis was obtained (Canadian Cannabis Survey, 2020). A gram of cannabis in a retail store bears the distribution fee, federal and provincial taxes, and retail mark-up on top of the wholesale price. At the outset of legalization, the price of legal cannabis was far higher than illicit cannabis. In Ontario, in early 2019 the average price per gram was estimated to be about 36 percent cheaper in the illicit market. The substantial price difference kept many people away from the legal sources in the early days of legalization. However, prices dropped after the first few months, and by the middle of 2020 were on par with the illicit market (Ontario Cannabis Store, 2021).

The slow roll-of retail shops also impacted uptake of the legal market. Although consumers were initially able to purchase cannabis online from provincial retailers, the retail shops were slow to open. In Ontario, Canada's largest province, the first retail store did not open until April 2019, a full six months after legalization. Currently there are 800 private cannabis retailers in that province; by the middle of 2021 there were more than 1,900 retail stores spread across Canada (Mir, 2021). This increase in retail shops parallels the uptick in legal sales noted above, which, however, are still far below the target goal of "keeping profits out of the hands of criminals" (Health Canada, 2016). The availability and quality of products in the legal market also impacted its uptake. To decrease the regulatory burden, extracts, edibles, drinks, or oil-based vaporizers were not permitted for sale for a full year after legalization came into effect. This left a large gap in the market that illicit sources continued to fill. In terms of quality, when consumers did try legal dried flower, they often found it lacking (Aversa et al., 2021). Cannabis degrades over time and many people buying legal cannabis in October 2018 found that their cannabis had been packaged or grown more than six months earlier. Even when cultivators supplied fresh cannabis, the results were underwhelming to many (Subramaniam, 2019).

Another missing piece of the consumer capture and quality puzzle is slow inclusion of the smaller 'legacy' cultivators (i.e., those operating before legalization) and their 'craft' cannabis products, with which many consumers were already familiar. While micro-cultivation and processing licenses in the Cannabis Act provides an avenue for smaller production enterprises to enter the legal market, the regulatory framework requires a sophisticated operation with numerous staff, large financial reserves, and overcoming extensive bureaucratic hurdles. All without the guarantee that a provincial wholesaler will even stock the eventual product. All those risks and barriers to entry are compounded by the fact that licensing for these micro-businesses did not get underway until a year into legalization. The first micro-cultivator was approved in mid-2019, and as of March 2021, there were still only around 200 micro-cultivators in Canada (Brown, 2021).

By not allowing direct sales from cultivators to retailers, the regulations mandating central distribution in most provinces have created difficulties for retailers trying to curate their products to meet consumers' preferences. This legislative barrier has acted to sever the relationships between retailers and cultivators that were such central part of the Compassion Club and dispensary model. These issues were anticipated and communicated to policy makers in consultations before legislation was drafted but went unheeded at the time. In recognition of the challenges for both small scales cultivators and retailers, as well as consumer demand, some efforts at remediating the limited interaction between cultivators, retailers, and consumers are taking place. Both the provinces of British Columbia and Ontario are moving forward with 'farmgate' sales that will allow cultivators to sell cannabis directly to consumers at their production locations (BNN Bloomberg, 2021), and British Columbia is creating an avenue for direct sales from small-scale licensed producer to retailers in 2022. A program is also being implemented in British Columbia to highlight Indigenous cultivators' products through an Indigenous Shelf Space Program at provincial and private retail locations (BC Gov News, 2020).

Conclusion

We have highlighted in this chapter how the non-profit and relational approach taken by both the Compassion Clubs and CSC models embody a shared sense of community and values. Born in the era of prohibition and operating on the margins of the law, these models both had the flexibility to innovate and contribute to a vision of a legal cannabis landscape in various countries on several continents. Unfortunately, Canada's initial foray into legalization has forgone the foundational components of Compassion Clubs. Cannabis was seen as a new commodity rather than a pre-existing good at the nexus of well-established relationships and practices. The relationships between Compassion Club operators, cannabis cultivators, and consumers were lost in the new regulatory structures, layers of bureaucracy, and rampant commercialization.

The transactional space created by Canada's legalization has placed an especially heavy burden on medical cannabis patients and marginalized members of society. Regulations not only omit Compassion Clubs and medically focused dispensaries, but they also curtail non-medical retailers' ability to cater to the needs of individuals using cannabis for medical purposes and those with lower incomes, and place increased taxes on cannabis in both the legal medical and non-medical markets. One response to these barriers to access and affordability has been the emergence of new unsanctioned cannabis distribution programs that provide free cannabis to Canada's most vulnerable communities (Valleriani et al., 2020). Their existence highlights the need for more equitable legal models of medical cannabis access within a legalized context.

Canada will be reflecting on the first three years of legalization as part of a legislatively mandated review of the Cannabis Act in the fall of 2021, and a five-year review of the medical cannabis program under the Act in 2023. These will provide opportunities to consider the benefits of non-profit models of production and distribution as a middle ground between prohibition and commercialization and to reinvigorate the relational elements of cannabis distribution that were suppressed in the initial legislation. This is also a time to work towards improved patient access to cannabis, and to revisit the Cannabis Act in light of Canada's relationships with First Nations, Metis, and Inuit communities. Plans in some provinces to reconnect cultivators with consumers through 'farmgate' sales, and to reconnect retailers and cultivators through direct sales that by-pass government buyers and distributors may help re-establish some of the relationships that had been severed.

At this time of transition toward cannabis legalization occurring across the globe, there is an important window to anticipate and prepare for the influx of commercial models, and the impact this could have on the CSCs and the values, practices, and relationships they foster. In order to protect this model, or potential other consumer or member-driven models, and ensure that they are not supplanted by commercialization, policy makers must commit to prioritizing a values-based cannabis model over profits, tax revenues, and stock prices. This includes supporting small businesses, non-profits, and cooperatives, emphasizing harm reduction, creating equitable economic opportunities, and promoting environmental sustainability. The success of legalized models will in part be measured by their financial profitability for businesses and governments. However, true success will likely depend on other factors, including whether and how legalization builds on the pre-existing models that base relationships between producers, retailers, and consumers on something more than the exchange of money.

References

Alonso, M. B. (2011). *Cannabis social clubs in Spain: A normalizing alternative underway*. Series on Legislative Reform of Drug Policies 9. Amsterdam: Transnational Institute.

Aversa, J., Jacobson, J., Hernandez, T., Cleave, E., Macdonald, M., & Dizonno, S. (2021). The social media response to the rollout of legalized cannabis retail in Ontario, Canada. *Journal of Retailing and Consumer Services*, 61, 102580. doi:10.1016/j.jretconser.2021.102580.

BBC News (19 July 2019). Toronto walls off illegal pot shops with concrete blocks. *BBC News*. Retrieved from: https://www.bbc.com/news/world-us-canada-49024678 (last accessed 27 September 2021)

BC Gov News (20 September 2020). New sales program to benefit cannabis producers, Indigenous businesses. *BC Gov News*. Retrieved from: https://news.gov.bc.ca/releases/2020PSSG0054-001830 (last accessed 27 September 2021)

Bear, D. (2017). From Toques to Tokes: Two challenges facing nationwide legalization of cannabis in Canada. *International Journal of Drug Policy*, 42, 97–101. doi:10.1016/j.drugpo.2017.03.002.

Belackova, V., & Wilkins, C. (2018). Consumer agency in cannabis supply- Exploring auto-regulatory documents of the cannabis social clubs in Spain. *International Journal of Drug Policy*, 54, 26–43. doi:10.1016/j.drugpo.2017.12.018.

Belle-Isle, L., Walsh, Z., Callaway, R., Lucas, P., Capler, R., Kay, R., & Holtzman, S. (2014). Barriers to access for Canadians who use cannabis for therapeutic purposes. *International Journal of Drug Policy*, 25(4), 691–699. doi:10.1016/j.drugpo.2014.02.009.

BNN Bloomberg (26 March 2021). Cannabis Canada Weekly: Ontario readies farm-gate stores, pot stocks enjoy another strong quarter. *BNN Bloomberg*. Retrieved from: https://www.bnnbloomberg.ca/cannabis-canada-weekly-ontario-readies-farmgate-stores-pot-stocks-enjoy-another-strong-quarter-1.1583072 (last accessed 27 September 2021)

Boidi, M. F., Queirolo, R., & Cruz, J. M. (2016). Cannabis consumption patterns among frequent consumers in Uruguay. *International Journal of Drug Policy*, 34, 34–40. doi:10.1016/j.drugpo.2016.05.008.

Brown, D. (7 May 2021). 200 micros now licensed in Canada. *StratCann*. Retrieved from: https://stratcann.com/2021/05/07/200-micros-now-licensed-in-canada (last accessed 27 September 2021).

Cain, P. (20 April 2016). Pot dispensaries are sprouting up all over Canada. Here's why. *Global News*. Retrieved from: https://globalnews.ca/news/2645660/in-canadas-illegal-pot-market-a-legalized-future-takes-shape (last accessed 23 March 2021).

Canadian Cannabis Survey (2020). *Canadian Cannabis Survey 2020 Summary*. Retrieved from: https://www.canada.ca/en/health-canada/services/drugs-medication/cannabis/research-data/canadian-cannabis-survey-2020-summary.html (last accessed 27 September 2021).

Canadian Press (10 December 2018). Shoppers Drug Mart granted licence to sell medical marijuana online. *CBC*. Retrieved from: https://www.cbc.ca/news/canada/toronto/shoppers-medical-cannabis-1.4938506 (last accessed 27 September 2021).

Cannabis Act (2018). S.C. 2018, c. 16). June 21, 2018. Retrieved from: https://laws-lois.justice.gc.ca/eng/acts/c-24.5 (last accessed 24 October 2021).

Cannabis Regulations (2018). CRC (SOR/2018–144) Retrieved from: https://laws-lois.justice.gc.ca/eng/regulations/SOR-2018-144/ (last accessed 24 October 2021).

Capler, R. (2010). Canadian compassion clubs. In J. Holland (Ed.), *The Pot Book: A complete guide to cannabis* (pp. 432–440). Rochester, VT: Park Street Press.

Capler, R. (2020). Can medical cannabis dispensaries be saved in Canada? *American Journal of Endocannabinoid Medicine*, 2(1), 32–36.

Capler, R., Boyd, N., & Macpherson, D. (2016). Organized crime in the cannabis market: evidence and implications. *Canadian Drug Policy Coalition*. Retrieved from: https://drugpolicy.ca/wp-content/uploads/2016/11/CDPC_Submission_Cannabis-and-Organized-Crime_Aug9-2016_Full-Final-1.pdf (last accessed 27 September 2021)

Capler, R., & Lucas, P. (2006). *Guidelines for the community-based distribution of medical cannabis in Canada*. Vancouver, BC: BC Compassion Club Society & Vancouver Island Compassion Society.

Capler, R., Walsh, Z., Crosby, K., Belle-Isle, L., Holtzman, S., Lucas, P., & Callaway, R. (2017). Are dispensaries indispensable? Patient experiences of access to cannabis from medical cannabis dispensaries in Canada. *International Journal of Drug Policy*, 47, 1–8. doi:10.1016/j.drugpo.2017.05.046.

Capler, R., Walsh, Z., & Lucas, P. (2020). The Medical Cannabis Standards Engagement Evaluation and Dissemination (SEED) project: A community-based research approach to self-regulating medical cannabis dispensaries in Canada. *International Journal of Drug Policy*, 78. doi:10.1016/j.drugpo.2020.102708.

CBC/Radio Canada (4 June 2021). Police raid 3 cannabis dispensaries on the Millbrook First Nation. *CBCnews*. Retrieved from: https://www.cbc.ca/news/canada/nova-scotia/police-raid-cannabis-dispensaries-on-the-millbrook-first-nation-1.6053307 (last accessed 27 September 2021)

City of Vancouver (2015). License by-law amending by-law re: retail dealer – medical marijuana-related. Retrieved from: http://former.vancouver.ca/ctyclerk/cclerk/20150624/documents/ptecbylaws.pdf. (last accessed 27 September 2021).

Controlled Drugs and Substances Act (1996). S.C. c. 19 (1996). Retrieved from: http://laws-lois.justice.gc.ca/eng/acts/C-38.8 (last accessed 27 September 2021).

Decorte, T. (2015). Cannabis social clubs in Belgium: Organizational strengths and weaknesses, and threats to the model. *International Journal of Drug Policy*, 26(2), 122–130. doi:10.1016/j.drugpo.2014.07.016.

Decorte, T., Pardal, M., Queirolo, R., Boidi, M. F., Avilés, C. S., & Franquero, Ò. P. (2017). Regulating Cannabis Social Clubs: A comparative analysis of legal and self-regulatory practices in Spain, Belgium and Uruguay. *International Journal of Drug Policy*, 43, 44–56. doi:10.1016/j.drugpo.2016.12.020.

Deschamps, T. (2 October 2020). Aurora increases executive compensation after lay-offs, $3.3B in losses. *CBC*. Retrieved from: https://www.cbc.ca/news/canada/edmonton/aurora-increases-executive-compensation-after-layoffs-3-3b-in-losses-1.5748958 (last accessed 27 September 2021).

DiMatteo, E. (29 January 2018). The ex-cops, politicians and friends of Bill Blair cashing in on legal weed. *Now Magazine*. Retrieved from: https://nowtoronto.com/news/cops-politicians-cashing-in-on-cannabis (last accessed 27 September 2021).

Dylan, B. (1966). 'Absolutely Sweet Marie'. On *Blonde on Blonde*.

Eagland, N. (5 March 2020). Laid-off workers at Canopy's pot greenhouses prepare for flights home. *Vancouver Sun*. Retrieved from: https://vancouversun.com/news/local-news/laid-off-workers-at-canopys-pot-greenhouses-prepare-for-flights-home (last accessed 27 September 2021).

ENCOD (European Coalition for Just and Effective Drug Policies) (2011). Retrieved from: https://encod.org/the-european-guidelines-for-cannabis-social-clubs (last accessed 1 March 2021).

George-Cosh, D. (23 January 2021). Cannabis Canada Weekly: A billion grams of unsold legal pot may spell further woes for the industry. *BNN Bloomberg*. Retrieved from: https://www.bnnbloomberg.ca/cannabis-canada-weekly-a-billion-grams-of-un

sold-legal-pot-may-spell-further-woes-for-the-industry-1.1552770 (last accessed 27 September 2021).

Government of Canada (2001) Marihuana medical access regulations. Pub. L. No. SOR/2001–2227. Retrieved from: https://www.canlii.org/en/ca/laws/regu/sor-2001-227/107866/sor-2001-227.html (last accessed 24 October 2021).

Government of Canada (2013). Marihuana for medical purposes regulations. *Canada Gazette Part II*, 147(13). Retrieved from: http://gazette.gc.ca/rp-pr/p2/2013/2013-06-19/html/sor-dors119-eng.php (last accessed 29 September 2021).

Government of Canada (2016). Access to cannabis for medical purposes regulations. *Canada Gazette Part II*, 150(17). Retrieved from: http://gazette.gc.ca/rp-pr/p2/2016/2016-08-24/html/sor-dors230-eng.php (last accessed 29 September 2021).

Health Canada (2016). Plenary Statement for the Honourable Jane Philpott Minister of Health – UNGASS on the World Drug Problem. Retrieved from: https://www.canada.ca/en/health-canada/news/2016/04/plenary-statement-for-the-honourable-jane-philpott-minister-of-health-ungass-on-the-world-drug-problem.html (last accessed 29 September 2021).

Health Canada (2019). ARCHIVED – market data under the Access to Cannabis for Medical Purposes Regulations. Retrieved from: https://www.canada.ca/en/health-canada/services/drugs-medication/cannabis/licensed-producers/market-data.html (last accessed 29 September 2021).

Health Canada (2021). Canadian cannabis survey 2020: Summary. Retrieved from: https://www.canada.ca/en/health-canada/services/drugs-medication/cannabis/research-data/canadian-cannabis-survey-2020-summary.html (last accessed 29 September 2021).

Hitzigv. Canada (2003). ONCA C39532; C39738; C39740.

Jansseune, L., Pardal, M., Decorte, T. & Parés, O. (2019). Revisiting the birthplace of the cannabis social Club Model and the role played by Cannabis Social Club Federations. *Journal of Drug Issues*, 49(2), 338–354. doi:10.1177/0022042618815690.

Kerr, T., Small, W., Peeace, W., Douglas, D., Pierre, A., & Wood, E. (2006). Harm reduction by a "user-run" organization: A case study of the Vancouver Area Network of Drug Users (VANDU). *International Journal of Drug Policy*, 17(2), 61–69. doi:10.1016/j.drugpo.2006.01.003.

Koutouki, K., & Lofts, K. (2018). Cannabis, reconciliation, and the rights of Indigenous Peoples: Prospects and challenges for cannabis legalization in Canada. *Alberta law Review*, 56, 709. doi:10.29173/alr2519.

Kupferman, S. (2016). Toronto police are raiding post dispensaries throughout the city. *Toronto Life*. Retrieved from: https://torontolife.com/city/toronto-police-are-raiding-pot-dispensaries-throughout-the-city/.(last accessed 24 October 2021).

Lamers, M. (19 January 2019). Canadian marijuana industry targets alcohol, mainstream executives to steer growth. MJ Business Daily. Retrieved from: https://mjbizdaily.com/canadian-marijuana-industry-alcohol-cpg-executives/ (last accessed 24 October 2021).

Le Dain, G. (1972). Commission of inquiry into the non-medical use of drugs – treatment report. Retrieved from: https://www.druglibrary.org/schaffer/Library/studies/ledain/ldctoc.html (last accessed 29 September 2021).

Leafly (2020). Leafly Jobs Report 2020 1–10. Retrieved from: https://leafly-cms-production.imgix.net/wp-content/uploads/2020/02/06145710/Leafly-2020-Jobs-Report.pdf (last accessed 29 September 2021).

Mahamad, S., & Hammond, D. (2019). Retail price and availability of illicit cannabis in Canada. *Addictive Behaviors*, 90, 402–408. doi:10.1016/j.addbeh.2018.12.001.
Mir, S. (2021). *Taking a walk through Canada's retail landscape.* Toronto, ON: Canaccord Genuity Corp.
Ontario Cannabis Store (2021). A Quarterly Review: April 1–June 30, 2020. Ontario's first fiscal quarter of 2020–2021. Cannabis operations. Retrieved from: https://cdn.shopify.com/s/files/1/2636/1928/files/OCS-InsightsReport_Q1-2020.pdf?v=1604697127 (last accessed 27 March 2022).
Pardal, M. (2018). An analysis of Belgian Cannabis Social Clubs' supply practices: A shapeshifting model? *International Journal of Drug Policy*, 57, 32–41. doi:10.1016/j.drugpo.2018.03.027.
Pardal, M., & Bawin, F. (2018). The supply of cannabis for medical use through cannabis social clubs in Belgium. *Contemporary Drug Problems.* 45(2), 127–145. doi:10.1177/0091450918768545.
Pardal, M., Bone, M., Parés, O., & Johansson, J. (2020). Mapping Cannabis Social Clubs in Europe. *European Journal of Criminology.* doi:10.1177/1477370820941392.
Penn, R. A. (2014). Establishing expertise: Canadian community-based medical cannabis dispensaries as embodied health movement organisations. *International Journal of Drug Policy*, 25 (3), 372–377. doi:10.1016/j.drugpo.2013.12.003.
Queirolo, R., Boidi, M. F., & Cruz, J. M. (2016). Cannabis clubs in Uruguay: The challenges of regulation. *International Journal of Drug Policy*, 34, 41–48. doi:10.1016/j.drugpo.2016.05.015.
R. v. Beren and Swallow. (2009). BCSC 429 (CanLII) – 2009-2002-02 Supreme Court of British Columbia.
R. v. Parker. (2000). CanLII 5762 (ON CA).
R. v. Wakeford. (1998). O.J. No. 3 Ont. Gen. Div.
Senate of Canada (2002). *Cannabis: Our position for a Canadian public policy.* Ottawa: Senate Special Committee on Illegal Drugs.
Skerritt, J. (19 March 2018). Marijuana the new gold as former mining companies flock to pot. *BNN Bloomberg.* Retrieved from: https://www.bnnbloomberg.ca/marijuana-is-the-new-gold-as-former-mining-companies-go-to-pot-1.1031028. (last accessed 29 September 2021).
Small, W., Moore, D., Shoveller, J., Wood, E., & Kerr, T. (2012). Perceptions of risk and safety within injection settings: Injection drug users' reasons for attending a supervised injecting facility in Vancouver, Canada. *Health, Risk & Society*, 14(4), 307–324. doi:10.1080/13698575.2012.680950.
Statistics Canada (2021a). Gross domestic product (GDP) at basic prices, by industry, monthly. Retrieved from: https://www150.statcan.gc.ca/t1/tbl1/en/tv.action?pid=3610043401 (last accessed 29 September 2021)
Statistics Canada (2021b). Detailed household final consumption expenditure, Canada, quarterly. Retrieved from: https://www150.statcan.gc.ca/t1/tbl1/en/tv.action?pid=3610012401 (last accessed 29 September 2021).
Subramaniam, V. (15 October 2019). A year in the weeds: Why the cannabis industry didn't take off the way everyone planned. *Financial Post.* Retrieved from: https://financialpost.com/cannabis/cannabis-news/cannabis-legalization/a-year-in-the-weeds-why-the-cannabis-industry-didnt-take-off-the-way-everyone-planned (last accessed 29 September 2021).
Tumilty, R. (2 February 2020). Cannabis taxes not bringing the cash government expected. *National Post.* Retrieved from: https://nationalpost.com/news/politics/ca

nnabis-taxes-not-bringing-the-cash-government-expected (last accessed 29 September 2021).

Valleriani, J., Haines-Saah, R., Capler, R., Bluthenthal, R., Socias, M. E., Milloy, M. J., Kerr, T., & McNeil, R. (2020). The emergence of innovative cannabis distribution projects in the downtown eastside of Vancouver, Canada. *International Journal of Drug Policy*, 79, 102737. doi:10.1016/j.drugpo.2020.102737.

11 Drug Social Clubs – the next social club generation?

Vendula Belackova, Marta Rychert, Chris Wilkins and Tom Decorte

Introduction

There is an emerging debate about whether and how other (illegal) psychoactive substances other than cannabis should be regulated and made available to people who choose to use them (Emerson, 2019; Global Commission on Drug Policy, 2018; Karel, 1991). This includes debate about regulated production and access to psychedelics (Australian Psychedelic Society, 2017; Haden, et al., 2016), stimulant-type-drugs (Transform, 2019), and opioids (Tyndall, 2018). A recent example of the expansion of a regulated market model to other drugs is the attempt to implement a regulated market for new psychoactive substances (NPS) ('legal highs') in New Zealand (Rychert et al., 2018; Wilkins, 2014).

A central question is whether grassroots initiatives could emerge for the consumption and acquisition of psychoactive substances other than cannabis. In other words, whether 'Drug Social Clubs' (DSC) are potentially viable. Could DSCs emerge that incorporate the defining principles of Cannabis Social Clubs (CSCs), that is, being primarily grassroots, harm reduction, and self-supply (i.e. not-for-profit) orientated consumer organizations?

Cannabis Social Clubs (CSCs) are known as not-for-profit, member-only associations of people who use cannabis, who combine to grow cannabis for personal use of the said members, and who endeavor to follow responsible use or harm-reduction principles (Barriuso, 2011; CATFAC, 2014; ENCOD, 2011). To date, these initiatives have relied largely on self-regulation (defined by individual CSCs or their federations), while overtly advocating to be regulated from the side of the authorities (Belackova & Wilkins, 2018; Jansseune et al., 2019).

There are several characteristics that define CSCs and make them distinct from other forms of drug use and supply organization. Firstly, CSCs have been formed by people who use cannabis with the objective of self-supplying their members with the drug and advocate on their behalf (Arana & Sánchez, 2011; Barriuso, 2011; Decorte, 2015; Gartner et al., 2018). The majority of CSCs in Europe cater primarily for recreational cannabis use, but some also provide for medical use as well (Decorte et al., 2020). As a recent study of European CSCs revealed, they tend to be officially registered with the authorities, i.e. follow

DOI: 10.4324/9781003055679-11

national laws for non-profit organizations with established governance structures (Pardal et al., 2020). While the objectives declared by the non-profit organizations might differ based on the legal context (e.g. whether cannabis production for the use of their members is considered legal), their defining principle is that they offer participatory governance in the CSC matters (Belackova & Wilkins, 2018; Parés & Bouso, 2015). The social aspect of CSCs pertains to 'community' organization, with social bonds being an important motivator for participation among the members (Marín-Gutiérrez & Hinojosa-Becerra, this volume). Also, access to the club is not public and individuals might need to be vouched for by existing members (Decorte et al., 2020). Finally, the peer-to-peer nature of the environment seems to facilitate effective delivery of harm-reduction messaging and practice (Belackova et al., 2016; Pardal et al., 2020; Trautmann, 1995).

The CSC model has been described as a 'middle ground' option for cannabis law reform, positioned between complete prohibition of cannabis supply and legal profit-driven commercial markets. Under prohibition, CSCs offer an alternative to illicit sources, while also leading to increased cannabis quality, safety, and knowledge of the product as well as security to the members (Álvarez et al., this volume; Barriuso, 2011; Belackova et al., 2016). In the North-American context, social or compassion clubs have been established as a means of accessing medicines that are not available to people in need (Feldman & Mandel, 1998). When deployed as a source of supply in places where cannabis is legalized, CSCs can offer an alternative to the commercial cannabis industry. This is important because profit-seeking behavior, notably among the large-scale commercial cannabis industry, seems to focus on expanding the market and targeting vulnerable people who are likely to become dependent users (Hall et al., 2019; Subritzky et al., 2016).

In this chapter, we first discuss the factors that stimulate and shape the origin, growth, and safe practice of CSCs. Next, we explore whether they might emerge in relation to other drug types.

Factors that shape the origin, growth, and safe practices of Cannabis Social Clubs

CSCs have mainly emerged as grassroots movements, usually operating in legal grey areas when using the space provided by cannabis decriminalization policies and related provisions for home cultivation for personal use. The CSC model originated in Spain, with the first CSC established in 2001 (Barriuso, 2011; Pardal, this volume). An important step in promoting the model among people who use cannabis has been the adoption of Cannabis Social Club guidelines by a European advocacy group: the European Coalition for Just and Effective Drug Policies (ENCOD, 2011).[1] Organizations which refer to themselves as CSCs now operate in a number of other countries, including Belgium (Pardal & Decorte, 2018), the UK (Harper, 2020), ten other European countries (Blickman, 2014; Pardal et al., 2020), and several Latin-American countries, including Uruguay (Bewley-Taylor et al., 2014; Decorte et al., 2017; Pardal, 2016).

When it comes to the development of CSCs in Spain where the movement originated, it has never been illegal to use and possess drugs for personal consumption in private, and its Supreme Court has ruled that even shared consumption among people dependent on drugs was lawful as long as it occurred in private settings (Parés & Bouso, 2015). This has provided an important window to the cannabis club movement which has been guided by a legal interpretation that under such conditions, the operation of CSCs and the shared cultivation of cannabis by their members was lawful (Muñoz & Soto, 2001).

Uruguay is the only country in the world that established a formal legal framework for CSCs via a national law, as a part of the government policy on cannabis legalization in 2013. The uptake of the CSC model in Uruguay was initially plagued by bureaucratic and collective action problems, but overtime there has been a learning process in which some of the first CSCs taught the new clubs how to successfully form a CSC, resulting in a growing number of clubs (Pardal et al., 2019; Queirolo et al., 2016). While full legalization has protected the CSC members from law enforcement risks (compared to an uncertain situation for CSCs in countries where cannabis has been decriminalized), the rather tight regulations can also come with hardship; some clubs in Uruguay had argued in the past that limiting membership numbers together with numerous administrative requirements have made them financially unviable (Musto, this volume; Queirolo et al., 2016).

A number of self-regulatory practices has been put in place by the individual CSCs or their federations around cannabis cultivation, supply, and consumption. In Spain, these have included for instance maximum daily and maximum monthly amounts that can be retrieved by CSC members (e.g. 10g and 60g respectively), and the total amount cultivated by the club being based on estimates of consumption by CSC members (Belackova & Wilkins, 2018). Legislation has also been a guiding principle in determining CSC practice – in Belgium, a limit of one plant per member is derived from a non-enforcement policy of such cannabis quantity (Decorte, 2018). The majority of CSCs in Europe reported that they impose age limits and require endorsement from existing members for new participants (Pardal et al., 2020).

CSCs have been public advocates in the interest of people who use cannabis and have been praised for providing education and consumer advice among their members, thus contributing to harm-reduction efforts (Belackova et al., 2016; Jansseune et al., 2019; Pardal et al., 2020). There are also informal aspects of how CSCs can shape cannabis consumption; for instance, when operating consumption venues, they have encouraged tobacco-free smoking environment or alternate consumption methods (such as via medical-grade vaporizers), provided information about the different effects certain cannabis strains can have on sleep or daytime productivity, or conducted informal screening of the members for health and social issues (Belackova et al., 2016; Jansseune et al., 2019).

The uniqueness of CSCs might be the relative ease with which cannabis as a plant drug can be produced and cropped. CSCs have extended the existing practice among people who use cannabis to grow their own, in order to retrieve a safer and more affordable product than what is available on the illicit market, and to avoid this market entirely (Belackova et al., 2019; Decorte, 2008; Potter et al., 2016). Collective cannabis cultivation, as conducted in CSCs, has similar benefits to individual home growing and also can offer a greater variety of cannabis and consistency of supply to their members (Pardal et al., 2019). With this larger choice, some level of control over the production process, and with peer-led cannabis dispensing, CSC members seem to gain control over their consumption and management of mental health risks by deploying knowledge and choice over different cannabis varieties, e.g. those with higher CBD content or those with sedating vs. stimulating effects (Belackova et al., 2016; Parés et al., 2019). Yet, it should be noted that one fifth of CSCs in Europe said that they (also) bought cannabis on the illicit market in which case there might be less control over the quality of cannabis dispensed (Pardal et al., 2020). Also, not all organizations that refer to themselves as CSCs actually supply cannabis to their members; some limit their activities to information and advocacy, mainly when cannabis self-supply is against the law (Pardal et al., 2020).

To conclude, the following aspects seem to be of essence in considering whether models like CSCs could yield similar benefits with respect to other drugs:

1 Legal context around the possession, sharing, and production of psychoactive substances;
2 Existing self-organization, advocacy, and self-regulation among relevant peer groups;
3 Experience with creating safer consumption practices and environments;
4 Potential for a (safe) supply practice within the (drug) social club.

We explore these further and provide relevant examples where available, noting the specifics of different drug types and their potential for developing and maintaining an associative model comparable to CSCs.

Method

We conducted an exploratory narrative review of scientific and grey literature centered around the four areas specified above. This included research known to the authors, as well as specific Google Scholar searches with relevant key words in English and Spanish (e.g. "(drug) decriminalization" AND "possession" / "supply"/ "production"; "consumer" / "user" / "people who use drugs" / "peer" AND "self-organization" / "advocacy" / "self-regulation"; "harm reduction" / "safe consumption" AND "environment", "venue", "self-organization"; "opium" / "coca" / "cannabis" / "ayahuasca" AND "home production", "self-supply", "social supply"). In parallel, we conducted a set of consultations with several experts who were known to the authors and had insights pertaining to relevant grassroots movements. We discuss selected case studies that describe consumers' self-organizing practices in the use and supply of various psychoactive substances. The examples are by no means exhaustive. Our aim is to stimulate discussion and further research concerning the utilization of social club like models for drugs other than cannabis.

Factors for social clubs growth in the context of other drugs

Legal context around the possession, sharing, and production of particular drugs

There are multiple historical as well as contemporary examples of a 'club' model applied to psychoactive substances other than cannabis. A club model has been applied to legal 'vices' – alcohol, tobacco, or gambling. Historically, private clubs have played a role in transitioning from alcohol prohibition. In the Canadian province of New Brunswick, government-run liquor stores sold alcohol for consumption at home and a small number of private clubs were the only establishments where social consumption was allowed between 1945 and 1960 (among the members and on a non-profit basis) (Marquis, 2000). Similarly, the U.S. state of Kansas prohibited alcohol sales 'by drink' until 1987, with some exceptions made to private clubs (Dyson, 1964). Recently, a phenomenon of 'cooperative breweries' emerged in the U.S., providing a highly localized and socially embedded, grassroots economic opportunity for microbreweries or tap-rooms which raise their capital within the community and like that, create a cooperative structure of member-owners (Henderson, 2019). While these have been notable in their community-building potential, their public health impact is unclear.

In Australia, and particularly New South Wales (NSW) around 1945–1960, (drinking) clubs were initially used to secure a private environment for higher social classes which further on invested into the community by e.g. funding hospital services; a privilege of unrestricted (alcohol) drinking hours or gambling was later on granted to them. As the membership bases have been expanding and the social objectives became marginal, clubs have taken over the gambling industry and become more commercially focused (Hing, 2006). The Australian case demonstrates that the incentives provided to clubs to fulfill their social objectives should be provided alongside with limiting their profit/making opportunities. The examples of such limits can include mandating a certain proportion of their revenue into prevention, harm reduction or community-level benefits, considering limits on their size, and/or implementing measures that prohibit advertising and other practices that may harm public health (Rychert & Wilkins, 2020).

When it comes to tobacco products, a recent proposal has suggested that private, non-profit clubs could be an option for supplying consumers with nicotine vaping devices in places where this has been classified for limited medicinal use or strictly banned (Gartner et al., 2018).

It appears that the legal interpretations of current laws, the extent of law enforcement on the ground, and/or the level of political and policy commitment to the continuation of prohibition would be fundamental factors for whether or not PWUD could take an active role in self-organizing to similar models in other psychoactive substances.

As for cannabis, at least 29 countries and states across the globe have decriminalized (i.e. when the offence makes part of administrative, rather than criminal code) or depenalized (i.e. when judges and prosecutors are instructed not to apply criminal sanctions) cannabis possession (Eastwood et al., 2016). When it comes to cannabis cultivation, the Czech Republic, three Australian states, Jamaica, and Spain decriminalized home cannabis cultivation by law, while Belgium and the Netherlands do not prosecute cultivation of a small number of cannabis plants (one plant or five outdoor plants respectively). Colombia, Costa Rica, Brazil, Chile, and Georgia have adopted some form of depenalization of (small-scale) cannabis cultivation for personal use. Two countries (Mexico and South Africa) have cancelled all criminal or administrative penalties pertaining to cannabis cultivation (Belackova et al., 2019). Nine U.S. states, Canada, and Uruguay have legalized cannabis cultivation (i. e. explicitly allowed for cannabis production when conducted under specified regulations), alongside with other legal supply options except for three U.S. states which legalized home cultivation only. Additionally, five U.S. states have legalized sharing or gifting of up to an ounce (28 grams) of cannabis, and cannabis sharing has been tolerated in the Netherlands and in Spain (criminal sanctions for sales up to ten grams of cannabis are not enforced in the former and sharing among fellow users is depenalized in the latter) (Belackova et al., 2019).

Indeed, decriminalization of the possession of other psychoactive substances has been underway in some countries. Portugal has been the most renowned country to decriminalize the use and personal possession of any psychoactive drug, with strong evaluation design demonstrating positive outcomes of this policy (Hughes & Stevens, 2012). Some form of 'all drug' decriminalization or depenalization, generally pertaining to personal possession of small amounts (sometimes restricted to private spaces) has taken place in Argentina, Armenia, Chile, Colombia, Costa Rica, Croatia, Czech Republic, Ecuador, Estonia, Germany, Mexico, the Netherlands, Paraguay, Peru, Poland, and Spain (Eastwood et al., 2016). Recently, ballot initiatives to decriminalize psilocybin mushrooms have been introduced in some U.S. states; in parallel, several trials for the use of psychedelics in psychotherapy are being pursued (Aday et al., 2019; Webster, 2019).

When it comes to production of other drugs, cultivation of a small number of psychoactive plants has been decriminalized in the Czech Republic since 2010 (Belackova & Stefunkova, 2018). Other than cannabis, these plants include psilocybin mushrooms, coca plants, and plants containing DMT or mescaline (i.e. ayahuasca plants or peyote cacti) (Zeman, 2010). In the Netherlands, psilocybin mushrooms were not subjected to any control until 1998 and were freely sold in smart shops; yet in that year, the Dutch Supreme Court decided that drying this produce resulted in the production of an illicit drug and further on in 2008, psilocybin mushrooms in any form were added on a list of prohibited substances (Van den Plas, 2011). Yet, the legislation did not refer to psilocybin truffles that grow underneath the soil; as such, these can be produced and shared and remain being sold (Prohibition Partners, 2020) and since 2019 have even been subjected to a value-added tax (Fiscal Vanmorgen, 2019).

In countries like the Czech Republic, where the emphasis of decriminalization policy is on personal use, sharing still constitutes a criminal offence (Belackova & Stefunkova, 2018; Mravčík, 2015). Yet, the above listed overview of decriminalization policies across the globe has listed Armenia as an example of a country where 'social supply' in small amounts is not a crime (Eastwood et al., 2016). Indeed, in the Spanish legal context, decriminalization pertains particularly to the private circumstances of drug consumption, rather than personal use (Sánchez & Collins, 2018). As such, the Spanish Supreme Court decision has stipulated that drug sharing among heroin and cocaine users should not be prosecuted; a ruling which, in fact, gave basis to the interpretation that CSCs are within the scope of the law in Spain (Muñoz & Soto, 2001; Parés & Bouso, 2015). Moreover, a recent legal interpretation has also supported clubs similar to CSCs for the purpose of using and sourcing ayahuasca in Spain (Muñoz & Pardo, 2019). It pointed to the fact that the ayahuasca plant in itself is not prohibited by the international drug conventions (or the Spanish legislation), and in some countries, it has been considered legal in the context of traditional use.

There seem to be opportunities in regard to international drug treaties to decriminalize or even legalize cultivation of plant drugs and, potentially, extraction of their respective psychoactive compounds.. Apart from opium, coca, and cannabis, no other psychoactive plant is specifically controlled by the United Nations conventions (Walsh, 2017). Notwithstanding, given that several plants worldwide contain psychotropic drugs that are controlled by these conventions, countries might chose to go further in prohibiting such plants (e.g. ayahuasca, psilocybin mushrooms, coca bush, some types of cacti, or khat) or, more commonly, the preparations made from these (Van den Plas, 2011). As an example, psilocybin mushrooms were legal to produce in the UK and ayahuasca was legal to possess and consume in France until their governments decided to explicitly prohibit these by the law in 2005 (Van den Plas, 2011). To advocate for the legalization of use and supply of psychoactive plants on the national level, arguments for religious freedom or indigenous and human rights have been used in the past (Jelsma, 2011; Sánchez & Bouso, 2015; Sandberg, 2011).[2] It is not clear though whether such arguments hold when the plant is taken out of the geographic region where the traditional use originated into other countries (Sánchez & Bouso, 2015).

Existing self-organization, advocacy, and self-regulation among people who use drugs

There has been a number of examples among PWUD of grassroots initiatives to self-organize (Hunt et al., 2010). Peer-based organizations have emerged among dance party-scene attendants and street-based PWUD (Hunt et al., 2010).[3]

Street or dependent PWUD have advocated for and collaborated with the authorities in the design and conduct of drug treatment across the United Kingdom, Australia, Canada, the Netherlands, and the United States (Ti et al., 2012). PWUD have also self-organized and collaborated with agencies in the development of harm-reduction programs (Friedman et al., 2007; Madden & Wodak, 2014; Trautmann, 1995), to educate, and provide peer support at the party scene (Goossens, 2008; Móró & Rácz, 2013), to advocate for the reform of drug policy (O'Gorman et al., 2014), and to improve public perception of PWUD, and reduce the stigma related to drug use (Chatwin, 2010).

These activities were not conducted in isolation and there has been a varying level of agency support across different countries. In Australia, organizations involving people who use drugs have developed with financial support from the government (Ryan, 2012). In the UK, the government enacted a policy requiring that drug services engage with locally based PWUD, practically prescribing for PWUD organizations to be created (Chatwin, 2010). In the Netherlands, on the other hand, consumer organizations were grassroots movements initially independent of external funding. This seemed to leave them with greater autonomy compared to later periods when they were funded from public budgets (Chatwin, 2010; Trautmann, 1995).

Experience with creating safer consumption practice and environments

PWUD-operated drug consumption environments have been established by a broad range of drug consumer groups. These include consumption environments that were set up by people who use traditional substances, recreational drugs at a dance parties and (sub-)cultural events, and even for injected drugs or drugs otherwise consumed in a risky way.

Some substances that had been used traditionally as a part of cultural practice or ritual have found their way into modern societies.[4] Enabled by their plant nature and legal status, this has been the case of ayahuasca in Europe and the Americas which we describe later, or kava in New Zealand, Australia, and the United States. Kava is a mildly intoxicating drink made from roots of a pepper plant Piper Methysticum. It is traditionally used as a ceremonial drink in Pacific cultures; the ceremony follows strict, locally specific protocols, including the sharing of kava from a wooden bowl and absence of women (except for when pouring the drink) (Tecun, 2017). Pacific diaspora migrating to western countries has brought the practice of drinking kava with them, somewhat diluting the strict protocols and bringing the ritual into a more relaxed social space (Nosa & Ofanoa, 2009). There has also been an uptake of social drinking of kava beyond Pacific communities. For example, a not-for-profit kava social club built around a group of friends and their social networks has been operating in Auckland (New Zealand) since 2011. First established as an informal student association, over the years the club organized hundreds of meetings to sample kava, introduced new cultivars, and engaged in social discussions (Kava Society, n.d.). The club members' interest in accessing different varieties of kava plants and the social aspect of communal kava drinking appear to be the primary attractions of the Auckland kava club. Part of the more recent club evolution involves opening of an online kava shop which has been possible because the sale and supply of kava is legal when under food laws in New Zealand (Rychert & Wilkins, 2016).

Similarly, the remedial and religious use of ayahuasca has been introduced from the traditional societies in South America into the western world (Luna, 2011; Sánchez & Bouso, 2015). The specifics of ayahuasca use, perhaps similar to kava, is that its use has been limited to the context of a ritual and has not been found in recreational settings where drug use might be more individualized (Sánchez & Bouso, 2015). Ayahuasca use in Europe and the Americas has taken place under the auspices of Santo Daime[5] and other religious organizations (Groisman, 2009), commercially run retreats (Fu et al., 2020; Prayag et al., 2015), ayahuasca circles, and shamanic rituals or, as Feeney et al. (2018) describe, as a combination of the above. In Spain, the ritual has indeed been, among other options, introduced in the context of a social club. Established in 2013, the Association for the Study of the Effects of Ayahuasca has nearly 700 members and six staff members. New members are recruited via word of mouth; as a private, not-for-profit association, it complies with the regulations by not publicizing their activities. Each new member is interviewed about their motives to join the club and is screened by the staff of the club for physical and mental health issues. After paying the membership fee, the participants are included in a mailing list where they can get information about upcoming ayahuasca sessions. These span a couple of days and include safe space for the ritual, accommodation, meals, accompanying through the ritual, and integration sessions. The enclosed and non-commercial nature of the ayahuasca club can be seen in parallel with the more entrepreneurially run psychedelic retreats (Fu et al., 2020; Prayag et al., 2015). Such retreats generally operate in countries where psychedelic plants like ayahuasca, psilocybin mushrooms, or iboga remain uncontrolled or legal (Third Wave, 2019). Psychedelic retreats generally offer the use of these plants in the context of healing and personal growth and include therapeutic as well as integration components, but their conduct has been diverse and unregulated (Fleming, 2019).

Related to the use of psychedelic drugs is the emergence of 'transformational events' which are embedding psychedelic experiences and have, among other things, given rise to peer-based psychedelic support (Ruane, 2017a). Set up as chill-out spaces which provide a sanctuary from the sometimes overwhelming festival environment, the so-called sitters are volunteering there to provide care and comfort to people who are in acute drug-related discomfort (commonly referred to as 'bad trip'), yet not in situations assessed as requiring medical attention (Kranz, 2020; Ruane, 2017b). This adds onto the record of peer-support organizations who have engaged in education, chill-out-zones, or drug checking services in party settings in the past (Hunt et al., 2010). Also linked to the psychedelic movement is a relatively new phenomenon of the peer-based 'integration circles' which help their participants to process their experiences from using psychedelics (Swann, 2017). In comparison to the situation where the above-mentioned sitters intervene, the circle participants are not in an acute stage of intoxication or crisis; the aim of the circle is to incorporate their recent psychedelic experience into their personal development (Godasi, 2019).

Indeed, the party scene offers interesting examples of creating participatory spaces where drug use takes place. For instance, the so-called 'raves' which are often operated illegally and are known to rely on do-it-yourself (DIY) principles, i.e. created among participants and operated on non-commercial principles, have been largely linked to the consumption of ecstasy, LSD, and other stimulant or hallucinogenic substances (Peter, 2020). These grassroots events have been denoted as fostering community and solidarity among the participants via their ritualized nature to which the drug use can contribute. Anecdotally, several sound-systems who travel around Europe have supplied drugs on these events too; yet, a perspective offered from within the community says that typically, these were not perceived as drugs of addiction and supplying them was seen as part of the event organization to which substance use represents an inherent part (Wimmer, 2006). Despite prevalent drug and alcohol use, excessive intoxication is often seen as against the community norms (Kavanaugh & Anderson, 2008).

Several instances of peer-operated venues for the consumption of substances with greater risks have been documented too. Early research of the so-called 'shooting galleries', i.e. places that people who inject drugs would use for drug administration, pointed to their potential for spreading blood-borne viruses like HIV and Hepatitis C due to the existing viral load and evidence of sharing of drug paraphernalia (Chitwood et al., 1990; Murphy & Waldorf, 1991). Yet, even early research has seen the varied potential across these sites for safe injecting practices (Ouellet et al., 1991) and suggested that appropriate education is essential to reduce the risks taken at these sites (Des Jarlais & Friedman, 1990).

Over time, a safer model of peer-based consumption sites for (at present, illegally acquired) substances like heroin or crack cocaine that can be both smoked and inhaled has taken place. Peer-operated (safe) consumption sites which are run on the principles of harm reduction have been well documented in Canada (Jozaghi, 2015; Kerr et al., 2005; McNeil et al., 2014), United States (Davidson et al., 2018), or Italy (Bergamo et al., 2019). Yet, they have commonly lacked endorsement from the authorities. Only recently, in the face of the opioid overdose epidemic, several Canadian provinces authorized temporary peer-staffed Overdose Prevention Sites (OPS) (Wallace et al., 2019). These sites have managed to build on existing environments and relationships when they deploy peer-workers from within the community alongside with non-PWUD coordinators from established services. OPS have demonstrated a great record in preventing drug-related harm, yet the emerging research shows that more resources should be put in, including an appropriate remuneration and psychological support to the peers working on the frontline of the overdose crisis (Thomson et al., 2017).

PWUD operated (safer) supply practice

In order to avoid illicit drug markets with their uncertain quality and safety profiles, PWUD have supplied themselves. For instance, several psychoactive plants have been cultivated with ease in home settings or harvested in the wild. Yet, the contemporary literature suggests that synthetic drugs probably cannot be manufactured safely enough by the consumers so that the benefits of home production could outweigh its risks. Yet, alternative proposals for the supply of synthetic drugs to the consumers have emerged.

Harvesting natural plant-type drugs might appear to be more analogous to the CSC operation. A record of harvesting and using poppy for opium exists among PWUD who can use this as a (seasonal) alternative to their otherwise regular opioid use, potentially replacing injecting with oral or smoking routes of administration (Braye et al., 2007; Haber et al., 2019; Klusoňová et al., 2005). Also, self-supply of psilocybin mushrooms appears to be common among users (Oss & Oeric, 1992; Steinhardt, 2018). A recent online survey of 564 'natural psychoactive users' mainly from the United States and Spain revealed that a substantial proportion of those who have used psylocibin mushrooms, San Pedro cactus, and several other less known plant drugs have grown or harvested them (Aixalá et al., 2020). Methods of extraction of psychoactive compounds, for example ayahuasca, are also available, yet the resulting drug can have a residual and toxic content from the solvents used in the extraction process (Rossi et al., 2019).

Alternative proposals have emerged from consumer representatives to source safer forms of (powder) drugs than those available on the illegal market. An example is a proposal for 'heroin compassion clubs' in Canada which have been suggested as consumer cooperatives. In this model, the cooperative would source medical-grade heroin from a pharmaceutical producer and provide restricted access to its (opioid-dependent) members (Thomson et al., 2019). Similar to the peer-based Overdose Prevention Sites described above, or to a recently implemented program which distributes less potent pharmaceutical opioids via a dispensing machine (Tyndall, 2018), this model was proposed to reduce the risk of overdose pertaining to fentanyl and other high-potency opioids flooding the street market (Thomson et al., 2019). The model of a 'heroin compassion club' which was primarily designed by people with lived experience of drug use suggested the presence of experts on addiction treatment and representatives of support services in the eventual Board. Despite harm-reduction peer programs like OPS are now being legally sanctioned all across Canada, they can still be contrasted to professionally-staffed services known as Drug Consumption Rooms (DCRs) or Supervised Injecting Facilities (SIFs). OPS typically do not offer services like counselling or referrals to health and social programs (Wallace et al., 2019). Indeed, DCRs and SIFs are being considered at the very opposite side of the drug policy spectrum than structured treatment programs in Canada, the Netherlands, or Switzerland where participants can self-inject with pharmaceutical-grade heroin or similar compounds upon medical prescription (Strang & Fortson, 2004). Thus, bridging peer-based harm reduction with actual provision of a high-risk substance can be rather controversial.

Home production of synthetic drugs has taken place in many countries, perhaps to sustain people with dependence when traditional drug supply is low or not affordable (Abdala et al., 2006). This has typically taken the form of diverting over-the-counter opioids (Van Hout, 2014), production of methamphetamine from ephedrine-containing preparations (Sexton et al., 2006; Zabransky, 2007), or manufacture of drugs from industrial items such as GHB produced from solvents and cleaning agents (van Amsterdam et al., 2012). Home production of drugs from available pharmaceuticals has been especially prevalent in the former Soviet Union (Hearne et al., 2016). Yet, some processes in analytical chemistry carry substantial risks of explosion, toxicity or contamination (Santos et al., 2005; Sexton et al., 2006) and as such, cannot be recommended outside of certified laboratory settings. Also, an abundance of health risks pertaining to the use of home-produced drugs has been documented. For instance, when it comes to the infamous drug 'krokodil', its negative health consequences including mortality have been linked to the crude extraction procedures and the resulting presence of toxic by-products (Hearne et al., 2016). Another risk is the unknown concentration of drugs manufactured without access to analytical equipment. This has been noted, for instance, in relation to home-produced GHB where potency was shown to vary, posing significant risks due to a steep dose-response relationship (van Amsterdam et al., 2012). A recent study has revealed that it is a part of the consumer ethos in online discussion boards not to share complex drug production procedures, other than when it comes to a potential purification of adulterated drugs (Hearne et al., 2017).

Another potentially feasible source for consumer collectives could be darknet markets where illicit substances can be purchased in bulk and where reviews on the drug quality and purity and seller reliability are published (Aldridge & Decary-Hetu, 2016). This mode of acquisition has previously been used by a consumer association in Spain to purchase and collectively consume the hallucinogen 2C-B, as described in an observational study (González et al., 2015; Papaseit et al., 2018). According to personal communication with the study coordinator, the ethics committee approved researchers to study the emotional effects on people of taking 2C-B recreationally. Again, it is important to note that in Spain the shared use of drugs on private property is legal. Importantly, a drug-checking service was used to verify the content of the drug, both for the purpose of the research and for consumers` safety.

Discussion and conclusions

We have presented a number of examples of self-organization, self-regulation, and self-supply among street-based PWUD, recreational drug users, and party-scene attendants.

The aims of formal consumer groups include advocacy, representation in relevant programs, or simply reduction of use-related harms, both with or without financial and expert support from the authorities. The level of agency found across different drug consumer groups and the scope of their activities, as well as the existing record of self-supply behavior, suggest that it could be possible for PWUD to form organizations similar to CSCs. The particular examples of environments formed by PWUD in order to facilitate the (safe) consumption of psychoactive substances include the kava club in New Zealand, ayahuasca clubs in Spain, a variety of environments tailored to the use of psychedelics around the world (such as volunteer-based chill-out zones or peer-based integration circles), or peer-operated overdose prevention sites in Canada. Notwithstanding, not all peer-based consumption environments in the past have promoted safety, and thus policies seeking to authorize CSC operation should emphasize harm reduction and promote it as a core principle for peer organizations seeking to host drug social clubs.

We have described how several countries have now moved in the direction of decriminalizing possession and use of other drugs than cannabis, while others are considering it. When criminal risks and stigma towards PWUD are minimized, this might further facilitate the agency of consumer groups to advocate on behalf of their members or even aim for establishing (safer) consumption environments. In the Czech Republic and the Netherlands, the cultivation of plant drugs has indeed been decriminalized. This is well in line with international drug control treaties that do not specifically prohibit any plant drug other than cannabis, opium, or coca, despite many plants contain prohibited compounds. As can be seen in the case of ayahuasca, however, there are wide differences in terms of how the national legislation and court systems interpret this. In countries where the laws are permissive to natural drug production, not-for-profit and self-supply initiatives could well emerge for plant drugs (in places like the Netherlands, Spain or several Latin American countries, their commercial counterparts have already taken place). For extracted or synthetic drugs, alternatives have been proposed, such as in a Canadian proposal to source heroin from a licensed producer for the members of a compassion club, or in case of a Spanish social club buying a particular synthetic drug from the darknet and testing for its content before use.

The primary concern in 'handing' the responsibility over psychoactive substance use to the consumers might be around controlling safety, spread of drug use and dependency, and related health and social problems. Previous research has pointed to the importance of 'enabling environments' (Duff, 2010) where the harms from drug use can be minimized, as a counterpart to 'risk environments' (Rhodes, 2002). The example of OPS which are peer-staffed, harm-reduction spaces for injecting illicit drugs that have been authorized in Canada as one of the responses to the overdose crisis, as opposed to shooting galleries, which have historically been associated with several health and social risks, shows that groups of consumers can set up spaces which vary largely in terms of their norms around safety. The factors that influence the level of risk might be the legal context as well as education in harm reduction. At the same time, it is important to acknowledge that as was the historical case of the Dutch and other street-based organizations, and perhaps as is the case of the contemporary psychedelic sitters and integration circles, PWUD tend to be at the forefront of developing new harm-reduction initiatives, rather than lag behind.

Equally, consumer-operated drug supply could be a way to enhance safety. Focusing on plant drugs which can undergo a controlled growing process is one way to achieve that, but other means of achieving safer drug supply exist. For instance, the main motivation of the recent and, to date, not implemented Canadian proposal to supply members of a compassion club with pharmaceutical-grade heroin has been its lower propensity for overdose than with the (high potency) opioids currently sold on the illicit market (Thomson et al., 2019). Therefore, bulk purchase of substances from (certified) providers or with verified content, can represent a source of risk reduction. Indeed, people who use drugs have demonstrated their willingness to subject the drugs they are using to chemical analyses (Barratt et al., 2018; Kennedy et al., 2018; Krieger et al., 2018; Sherman et al., 2019). However, for vulnerable PWUD, a number of barriers to drug-checking programs exist (Bardwell et al., 2019b); perhaps drug social clubs could be an avenue to mitigate these barriers by ascertaining drug checking in bulk. In fact, recent research has pointed to the trend of potentially checking drug content before it reaches the consumers; a recent survey from United States revealed a practice of checking drug content for friends as well as customers (Palamar et al., 2019) and trusted dealers on illicit market were found to test drug batches and as such, prevent their customers` exposure to high-potency opioids (Carroll et al., 2020). Studies from Canada also suggested that drug suppliers should indeed be involved in drug checking and harm-reduction programming (Bardwell et al., 2019a; Kolla & Strike, 2020).

These novel approaches are in contrast to the previously established paradigm that drug dealers should be excluded from drug checking to prevent them from advertising their drugs as 'safe' (Brunt, 2017); in particular, this has been an explicit condition for using the long-standing Dutch drug checking service called DIMS (Smit-Rigter & Van der Gouwe, 2019). As any social club members would be in a double role of both consumers and suppliers (to themselves and their peers), their involvement in drug checking is probably less controversial, yet carries a similar risk of a potentially false perception of drug safety. For instance, not all drug-checking methods provide a quantitative assessment (i.e. information about drug potency) despite the presence of high-risk compounds might be a sufficiently strong warning message (Barratt & Ezard, 2016). Moreover, even when quantitative assessments are available, sampling of larger batches might be problematic (Bardwell et al, 2019a). Also, it should be noted that potency in itself might not be the main risk factor for, e.g. opioid, overdose (Darke, 2016). Notwithstanding, with good availability of drug checking, and establishment of adequate procedures drug social clubs could take a variety of steps to communicate the potential risks of using a particular drug batch to their members and rule out the use of identified risky or unwanted compounds.

A number of challenges to operating safe drug-consumption environments might emerge. These could be specific to the drug type and the consumer group. When it comes to the misuse of street drugs, there are obvious risks related to (opioid) overdose, injecting, and related blood-borne diseases, as well as dependence and the related chaotic lifestyles. Interlinking the club with support services and perhaps even assisting in organizational duties might be necessary. In party settings, the main risks seem to be related to binge use and polydrug use and any peer-run consumption venues would need to take a stand on managing those situations, ranging from peer-enacted norms about responsible use to emergency protocols for acute intoxication. Also, protocols around neighborhood nuisance are of essence; for example, management of intoxicated individuals, related noise, or rubbish disposal (the latter two pertaining especially to any outdoor environments). The dispensing staff at a drug social club would have an important role in educating about the drug content and safer modes of administration. When it comes to the broader group of psychedelics, there are risks pertaining to mental health, both in acute and chronic manner. While psychedelic sitters and integration circles have been implemented, there seems to be additional space for providing specific advice to the consumers before taking particular substances. As our overview suggests, some of the risks pertaining to drug consumption have been addressed by drug using peers and organizations in the past and represent an avenue of positive examples to be developed further.

Our findings lead us to conclude that with the existing record among the peer movement, social clubs might be a feasible model under which a range of activities could yield a safer environment for the use and supply of a wide spectrum of psychoactive substances. As outlined in Table 11.1, various forms of self-organization, advocacy, self-regulation, consumption environments, and supply models could take place among PWUD who consume drugs recreationally, for the purpose of personal transformation, and/or in an intensive manner.

Yet, it appears that for any grassroots movement to be pursued in the path of drug social clubs, the legal and administrative framework is of essence. Despite social clubs being described as a 'middle-ground' option, (half-way) decriminalization policies per se might not be a sufficient impetus to drive their creation. Countries like Portugal, the Czech Republic, or the Netherlands have decriminalized all drug use and personal possession decades ago, and both the Czech Republic and the Netherlands also decriminalized personal cannabis cultivation (Belackova & Stefunkova, 2018; Hughes & Stevens,

Table 11.1 Functions and activities of potential drug social clubs per PWUD group.

FUNCTION	*POSSIBLE FORMS AND ACTIVITIES*	*Consumer groups*[1]	*PWUD who seek personal transformation (e.g. so-called psychonauts)*	*People who inject drugs (PWID) or other high-risk drug users (HRDU)*	*People who use drugs recreationally or for other reasons*
		SUBSTANCE TYPE[1]	*Psychedelics*	*Stimulants, opioids, cannabis**	*Cannabis, ecstasy, cocaine, other stimulants, psychedelics*
SELF-ORGANISATION	Unofficial consumer groups		YES/NO[1]	YES/NO[1]	YES/NO[1]
	Officially registered consumer associations operating on a self-sustained basis		YES	NO[2]	YES
	Officially registered consumer associations linked to government funding and expert support		YES/NO[2]	YES	YES/NO[2]
ADVOCACY AND SELF-REGULATION	Policy reform advocacy		YES	YES	YES
	Advocacy for improvement of services/ design of treatment		YES[3]	YES	YES[3]
	Advocacy for reduction of stigma/normalization of use		YES	YES	YES
	Information about safer modes of drug use and administration		YES	YES	YES
	Peer-based harm-reduction interventions/ psychedelic integration		YES	YES	YES
CONSUMPTION ENVIRONMENT	(Safer) space for individual drug consumption		YES	YES	YES
	Collective ritual/ceremonial consumption		YES	YES/NO	YES
	Special events for socialization and/or drug consumption		YES	YES	YES

FUNCTION	*POSSIBLE FORMS AND ACTIVITIES*	*Consumer groups*[1]	*PWUD who seek personal transformation (e.g. so-called psychonauts)*	*People who inject drugs (PWID) or other high-risk drug users (HRDU)*	*People who use drugs recreationally or for other reasons*
		SUBSTANCE TYPE[1]	*Psychedelics*	*Stimulants, opioids, cannabis**	*Cannabis, ecstasy, cocaine, other stimulants, psychedelics*
SUPPLY	Cultivation of plants		YES	YES	YES
	Rather simple processing of plants into other products		YES	YES	YES
	Synthetic drug production		YES/NO[4]	YES/NO[4]	YES/NO[4]
	Obtained from informal/illegal markets when drug testing is available		YES/NO[5]	YES/NO[5]	YES/NO[5]
	Obtained from certified producers		YES	YES	YES
	Distribution on selected times/events only		YES	NO	YES
	Dispensing within opening hours from the social club		YES	YES	YES

Notes:

[1] There exists an overlap between the proposed consumer groups as well as the type of substances that are used within them; in this table, we assume drug social clubs being primarily driven by consumer groups which might be centered around a single substance or a multitude of drugs. Yet, given the unique (self) supply environments for particular substances and the specific legal contexts surrounding them, an alternate division could be presented where a multitude of e.g. cocaine social clubs emerges such that primarily cater for either recreational or high-risk PWUD, or where different PWUD groups are accounted for at once. Also, we decided not to include medicinal users as a specific category of PWUD, because health (e.g. mental health, substitution for the drug of dependence, pain management) might be one of the reasons for drug use across all the presented groups.

[2] Social clubs involving PWID or other HRDU would likely require involvement of experts and funding if operating consumption environments and/or supplying drugs (in case of other types of PWUD, these might be beneficial too).

[3] While recreational and transformative drug use are not directly linked to the need for drug treatment, they might be important stakeholders for mental health programs or drug checking services.

[4] Complex chemical processes would likely require operation of a certified laboratory which might not be within the scope of a drug social club.

[5] While checking for absence of known harmful adulterants such as high-potency opioids might be a feasible procedure to reduce risks, obtaining information about the exact compounds present in the batch and their concentration would be more complicated. This is particularly risky with respect to the multitude of new psychoactive substances on the market with a wide range of effective and potentially toxic doses.

YES – has been documented or can be seen as feasible / NO – probably or certainly not feasible; please see commentary below.

*Cannabis has been included as a drug used by PWID and HRDU, because its use is prevalent in these groups of PWUD; in particular, there have been recent movements among street opioid users in Vancouver, Canada to self-supply with cannabis in order to manage opioid withdrawal and potentially reduce their risk of overdose (Valleriani et al., 2020).

2007; Van Solinge, 1999). Yet, Portugal has not seen any form of social club-type movement with cannabis or other substances, and their appearance in the latter two countries has been rare (Pardal et al., 2020). Also, even favorable legal interpretations for CSCs in places like Spain have not deterred the authorities from intervening against CSCs (Arana, 2019; Jansseune et al., 2019) and, on the contrary, the lack of clear regulations has created an environment where the CSC model can be taken over by profit-seeking organizations (Decorte, 2018). The risk of full-scale legalization as in the case of Uruguay, on the other hand, is that the authorities set up requirements that may make the model not economically viable, as some CSCs had argued in the past (Queirolo et al., 2016). As such, authorities should avoid 'over-regulation' of a model which primarily must rely on consumer initiative and agency, such as avoiding technical requirements on cultivation sites that would normally require significant investment capital or not imposing such caps on the CSC size which would yield the cost of cannabis being substantially higher than its legal or illicit alternatives. To conclude, a mix of strong peer movement, feasibility of drug self-supply, and of favorable policy environment will be instrumental for drug social clubs to emerge and sustain their activities.

Acknowledgements

We would like to thank the following people for their valuable input into this chapter, namely Òscar Parés (ICCERS), Pep Cunyat (Association for the Study of Effects of Ayahuasca), Debora Gonzales (PHI Association for the Study of States of Consciousness), Martin Pazitny (Slovac Psychedelic Society), Ana Afuera (ENCOD), Antoniu Llort (ARSU – Associaciació Reus Som Útils).

Notes

1 These guidelines have recently been updated (ENCOD, 2020).
2 For example, ayahuasca use in the context of Santo Daime church, cannabis in Rastafarian religion, or coca leaf among indigenous populations in several Latin-American countries (Jelsma, 2011; Sandberg, 2011).
3 The examples of consumer organizations that have been described in the literature include the Vancouver Area Network of Drug Users in Canada (Kerr et al., 2006), The Australian Illicit Drug Users League (AIVL) (Madden & Wodak, 2014), or the Dutch Medical-Social Service for Heroin Users (MDHG) (Chatwin, 2010). Founded in 2006, the International Network of People Who Use Drugs (INPUD) has become the leading organization that represents people who use drugs on a global scale. INPUD currently enlists more than 50 national-level organizations across 25 countries on its webpage. Many other organizations might be founded and operated by people who use drugs, but their drug use might not be disclosed.
4 On the contrary, some psychoactive drugs which have had significant use in their places of origin never did spread into western societies, at least not beyond their limited use by migrant groups like in the case of khat (Anderson et al., 2020).
5 Santo Daime is a syncretic religion founded in the 1930s in a Brazilian Amazonian state and incorporates elements of several religious or spiritual traditions including Christianity, Spiritism, and shamanism. Ayahusca is being consumed during its ceremonies.

References

Abdala, N., Grund, J. P. C., Tolstov, Y., Kozlov, A. P., & Heimer, R. (2006). Can home-made injectable opiates contribute to the HIV epidemic among injection drug users in the countries of the former Soviet Union? *Addiction*, 101(5), 731–737. doi:10.1111/j.1360-0443.2006.01409.x.

Aday, J. S., Davoli, C. C., & Bloesch, E. K. (2019). 2018: A watershed year for psychedelic science. *Drug Science, Policy and Law*, 5, 2050324519872284. doi:10.1177/2050324519872284.

Aixalá, M., Ona, G., Parés, Ò., & Bouso, J. C. (2020). Patterns of use, desired effects, and mental health status of a sample of natural psychoactive drug users. *Drugs: Education, Prevention and Policy*, 27(3), 191–198. doi:10.1080/09687637.2019.1611739.

Aldridge, J., & Decary-Hetu, D. (2016). Cryptomarkets and the future of illicit drug markets. In J. Mounteney, A. Bo, & A. Oteo (Eds.), *The internet and drug markets*, 23–30. European Monitoring Centre for Drugs and Drug Addiction: Insights. Luxembourg: Publications Office of the European Union.

Aldridge, J., Stevens, A., & Barratt, M. J. (2018). Will growth in cryptomarket drug buying increase the harms of illicit drugs? *Addiction*, 113(5), 789–796. doi:10.1111/add.13899.

Anderson, D., Beckerleg, S., Hailu, D., & Klein, A. (2020). *The khat controversy: Stimulating the debate on drugs*. London: Routledge.

Arana, X. (2019). Cannabis regulation in Europe: Country report Spain. Retrieved from: https://www.tni.org/files/publication-downloads/cr_spain_final.pdf (last accessed 28 September 2021).

Arana, X., & Sánchez, V. (2011). Cannabis cultivation in Spain – The case of Cannabis Social Clubs. In T. Decorte, G. R. Potter, & M. Bouchard (Eds.), *World wide weed: Global trends in cannabis cultivation and its control*. London: Ashgate.

Australian Psychedelic Society. (2017). Submission to the Victorian inquiry into drug law reform. Retrieved from: https://www.parliament.vic.gov.au/images/stories/committees/lrrcsc/Drugs_/Submissions/187_2017.03.17_-_The_Australian_Psychedelic_Society_-_submission.pdf (last accessed 28 September 2021).

Bancroft, A., & Reid, P. S. (2016). Concepts of illicit drug quality among darknet market users: Purity, embodied experience, craft and chemical knowledge. *International Journal of Drug Policy*, 35, 42–49. doi:10.1016/j.drugpo.2015.11.008.

Bardwell, G., Boyd, J., Arredondo, J., McNeil, R., & Kerr, T. (2019a). Trusting the source: The potential role of drug dealers in reducing drug-related harms via drug checking. *Drug and Alcohol Dependence*, 198, 1–6. doi:10.1016/j.drugalcdep.2019.01.035.

Bardwell, G., Boyd, J., Tupper, K. W., & Kerr, T. (2019b). "We don't got that kind of time, man. We're trying to get high!": Exploring potential use of drug checking technologies among structurally vulnerable people who use drugs. *International Journal of Drug Policy*, 71, 125–132. doi:10.1016/j.drugpo.2019.06.018.

Barratt, M. J., Bruno, R., Ezard, N., & Ritter, A. (2018). Pill testing or drug checking in Australia: acceptability of service design features. *Drug and Alcohol Review*, 37 (2), 226–236. doi:10.1111/dar.12576.

Barratt, M. J., & Ezard, N. (2016). Drug checking interventions can track the nature and size of the discrepancy between self-report and actual drugs consumed. *Addiction*, 111(3), 558–559. doi:10.1111/add.13194.

Barriuso, A. M. (2011). *Cannabis social clubs in Spain: A normalizing alternative underway*. Series on Legislative Reform of Drug Policies (Vol. 9). Amsterdam: Transnational Institute.

Belackova, V., Roubalova, M., & van de Ven, K. (2019). Overview of "home" cultivation policies and the case for community-based cannabis supply. *International Journal of Drug Policy*, 71, 36–46. doi:10.1016/j.drugpo.2019.05.021.

Belackova, V., & Stefunkova, M. (2018). Interpreting the Czech drug decriminalization: The glass is half full – Response to Cerveny, J., Chomynova, P., Mravcik, V., & van Ours, J. C. (2017). Cannabis decriminalization and the age of onset of cannabis use. *International Journal of Drug Policy*, 52, 102–105. doi:10.1016/j.drugpo.2017.02.014.

Belackova, V., Tomkova, A., & Zabransky, T. (2016). Qualitative research in Spanish Cannabis Social Clubs:"The moment you enter the door, you are minimising the risks". *International Journal of Drug Policy* (34), 49–57. doi:10.1016/j.drugpo.2016.04.009.

Belackova, V., & Wilkins, C. (2018). Consumer agency in cannabis supply – Exploring auto-regulatory documents of the cannabis social clubs in Spain. *International Journal of Drug Policy*, 54, 26–34. doi:10.1016/j.drugpo.2017.12.018.

Bergamo, S., Parisi, G., & Jarre, P. (2019). Harm reduction in Italy: the experience of an unsanctioned supervised injection facility run by drug users. *Drugs and Alcohol Today*, 19(2), 59–71. doi:10.1108/DAT-03-2018-0011.

Bewley-Taylor, D., Blickman, T., & Jelsma, M. (2014). The rise and decline of cannabis prohibition: The history of cannabis in the UN drug control system and options for reform. Retrieved from: https://www.tni.org/files/download/rise_and_decline_web.pdf (last accessed 28 September 2021).

Blickman, T. (2014). Cannabis policy reform in Europe: Bottom up rather than top down. *Series on Legislative Reform of Drug Policies*, 28 (December), 1–24.

Braye, K., Harwood, T., Inder, R., Beasley, R., & Robinson, G. (2007). Poppy seed tea and opiate abuse in New Zealand. *Drug and Alcohol Review*, 26(2), 215–219. doi:10.1080/09595230601146637.

Brunt, T. M. (2017). *Drug checking as a harm reduction tool for recreational drug users: opportunities and challenges Background paper commissioned by the EMCDDA for Health and social responses to drug problems: a European guide*. Lisbon: European Monitoring Centre for Drugs and Drug Addiction.

Carroll, J. J., Rich, J. D., & Green, T. C. (2020). The protective effect of trusted dealers against opioid overdose in the US. *International Journal of Drug Policy*, 78, 102695. doi:10.1016/j.drugpo.2020.102695.

CATFAC. (2014). Código de Buenas Prácticas para Asociaciones Cannàbicas. Retrieved from: http://catfac.org/wp-content/uploads/2014/10/C%C3%B3digo-de-Buenas-Pr%C3%A1cticas-2015.pdf (last accessed 28 September 2021).

Chatwin, C. (2010). User involvement in the illegal drugs field: what can Britain learn from European experiences? *Safer Communities*, 9(4), 51. doi:10.5042/sc.2010.0585.

Chitwood, D. D., McCoy, C. B., Inciardi, J. A., McBride, D. C., Comerford, M., Trapido, E., McCoy, V., Page, B., Griffin, J., Fletcher, M. A. & Ashman, M. A. (1990). HIV seropositivity of needles from shooting galleries in south Florida. *American Journal of Public Health*, 80(2), 150–152. doi:10.2105/AJPH.80.2.150.

Darke, S. (2016). Heroin overdose. *Addiction*, 111(11), 2060–2063. doi:10.1111/add.13516.

Davidson, P. J., Lopez, A. M., & Kral, A. H. (2018). Using drugs in un/safe spaces: impact of perceived illegality on an underground supervised injecting facility in the United States. *International Journal of Drug Policy*, 53, 37–44. doi:10.1016/j.drugpo.2017.12.005. Decorte, T. (2008). Domestic cannabis cultivation in Belgium: The (un) intended effects of the national drug policy on the cannabis market. In D.

Korf (Ed.), *Cannabis in Europe: Dynamics in perception, policy and markets*, 69–86. Lengerich, Germany: Pabst Science Publishers.

Decorte, T. (2015). Cannabis social clubs in Belgium: Organizational strengths and weaknesses, and threats to the model. *International Journal of Drug Policy*, 26(2), 122–130. doi:10.1016/j.drugpo.2014.07.016.

Decorte, T. (2018). *Regulating Cannabis: A detailed scenario for a nonprofit Cannabis market*. Bloomington, IN: Archway Publishing.

Decorte, T., Lenton, S., & Wilkins, C. (2020). *Legalizing cannabis: Experiences, lessons and scenarios*. New York: Routledge.

Decorte, T., Pardal, M., Queirolo, R., Boidi, M. F., Sánchez Avilés, C., & Parés, Ó. F. (2017). Regulating Cannabis Social Clubs: A comparative analysis of legal and self-regulatory practices in Spain, Belgium and Uruguay. *International Journal of Drug Policy*, 43, 44–56. doi:10.1016/j.drugpo.2016.12.020.

Des Jarlais, D. C., & Friedman, S. R. (1990). Shooting galleries and AIDS: Infection probabilities and 'tough' policies. *American Journal of Public Health*, 80(2), 142–144.

Duff, C. (2010). Enabling places and enabling resources: New directions for harm reduction research and practice. *Drug and Alcohol Review*, 29(3), 337–344. doi:10.1111/j.1465-3362.2010.00187.x.

Dyson, E. (1964). Liquor regulation, racial discrimination, and private clubs in Kansas. *University of Kansas Law Review*, 13, 135.

Eastwood, N., Fox, E., & Rosmarin, A. (2016). *A quiet revolution: Drug decriminalisation across the globe*. London: Transform, Release.

Emerson, B. (2019). Regulation of illegal drugs – no longer what?, but how? *Journal of Illicit Economies and Development*, 1(3), 251–254. doi:10.31389/jied.19.

ENCOD. (2011). Code of conduct for European Cannabis Social Clubs. Retrieved from http://www.encod.org/info/CODE-OF-CONDUCT-FOR-EUROPEAN.html (last accessed 28 September 2021).

ENCOD. (2020). A regulatory model for cannabis access Guidelines European Social Clubs. European Coalition for Just and Effective Drug Policies. Retrieved from: https://www.akzept.eu/wp-content/uploads/2020/12/Guidelines-European-Cannabis-Social-Clubs-published.pdf (last accessed 3 November 2021).

Feeney, K., Labate, B. C., & Hudson, J. H. (2018). Bubbling with controversy: Legal challenges for ceremonial ayahuasca circles in the United States. In B. C. Labate & C. Cavnar (Eds.), *Plant medicines, healing and psychedelic science*, 87–111. New York: Springer.

Feldman, H. W., & Mandel, J. (1998). Providing medical marijuana: The importance of cannabis clubs. *Journal of Psychoactive Drugs*, 30(2), 179–186. doi:10.1080/02791072.1998.10399688.

Fiscal Vanmorgen. (16 September 2019). 21% BTW voor de levering van magische truffels. *MOCuitgevers*. Retrieved from: https://www.taxlive.nl/nl/documenten/nieuws/21-btw-voor-de-levering-van-magische-truffels/ (last accessed 3 November 2021).

Fleming, A. (2019). A psychedelic retreat proves a healing trip. *The Guardian*. Retrieved from: https://www.theguardian.com/lifeandstyle/2019/nov/16/a-psychedelic-retreat-proves-a-healing-trip (last accessed 28 September 2021).

Friedman, S. R., de Jong, W., Rossi, D., Touzé, G., Rockwell, R., Des Jarlais, D. C., & Elovich, R. (2007). Harm reduction theory: Users' culture, micro-social indigenous harm reduction, and the self-organization and outside-organizing of users' groups. *International Journal of Drug Policy*, 18(2), 107–117. doi:10.1016/j.drugpo.2006.11.006.

Fu, C.-C. A., Morales, M. L., & Cabada, M. M. (2020). Ayahuasca experiences for sale on the internet – systematic analysis of health information provided to travelers in commercial websites. *Journal of Travel Medicine*. doi:10.1093/jtm/taaa142.

Gartner, C., Bromberg, M., Musgrove, T., & Luong, K. (2018). Vape club: Exploring non-profit regulatory models for the supply of vaporised nicotine products. *International Journal of Environment Research and Public Health*, 15(8). doi:10.3390/ijerph15081744.

Global Commission on Drug Policy. (2018). Regulation: The responsible control of drugs. Geneva: Global Commission on Drug Policy. Retrieved from: https://www.globalcommissionondrugs.org/reports/regulation-the-responsible-control-of-drugs (last accessed 2 November 2021).

Godasi, S. (2019). A guide to starting a community psychedelic integration circle: PsychedelicSupport.com. Retrieved from: https://psychedelic.support/resources/guide-community-psychedelic-integration-circle/#:~:text=In%20May%202017%2C%20the%20first,individuals%20who%20use%20psychedelic%20substances (last accessed 20 March 2022).

González, D., Torrens, M., & Farré, M. (2015). Acute effects of the novel psychoactive drug 2C-B on emotions. *BioMed Research International, 2015*. doi:10.1155/2015/643878.

Goossens, S. (2008). Drug user activism: an overview. In G. Bröring & E. Schatz (Eds.), *Empowerment and self-organisations of drug users: Experiences and lessons learnt*. Amsterdam: Foundation Regenboog AMOC.

Groisman, A. (2009). Trajectories, frontiers, and reparations in the expansion of Santo Daime to Europe. In A. Groisman, *Transnational transcendence: Essays on religion and globalization*, 185–204. doi:10.1525/9780520943650-009.

Haber, I., Pergolizzi, J., & LeQuang, J. A. (2019). Poppy seed tea: a short review and case study. *Pain and Therapy*, 8(1), 151–155. doi:10.1007/s40122–40019–0113–0115.

Haden, M., Emerson, B., & Tupper, K. W. (2016). A public-health-based vision for the management and regulation of psychedelics. *Journal of Psychoactive Drugs*, 48(4), 243–252. doi:10.1080/02791072.2016.1202459.

Hall, W., Stjepanović, D., Caulkins, J., Lynskey, M., Leung, J., Campbell, G., & Degenhardt, L. (2019). Public health implications of legalising the production and sale of cannabis for medicinal and recreational use. *The Lancet*, 394(10208), 1580–1590. doi:10.1016/S0140-6736(19)31789–31781.

Harper, S. (2020). In their own words: The story of the UK's Cannabis Social Clubs. Retrieved from: https://volteface.me/feature/story-of-ukcsc/ (last accessed 28 September 2021).

Hearne, E., Alves, E. A., Van Hout, M. C., & Grund, J.-P. C. (2017). Home manufacture of drugs: An online investigation and a toxicological reality check of online discussions on drug chemistry. *Journal of Psychoactive Drugs*, 49(4), 279–288. doi:10.1080/02791072.2017.1320735.

Hearne, E., Grund, J.-P. C., Van Hout, M. C., & McVeigh, J. (2016). A scoping review of home-produced heroin and amphetamine-type stimulant substitutes: implications for prevention, treatment, and policy. *Harm Reduction Journal*, 13(1), 14. doi:10.1186/s12954–12016–0105–0102.

Henderson, L. (2019). Brewing up community: Exploring the potential of cooperative breweries for community development. Retrieved from: https://lib.dr.iastate.edu/cgi/viewcontent.cgi?article=1473&context=creativecomponents (last accessed 4 November 2021).

Hing, N. (2006). A history of machine gambling in the NSW club industry: from community benefit to commercialisation. *International Journal of Hospitality & Tourism Administration*, 7(2–3), 83–107. doi:10.1300/J149v07n02_05.

Hughes, C. E., & Stevens, A. (2007). The effects of decriminalization of drug use in Portugal. Oxford: Beckley Foundation. Retrieved from: https://core.ac.uk/download/pdf/91904.pdf (last accessed 28 September 2021).

Hughes, C. E., & Stevens, A. (2012). A resounding success or a disastrous failure: Re-examining the interpretation of evidence on the Portuguese decriminalisation of illicit drugs. *Drug and Alcohol Review*, 31(1), 101–113. doi:10.1111/j.1465-3362.2011.00383.x.

Hunt, N., Albert, E., & Sánchez, V. M. (2010). User involvement and user organising in harm reduction. In EMCDDA (Ed.), *Harm reduction: Evidence, impacts and challenges*, 333–354. Luxembourg: Publication Office of the European Union.

Jansseune, L., Pardal, M., Decorte, T., & Parés, Ó. F. (2019). Revisiting the birthplace of the Cannabis Social Club model and the role played by Cannabis Social Club federations. *Journal of Drug Issues*, 49(2), 338–354. doi:10.1177/0022042618815690.

Jelsma, M. (2011). Lifting the ban on coca chewing: Bolivia's proposal to amend the 1961 Single Convention. In Transnational Institute (Ed.), *Amsterdam: Transnational Institute*. Series on Legislative Reform of Drug Policies, 11. Amsterdam: Transnational Institute.

Jozaghi, E. (2015). Exploring the role of an unsanctioned, supervised peer driven injection facility in reducing HIV and hepatitis C infections in people that require assistance during injection. *Health & Justice*, 3(1), 16. doi:10.1186/s40352-40015-0028-0.

Karel, R. B. (1991). A model legalization proposal. In J. A. Inciardi (Ed.), *The drug legalisation debate*. Newbury Park, CA: Sage.

Kava Society. (n.d.). Our story. Retrieved from: https://kavasociety.nz/our-story (last accessed 5 February 2021).

Kavanaugh, P. R., & Anderson, T. L. (2008). Solidarity and drug use in the electronic dance music scene. *The Sociological Quarterly*, 49(1), 181–208. doi:10.1111/j.1533-8525.2007.00111.x.

Kennedy, M. C., Scheim, A., Rachlis, B., Mitra, S., Bardwell, G., Rourke, S., & Kerr, T. (2018). Willingness to use drug checking within future supervised injection services among people who inject drugs in a mid-sized Canadian city. *Drug and Alcohol Dependence*, 185, 248–252. doi:10.1016/j.drugalcdep.2017.12.026.

Kerr, T., Oleson, M., Tyndall, M. W., Montaner, J., & Wood, E. (2005). A description of a peer-run supervised injection site for injection drug users. *Journal of Urban Health*, 82(2), 267–275. doi:10.1093/jurban/jti050.

Kerr, T., Small, W., Peeace, W., Douglas, D., Pierre, A., & Wood, E. (2006). Harm reduction by a "user-run" organization: A case study of the Vancouver Area Network of Drug Users (VANDU). *International Journal of Drug Policy*, 17(2), 61–69. doi:10.1016/j.drugpo.2006.01.003.

Klusoňová, H., Vlková, J., & Višňovsky, P. (2005). Natural opium as one of the possibilities for drug abusers. *Biomedical Papers*, 149(2), 481–483. doi:10.5507/bp.2005.085.

Kolla, G., & Strike, C. (2020). Practices of care among people who buy, use, and sell drugs in community settings. *Harm Reduction Journal*, 17, 1–12. doi:10.1186/s12954-020-00372-5.

Kranz, M. (2020). Harm reduction at music festivals: How peer organisations support the wellbeing of partygoers. Retrieved from: https://www.theseus.fi/handle/10024/302862 (last accessed 2 November 2021).

Krieger, M. S., Yedinak, J. L., Buxton, J. A., Lysyshyn, M., Bernstein, E., Rich, J. D., Green, T. C., Hadland, S. E., Marshall, B. D. (2018). High willingness to use rapid fentanyl test strips among young adults who use drugs. *Harm Reduction Journal*, 15 (1), 7. doi:10.1186/s12954-018-0213-2.

Luna, E. L. (2011). Some reflections on the global expansion of ayahuasca. In B. C. Labate & H. Jungaberle (Eds.), *The internationalization of ayahuasca*, 123–129. Zurich; Berlin: Lit Verlag.

Madden, A., & Wodak, A. (2014). Australia's response to HIV among people who inject drugs. *AIDS Education and Prevention*, 26(3), 234–244. doi:10.1521/aeap.2014.26.3.234.

Marquis, G. (2000). Civilized drinking: Alcohol and society in New Brunswick, 1945–1975. *Journal of the Canadian Historical Association/Revue de la Société historique du Canada*, 11(1), 173–203. doi:10.7202/031136ar.

McNeil, R., Small, W., Lampkin, H., Shannon, K., & Kerr, T. (2014). "People knew they could come here to get help": An ethnographic study of assisted injection practices at a peer-run 'unsanctioned'supervised drug consumption room in a Canadian setting. *AIDS and Behavior*, 18(3), 473–485. doi:10.1007/s10461-013-0540-y.

Móró, L., & Rácz, J. (2013). Online drug user-led harm reduction in Hungary: A review of "Daath". *Harm Reduction Journal*, 10(1), 1–11.

Mravčík, V. (2015). (De)criminalisation of possession of drugs for personal use – A view from the Czech Republic. *International Journal of Drug Policy*, 26(7), 705–707. doi:10.1016/j.drugpo.2015.01.022.

Muñoz, S. J., & Pardo, M. A. (2019). El estatuto legal de la ayahuasca en España: la relevancia penal de los comportamientos relacionados con su consumo y posesión. In Tirant lo Blanch Editorial Committee (Ed.), *El estatuto legal de la ayahuasca en España*, 1–184. Valencia: Tirant lo Blanch.

Muñoz, S. J., & Soto, S. (2001). El Uso terapéutico de cannabis y la creación de establecimientos para su adquisición y consumo [Therapeutic Use of Cannabis and Creation of Establisments for Its Acquisition and Consumption]. *Revista de Derecho Penal y Criminología*, (7), 49–94.

Murphy, S., & Waldorf, D. (1991). Kickin' down to the street doc: shooting galleries in the San Francisco Bay Area. *Contemporary Drug Problems*, 18, 9.

Nosa, V., & Ofanoa, M. (2009). The social, cultural and medicinal use of Kava for twelve Tongan born men living in Auckland, New Zealand. *Pacific Health Dialog*, 15(1), 96.

O'Gorman, A., Quigley, E., Zobel, F., & Moore, K. (2014). Peer, professional, and public: An analysis of the drugs policy advocacy community in Europe. *International Journal of Drug Policy*, 25(5), 1001–1008. doi:10.1016/j.drugpo.2014.04.020.

Oss, O., & Oeric, O. (1992). *Psilocybin, magic mushroom grower's guide: A handbook for psilocybin enthusiasts.* Oakland, CA: Quick American Publishing.

Ouellet, L. J., Jimenez, A. D., Johnson, W. A., & Wiebel, W. W. (1991). Shooting galleries and HIV disease: Variations in places for injecting illicit drugs. *Crime & Delinquency*, 37(1), 64–85. doi:10.1177/0011128791037001006.

Palamar, J. J., Acosta, P., Sutherland, R., Shedlin, M. G., & Barratt, M. J. (2019). Adulterants and altruism: A qualitative investigation of "drug checkers" in North America. *International Journal of Drug Policy*, 74, 160–169. doi:10.1016/j.drugpo.2019.09.017.

Papaseit, E., Farré, M., Pérez-Mañá, C., Torrens, M., Ventura, M., Pujadas, M., De La Torre, R., & González, D. (2018). Acute pharmacological effects of 2C-B in humans: an observational study. *Frontiers in Pharmacology*, 9, 206. doi:10.3389/fphar.2018.00206.

Pardal, M. (2016). Cannabis Social Clubs through the lens of the drug user movement. *Tijdschrift over Cultuur & Criminaliteit*, 6, 47–58. doi:10.5553/TCC/221195072016006002003.

Pardal, M., & Decorte, T. (2018). Cannabis use and supply patterns among Belgian Cannabis Social Club members. *Journal of drug issues*, 48(4), 689–709. doi:10.1177/0022042618791295.

Pardal, M., Decorte, T., Bone, M., Parés, Ó. F., & Johansson, J. (2020). Mapping Cannabis Social Clubs in Europe. *European Journal of Criminology*, 1–24. doi:10.1177/1477370820941392.

Pardal, M., Queirolo, R., Álvarez, E., & Repetto, L. (2019). Uruguayan cannabis social clubs: from activism to dispensaries? *International Journal of Drug Policy*, 73, 49–57. doi:10.1016/j.drugpo.2019.06.022.

Parés, Ó. F., & Bouso, J. C. S. (2015). Innovation born of necessity: Pioneering drug policy in Catalonia. In Global Drug Policy Program (Ed.), *Lessons for Drug Policy Series*, 66. New York: Open Society Foundation.

Parés, Ó. F., Jubert-Cortiella, X., Olivares-Gálvez, S., Díaz-Castellano, A., Jiménez-Garrido, D. F., & Bouso, J. C. (2019). Use and habits of the protagonists of the story: Cannabis Social Clubs in Barcelona. *Journal of Drug Issues*, 49(4), 607–624. doi:10.1177/0022042619852780.

Peter, B. (2020). Raves in the twenty-first century. In E. Mazierska., L. Gillon,. & T. Rigg (Eds.), *The future of live music*, London: Bloomsbury Academic.

Potter, G. R., Barratt, M. J., Malm, A., Bouchard, M., Blok, T., Christensen, A.S., Decorte, T., Frank, V. K., Hakkarainen, P., Klein, A., Lenton, S., Perälä, J., Werse, B., & Wouters, M. (2016). Global patterns of domestic cannabis cultivation: Sample characteristics and patterns of growing across eleven countries. In B. Werse & C. Bernard (Eds.), *Friendly business: International views on social supply, self-supply and small-scale drug dealing*, 163–196. Wiesbaden: Springer Fachmedien Wiesbaden.

Prayag, G., Mura, P., Hall, M., & Fontaine, J. (2015). Drug or spirituality seekers? Consuming ayahuasca. *Annals of Tourism Research*, 52, 175–177. doi:10.1016/j.annals.2015.03.008.

Prohibition Partners. (2020). *PSYCH: The psychedelics as medicine report*. London; Barcelona; Dublin: Prohibition Partners.

Queirolo, R., Boidi, M. F., & Cruz, J. M. (2016). Cannabis clubs in Uruguay: The challenges of regulation. *International Journal of Drug Policy*, 34, 41–48. doi:10.1016/j.drugpo.2016.05.015.

Rhodes, T. (2002). The 'risk environment': a framework for understanding and reducing drug-related harm. *International Journal of Drug Policy*, 13(2), 85–94. doi:10.1016/S0955-3959(02)00007–00005.

Rossi, G. N., Crevelin, E. J., de Oliveira Silveira, G., Eugênia Costa Queiroz, M., Yonamine, M., Cecilio Hallak, J. E., & Guimarães dos Santos, R. (2019). Internet method for the extraction of N, N-dimethyltryptamine from Mimosa hostilis roots: Does it really extract dimethyltryptamine? *Journal of Psychedelic Studies*, 3(1), 1–6. doi:10.1556/2054.2019.009.

Ruane, D. (2017a). Harm reduction or psychedelic support? Caring for drug-related crises at transformational festivals. *Dancecult: Journal of Electronic Dance Music Culture*, 7(1), 55–75. doi:10.12801/1947-5403.2015.07.01.03.

Ruane, D. (2017b). Trip hazards: drug-related crisis, peer support and control at transformational festivals [Doctoral thesis, University of Kent].

Ryan, J. (2012). Committeeville and drug users as social change agents. *Substance Use & Misuse*, 47(5), 601–604. doi:10.3109/10826084.2012.653253.

Rychert, M., & Wilkins, C. (2016). What products are considered psychoactive under New Zealand's legal market for new psychoactive substances (NPS, 'legal highs')? Implications for law enforcement and penalties. *Drug Testing and Analysis*, 8(8), 768–778. doi:10.1002/dta.1943.

Rychert, M., & Wilkins, C. (2020). "You have to make some money before you can do some good": Balancing the commercial, social and public health objectives in a "community enterprise" regulatory model for alcohol and cannabis. *International Journal of Drug Policy*, 77, 102689. doi:10.1016/j.drugpo.2020.102689.

Rychert, M., Wilkins, C., & Witten, K. (2018). "Lost in translation": Issues with the establishment of a legal market for "low risk" psychoactive products ("legal highs") in New Zealand. *Drugs: education, prevention and policy*, 25(3), 254–261. doi:10.1080/09687637.2017.1282422.

Sánchez, C., & Bouso, J. C. (2015). *Ayahuasca: From the Amazon to the global village.* Amsterdam: Transnational Institute.

Sánchez, C., & Collins, M. (2018). Better to ask forgiveness than permission: Spain's sub-national approach to drug policy. *Policy Brief*, 12 (June), 1–25.

Sandberg, R. (2011). Judging religious drug use: The misuse of the definition of "religion". In B. C. Labate & H. Jungaberle (Eds.), *The internationalization of ayahuasca*, 327–338. Zurich; Berlin: Lit Verlag.

Santos, A. P., Wilson, A. K., Hornung, C. A., Polk Jr, H. C., Rodriguez, J. L., & Franklin, G. A. (2005). Methamphetamine laboratory explosions: a new and emerging burn injury. *Journal of Burn Care & Research*, 26(3), 228–232. doi:10.1097/01.BCR.0000162947.17782.64.

Sexton, R. L., Carlson, R. G., Leukefeld, C. G., & Booth, B. M. (2006). Patterns of illicit methamphetamine production (" cooking") and associated risks in the rural South: An ethnographic exploration. *Journal of Drug Issues*, 36(4), 853–876. doi:10.1177/002204260603600405.

Sherman, S. G., Morales, K. B., Park, J. N., McKenzie, M., Marshall, B. D., & Green, T. C. (2019). Acceptability of implementing community-based drug checking services for people who use drugs in three United States cities: Baltimore, Boston and Providence. *International Journal of Drug Policy*, 68, 46–53. doi:10.1016/j.drugpo.2019.03.003.

Smit-Rigter, L., & Van der Gouwe, D. (2019). *The Drugs Information and Monitoring System (DIMS): Factsheet on drug checking in the Netherlands.* Utrecht: Trimbos Institute.

Steinhardt, J. (2018). Psychedelic naturalism and interspecies alliance: Views from the emerging do-it-yourself mycology movement. In B. C. Labate & C. Cavnar (Eds.). *Plant medicines, healing and psychedelic science*, 167–184. Berlin: Springer.

Strang, J., & Fortson, R. (2004). Supervised fixing rooms, supervised injectable maintenance clinics – understanding the difference. *British Medical Journal*, 328(7431), 102–103. doi:10.1136/bmj.328.7431.102.

Subritzky, T., Lenton, S., & Pettigrew, S. (2016). Legal cannabis industry adopting strategies of the tobacco industry. *Drug and Alcohol Review*, 35(5), 511–513. doi:10.1111/dar.12459.

Swann, J. (2017). The support groups that help people process psychedelic trips: Vice.com. Retrieved from: https://www.vice.com/en/article/jpzvvd/the-support-groups-that-help-people-process-psychedelic-trips (last accessed 2 November 2021).

Tecun, A. (2017). Tongan kava: Performance, adaptation, and identity in diaspora. *Performance of the Real E-journal*, 1(1), 52–64.

Third Wave. (2019). An introduction to psychedelic retreat centers: The third wave. Retrieved from: https://thethirdwave.co/psychedelic-retreats/ (last accessed 3 November 2021).

Thomson, E., Lampkin, H., Maynard, R., Karamouzian, M., & Jozaghi, E. (2017). The lessons learned from the fentanyl overdose crises in British Columbia, Canada. *Addiction*, 112(11), 2068–2070. doi:10.14288/1.0372517.

Thomson, E., Wilson, D., Mullins, G., Livingston, A., Shaver, L., McBain, L., Wagner, E., Hollet, K., Johnson, C., Brar, R., Sutherland, C., Wood, E., & Ahamad, K. (2019). *Heroin Compassion Clubs A cooperative model to reduce opioid overdose deaths & disrupt organized crime's role in fentanyl, money laundering & housing unaffordability.* Vancouver: British Columbia Centre on Substance Use (BCCSU).

Ti, L., Tzemis, D., & Buxton, J. A. (2012). Engaging people who use drugs in policy and program development: a review of the literature. *Substance abuse treatment, prevention, and policy*, 7(1), 1–9.

Transform. (2019). Let`s talk about stimulants: Transform Drug Policy Foundation. Retrieved from: https://transformdrugs.org/blog/its-time-to-regulate-stimulants (last accessed 2 November 2021).

Trautmann, F. (1995). Peer support as a method of risk reduction in injecting drug-user communities: Experiences in dutch projects and the "european peer support project". *Journal of Drug Issues*, 25(3), 617–628. doi:10.1177/002204269502500307.

Tyndall, M. (2018). An emergency response to the opioid overdose crisis in Canada: A regulated opioid distribution program. *CMAJ*, 190(2), E35–E36. doi:10.1503/cmaj.171060.

Valleriani, J., Haines-Saah, R., Capler, R., Bluthenthal, R., Socias, M. E., Milloy, M., & McNeil, R. (2020). The emergence of innovative cannabis distribution projects in the downtown eastside of Vancouver, Canada. *International Journal of Drug Policy*, 79, 102737.

van Amsterdam, J. G., van Laar, M., Brunt, T. M., & van den Brink, W. (2012). Risk assessment of gamma-hydroxybutyric acid (GHB) in the Netherlands. *Regulatory Toxicology and Pharmacology*, 63(1), 55–63. doi:10.1016/j.yrtph.2012.03.005.

Van den Plas, A. (2011). Ayahuasca under international law: The Santo Daime churches in the Netherlands. In B. C. Labate & H. Jungaberle (Eds.), *The internationalization of ayahuasca*, 327–338). Zurich; Berlin: Lit Verlag.

Van Het Loo, M., Van Beusekom, I., & Kahan, J. P. (2002). Decriminalization of drug use in Portugal: The development of a policy. *The ANNALS of the American academy of political and social science*, 582(1), 49–63. Retrieved from: http://ann.sagepub.com/content/582/1/49.short (last accessed 28 September 2021).

Van Hout, M. C. (2014). Kitchen chemistry: A scoping review of the diversionary use of pharmaceuticals for non-medicinal use and home production of drug solutions. *Drug Testing and Analysis*, 6(7–8),778–787. doi:10.1002/dta.1622.

Van Solinge, T. B. (1999). Dutch drug policy in a European context. *Journal of Drug Issues*, 29(3), 511–528. doi:10.1177/002204269902900305.

Wallace, B., Pagan, F., & Pauly, B. B. (2019). The implementation of overdose prevention sites as a novel and nimble response during an illegal drug overdose public health emergency. *International Journal of Drug Policy*, 66, 64–72. doi:10.1016/j.drugpo.2019.01.017.

Walsh, C. (2017). Caught in the crossfire: Plant medicines and the Psychoactive Substances Act 2016. *Journal of Psychedelic Studies*, 1(2), 41–49. doi:10.1556/2054.01.2017.010.

Webster, P. (2019). Denver votes to decriminalise psilocybin mushrooms. *The Lancet*, 393(10185). doi:10.1016/S0140-6736(19)31082–31087.

Wilkins, C. (2014). The interim regulated legal market for NPS ('legal high') products in New Zealand: The impact of new retail restrictions and product licensing. *Drug Testing and Analysis*, 6, 7–8, 868–875. doi:10.1002/dta.1643.

Wimmer, L. (2006). Freetekno a Czechtek 2005 [Bachelor's thesis, Charles University, Prague].

Zabransky, T. (2007). Methamphetamine in the Czech Republic. *Journal of Drug Issues*, 37(1), 155–180. doi:10.1177/002204260703700108.

Zeman, P. (2010). *Nový trestní zákoník: Změny v postihu (nejen) drogové kriminality Zaostřeno na drogy* [Focus on Drugs]. Vol. 8, 1–20. Prague: Office of the Government of the Czech Republic.

Index

activism 1–2, 9–10, 19, 43–45, 49, 57–58, 61, 64, 95, 126, 193: demonstration 9, 29, 82–85, 89, 120; transnationalization 19–20, 34; social movement 19, 43, 80, 89, 115–116, 120; social movement organization 19, 115

CSC Federation 4–5, 23–24, 26, 43, 49, 52, 74, 85, 104, 122
CSC members 9, 40, 45, 52, 75–76, 93, 98–100, 104, 108–109, 125, 134, 143–144, 194, 211–212
CSC variants 4, 7, 23, 195

illicit market 33, 47, 78, 80, 88, 110, 133, 136, 140, 146, 201, 212

grey market 102, 145, 162

harm reduction 2, 9, 23, 28–29, 50, 64, 102, 108–110, 138, 145, 195, 203, 210–211, 213, 216, 220, 222,

motivation 22–23, 33–34, 62, 191, 194

relationships: collaboration 9, 19–20, 24–26, 28–32, 80, 85; conflict 25–26, 32–33
regulatory framework 7, 40, 43, 45, 49–50, 52, 58, 94, 121, 144, 157, 189, 200, 202,
repertoire of action 19, 115: assembly meetings 78, 87, 102, 104, 108; see activism; 'Cannabis Cups' 27, 79–80; collective cultivation 3–4, 9–10, 39, 78, 87, 120–121; social and cultural activities 4, 50, 54, 76; workshops 9, 19, 28, 77, 80, 85, 102, 104, 108

supply models for cannabis 1, 39, 94–95, 98–100, 102, 107, 134, 137, 145, 148, 195

For Product Safety Concerns and Information please contact our EU
representative GPSR@taylorandfrancis.com
Taylor & Francis Verlag GmbH, Kaufingerstraße 24, 80331 München, Germany

www.ingramcontent.com/pod-product-compliance
Ingram Content Group UK Ltd.
Pitfield, Milton Keynes, MK11 3LW, UK
UKHW020142200926
475702UK00005B/873
9780367519063